Managing the Mills

Labor Policy in the American Steel Industry During the Nonunion Era

Jonathan Rees

University Press of America,® Inc.
Dallas · Lanham · Boulder · New York · Oxford

4501 Forbes Boulevard
Suite 200
Lanham, Maryland 20706
UPA Acquisitions Department (301) 459-3366

PO Box 317
Oxford
OX2 9RU, UK

Printed in the United States of America
British Library Cataloging in Publication Information Available

Library of Congress Control Number: 2003114222
ISBN 0-7618-2705-6 clothbound : alk. ppr.)
ISBN 0-7618-2706-4 (paperback : alk. ppr.)

The paper used in this publication meets the minimum requirements of American National Standard for Information Sciences—Permanence of Paper for Printed Library Materials, ANSI Z39.48—1984

Contents

Acknowledgments

This book began life as my dissertation at the University of Wisconsin -Madison. For that reason, it is only fitting that the first person I thank is my dissertation advisor, J. Rogers Hollingsworth. He has done more than anybody else to shape the way I look at both history and industrial relations. Thanks also to the other members of my committee: John Cooper, Diane Lindstrom, Colleen Dunlavy and Paula Voos. Other University of Wisconsin professors who influenced this work in the dissertation stage include Tom Archdeacon, Stanley Kutler, Jonathan Zeitlin, Stuart Brandes and Paul Boyer. David Zonderman, now of North Carolina State University, also deserves mention. He was my first advisor at Wisconsin and he continued to be involved with this project long after he had to be, for which I am grateful.

When choosing a topic, my intention was to study anti-unionism, not the steel industry in particular. Therefore, I had to learn a great deal about steel and steel-making in order to write this. This is where two fellow graduate students working on steel topics I met early on proved so helpful to me. Mark Brown told me what to read in order to understand the background of the steel industry, the technology in particular. Jim Rose sent me material relating to his research on U.S. Steel's Duquesne Works. This work introduced me to most of the key sources on steel labor relations in the 1930s.

So many people have read part or all of this work as I tried to revise it from a dissertation to a published book that I've lost track of everybody. Those who had the greatest impact on what follows are Roger Horowitz of the Hagley Museum and Library, Tom Dicke and Steve McIntyre of Southwest Missouri State University and especially Bruce Kaufman of Georgia State University.

Thanks to Tom Tweedale, David Grace, Emily Weaver, Deirdre Weaver, Frank Brock, Robin Yaure and Nick Hirsch for providing space for me to sleep on my many research trips. Megan Balzer helped me with research assistance in this book's last stages. Sarah Towne assisted me in copy-editing the final product before it went to press. Any mistakes that remain are my own. Geri Koncilja did a great job helping me put the charts together in their present form.

Grants from the Hagley Museum and Library, the Rockefeller Archives Center and the University of Wisconsin–Madison History Department helped me complete my research. A working fellowship at the George Meany Memorial Archives facilitated my studies in the Washington, D.C. area.

Thanks to the Albert and Shirley Small Special Collections Library of the University of Virginia and Wallace Stettinius for permission to use materials from the Edward Stettinius Papers in Chapter Seven. Thanks to Rocky Mountain Steel Mills and the Bessemer Historical Society for allowing me access to material from the Colorado Fuel and Iron archives. The Hagley Museum and Library provided me with the illustration in Chapter Three.

Most importantly, I never would have been able to start let alone finish this project without the intellectual and emotional support of my late parents Albert and Marianne Rees. My father was a labor economist. Although I entered a different discipline, his influence had everything to do with my interest in labor and business history. I was particularly happy to be able to cite his work in Chapter Three. He will always be my model of what a scholar and a teacher should be. My mother also shaped my life in countless ways, even if her influence on this work is less obvious. This book is dedicated to both of their memories.

Jonathan Rees
Pueblo, Colorado
May 2003

Introduction

The Ethos of Individual Achievement and Corporate Labor Policy During the Nonunion Era

> The American Businessman was independent of his fellows. No individual could rule him. . . . However, he was the only individual entitled to this kind of freedom. His employees were subject to the arbitrary control of this divinity. Their only freedom consisted in the supposed opportunity of laborers to become American businessmen themselves.
>
> —Thurman W. Arnold, *The Folklore of Capitalism*, 1937.[1]

In 1912, United States Steel produced a motion picture entitled "An American in the Making." The Corporation showed it to thousands of employees. A company-written synopsis of the film begins as follows: "Every European liner that steams into New York Harbor brings in its steerage Americans in the making. Of the host of aliens who are annually filtered into this country through the pathway of Ellis Island, some are dire failures, some achieve vast wealth; but to one and all there are possibilities of comfort and happiness—if they have the ability and energy to utilize them." U.S. Steel describes this film as the story of "an ignorant Hungarian peasant, who, if he had remained in his native land, never would have arisen above the dull—worthless level of his surroundings." Instead, his passage was paid for by his brother, who had already settled in Gary, Indiana. The protagonist joins his brother there, working at a steel plant. Because he was "stupid and uneducated," he started out doing only manual labor. However, as he gained experience, "he found there were chances for advancement if he cared to take advantage of them." According to the synopsis, "This is not the story of a comet-like rise to riches," rather it depicts the ways in which an ordinary worker took advantage of the opportunities which his employer provided him in order to carve out a comfortable existence. "[T]o-day," the synopsis concludes, "he is an intelligent and industrious workman, and a happy husband and father, and, although he does not expect ever to become a millionaire, he has money in the bank and no apprehensions regarding his future."[2]

This tale illustrates the importance that American steelmakers attached to promoting individual initiative in their employees. Indeed, by the Gilded Age all of American culture seemed geared to telling every citizen how they too could be a success story. Scores of books and articles explained how anybody could become rich if he just worked hard enough. While some authors hearkened back to early-American sources such as the sermons of Puritan ministers and the writings of Benjamin Franklin, many depended upon the life stories of successful businessmen to make their points.[3] Many of these works were written by successful businessmen, including a few written by movers and shakers in the steel industry. By telling their stories themselves (or through ghost writers), successful steel producers justified their business practices and established themselves as worthy of the trappings of success. These tales of triumph over adversity had the added benefit of creating public sympathy for managers because a sizable portion of the population always dreamed about becoming successful businessmen.[4] "What this barefoot American boy has done others can do—and he tells you how," declared the editors of *The American Magazine* in a teaser for a series of articles on success by Bethlehem Steel Chairman Charles M. Schwab.[5]

The ubiquity of this idea in American culture suggests a fundamental principle that influenced the course of both labor and business history. Historians call it the ethos of individual achievement.[6] This is the belief that every worker should be rewarded for hard work by fulfilling his individual potential as a participant in the American capitalist system. To do otherwise would be to undermine the incentives that make American capitalism function. Under this conception, success must be unevenly distributed. If life is a game, the ethos of individual achievement dictates that only a few "deserving" people can be allowed to win at one time so as not to diminish the accomplishments of past winners. This notion also justified the control which employers wielded over their employees. Men who had proven their merit in American economic life believed they had conditions, organization by definition cost employers money. However, this is not the end of the story. In this work, I will argue that one must look at the ideological motivations for management's opposition in order to understand both the intensity and the precise form of the steel industry's anti-union labor policies. Understanding the intensity of the steel industry's opposition to unions is essential to understanding the course of labor relations in this sector of the economy. As James Holt argues, "The determination to resist the growth of trade unions by employers who possessed vast financial resources, who controlled a rapidly changing technology, and who were uninhibited by political constraints, may not have been the only reason for the collapse of unionism in the American steel industry, but it surely is the most important one."[31] With respect to form, I mean the methods which steelmakers used to prevent organization. Why did some steelmakers become welfare capitalists and offer high wages while others kept wages low and conditions bad in order to hold down costs? Since both strategies make economic sense, one must look to the ideological underpinnings of these policies in order to answer this question.

The labor policies of steel manufacturers were more influential than those of other industries because of the importance of steel to the American economy. From coal mining to cement making, steel manufacturers had links to many other enterprises as customers or as wholly owned subsidiaries of steel-producing firms. They used these connections to get other firms to fight organized labor. And for firms in other industries with high labor costs, which needed no convincing to oppose trade unions, the steel industry's labor policy served as a model. The most important labor policy leader in the steel industry was, inevitably, U.S. Steel. As Louis Brandeis argued in 1911, "[T]he influence of the Steel Corporation is such . . . that what it does in respect to labor is done practically by all in the industry."[32] As late as 1936, *Fortune* magazine declared, "Let U.S. Steel decide tomorrow that labor unions are good, and the nation's steel mills would be organized within a year."[33] The industries that looked to U.S. Steel for guidance on labor issues included the electrical industry, meat packing, agricultural machinery, automobiles, chemicals, baking and tobacco.[34]

By providing a better understanding of management labor policy in this key industry, this study offers many new insights into a critical chapter in the history of industrial relations in America. This analysis begins at the dawn of mass steel production in the United States. By examining

Andrew Carnegie's attitudes toward labor before and after the Homestead lockout, Chapter One of this study demonstrates his ideological consistency even though most historians, particularly those sympathetic to organized labor, generally attack him for hypocrisy. Furthermore, by putting events in Homestead in the context of the rest of the industry (rather than focusing exclusively on one plant), this chapter suggests that the importance of the Homestead lockout with regard to eliminating unions from the steel industry has been vastly exaggerated. Chapter Two considers the history and policies of the Amalgamated Association of Iron, Steel and Tin Workers. It explains not only how changing technological circumstances led to its gradual extinction, but how steel manufacturers put forward a vision of workplace relations that undercut the legitimacy of the union and thereby helped keep it from regaining its former strength. Chapter Three details the various methods by which employers made and kept their establishments nonunion. Many of the weapons that steel manufacturers chose in this fight had severe social and economic consequences for the firms that employed them as well as for the communities in which these firms operated. Nevertheless, steel manufacturers employed tactics like spying on their employees or instigating racial and ethnic hatred because their intense hostility to organized labor justified victory at all costs. Chapter Four examines welfare capitalism in the steel industry. Critics have assumed that its purpose was to co-opt workers into accepting their non-union status, but a close examination of management motivations for the implementation of key policies shows that expensive welfare programs embodied the self-help ideology of the firms who created them better than they improved labor relations.

Only with pressure from the federal government did the industry's opposition to trade unions begin to break down. This was a necessary prerequisite to the return of trade unionism to the American iron and steel industry after 1937. Chapter Five explains how this change began when the Wilson and Harding administrations forced employers to create the first company unions in the industry and put an end to the twelve-hour day. Chapter Six covers the struggle between steelmakers and the Roosevelt administration over Section 7(a) of the National Industrial Recovery Act and the aborted organizing campaign that it inspired. It argues that without government encouragement to workers to begin some form of collective bargaining, there would have been no campaign at all. Chapter Seven describes the central role of the National Labor Relations Act in United States Steel's decision to recognize the Steel Workers Organizing Committee in 1937. The firm's fear of government intervention in its industrial relations and the union's shrewd use of New Deal labor legislation are the main reasons for this change of heart. Chapter Eight examines the Little Steel Strike of 1937 and shows the influence of older management ideals on labor relations in the steel industry during World War II and beyond.

The time period this study covers follows the fall, absence, and return of trade unionism in an infamous nonunion industry. A strong union presence existed in steelmaking up until the mid-1870s. That organization began to disappear in the mid-1880s, and was mostly gone following the famous Homestead lockout of 1892. A new union, the Steel Workers Organizing Committee, successfully re-ignited organized labor in this industry starting in 1937. David Brody, in his classic 1960 history of labor relations during this period, *Steelworkers in America*, has dubbed this entire stretch of time the "Nonunion Era."[35] Despite the importance of steel to the American economy, this is the first work since Brody's devoted to examining labor relations in steel during this period on an industry-wide basis.

Unlike the economists who had dominated the writing of labor history up until that time, Brody argued that working people were subjects worthy of study in their own right, independent of their employers and their unions. But in doing this, he offers a one-dimensional explanation for management's anti-union policies. To Brody, the men who ran the steel industry during the Nonunion Era were relentless economizers, and little else. Brody summarized his argument about the centrality of cost-cutting near the beginning of the book. "[The] impulse for economy shaped American steel manufacture," he wrote:

> It inspired the inventiveness that mechanized the productive operations. It formed the calculating and objective mentality of the industry. It selected and hardened the managerial ranks. Its technological and psychological consequences, finally, defined the treatment of the steelworkers. Long hours, low wages, bleak conditions, anti-unionism, flowed alike from the economizing drive that made the American steel industry the wonder of the manufacturing world.[36]

Even Brody's former student Lizabeth Cohen believes that "Brody's fixed, simplistic" portrait of management psychology was "not adequate to his task."[37] Unfortunately, as Howell Harris explains, "Everything in *Steelworkers* rests on the grinding cost-consciousness Brody detects among steel company executives in the 1880s through 1900s."[38]

Undoubtedly, the desire to minimize costs had an enormous effect on the industry's labor policies, but the relationship between labor costs and profits is not so obvious. By 1910, the height of the Nonunion Era, there were few capital-intensive industries other than steelmaking for which labor costs formed such a small percentage of overall production expenses. American steel plants were among the most productive in the world, but many steelmakers still complained that practically all the cost of production was taken up by labor.[39] A firm that faced this situation might have decreased wages in order to lower total labor costs, but this action would have hurt overall productivity if these companies were then unable to attract quality workers capable of operating sophisticated capital equipment. On the other hand, if good wages attracted more productive workers, overall profits might actually have gone up, even if wages remained high. Both these paths were followed by different sectors of the steel industry during the Nonunion Era. U.S. Steel had a policy of matching union wage levels in order to discourage the unionization of its mills and to attract the best workers available. The large independent companies like Bethlehem Steel paid their workers less than the Corporation because, despite the limited cost of labor as an overall factor in production, the men who ran these companies believed that paying U.S. Steel's wage rates was unnecessary. Both policies make economic sense. This difference in policy demonstrates that an employer's decision where to set wages depends on more than just what seems rational.

The effect of unions on overall profitability also depended on particular circumstances. Economists call the increase in workers' wages directly attributable to unionization the union wage effect. The size of that effect will vary between industries and within facilities in the same industry depending upon other factors in the economy at large. If other factors compensate for the union wage effect and other less-tangible costs of unionization, firms can benefit from bargaining with organized labor under certain conditions. Unions have two faces: the monopoly face and the collective voice/institutional response face. Unions wield their monopoly power to raise wages, which leads to increased costs for employers. However, unions can also improve productive efficiency by facilitating better communication between employers and employees. When management uses these channels of communication, turnover decreases and the firm can be more flexible when dealing with a downturn in business. Not all employers experience these benefits, but the possibility of such gains can apply to even the most anti-union industries.[40]

Despite the intense hostility of steel manufacturers toward unionization, some firms still bargained collectively with their employees because they perceived a situation where benefits outweighed costs. Of these instances, the most important was Carnegie Steel's policy of signing contracts with the Amalgamated Association of Iron and Steel Workers, the chief union in this industry, until the mid-1880s. The firm did this because its technical advantages meant it could absorb higher labor costs than its competitors. A similar situation existed during the first decade of this century when U.S. Steel continued to recognize the Amalgamated Association in its sheet and tin plate mills in order to force new firms entering these fields to bear the additional cost of a union contract.[41] In 1937, U.S. Steel recognized the Steel Workers Organizing Committee (SWOC) in part to forego the costs of fighting that organization and pass them along to its competitors. This phenomenon is known as regulatory unionism, and its existence in the steel industry makes sweeping generalizations about the motives of managers who opposed unions inherently suspect.[42]

Brody described a nonunion labor policy that used a combination of repression and welfare capitalism to get steelworkers to acquiesce to bad conditions of employment. His conception of a nonunion employer unilaterally setting wages, hours and the pace of work depends on the industry's success at achieving this goal. However, critiquing Brody's book, William Lazonick argues, "To recognise that industrial relations remains an issue after such a thorough defeat of collective bargaining is to recognise that there are no objective criteria of cost minimisation and profit maximisation. The capitalist cannot manipulate wage rates and work-loads with impunity precisely because he still has to deal with a labour force, whether unionised or not. He has to get his workers to work for the company."[43] The absence of unions allowed employers to cut costs more easily, but power wielded in too antagonistic a fashion might have alienated employees enough so that their subsequent lack of effort would hurt the bottom line even more. Profits also would have fallen if the arbitrary use of power over labor led to a costly strike or a significant increase in turnover. Even the most gifted industrial relations professional would have had difficulty deciding how hard to push workers without creating a backlash. In fact, the many spontaneous strikes that occurred in the steel industry during the Nonunion Era indicate that employers often pushed their employees too hard. Exactly how vigorously could a steel manufacturer drive his workers? And how did a steel manufacturer decide when it was to his economic advantage to bargain with a union and when it was to his advantage to fight?

Even with the best information available, these vital economic questions were not easy to answer. Under such circumstances the values and beliefs of employers played an important role in management decision making. Faced with difficult decisions and no clear idea of the possible outcomes, steel manufacturers depended heavily on their conceptions of right and wrong to determine which economic factors would influence the creation of their labor policies. As Elbert Gary once explained to his Board of Directors, "From the standpoint of making the most money for the Corporation there might be one answer and from the standpoint of doing the right thing there might be another. . . . [I]f you are sure of your morals, good policy follows."[44] To Gary and others in his position, morality and economic interest were inexorably intertwined.

In order to make morally correct, economically beneficial decisions steelmakers consistently sought the freedom to control every aspect of their business, especially the terms and conditions under which they employed their workers.[45] Steel manufacturers believed they had a fundamental right to decide wages, hours, and whether to engage in collective bargaining entirely by themselves. With this power, the men who ran this industry could implement labor policies that increased profits and embodied their values. Management demanded this ability in exchange for its efforts to give their employees the chance to succeed.

Like the ethos of individual achievement, the desire for the freedom to control was an important part of American business ideology. It motivated businessmen from all walks of life, in all kinds of businesses. The importance of this ideal is clearly evident in the success literature of the industrializing age. For example, in his *One Hundred Lessons of Business*, Seymour Eaton's first lesson is for young men "to be 'masters of [their] own business' in every way." This first lesson is reinforced in many of the other lessons that follow.[46] Individual control may have been the surest route to economic success for talented businessmen, but to assume that this idea is entirely the result of profit motive oversimplifies the matter. Nineteenth century American culture did not glorify people who made their fortunes as silent investors in other people's businesses; it glorified the individual success story. Control over the business by a single individual was a necessary prerequisite for public acclaim and for attaining the cultural status of a Carnegie or Rockefeller, but not for substantial economic gain.

Another sign of the importance of the freedom to control to American business culture was the popularity of Taylorism. The desire of managers to dictate "the one best way" for employees to do their work spread to countless industries in the Teens and Twenties. Although steelmakers wanted to assume as much control over the conditions of the workplace as possible, to dictate the precise manner in which workers did their jobs was impossible because of the circumstances surrounding the production process.[47] This argument may seem nonsensical to readers familiar with Taylor's career. After all, didn't Taylor begin his career at Midvale Steel in the 1870s? And didn't he do his most famous work at Bethlehem Steel in the 1890s? In fact, Taylor's contributions to organization of work at both firms occurred primarily within the machine shops, not the steel mills. Taylor's work at Midvale Steel improved production in the cutting and shaping of the steel tires which were the company's most important product at that time; it did nothing to improve the production of the steel itself. Bethlehem Steel employed Taylor as a consultant between 1897 and 1901. He reorganized the machinists there and the unskilled workers in the rail yard, but never got to the majority of workers who actually produced steel.[48] In 1915, Horace Drury reported that, "The present owners [of Bethlehem Steel] say they have rid themselves of Taylor and his ideas, and declare in their irritation that they 'don't want to hear anything more about scientific management.'"[49] "[T]he system used at Bethlehem is not the so-called Scientific Management," reported one national magazine in 1916, "although in some respects the same principles are followed."[50] Other steel firms never took to Taylor's system of labor even after it became popular. "Compared to the number of time studies made in machine shops," explained the journal *Blast Furnace and Steel Plant* in 1916, "very few such studies are made in steel mills."[51] Taylor's experiments with high-speed-tool steel led to cutting tools that increased the productive efficiency of machine shops inside and outside the steel industry. However, they did nothing to increase the efficiency of steel production. Critics of organized labor adopted Taylor-inspired arguments about the inefficiency of trade unionism as scientific management grew in popularity, but steelmakers continued to cite their traditional prerogatives as managers in order to justify their opposition to organized labor well into the 1930s.[52]

A close examination of the steelmaking process shows that most jobs in a steel mill could not be regimented in the way that scientific management required. By the early twentieth century, mechanization had eliminated the need for many jobs that required only brute strength as a qualification. Firms now needed workers who possessed diagnostic skills that would help them coordinate continuous flow operations.[53] This new production process rendered the skills of former union members irrelevant, but it did not turn workers into the automatons that Taylor imagined. A few steelworkers were paid through a differential piece rate, a system commonly associated with Taylorism in the historical literature, but piece rates and incentive wages did not always indicate an employer's belief in the principles of scientific management.[54] In fact, American steelmakers tolerated an enormous amount of inefficiency in their operations because of strains inherent in the production process. One 1912 study found that workers in the blooming mill, blast furnace and open hearth departments of one Pittsburgh plant were idle for 47.9 percent of their working hours.[55] Employers could never expect their employees to work at peak efficiency because of the heat and strain of most steel mill jobs.

Even if they could not dictate every movement their employees made, steelmakers wanted to be able to impose the terms and conditions of employment under which employees worked. The potential economic benefits of such power should be obvious. Yet the desire for control was as much cultural as economic; though the cultural reasons for this objective were more subtle. Steel manufacturers saw the freedom to control as a way to cement their position at the top of the workplace social hierarchy. They considered themselves supremely qualified to run their businesses because of their personal success in rising to the top of their profession. Ordinary workers, on the other hand, had no right to exert any power over production because they had not succeeded. Trying to explain how labor unrest in the steel industry looked "from above to the employer," Ray Stannard Baker wrote in 1920:

> The idea . . . of crowds of ignorant workers, who have no knowledge of the problems involved, no training to deal with them, breaking in with extreme demands for a share of control of the management seems wildly destructive and disastrous. [Steel manufacturers] fear it desperately. . . . They regard it not only as meaning the destruction of their own power, and of the organization which they have built up so painfully through so many years, but as a complete overthrow of our institutions.[56]

Some contemporary observers thought steel manufacturers could dictate every aspect of the terms and conditions of employment to their employees, but the periodic strikes among the industry's nonunion employees strongly suggests that employers never entirely reached this ideal.[57]

In general, the course of labor relations in any industry is determined by both labor and management. I believe that in the same way that the experiences of African Americans and whites must be considered together in order to understand the history of American race relations, the same way that the experiences of men and women must be considered together in order to understand American social history, the history of both labor and management must be considered together in order to understand the course of American capitalism. This is particularly true with respect to the steel industry because of the immense power which steelmakers wielded over their employees. Therefore, in this work I offer a more nuanced portrait of the motivation for management's labor policies than currently exists, one that takes their social discourse on labor relations seriously. "Perhaps Brody's steelmasters were just 'economic men'" writes Howell Harris, "or perhaps there were questions not asked or improperly specified in Steelworkers, which should encourage younger scholars to broaden their research agendas beyond those suggested even in this most valuable work."[58] What follows in this book demonstrates that steelmasters were not just economic men.

Notes

1. Thurman W. Arnold, *The Folklore of Capitalism* (New Haven: Yale University Press, 1937), 35.

2. United States Steel Corporation, *Bureau of Safety, Sanitation and Welfare Bulletin*, No. 7, (December 1918): 5-6.

3. Judy Hilkey's *Character is Capital: Success Manuals and Manhood in Gilded Age America* (Chapel Hill: University of North Carolina Press, 1997) is a useful introduction to these materials. On the ideological antecedents of this ethos, see Hilkey, 3-6.

4. Sanford Jacoby, "American Exceptionalism Revisited," in *Masters to Managers*, Sanford Jacoby, ed. (New York: Columbia University Press, 1991):185-86.

5. *The American Magazine* 82, (October 1916): 20.

6. See, for example, Jacoby, "American Exceptionalism Revisited," 185.

7. L.T.C. Rolt, "Introduction," in Samuel Smiles, *Industrial Biography: Iron Workers and Tool Makers* (Newton, UK: David and Charles, 1967), vii.

8. Barnard Alderson, *Andrew Carnegie: The Man and His Work* (New York: Doubleday, Page & Co., 1902), 55.

9. Arundel Cotter, *United States Steel: A Corporation With a Soul* (Garden City, NY: Doubleday, Page & Company, 1921), 134.

10. I have deliberately chosen to refer to the United States Steel Corporation as "the Corporation," with a capital "C," because that is how journalists, politicians, labor, other steel executives and U.S. Steel officials referred to this firm. To me, this language conveys the importance of U.S. Steel in the steel industry and in the American economy overall.

11. For examples of Gary's claim, see John Kimberly Mumford, "This Land of Opportunity," *Harper's Weekly* 52 (13 June 1908): 23; Elbert Gary, "Workers' Partnership in Industry," *The World's Work* 48 (June 1924): 200.

12. In 1909, Elbert Gary of U.S. Steel founded the American Iron and Steel Institute (AISI) to facilitate communication between steel industry leaders in all area of business operations. Its members met twice a year to discuss and coordinate policies. At the turn of the century, the AISI was the only trade association in the iron and steel industry with a national constituency of manufacturers in every product line. It still exists today.

13. American Iron and Steel Institute, "The Men Who Make Steel," May 1936, 24.

14. John N. Ingham, *The Iron Barons* (Westport, CT: Greenwood Press, 1978), 37.

15. Gerald Eggert, *Steelmasters and Labor Reform, 1886-1923* (Pittsburgh: University of Pittsburgh Press, 1981), 19-20. Also see Frances W. Gregory and Irene D. Neu, "The American Industrial Elite in the 1870s: Their Social Origins," in *Men in Business*, William Miller, ed. (Cambridge: Harvard University Press, 1952), 202.

16. This belief explains numerous statements by steelmakers that young men did not need a college education in order to achieve business success. See Carnegie quoted in Joseph Frazier Wall, *Andrew Carnegie* (New York: Oxford University Press, 1970), 835; George Harvey, *Henry Clay Frick: The Man* (New York: Charles Scribner's Sons, 1928), 369-70 and Robert Hessen, *Steel Titan* (New York: Oxford University Press, 1975), 129.

17. Andrew Carnegie, "Dedication of the Carnegie Library at the Edgar Thomson Steel Works, Braddocks [sic]," March 30, 1889, 29.

18. Arthur H. Young, Speech to Meeting of U.S. Steel Representatives, March 31 1936, 1, Arthur H. Young Papers, Management Library, California Institute of Technology, Pasadena, CA. I am grateful to Jim Rose for providing me with all my material from the Young Papers.

19. S.B. Whipple, "Notes from Interviews in Preparation for a Biography of Charles M. Schwab," c. 1936, 71, Bethlehem Steel Corporation Papers, Box 17, Hagley Museum and Library, Wilmington, DE.

20. Andrew Carnegie, "Mr. Andrew Carnegie on Socialism, Labour and Home Rule," Aberdeen, Scotland, 1892, 10.

21. Elbert Gary, "Address at Annual Meeting of the American Iron and Steel Institute," May 28, 1920, 9.

22. Richard Hofstadter, *Social Darwinism in American Thought*, 2nd ed. (Boston: Beacon Press, 1955), 44-45.

23. Alun Munslow, "Andrew Carnegie and the Discourse of Cultural Hegemony," *Journal of American Studies* 22 (August 1988): 219-20. For a discussion of the differences between Carnegie's ideas and orthodox Social Darwinism, see Wall, *Andrew Carnegie*, 391-97.

24. William Brown Dickson, *History of Carnegie Veteran Association* (Montclair, NJ: Mountain Press, 1938), 150.

25. E.T. Weir, "'I Am What Mr. Roosevelt Calls an Economic Royalist'," *Fortune* 14 (October 1936):121.

26. Charles M. Schwab, "My 20,000 Partners," *American Magazine* 82 (December 1916): 74.

27. John Monk Saunders, "'It Ain't No Job For Lily-Fingers!,'" *The American Magazine* 101 (January 1926): 127.

28. Daniel T. Rodgers, *The Work Ethic in Industrial America, 1850-1920* (Chicago: University of Chicago Press, 1978), 28.

29. Michael John Nuwer, "Labor Market Structures in Historical Perspective: A Case Study of Technology and Labor Relations in the United States Iron and Steel Industry," Ph.D. Diss., University of Utah, 1985, 155.

30. John A. Fitch, *The Steel Workers* (Pittsburgh: University of Pittsburgh Press, 1989/Originally published by the Russell Sage Foundation, 1910), 148.

31. James Holt, "Trade Unionism in the British and U.S. Steel Industries, 1880-1914: A Comparative Study," *Labor History* 18 (Winter 1977): 34.

32. U.S., Congress, House, *Hearings Before the Committee on Investigation of United States Steel Corporation* (in 8 vols.) [Stanley Committee Hearings], 62nd Cong., 2nd Sess., 1911-12, 2836.

33. *Fortune* 13 (May 1936): 94.

34. Don D. Lescohier, "Working Conditions," in *History of Labour in the United States, 1896-1932*, Vol. 3, John R. Commons, ed. (New York: Macmillan Company, 1935), 298.

35. David Brody, *Steelworkers in America: The Nonunion Era* (Urbana: University of Illinois Press, 1998/ Originally published by Harvard University Press, 1960).

Brody's book goes only through the 1920s. I will use the term the "Nonunion Era" to extend from 1892 to 1937, the year U.S. Steel's agreement with the Steel Workers Organizing Committee first returned a significant portion of the industry's workforce to the union fold.

36. Brody, *Steelworkers in America*, 2.
Scholars examining labor relations in the steel industry since Brody have invariably used this argument about management motivation in their own work. These include Joseph Frazier Wall, Paul Krause and John P. Hoerr. See Wall, *Andrew Carnegie*, 337-38; Paul Krause, *The Battle for Homestead, 1880-1892* (Pittsburgh: University of Pittsburgh Press, 1992), 286; John P. Hoerr, *And the Wolf Finally Came* (Pittsburgh: University of Pittsburgh Press, 1988), 86. Brody cites his earlier analysis to explain the steel industry's labor policies in *Labor in Crisis*, 2nd ed. (Urbana: University of Illinois Press, 1987), 15.

37. Lizabeth Cohen, "Commentary," in Brody, *Steelworkers in America*, 298.
Cohen's commentary on Steelworkers in America, as well the commentary of other authors on this same book, originally appeared as "Symposium on David Brody, *Steelworkers in America: The Nonunion Era*, and the Beginnings of the New Labor History," *Labor History* 34 (Fall 1993): 457-514. The symposium is reprinted in its entirety in the University of Illinois Press edition of *Steelworkers in America*.

38. Howell John Harris, "Commentary," in Brody, *Steelworkers in America*, 311.

39. United States Commissioner of Labor, *Report on Conditions of Employment in the Iron and Steel Industry*, Vol. 3, Senate Document No. 110, 62nd Cong., 1st Sess., 1913, 276; Robert C. Allen, "International Competition in Iron and Steel, 1850-1913," *Journal of Economic History* 39 (December 1979): 919.

40. Richard B. Freeman and James L. Medoff, *What Do Unions Do?* (New York: Basic Books, 1984), 5-11.

41. Brody, *Steelworkers in America*, 70.

42. For examples of regulatory unionism in many industries, see Colin Gordon, *New Deals* (New York: Cambridge University Press, 1994), 87-128.

43. William H. Lazonick, "Technological Changes and the Control of Work: The Development of Capital-Labour Relations in US Mass Production Industries," in *Managerial Strategies and Industrial Relations: An Historical and Comparative Study*, Craig R. Littler and Howard F. Gospel, eds. (London: Heinemann Educational Books, 1983), 117.

44. "From minutes of Presidents Meeting, Feb. 25th, 1910," William Brown Dickson Papers, Box 7, Historical Collections & Labor Archives, Pattee Library, Pennsylvania State University, State College, PA.

45. I borrow the term "freedom to control" from Rowland Berthoff, "The 'Freedom to Control' in American Business History," in *A Festschrift for Frederick B. Artz*, David H. Pinckney and Theodore Ropp eds. (Durham, NC: Duke University Press, 1964), 158-180.

Fitch argues that steelmakers sought to destroy unionism in this industry to achieve "administrative control" [Fitch, *The Steel Workers*, 205]. However, he implies this desire was ultimately the result of economic motivations exclusively. Therefore, I have chosen a slightly different terminology.

46. Seymour Eaton, *One Hundred Lessons in Business*, quoted in Pamela Walker Laird, *Advertising Progress* (Baltimore: The Johns Hopkins University Press, 1998), 40-41.

47. The best-known article on Taylorism in the steel industry is Katherine Stone, "The Origins of Job Structures in the Steel Industry," *Review of Radical Political Economics* 6 (Summer 1974): 61-97. She cites the prevalence of articles about scientific management in the journal *Iron Age* as proof of the popularity of Taylorism throughout the steel industry. However, the five articles she cites by date discuss scientific management in machine shops, a machine tool company, a paint barrel producer, dockyards and automobile engine assembly. This is not surprising because the readership of *Iron Age* included not just steelmakers, but consumers of steel like hardware manufacturers and machine shops. She offers two examples of Taylorism at Bethlehem Steel, but they concern that company's shipbuilding operations and the 1910 steel strike which started among machinists. Stone equates piece work for a limited number of steelworkers and workers in related industries with scientific management throughout the steel industry. A closer examination of the literature on industrial relations in the basic steel industry would demonstrate that this conclusion is inaccurate.

48. Robert Kanigel, *The One Best Way: Frederick Winslow Taylor and the Enigma of Efficiency* (New York: Viking, 1997), 210-14, 309-15, 347-55.

49. Horace Drury, *Scientific Management: A History and Criticism* (New York: Columbia University Press, 1915), 121.

50. *Collier's* 57 (May 13, 1916): 4.

51. *Blast Furnace and Steel Plant* 5 (September 1916), 429.

52. Mark Koerner, "The Menace of Labor: Anti-Union Thought in the Progressive Era, 1901-1917," Ph.D. Diss., University of Wisconsin–Madison, 1995, 285.

53. Charles Reitell, "Machinery and its Benefits to Labor in the Crude Iron and Steel Industries," Ph.D. Diss., University of Pennsylvania, (Menasha, WI: The Collegiate Press, 1917), 20; Michael Nuwer, "From Batch to Flow: Production Technology and Work-Force Skills in the Steel Industry, 1880-1920," *Technology and Culture* 29, (October 1988), 815-37.

54. Daniel Nelson, "Scientific Management and the Workplace, 1920-1935," in *Masters to Managers*, 74-89.

55. *Iron Age* 89, 1 February 1912, 312.

56. Ray Stannard Baker, *The New Industrial Unrest*, (Garden City, NY: Doubleday, Page & Company, 1920), 13, 24-25.

57. John A. Fitch, "The Labor Policies of Unrestricted Capital," *The Survey* 28 (6 April 1912): 27.

58. Harris, in Brody, *Steelworkers in America*, 316. In his response to the symposium, David Brody agrees with this criticism. See, David Brody, "Response," in Brody, *Steelworkers in America*, 344.

Chapter One

Andrew Carnegie and the Origins of the Nonunion Era

> The first employer who reduces labor [costs] is labor's enemy; but the last employer to reduce labor [costs] may be labor's staunchest friend.
>
> —Andrew Carnegie, 1889.[1]

Today, most Americans remember Andrew Carnegie for his philanthropy. Countless libraries, Carnegie Hall in New York City, the Carnegie Institute of Technology (now Carnegie-Mellon University); all are monuments to his generosity. Anyone familiar with U.S. history knows that he made his money by building the largest steel company in the world during the late-nineteenth century. Before he became the greatest philanthropist of his era, most people knew Andrew Carnegie not so much for his business activities but as a model of success. As a biographer, Barnard Alderson, wrote in 1902, "[T]he rising generation, as they follow the gradual growth of [Carnegie's] fortunes, and the development of his character, may gather from an account of the winning of his wealth a strong incentive to creative enterprise."[2] Ordinary Americans did not care who controlled the steel industry. Most people did not have a Carnegie library in their town, and if they did they did not necessarily use it. However, every American knew that Andrew Carnegie had gone from rags to riches through hard work and sacrifice. He was living proof that Horatio Alger stories could come true. Even before Carnegie retired from business in 1901, his life had become the archetype of the American dream.

"Whatever I engage in I must push inordinately," wrote Carnegie in a memo to himself at the age of thirty-three, "therefor [sic] should I be careful to choose that life which will be most elevating in its character."[3] Born in Dunfermline, Scotland, in 1835, to a master weaver and the daughter of a cobbler, Carnegie and his family emigrated to the United States in 1848 because of the difficulties that the rise of the English factory system created for his father's career. Unable to support the family in America, Andrew went to work as a bobbin boy in a textile mill. Later, he moved on to become the bill clerk of the factory. He quit that job at age fourteen to work in a telegraph office. It was in this capacity that Thomas Scott, superintendent of the Pennsylvania Railroad, noticed him. Scott asked Carnegie to be his clerk and telegraph operator, an offer that proved to be Carnegie's big break. Using the surplus of his vastly increased salary, Carnegie invested in a number of different ventures recommended to him by Scott and other businessmen he met in the course of his duties. Having risen to the position of superintendent of the Pennsylvania Railroad's Pittsburgh division, he quit the company after fourteen years to devote all of his energy to his investments. Carnegie first entered the enterprise that would come to be known as Carnegie Steel[4] in 1863, when he joined a partnership with two childhood friends. The firm grew rapidly as Carnegie became more involved in iron and steelmaking. Carnegie's work ethic, his commitment to cutting-edge technology and his talent for picking gifted partners helped make Carnegie Steel the dominant steel concern of the late nineteenth century. When Carnegie sold his firm to the founders of United States Steel in 1901, the proceeds made him the richest man in the world.[5]

Carnegie's writing played an important role in publicizing his life story. No employer in any major industry has ever offered as much explanation of his views on American culture and society as Andrew Carnegie. According to Alun Munslow, "The hero of Carnegie's business discourse was the entrepreneur"; which makes sense when one recognizes that much of his writing on business was autobiographical.[6] But Carnegie did not restrict himself to writing on business. Carnegie authored eight books, sixty-three magazine articles, and had ten major addresses published in pamphlet form during his lifetime. The subjects of these works ranged from "The Negro in America" to a biography of the inventor James Watt. His books sold well and his articles appeared in a wide range of popular and scholarly journals in both America and Great Britain.[7]

Andrew Carnegie's words helped make him famous, but they frequently served as a way for critics to attack him. His writings on labor policy proved particularly controversial. In 1886, Carnegie wrote two essays for the magazine *Forum* which seemed to support trade unions. Often-quoted parts of these articles do indeed show Carnegie as far more liberal on labor questions than any of his contemporaries. For instance, in "An Employer's View of the Labor Question" he wrote, "My experience has been that trade-unions, upon the whole are beneficial to both labor and capital."[8] In "Results of the Labor Struggle," Carnegie explained, "There is an unwritten law among the best workmen: 'Thou shalt not take thy neighbor's job.' No wise employer will lightly lose his old employees."[9] Here, it seemed, an important industrialist had answered the labor question in a manner that labor had actually supported. The two *Forum* essays made Carnegie a hero to the working classes. For example, in commemoration of these sentiments, the Brotherhood of Locomotive Engineers named a division after him and made him an honorary member of the union.[10]

The words in these essays would come back to haunt Carnegie again and again after the famous Homestead lockout. On July 6, 1892, seven workers and three Pinkerton guards died in a gun battle on the banks of the Monongahela River, near Carnegie Steel's Homestead Works. It was one of the bloodiest labor disturbances of an era that saw many bloody labor disturbances. Even though Carnegie was in Scotland at the time of the violence, his *Forum* articles allowed his enemies to portray him as a hypocrite for allowing the hiring of Pinkerton guards for his company's works. "Count no man happy until he is dead," wrote the *St. Louis Post-Dispatch* in an editorial reprinted all over the country shortly after the violence at Homestead ended:

> Three months ago Andrew Carnegie was a man to be envied. Today he is an object of mingled pity and contempt. In the estimation of nine-tenths of the thinking people on both sides of the ocean he had not only given the lie to all his antecedents, but confessed himself a moral coward. One would naturally suppose that if he had a grain of consistency, not to say decency, in his composition, he would favor rather than oppose the organization of trades-unions among his own working people at Homestead. One would naturally suppose that if he had a grain of manhood, not to say courage, in his composition, he would at least be willing to face the consequences of his inconsistency.[11]

Historians have attacked Carnegie along these same lines. "His writings and speeches," writes Leon Wolff, echoing a familiar theme, "were pro-union, liberal, humane, philanthropic, enlightened. The policies of his company were in stark contrast. . . . The cleavage between theory and practice was bewildering."[12] Paul Krause, author of the most recent monograph on the Homestead lockout, argues that Carnegie never supported unions and that the *Forum* articles were just self-serving propaganda.[13]

Contrary to popular opinion, Carnegie neither unequivocally opposed organized labor throughout his career nor was he of two minds on this subject. When unions were willing to submit to management authority he bargained with them; when adverse economic circumstances led unions to demand better wages and working conditions he ousted them. Before the mid-1880s, Carnegie accepted the presence of the Amalgamated Association of Iron and Steel Workers in key mills and signed contracts with them during periods of labor strife because this allowed him to run his business the way he wanted and because he believed a reliable supply of skilled labor gave him an advantage over his competitors. After 1886, Carnegie gradually backed away from his earlier support of the union. His dispute with trade unions over the conditions of employment at his mills culminated in the Homestead lockout. His firm's actions in that dispute appeared hypocritical to workers who remembered Carnegie's praise for unions in his 1886 essays, but close readers should not have been surprised.

Besides charges of hypocrisy, many commentators have blamed Andrew Carnegie for the collapse of the Amalgamated Association. As early as 1910, John A. Fitch wrote, "Where the great Carnegie Steel company led, the others had to follow; from this time on [1892] we find the union being steadily but surely crowded out of the steel industry."[14] Katherine Stone, in a highly-influential article, echoes Fitch's causation scheme: "The Homestead strike was the turning point for the Amalgamated Association throughout the country. Other employers, newly invigorated by Frick's performance, took a hard line against the union."[15] David Brody made the same argument in *Steelworkers in America*.[16] However, this common assessment of the impact of one of the most important disputes in American labor history cannot survive close scrutiny. Rather than being one of the first steelmakers to take on the Amalgamated Association, Carnegie Steel was one of the last. Apart from employer opposition, technological change had already weakened the

Amalgamated Association considerably when Carnegie forced the union from the last of his mills. In fact, since the technology of steelmaking gradually eliminated the need for the special skills that its members possessed, the union would have faded from view even if the Homestead lockout had never occurred.

To prove these points it is necessary to examine the economic and ideological issues affecting Andrew Carnegie's labor policy, while comparing them with the labor policies of the rest of the steel industry. By doing this, it will be possible to put the Homestead lockout in its proper context, independent of the mythology that now surrounds it.[17] Post-Homestead critics of Carnegie tend to let the strike color their assessment of his earlier policies, thereby ignoring the many actions which made him a popular figure in labor circles even while the strike was unfolding. This does not mean that Andrew Carnegie should be absolved of responsibility for the Homestead tragedy. At the very least, Carnegie explicitly endorsed the goal of eradicating the union and tacitly endorsed the tactics employed by his partner Henry Clay Frick, including the deployment of Pinkertons, which led directly to the violence that killed ten people. Nevertheless, Carnegie's philosophy of labor did not really change between 1886 and 1892. His primary concern throughout these years remained the freedom to control the terms and conditions of employment throughout his mills.

The "Friend" of Labor

Andrew Carnegie's views on labor matters were not always influential. In late 1884, he delivered an off-the-cuff speech before the Nineteenth Century Club in New York City, during which he proclaimed himself "a socialist and an advocate of socialist principles." *The New York Times*, following up on the story, asked Carnegie to confirm whether his views had been accurately conveyed in news reports about the speech. Carnegie responded as follows: "I believe socialism is the grandest theory ever presented, and I am sure some day it will rule the world. Then we will have the millennium." Such sentiments were widely interpreted as dangerously radical for a man of his stature, but a complete reading of his statements suggests otherwise. When questioned, Carnegie responded that workers' control of industry would only happen in the distant future. "Speaking of the present position of the working man," he told the *Times*,

"I believe co-operation is his hope."[18] Furthermore, when Carnegie transcribed his remarks for publication as a privately circulated pamphlet he left out all references to socialism, perhaps because of the uproar the use of the word created in the New York media. Only two days after the interview with Carnegie appeared, the *Times* reported that his workmen were "trying their best to reconcile the idealistic views" expressed by their employer "with the industrial establishments in which he is the leading spirit."[19] This was not the first time that Andrew Carnegie's words would confuse working-class readers.

The 1886 *Forum* articles were the most controversial writings of Andrew Carnegie's long literary career; but like his allegiance to socialism, these essays also need to be considered in their full context to be completely understood. In the *Forum* essays, Carnegie detailed a labor relations philosophy based on cooperation, but he clearly intended that that cooperation would occur on management's terms:

> [I]t may be laid down as a rule that the more intelligent the workman the fewer the contests with employers. It is not the intelligent workman, who knows that labor without its brother capital is helpless, but the blatant ignorant man, who regards capital as the natural enemy of labor, who does so much to embitter the relations between employer and employed; and the power of this ignorant demagogue arises chiefly from the lack of proper organization among the men through which their real voice can be expressed.[20]

The "organization among the men" which Carnegie refers to here is a union, but his role for organization was highly circumscribed. Unions must, "in their very nature," he wrote, "become more conservative than the mass of men they represent; [otherwise] they go to pieces through their own extravagance."[21] By late-nineteenth-century standards any endorsement of worker organization from a man in Carnegie's position deserves attention. Nevertheless, rather than being radical, the principles embodied in Carnegie's *Forum* essays derived from labor policies that had already made him a very rich man.

During the 1870s and early-1880s, while his competitors worked hard to cut labor costs, Carnegie practiced an expensive, paternalistic labor policy which benefited him more in the longer term than the anti-union labor policy of competitors. The most important aspect of this policy was high wages. Although this meant higher up front labor costs, paying high wages to attract good workers and keep them proved successful enough for Carnegie to maintain this policy for over a decade. Because the production process at this time required efficient, skilled workers, Carnegie willingly paid them a premium. In 1879, Carnegie introduced the eight-hour day at his Edgar Thomson Works. He did the same in some departments at Homestead after he purchased that plant in 1882. Carnegie did not implement these policies in response to worker requests; he did this because the Superintendent of the Edgar Thomson Works, Captain William R. Jones, convinced him that a fresh crew of men every eight hours would produce better results. In the mid-1880s, Carnegie also began to experiment with welfare capitalist schemes, like selling coal to employees at below-market prices. Although never as elaborate as the welfare programs that U.S. Steel created after the turn of the century, the idea of doing anything for one's workers beyond paying them a wage was novel at that time.[22] In short, from the late-1870s to late-1880s, Andrew Carnegie was the best friend labor had in the steel industry, albeit a friend of convenience.

Another important manifestation of Carnegie's cultivation of skilled workers was his cooperation with unions, specifically the Amalgamated Association of Iron and Steel Workers. "I am a firm friend of the Amalgamated Association," proclaimed Carnegie in 1885, "and no one ever heard of my having trouble with them."[23] The Amalgamated Association was the only important trade union in the steel industry between its institution in 1876 and 1937. This union formed in the merger of four separate craft unions: the United Sons of Vulcan; the Associated Brotherhood of Iron and Steel Heaters, Rollers and Roughers of the United States; the Iron and Steel Roll Hands' Union; and the United Nailers.[24] For most of the nineteenth century, iron manufacturers had no choice but to cede some control to their organized employees because these unionized workers possessed indispensable skills.[25] Pig iron produced by a blast furnace varied considerably from batch to batch. Only experienced craftsmen knew exactly how long and at what temperature to work the product in order to achieve the desired uniform consistency. The men who did this stirred the material coming out of the blast furnace to separate the iron from the impurities. They were known as puddlers. Puddlers made many informed judgments like these during the production process. Despite frequent efforts to do so, manufacturers could find no substitute for the skilled puddler.[26] Because this process depended on the involvement of individual workmen from beginning to end, the only way for an iron manufacturer to expand production was to build more furnaces and hire more puddlers. Skilled workers used their power over the production process to gain benefits like control over their hours of employment, the right to choose their own helpers and, of course, union recognition.[27]

The most obvious economic manifestation of the Amalgamated Association's power was its ability to limit production. Until 1905, the union required that the contracts it signed included restrictions on the amount of steel in each heat and the number of heats per shift in puddling mills, restrictions on the number of bars rolled each shift in sheet mills and restrictions on the amount of tin plate produced in plate mills. The union justified these restrictions as protection for the health of its membership because if an individual worker could not keep up the pace of his teammates in production, he would experience stress and overexertion.[28] Employers, on the other hand, wanted workers to distinguish themselves from their colleagues. This gave them the opportunity to identify their most deserving employees so that they could be moved to higher positions in the firm as well as generate more product to sell.

Starting in the 1870s, the Amalgamated Association created a common wage scale for every sector of the industry each year and presented it to those manufacturers who recognized the union. Those firms that did not reach an agreement with the union faced the prospect of strikes. The union worked out its scales with the Pittsburgh manufacturers; then those scales were usually accepted by other manufacturers outside the region. Once one firm signed, pressure grew on other firms to follow because in the event of a strike they could lose business to competitors that continued producing steel. Employers outside the region often complained bitterly that their Pittsburgh brethren, led by Carnegie, settled with the union too easily. "The Pittsburgh manufacturers have no enviable reputation among the iron manufacturers of other sections of the country," remarked the journal *Iron Age* in 1885, "and if in the face of the weakness of the Amalgamated Association they suffer defeat, they certainly cannot take exception if the respect in which they are held by the iron trade of the country is not increased."[29]

Before 1888, Carnegie was always one of the first manufacturers to sign the Amalgamated Association's scales, even when labor disputes closed down other firms.[30] In the steel sector of the industry, Carnegie Steel was practically the only manufacturing establishment to sign the union scale. Despite the fact that the Amalgamated Association lost eleven of the thirteen lockouts or strikes that it participated in between 1881 and 1885, the Carnegie mills still bargained with the union. As the president of the Amalgamated Association described the situation in 1884, "Every strike that has thus far taken place in our Bessemer steel mills has gone against us. . . . But one Bessemer works only has succeeded in maintaining its position with any degree of dignity and respect and that is the Edgar Thomson Steel Works at Braddock."[31] Carnegie did this because the technological superiority and enormous production capacity of his Edgar Thomson mill meant that his firm did not need to cut labor costs to compete. In fact, Carnegie had an interest in keeping the Amalgamated Association strong because if labor costs were high throughout the industry, his firm could undersell its competitors by exploiting other important advantages.[32]

Completed in 1875, the Edgar Thomson Works in Braddock, Pennsylvania, became the prototype for all subsequent Bessemer plants no matter what company owned them. Unlike previous Bessemer works which had to be fit within preexisting plant structures, engineer Alexander Holley designed Edgar Thomson from the ground up. The layout of the plant made the delivery of raw materials easier and streamlined production once processing began by hastening the delivery of pig iron from the blast furnace to the Bessemer converters. This increased efficiency, increased production and decreased the plant's need for labor.[33] The use of a technique known as "hard driving" also increased the productive capacity of Carnegie's mills.[34] This meant each furnace would be run at maximum output for as long as it could still produce, even if this permanently damaged the equipment. Management did this because it believed that the extra profit from running in this manner would more than compensate for replacement costs of capital. Throughout his business career, Carnegie tried to exploit his advantages so as to undercut competitors. According to a former vice-president, "The advantage of Carnegie management was that even at reduced prices, a profit could still be made, and decreased earnings were regarded as preferable to suspended operations. It was the recognized Carnegie policy—'Take orders and run full.'"[35] Yet in order to maintain its breakneck production pace, the firm had to have skilled workers willing to run its facilities. Consistently signing the Amalgamated Association scale ensured that the necessary skilled labor would always be available. This way, the union could not control the fate of Carnegie Steel by shutting it down with a strike.

A Friendship in Peril

In 1889, at a speech in Braddock dedicating his first library in America, Andrew Carnegie explained to the no-longer-organized workers there the reasons behind his decision to operate the mill non-union:

> You all know that for twenty years, ever since we began manufacturing, we have invariably signed the iron scale, because our competitors generally had to sign it and pay the same wages to labor. If a uniform scale could be enforced in the steel mills of this country, we would gladly pay hundreds of thousands of dollars to secure it. The Amalgamated Association is, unfortunately, no longer able to enforce its decrees even in the Pittsburgh mills to say nothing of the strong competing mills at Harrisburgh and Johnstown. Already there are no less than five non-union mills in Pittsburgh, and every mill that resolves to throw over the Amalgamated Association succeeds in doing so without difficulty. These non-union mills, beyond the reach of the Amalgamated Association, have us at their mercy.[36]

This effort by Carnegie to blame the weakness of the Amalgamated for his labor policies was disingenuous. Certainly Carnegie had always been concerned about high labor costs, but many of his competitors had been running non-union for a long time when he made this speech. Carnegie's arch-rival, Cambria Steel, had not had a union in its mills for fifteen years.[37] Four years earlier Carnegie bragged about being the Amalgamated Association's friend. Why did he start to backslide from that position in 1889? And why did he wait three more years before delivering the final blow at Homestead?

Developments in the marketplace and in the industry between 1885 and 1892 made jettisoning the union the only way Carnegie could continue to set wages and working conditions in the late-1880s. Before this period, most steel produced in this country went to make steel rails, but profit margins on this key product dropped considerably when the price of steel rails collapsed around 1885, primarily because of overproduction.[38] Furthermore, changes within the industry destroyed the viability of Carnegie's take orders and run full strategy. Carnegie Steel once had by far the greatest production capacity in the world, but by the late 1880s this was no longer the case. Several mills across the country could match Carnegie's capacity, the most noteworthy being the Duquesne Works of the Allegheny Bessemer Steel Company. When three firms merged to form the Illinois Steel Company in 1889, its production capacity surpassed that of the Carnegie mills.[39] In response, Carnegie spent $3 million on improvements during these years in an effort to maintain his competitive advantage. This resulted in a crisis of overproduction. As Carnegie predicted in 1888, "With a capacity to manufacture double the amount of rails required, the steel rail mills of this country have nothing to look forward to for some time but a severe struggle to run part of their works and maintain their organizations."[40]

The rail market experienced a downturn in the late 1880s not only because of overproduction at high-capacity mills, but because of changes in the nature of the demand for steel. In the early 1880s, over 90 percent of rolled steel produced in the United States went to rails. By 1890, that proportion fell to 50 percent.[41] The fastest emerging market for steel was for structural shapes to build skyscrapers. Carnegie wanted to use the same production strategy that he had always used, but he no longer had the same advantages. "We could get all the business we could do in building beams if we put [the] price down," he wrote in 1889;[42] but in this new market, economizing did not necessarily produce higher returns. Structural shapes required high-quality steel, not low-quality steel produced in large amounts (the formula which had made Carnegie Steel successful early in its history). Faced with these new manufacturing problems, Carnegie's high labor costs became increasingly burdensome.[43]

His solution to the problems of a changing industry was the sliding scale. Under a sliding scale, the compensation unionized workers received for what they produced would rise and fall with the market price instead of being locked into a particular rate for a set period of time.[44] Since skilled workers were the people most likely to work on a scale, they stood to lose the most from this new flexible tonnage rate, particularly at a time of falling prices. To Carnegie, however, the sliding scale was good for everybody. In his *Forum* essays, he wrote that the enactment of the sliding scale would mean employers and employees would be "in the same boat, rejoicing together in their prosperity, and calling into play their fortitude together in adversity . . . instead of a feeling of antagonism there will be a feeling of partnership." The automatic readjustment of wages would eliminate the need for the yearly renegotiation of the scale. This in turn would limit the opportunities for the strikes and lockouts that inevitably went with those talks. Carnegie considered strikes and lockouts "ridiculous affair[s]," which needed to be eliminated the same way that duels had been outlawed earlier in the nineteenth century.

Of course, a union that does not strike foregoes one of its most powerful weapons and workers who accepted the sliding scale could not strike. In fact, when Carnegie first endorsed this idea he did so not to improve the lot of workers, but to force them to accept wage cuts. "In depressed times," he wrote, "enormous concessions upon the published card prices have been necessary to effect sales, and in these the workmen have not shared with their employers."[45] Furthermore, because of Carnegie's accelerated system of production, employees could theoretically work harder and still receive less money if the massive output they produced drove down prices.

Organized labor in the steel industry initially opposed Carnegie's proposal, but the sliding scale was not necessarily anti-union. The Sons of Vulcan, the skilled ironworkers union that championed this idea during the 1860s and early 1870s, believed this practice ensured that its members would receive a fair return on their labor. By 1891, the Amalgamated Association decided that it should attempt to establish a sliding scale in all the steel mills under its jurisdiction.[46] For Carnegie, however, the sliding scale and the Amalgamated Association served the same function: both could keep workers on the job. The sliding scale offered Carnegie the same guarantee of labor that a union contract provided because it eliminated the need for negotiations. Workers were locked into the sliding scale for years at a time. Furthermore, the sliding scale helped the firm keep its production costs down because wage rates moved up or down with the price of production. The sliding scale was a manifestation of cooperation between labor and management that permitted the company to remain profitable whether or not it recognized a union. In instances where unions stood in the way of cooperation, the sliding scale threatened the role which Carnegie's *Forum* essays laid out for them. In time, this policy would also threaten the existence of unions in the industry.

Since market changes had their greatest impact on steel rail production, it is no wonder that Carnegie picked the Edgar Thomson mill at Braddock as the first place to put the sliding scale into practice. Nonunion when first built, Carnegie recognized the Amalgamated Association there in 1882 in order to get a jump on his competition during an industry-wide strike. In 1885, Carnegie first complained publicly about labor costs in Braddock. He blamed the Amalgamated for not organizing other Bessemer rail mills, which would have equalized labor costs across the steel sector of the industry. Carnegie did not move against unionized workers in their entirety at Braddock until 1888, by which time the Amalgamated had been replaced in the mill by the Knights of Labor. Even then, he did not initially set out to break the union. In January, all but two of the plant furnaces shut down because of lack of orders. In March, Carnegie offered representatives of the Knights the chance to work with a wage cut under the sliding scale if they accepted the return of the twelve-hour day. Only after they rejected this offer did Carnegie hire replacement workers and Pinkertons to guard them. Then, he imposed his terms unilaterally. Although the Edgar Thomson mill operated nonunion from that point on, the Amalgamated did not see this as the start of an anti-union campaign. In fact, the union sympathized with Carnegie's position, arguing that the eight-hour day put Edgar Thomson at an unreasonable disadvantage as long as other mills still worked their employees twelve hours.[47] Carnegie also did his best to assuage the fears of union members, telling a reporter from the Pittsburgh journal *American Manufacturer* that "he had not lost faith in organized labor, and felt sure that eventually the Braddock men would see their mistake."[48]

In 1889, Carnegie Steel refused to sign the union scale at its Homestead plant. Initially the company did not drive the union out of the plant; it laid workers off so that its total labor cost would go down. By the time negotiations started, management's position had hardened. At that point, it wanted the conditions of employment at Braddock instituted at Homestead: individual agreements with employees (meaning no union) and a sliding scale. The firm also demanded that the termination date of the contracts be changed from summer to winter, a time when most employees could not have risked walking a picket line. In June, a delegation from the Amalgamated Association convention toured the Homestead plant at the invitation of its superintendent, Charles M. Schwab. Although the convention passed a motion thanking the company for "the kindness and luxuries . . . bestowed on the delegates," the workers still refused to accept the company's terms and struck on July 1st. Rather than close the plant and wait for the workers to return, as Carnegie had recommended in the *Forum*, William Abbott, the manager in charge of negotiations while Carnegie was out of the country, hired replacements and tried to bring them into the plant under protection of the local sheriff. On successive days, management made two different attempts to restart the plant, but each time angry crowds turned back the replacements and the police charged with protecting these new workers. Shortly after the second attempt failed, the firm and the union reached a settlement. Carnegie Steel dropped the question of individual contracts and the new termination date. In return, the workers at Homestead agreed to work under the sliding scale for three years rather than the usual one.[49]

Most historians view the 1889 Homestead Strike as a dress rehearsal for the 1892 Homestead lockout, but this comparison shows the tendency of commentators to read history backwards. Judgments about the success or failure of both sides in this conflict have been made with an eye to their position when the final showdown came three years later. For instance, James Howard Bridge, who supported the actions of management in 1892, saw the outcome of the 1889 strike a "defeat." [50] Paul Krause, presenting this strike as part of a long line of Andrew Carnegie's misdeeds, calls the strike a "successful reconnaissance."[51] But in 1889, a final showdown was by no means inevitable.

The 1889 strike settlement did not mark the end of the first battle in a long war as much as a return to peaceful coexistence. Even though Carnegie was not directly involved in negotiations, the settlement was entirely consistent with Carnegie's pre-strike labor policy. The firm got the workers to accept the sliding scale, just as the Edgar Thomson workers had. Although the firm dropped the demand for individual contracts, Carnegie could not have been too concerned about this since he had already dealt with the Amalgamated Association for as long as he had owned the Homestead plant. Furthermore, at least one steel manufacturer later complained because the wages under the sliding scale at the beginning of the contract proved to be substantially lower than the wages paid under the scale signed by the rest of the industry.[52]

The long-term contract was management's idea.[53] The Amalgamated Association's scale at all but one other mill under its jurisdiction ran for one year, from July 1 to June 30. Carnegie wanted a three-year contract in order to avoid the problem of renegotiating the scale each year.[54] This way the firm would have skilled labor when other firms could possibly be shut down in a dispute with the union.[55] Although he was concerned about the precedent of giving in to strikers, Carnegie's reaction to the settlement was generally positive. "I am glad however that we will have three years of peace under the sliding scale," Carnegie wrote Abbott. "[Y]our statement . . . about this was to the point—admirable—[the] scale can be made fair where it is not and then we are at peace."[56] In short, breaking the union was not Carnegie's top priority in 1889. Management still believed that it was more important not to have production interrupted by a strike than to make the Homestead works union-free. If Carnegie had already decided that the Amalgamated had to go, his firm would never have signed a unique long-term agreement with the union.

How Strong Was the Amalgamated Association?

Even though management considered its 1889 contract at Homestead a victory, many historians view it as one sign of the Amalgamated Association's strength. Writing in 1918, John R. Commons and Associates called the Amalgamated "the strongest trade union in the entire history of the American labour movement."[57] Katherine Stone describes this same organization as "the strongest union of its day."[58] These interpretations accentuate the perceived impact of the Homestead lockout on the rest of the steel industry, but obscure a larger reality. Such assessments of the Amalgamated Association are based on either the strength of the union at Homestead or the strength of the union in the Pittsburgh area. This supposition is highly misleading because before 1892 the union was never as strong in any other mill as it was in Homestead and never as strong in any other district as it was in Pittsburgh.[59] Following this same faulty logic, Sharon Trusilo refers to the period from late 1888 to 1892 as "the years of the [Amalgamated Association's] greatest prosperity and success," but even in Pittsburgh, changes in the production process and the market were already cutting substantially into the union's power base.[60]

In order to judge the Amalgamated Association's strength throughout the country accurately, it is important to differentiate between two sectors of the industry. Iron and steel, although closely related, are not the same thing. Both substances begin in a blast furnace, but steel is refined in an additional step so that most of the carbon is limited to approximately 1 percent of the substance and mixed evenly throughout.[61] After its invention in 1856, the Bessemer converter became the most efficient way to make steel. Essentially, Henry Bessemer's insight was to create a device that would blow air through unrefined pig iron in order to increase its heat and remove the impurities without puddling. The metal produced by the Bessemer process was more malleable and set harder than ordinary wrought iron (and puddling remained a necessity for producing iron). Innovations in design made by the industrial engineer Alexander Holley in the 1860s and 1870s led to the first successful

Bessemer mills in America. By 1876, there were thirteen Bessemer mills in the United States, eleven of them built by Holley, including Andrew Carnegie's groundbreaking Edgar Thomson Works. Unlike iron, which could only be produced in small batches, the Bessemer method eliminated the need for puddling, thereby making the mass production of steel possible for the first time. While a typical iron rail mill could produce only 12,000 tons of product per year, a new Bessemer works could produce 114,000 tons. Since these products were substitutable for one another, even a small number of new steel plants significantly changed the market for both iron and steel.[62]

New Bessemer works and further improvements in the productive efficiency at older works such as Edgar Thomson contributed to a huge increase in the amount of steel manufactured in the United States.[63] Total Bessemer rail production in the United States went from 6,451 tons in 1868 to 1,187,770 in 1881. Annual production at the typical Bessemer mill went from 10,000 tons per year in 1868 to 172,000 tons per year in 1880. As production increased, the price of steel rails for railroads dropped from $120/ton in 1873 to $42/ton in 1878, thereby creating a market for steel where none had existed before. Even before the Amalgamated Association formed in 1876, Bessemer technology had already begun to eliminate jobs for puddlers as steel replaced iron in more and more markets where iron had once dominated. By 1877, the number of Bessemer steel rails produced in this country surpassed that of iron rails for the first time. In 1892, nationwide steel production surpassed that of iron for the first time. [64] "The change from iron to steel has been gradual and therefore hardly realized by the mill owners," wrote one manufacturer this same year; but by that point, it was already obvious to all observers that steel represented the future of the industry.[65]

The power of the Amalgamated Association was overwhelmingly concentrated in the iron-producing sector of the industry, which became increasingly irrelevant as the size of the steel sector grew ever larger. The reason the Amalgamated Association was stronger in the older sector had to do with the difference between iron and steel producing technology. The first Bessemer steel plants hired many men who had no experience in the iron industry. Employers could do this because innovations in steelmaking made it easy to train immigrants and other less-skilled workers to replace skilled union men, while iron still had to be puddled by hand. It took one to two years to learn puddling, but a common laborer could become a skilled steelworker in as little as six to eight weeks.[66] As *Iron Age* put it in 1892, "A man need not have spent a life time in a rolling mill to become an expert in the duties for which it calls."[67] Because the Amalgamated Association had always concentrated its organizing efforts on highly-skilled workers, less-skilled workers tended to view the union with contempt. Therefore, the increased need for less-skilled labor damaged the long-term viability of the organization. In a few instances during the 1880s, employers trained less-skilled steelworkers to permanently replace Amalgamated Association members trying to organize their mills.[68]

Because the circumstances that workers faced in the iron and steel sectors of the industry were so different, it is important to consider the strength of the union in each one separately. Although strong in the iron industry, the Amalgamated Association was never able to organize even half the steelworkers in the Pittsburgh district, the union's strongest. In fact, at its peak in 1891, only twenty-five percent of steelworkers eligible for Amalgamated membership nationwide were in the union. Even at Homestead, a few months before the strike began less than 400 of the 2000 workers at the plant eligible to join the union were actually members. As early as 1885, the signing of the scale was irrelevant to most steel firms across the industry because they already ran nonunion. Steelmakers tended to build entirely new mills and keep the Amalgamated out. In this manner, steel manufacturers outflanked the skilled workers who had wielded a considerable amount of power on the shop floor up to that point in time.[69]

After 1889, the situation of the Amalgamated Association changed dramatically for the worse. The union reached its high point in membership in 1891, 24,068; but by 1893, that figure had dropped by almost a half to 13,613.[70] Yet these numbers obscure a sharper drop in membership in the iron and steel sector of the industry. At the same time membership in the iron and steel sector of the economy decreased, membership in the tin plate sector of the industry increased sharply. Tin plate is steel rolled into thin sheets and dipped in tin. Its primary use was for cans or as roofing material. In 1890, the United States was completely dependent upon Wales for its tin plate; it produced virtually none of its own. High duties on tin plate, passed as part of the McKinley Tariff of 1890, caused imports of Welsh tin plate to dry up and jump-started a domestic tin plate industry. In the first quarter of operations after the tariff took effect on July 1, 1891, United States manufacturers produced 826,922 pounds of tin plate. That production practically doubled for each of the next two quarters, to 3,004,087 pounds. By 1896, American tin plate production exceeded imports from Wales for the first time. For this reason, the American Iron and Steel Association later concluded, "The McKinley Tariff is entitled to the whole credit for establishing this new industry."[71] The skilled labor that made this increase in production possible came from Wales. Welshmen joined the Amalgamated Association in large numbers because of the strong tradition of trade unionism in their home country. Although the exact number of tin plate workers who joined the union is impossible to discern, it may be as many as several thousand. Those who were not Welsh were often Amalgamated men displaced from nonunion rolling mills. Growth in employment for tin workers compensated for shrinking membership rolls in other sectors of the industry.[72] If tin plate production had not taken off when it did, the decline in the Amalgamated Association's membership would have occurred earlier and been more pronounced than the total membership numbers indicate.

The Amalgamated Association was also shaken by internal discord brought on by tensions between skilled and less-skilled workers in the years before Homestead. The union amended its constitution in 1889 to allow unskilled workers into its ranks. This new rule meant the Amalgamated could recruit new members without organizing new mills by organizing more thoroughly the mills it already controlled. In fact, enough unskilled workers joined the union that the highly skilled men started to complain that the national union no longer represented their interests. At the same time, the less-skilled members of the Amalgamated resented the way in which the skilled men dominated the local lodges.[73] Because of these tensions, *American Manufacturer* could describe the union's situation a few weeks before the scale expired in 1892 as follows: "At this moment, [the Amalgamated] is weaker than it has been for years. We do not mean by this to say that its membership is less, but in the present interest of its members, in the organization, in prestige, in accumulated funds, and in esprit du corps it is weaker than at any time since its formation."[74]

Compounding these problems (or perhaps because of them), the Amalgamated Association suffered a long series of setbacks at mills across the country beginning in the late-1880s.[75] But unlike most of the strikes the union had lost in the past, the Amalgamated lost these mills permanently. Under the weight of increased competition, iron and steel manufacturers in every region of the country moved to cut back on their labor costs by running nonunion with increasing frequency. In Pittsburgh, the smaller iron-making operations grew increasingly hostile to the union in their midst because they faced escalating competition with nonunion steel firms. By the late 1880s, the results of this new mentality began to show. In 1888, three Pittsburgh firms (Spang, Chalfant and Company; Singer, Nimick and Company; and Dilworth, Porter and Company) all rejected the Amalgamated scale and began to operate on a nonunion basis.[76] Just these few nonunion iron mills in the Amalgamated Association's strongest district were enough to cause the union concern; as evidenced by the *National Labor Tribune's* warning to its readers in 1889, "[I]t is bad policy to permit nonunionism to exist in small spots. Such spots should be converted to the only right policy as soon as one of them appears, for the tendency of even a small one is to grow larger and in time spread."[77] In the years leading up to the Homestead strike, this prediction would prove increasingly prophetic.

The Allegheny Bessemer Steel Company opened a new large-capacity steel mill in Duquesne, near Pittsburgh, in early 1889. The firm wanted to pay below union scale because it was in direct competition with Carnegie Steel, but the employees walked off the job in response to low wages. When management permanently discharged thirty strike leaders, the workers formed an Amalgamated Association lodge. At this point, the company hired replacements and Pinkertons to protect them. The mill began producing rails again by early May. However, the strike did help to destroy the financial position of the company. The firm sold out to Carnegie Steel in 1890 to become that concern's second nonunion mill. Also in 1890, the Carbon Iron Company of Pittsburgh, the Braddock Wire Company, the Bellefonte Iron and Nail Company, the Ellis and Lessig Steel and Iron Company of Pottstown, and the Iowa Barb Wire Company of Allentown all rejected the Amalgamated scale and started to operate on a nonunion basis.[78]

In 1891, the Amalgamated Association lost strikes at iron and steel mills across the eastern region. Outside Pennsylvania, the Elmira Iron and Steel Company of Elmira, New York, and the Riverside Iron Company of New Castle, Delaware, both defeated the union. In eastern Pennsylvania, the Amalgamated lost disputes at the Norristown Iron Works, the Lochiel Iron Company of Harrisburg, the Lebanon Iron Company, the Lebanon Rolling Mill, the East Lebanon Iron Company, the Hamburg Rolling Mill Company, the Pottsville Iron and Steel Company, the Gibraltar Iron Works in Bucks County, the Taggart and Howells Rolling

Mill in Northumberland, the Pencoyd Iron and Steel Company, and the Catasauqua Rolling Mill. The Pennsylvania Steel Company won a two-week strike by 2,000 workers at Steelton, Pennsylvania, and declared its new mill at Sparrow's Point, Maryland, an open shop at the same time. This dispute deserves special attention because management hired Pinkerton guards to protect their mills and several hundred Black replacement workers to defeat the strikers. Over the next year, these eastern mills exploited their lower labor costs to penetrate markets in western Pennsylvania that had previously been dominated by Pittsburgh firms. This only increased the pressure on western Pennsylvania manufacturers to jettison the union.[79]

Around Pittsburgh in 1891, Moorhead Brothers & Company of Sharpsburg locked out its workers even though a company representative had sat on the conference committee that had negotiated that year's scale. At Duquesne and McKeesport, workers again tried to organize but failed. Even though the Amalgamated Association did manage to organize the Illinois Steel Company in Chicago in 1891, one trade journal nonetheless reported, "It is claimed that this has been the worst year in the history of the organization. The manufacturers also say there will be more trouble for the Amalgamated next year if they do not adopt more equitable schedules and if the mills now making the effort to resume with non-union men are entirely successful."[80]

In 1892, the conflict between management and the union continued to spread. Because the market for steel remained depressed, both sides expected trouble as the time to renegotiate the scale approached. The price of many different iron and steel products sunk to new lows. Among these were steel rails, the price of which dropped even lower than in 1889. Furthermore, the crisis of overproduction that first sent shock waves through the industry in the late-1880s intensified. Even though more pig iron was produced in 1890 than in 1892, the industry's potential production capacity actually grew by 3 million gross tons over those years.[81] "The iron trade continues in a demoralized condition," reported the Pittsburgh correspondent of the *Engineering and Mining Journal* in March 1892. "The outlook at present is by no means a favorable one."[82] Despite the poor state of the industry, the Amalgamated Association submitted a wage scale that was essentially the same as the one it had submitted the year before to manufacturers who were in no mood to bargain.[83]

Virtually every firm in both the iron and steel sectors of the industry found the Amalgamated Association scale unacceptable in 1892. Most companies that had previously signed the scale refused that year. In fact, manufacturers from every sector of the industry and every region of the country began proposing deep wage cuts even before the union first offered its scale. During early negotiations, the manufacturers of the Mahoning and Shenango valleys in Ohio demanded a fifteen to sixty percent decrease for their unionized employees. Around Pittsburgh, the manufacturers surprised the Amalgamated by presenting their own wage scale before receiving the scale from the union. It included wage cuts even deeper than the ones proposed in Ohio. Union shops around Philadelphia also refused to sign. In sectors where the union remained strong, like sheet steel, manufacturers tended to settle without a strike. Even Carnegie Steel signed a special scale for its two iron plants: Union Mills and Beaver Falls. "We have no especial objection to the Amalgamated Association in these mills," a company official later explained, "for the reason that the product for the main part is merchant iron and steel, in the manufacture of which we compete with similar union mills all over the country." The sectors of the industry in which the union was weakest were those where manufacturers were most likely to fight.[84]

Many steel manufacturers besides Carnegie Steel took on the union in the summer of 1892 because companies throughout the industry perceived the Amalgamated Association as vulnerable. "At the great majority of the iron and steel mills west of the Alleghenies not a fire is burning nor a wheel is turning today," reported *the Bulletin of the American Iron and Steel Association* shortly after the old Amalgamated scale expired on July 1st.[85] In the struggle that followed, steelmakers across the country managed to permanently banish the Amalgamated from their facilities. By August, there were more nonunion mills up and running across the country than at any time in the previous twenty years. In September, Iron Age printed a substantial list of nonunion firms in the iron and steel industry. The journal explained its data as follows:

> Our tables enumerate non-union rolling mills employing not less than 70,000 men. . . . In addition we have confidential data from 13 mills having a monthly tonnage of 36,150 tons and employing 10,715 men. . . . We have gone over carefully the non-union mills from which no reports have been received, estimating from the equipment and product, and taking into consideration the returns from similar

> works from which data are available, and find . . . the total number of men working in non-union works in the United States up to 100,000 men.
>
> A study of the products made by these non-union mills will show they embrace every line of work in the whole range.[86]

However, the struggle between labor and management at one mill had already drawn all the attention away from industrial relations at every other firm. That fight was at Homestead.

A Friend No More

A lot of ink has been spilled over the question of who was responsible for the violence at Homestead—Andrew Carnegie, or his colleague Henry Clay Frick. The answer to this question is undoubtedly both of them. Born in 1849, Frick grew up on his grandfather's farm in West Overton, Ohio. His family was rich, not from farming, but from producing rye whiskey. Although not a self-made man, Frick, like Carnegie, had a strong drive to succeed. Upon being told that his grandfather was worth one half a million dollars, Frick resolved "to be worth [one million] before I die."[87] Like Carnegie, Frick believed strongly in Social Darwinism. Like Carnegie, Frick's career trajectory demonstrates his resolve. After eight years of formal education (including a brief stint in college), Frick secured a job in his uncle's general store working as a clerk. From there he became chief bookkeeper at a local distillery. Using money he saved in salary and borrowed from relatives, Frick began to buy coal lands in 1859. He organized the Henry Clay Frick Coke Company in 1871, and the business quickly grew, selling all the coal it could produce, mostly to the rapidly growing steel industry. Due to his detailed bookkeeping, Frick knew he made his first million when he was thirty. By 1880, H.C. Frick dominated the regional coal industry. When Carnegie decided that his firm should be vertically integrated so as to protect his supply of coal, he began to buy up stock in Frick's firm. Although Carnegie controlled approximately 50% of Frick's firm by the mid-1880s, Frick continued to run the coal company. In 1889, Carnegie brought Frick in as a partner and named him chairman of Carnegie Steel.[88]

By 1892, Henry Clay Frick had a reputation for breaking trade unions. That reputation came from his long fight against the miners' union in the

H.C. Frick Coke Company coal fields. In a famous 1887 coal strike, Frick employed replacement workers and Pinkerton guards to protect them. He also evicted strikers from company housing and used other strongarm tactics.[89] Carnegie undoubtedly knew of Frick's actions because at the time of this strike he was part owner of the coal company. Therefore, when he wrote Frick on May 4th, 1892, "We all approve of anything you do, not stopping short of approval of a contest. We are with you to the end," he undoubtedly knew what to expect.[90] If there had been no violence at Homestead, Frick's choice of tactics probably would never have become an issue.

Because both men agreed that the union had to go, Carnegie Steel bargained harder than it ever had before in the months preceding the expiration of the 1889 contract. Management and labor were far apart at the beginning of negotiations and they never got together. In March, the Amalgamated Association made its first offer for a new scale, which included a ten percent wage increase for most departments. Management found the offer unacceptable. On April 4th, Carnegie sent Frick a draft of a notice to be given to Homestead employees. The key sentences read as follows: "As the vast majority of our employees are Non-Union, the Firm has decided that the minority must give place to the majority. These works therefore, will be necessarily Non-Union after the expiration of the present agreement." Frick, not yet willing to provoke open conflict, never posted the notice. Instead, he offered the union terms he knew it would never accept; then rather than negotiate from that position, Frick waited until the scale expired before making the company's intentions known.[91]

The issue at the heart of the lockout was the company's desire to control the production process. As Frick explained shortly after the violence, "It is whether the Carnegie Steel Company or the Amalgamated association [sic] shall have absolute control over our plant."[92] Notice there is no middle ground. Frick wanted complete control. This reflects, as Thomas Misa explains, "a social choice to retain profits rather than distribute them as wages," not a prerequisite for technological improvements since technological improvements at Homestead had already successfully begun. Carnegie agreed with this choice because of his growing distaste for unions that came about in large part because of this dispute. "All anxiety gone since you stand firm," he wrote Frick, "Never employ one of these rioters. Let grass grow over works. Must not fail now." [93] The emphasis on control and the vehemence of these statements suggest the manner in which the actions of the strikers rattled the cultural sensibilities of both men. The displaced workers were not just unreliable workers, they were rabble who did not deserve a second chance to be employed at the jobs the company had once graciously provided. Even when the strikers offered to accept the terms of the company's last offer and go back to work, Frick refused them because he was more concerned with eliminating the presence of the union at Homestead than he was about the wage rate which the company paid its employees. Management's hostility would eventual be reflected in the hardened anti-union position of Carnegie Steel alumni during the early-twentieth century.

In the months following the violence, Carnegie and Frick's views on the lockout began to diverge. However, it should be noted that their argument was over methods rather than results. Publicly, Carnegie continued to back Frick, declaring his faith in him during his first public speech on the Homestead dispute in January 1893. Privately, he began to back away. In a reply to a letter of sympathy from British Prime Minister William Gladstone, Carnegie wrote, "Our firm offered all it could offer, even generous terms. . . . They went as far as I could have wished but the false step was made in trying to run the works with new men." [94] Only after the magnitude of the public outrage began to affect his own reputation did Carnegie begin to question Frick's judgment. This difference of opinion on Homestead contributed to a complete break between the two men in 1899.[95]

With the passage of years, Carnegie began to express his regret for the violence at Homestead publicly. But rather than defend the aspects of his earlier writings that supported his later policies, Carnegie misrepresented facts in such a way so as to appear that he still believed in the aspects of the *Forum* essays that had once made him so popular with labor. Testifying before Congress in 1911, Carnegie claimed that Homestead was the only time Carnegie Steel had ever employed Pinkertons even though the firm had made use of Pinkertons at Braddock in 1888 and had tried to have the militia brought in at Homestead in 1889. While preparing his autobiography, Carnegie had a top executive searching for weeks to a find a telegram that he remembered the workers sent him before the strike. It supposedly read, "Kind master, tell us what you wish us to do and we will do it for you." No such telegram ever surfaced, but Carnegie used the story in his autobiography anyway.[96] Whether these incidents were deliberate deception or merely self-delusion, they are consistent with a man who felt guilty about something.

Carnegie never tried to clear up the general misimpression of his views on unions, perhaps because he liked the accolades that the selective quotation of his *Forum* essays had brought him.

Even after Homestead, Carnegie still stressed cooperation as the most important quality of any labor management relationship. "The best of all unions," he told the assembled crowd when he opened the Carnegie Library of Homestead in 1898, "is such a happy union as prevails between the firm and its men, the two high contracting parties representing kind friendly capital and self-respecting labor."[97] Yet by that time his workers recognized that the cooperation that Carnegie championed was cooperation on management's terms. The support Andrew Carnegie had shown the Amalgamated Association disappeared when it became apparent that even a conservative union was a financial liability in a largely nonunion industry. Carnegie Steel's internal espionage system stopped two later organizing attempts at Homestead, and thereby kept the power equation tilted towards management. These post-lockout labor policies were the direct antecedents to the draconian excesses of the Nonunion Era.

Despite his regrets, Carnegie never acknowledged his contribution to the tragedy of July 6, 1892. To have done so would have justified the numerous attacks on his character that followed the violence. A passage from his autobiography shows that Carnegie felt his critics had treated him unfairly, "I knew myself to be warmly sympathetic to the workingman, but throughout the country it was naturally the reverse, owing to the Homestead riot. The Carnegie Works meant to the public Mr. Carnegie's war upon labor's just earnings."[98] Homestead had become a symbol in the national debate over the merits of trade unionism. The misunderstanding that had once made Carnegie popular with labor only increased resentment against Carnegie after Homestead. Workers recognized the importance of Carnegie's complicity in crushing the union. The businessman who had claimed to be labor's friend became labor's worst enemy. Rather than defend his real philosophy of labor, Carnegie used philanthropy to assuage his guilt.[99] The men who controlled the steel industry after Carnegie's retirement built an unambiguous defense of their antiunion labor policies based on the notion that their achievements in society justified their complete control of all business operations. After the turn of the century, they completed the process that Carnegie had hastened by removing the Amalgamated Association from their mills.

Notes

1. Andrew Carnegie, "Dedication of the Carnegie Library at the Edgar Thomson Steel Rail Works, Braddocks [sic]," March 30, 1889, 17.

2. Barnard Alderson, *Andrew Carnegie: The Man and His Work* (New York: Doubleday, Page & Company, 1902), vii.

3. Andrew Carnegie, "Memorandum of 1868," in *The Andrew Carnegie Reader*, Joseph Frazier Wall, ed. (Pittsburgh: University of Pittsburgh Press, 1992), 41.

4. Carnegie's interests were organized into many different subsidiaries and reorganized often. The most important were Carnegie, Phipps & Co., organized in 1874; Carnegie Brothers & Company, organized in 1881; and the first complete consolidation of Carnegie's holdings, Carnegie Steel Company, organized just days before the Homestead tragedy in 1892. For sake of simplicity, I will refer to the enterprise as the Carnegie Steel Company in this work no matter what period of its history is being discussed.

5. The definitive Andrew Carnegie biography is Joseph Frazier Wall, *Andrew Carnegie* (New York, Oxford University Press, 1970).

6. Alun Munslow, "Andrew Carnegie and the Discourse of Cultural Hegemony," *Journal of American Studies* 22 (August 1988): 217.

7. Joseph Frazier Wall, "Introduction," in *The Andrew Carnegie Reader*, x-xi.

8. Andrew Carnegie, "An Employer's View of the Labor Question, in *The Andrew Carnegie Reader,* 96.

9. Andrew Carnegie, "Results of the Labor Struggle," in *The Andrew Carnegie Reader*, 112.

10. Wall, *Andrew Carnegie*, 526.

11. *St. Louis Post Dispatch* quoted in Wall, *Andrew Carnegie*, 572.

12. Leon Wolff, *Lockout* (New York: Harper & Row, 1965), 64.

13. Paul Krause, *The Battle for Homestead, 1880-1892* (Pittsburgh: University of Pittsburgh Press, 1992), 233-35.

14. John A. Fitch, *The Steel Workers* (Pittsburgh: University of Pittsburgh Press, 1989/Originally published by the Russell Sage Foundation, 1910), 132.

15. Katherine Stone, "The Origins of Job Structures in the Steel Industry," *Review of Radical Political Economics* 6 (Summer 1974): 66.

16. David Brody, *Steelworkers in America* (Urbana: University of Illinois Press, 1998/ Originally published by Harvard University Press, 1960), 57-58. Paul Krause makes the same argument in *The Battle for Homestead* on page 361.

17. The classic descriptions of the Homestead lockout include Myron Stowell, *"Fort Frick" or the Siege of Homestead* (Pittsburgh: Pittsburgh Printing Company, 1893); Arthur G. Burgoyne, *The Homestead Strike of 1892* (Pittsburgh:

University of Pittsburgh Press, 1979/Originally published by Rawsthorne Engraving and Printing Company, 1893); J. Bernard Hogg, "The Homestead Strike of 1892," Ph.D. Diss., University of Chicago, 1943) and Wolff. Although I disagree with some parts of his analysis of Andrew Carnegie's labor policies, Paul Krause's *The Battle for Homestead* is still the best treatment of the Homestead lockout yet written.

18. *New York Times*, 2 and 4 January 1885.

19. *John Swinton's Paper*, 11 January 1885.

20. Carnegie, "An Employer's View of the Labor Question," 96.

21. Carnegie, "Results of the Labor Struggle," 112.

22. Wall, *Andrew Carnegie*, 520-22; John Ingham, *Making Iron and Steel* (Columbus: Ohio State University Press, 1991),137; Fitch, *The Steel Workers*, 193.

23. *New York Times*, 2 January 1885

24. Jesse Robinson, *The Amalgamated Association of Iron, Steel and Tin Workers* (Baltimore: The Johns Hopkins University Press, 1920), 10.

25. Michael Nuwer, "From Batch to Flow: Production Technology and Work-Force Skills in the Steel Industry, 1880-1920," *Technology and Culture* 29 (October 1988): 812-15.

26. Francis G. Couvares, *The Remaking of Pittsburgh: Class and Culture in an Industrializing City, 1879-1914* (Albany: State University of New York Press, 1984), 11, 13; Michael W. Santos, "Laboring on the Periphery: Managers and Workers at the A.M. Byers Company, 1900-1956, *Business History Review* 61 (Spring 1987): 116, n. 7.

27. For more on workers' control in the iron industry, see David Montgomery, *Workers' Control in America* (New York: Cambridge University Press, 1979), 11-12; For a step-by-step recounting of the ironmaking process, see Michael John Nuwer, "Labor Market Structures in Historical Perspective: A Case Study of Technology and Labor Relations in the United States Iron and Steel Industry, 1860-1940," Ph.D. Diss., University of Utah, 1985, 38-44.

28. Robinson, 114-15.

29. *American Manufacturer* 36 (5 June 1885), 10; *Iron Age* quoted in *National Labor Tribune*, 27 (June 1885).

30. John A. Fitch, *The Steel Workers*, Appendix II, "The Amalgamated Association," 255; Hogg, 25, n. 8.

31. Mary Ellen Freifeld, "The Emergence of the American Working Classes: The Roots of Division, 1865-1885," Ph.D. Diss., New York University, 1980, 469; William Weihe quoted in Freifeld, 533.

32. James Howard Bridge, *The Inside History of the Carnegie Steel Company* (Pittsburgh: University of Pittsburgh Press, 1991/Originally published by Aldine Book Company, 1903), 186.

33. Thomas J. Misa, *A Nation of Steel* (Baltimore: The Johns Hopkins University Press, 1995), 23-28.

34. Peter Temin, *Iron and Steel in Nineteenth-Century America* (Cambridge, MA: MIT Press, 1964), 157.

35. Lawrence C. Phipps quoted in William Brown Dickson, *History of the Carnegie Veteran Association* (Montclair, NJ: Mountain Press, 1938), 26.

36. Carnegie, "Dedication," 16.

37. Herbert Gutman, "Two Lockouts in Pennsylvania, 1873-1874," in *Work, Culture and Society in Industrializing America* (New York: Vintage Books, 1977), 324.

38. Brody, *Steelworkers in America*, 3.

39. Victor S. Clark, *History of Manufactures in the United States*, Vol. 2, (New York: McGraw Hill, 1929), 237.

40. *Iron Age* 41, 24 (May 1888): 847.

41. Temin, 222-23.

42. Andrew Carnegie to W.L. Abbott, June 1889, Andrew Carnegie Papers, Vol. 10, Library of Congress, Washington, D.C.

43. Misa, *A Nation of Steel*, 70.

44. The idea of a sliding scale did not originate with Andrew Carnegie; it first appeared on the Pittsburgh scene in 1865. Carnegie did, however, champion the idea at a time when it had fallen out of favor. See Krause, *The Battle for Homestead*, 94-95, 106.

45. Carnegie, "An Employer's View of the Labor Question," 93, 99-100.

46. Fitch, *The Steel Workers*, 122.

47. Fitch, *The Steel Workers*, 114-18; *Iron Age* 41, 5 and 12 May 1888, 10 May 1888; *National Labor Tribune*, 4, 14 and 28 April 1888.

48. *American Manufacturer* 42, 4 May 1888.

49. Andrew Carnegie to W.L. Abbott, December 29, 1888; Andrew Carnegie Papers, Vol. 10; Amalgamated Association, *Journal of Proceedings*, 1889, 2600; Hogg, 32-37; *Iron Age* 43, 23 May 1889, 27 June 1889.

50. Bridge, 200-01.

51. Krause, *The Battle for Homestead*, 250.

52. *Iron Age* 52 (20 July 1893). 111.

53. Carnegie Steel also proposed long-term contracts in 1888 at Edgar Thomson and at Homestead in 1892, but the lockouts at both places made this position moot.

54. Robinson, 149.

55. U.S. Congress, House, *Hearings Before the Committee on Investigation of United States Steel Corporation* (in 8 Vols.) [The Stanley Committee], 62nd Cong., 2nd Sess., 1911-1912, 2524.

56. Andrew Carnegie to W.L. Abbott, August 7, 1889, Andrew Carnegie Papers, Vol. 10.

57. Henry E. Hoagland, "Humanitarianism," *History of Labour in the United States*, Vol. 2 (New York: Macmillan, 1918), 495-96.

58. Stone, 64.
It is worth noting that Katherine Stone's article is based on the idea that modern job structures were created when the worker-controlled labor system of the nineteenth century was overthrown. However, virtually all of her evidence of worker influence in the early steel industry comes from the Homestead plant.

59. As A.F. Huston, Vice-President of the Lukens Steel Company told the *Boston Herald* in July 1892, "Iron and steel labor in Pittsburgh and vicinity commands higher wages than in any place east of it. The reason for this is that the Amalgamated Association is stronger in the western part of Pennsylvania than anywhere else (quoted in Horace B. Davis, *Labor and Steel* (New York: International Publishers, 1933), 229)."

60. Sharon Trusilo, "The Amalgamated Association of Iron and Steel Workers," in *"The River Ran Red": Homestead 1892,* David P. Demarest, Jr. ed. (Pittsburgh: University of Pittsburgh Press, 1992), 17.

61. Pig iron is the product created by a blast furnace. Remove some of the carbon from it, the product is steel. Remove all the carbon from it and the product is wrought iron. Steel, therefore, is an intermediate compound.

62. Misa, *A Nation of Steel*, 5-15, 22; Freifeld, 472. For a step-by-step recounting of Bessemer production, see Nuwer, "Labor Market Structures in Historical Perspective," 47-50.

63. For details on these improvements, see Misa, *A Nation of Steel*, 26-28.

64. American Iron and Steel Association, *Annual Statistical Report*, 1885, 26-27; Clark, Vol. 2, 265; John W. Bennett, "Iron Workers in Woods Run and Johnstown: The Union Era, 1865-1895," Unpublished Ph.D. Dissertation, University of Pittsburgh, 1977, 3-4.

65. *National Labor Tribune*, 5 March 1892.

66. H.E. Hoagland, "Trade Unionism in the Iron Industry: A Decadent Organization," *Quarterly Journal of Economics* 31 (August 1917): 681-82; Nuwer, "From Batch to Flow," 830; Stone, 75.

67. H.E. Hoagland, "Trade Unionism in the Iron Industry: A Decadent Organization," *Quarterly Journal of Economics* 31 (August 1917): 681-82; Nuwer, "From Batch to Flow," 830; Stone, 75; *Iron Age* 50, 9 September 1892, 581.

68. Nuwer, "Labor Market Structures," 127-28.

69. Fitch, *The Steel Workers*, 87, 89; Krause, *The Battle for Homestead*, 289; Edward Bemis, "The Homestead Strike," *Journal of Political Economy* 2 (June 1894): 372; *American Manufacturer* 36, 5 June 1885, 10-11; Couvares, 85.

70. Robinson, 21.

71. Ira Ayer, "Special Report to the Secretary of the Treasury . . . Relative to the Manufacture of Tin and Terne Plate," Government Printing Office, April 26, 1892, 7-8; Carroll W. Pursell, Jr., "Tariff and Technology: The Foundation and Development of the American Tin-Plate Industry, 1872-1900," *Tech-*

nology and Culture 3 (Summer 1962): 273; American Iron and Steel Association, *Annual Statistical Report*, 1892, 19.

72. D.E. Dunbar, *The Tin-Plate Industry: A Comparative Study of Its Growth in the United States and in Wales* (Boston: Houghton Mifflin Company, 1915), 53; Brody, *Steelworkers in America*, 60.

73. On tensions inside the Amalgamated Association see Bennett, 56-57 and Steven Cohen, "Reconciling Industrial Conflict and Democracy: The "Pittsburgh Survey" and the Growth of Social Research in the United States," Ph.D. Diss., Columbia University, 1981, 86-88.

74. *American Manufacturer* 50 (10 June 1892), 1035.

75. Paul Krause, in Appendix L of *The Battle for Homestead* [pp. 404-05], offers a chart titled "Selected Disputes in Greater Pittsburgh, Metalmaking Industries, 1867-1892." He cautions readers, "The table is by no means exhaustive; in virtually every year, there were important confrontations in the mills of Pittsburgh." Nevertheless, Krause's failure to consider conflicts at smaller Pittsburgh mills or any mill outside of Pittsburgh is symptomatic of his narrow focus.

76. Amalgamated Association, *Journal of Proceedings*, 1889, 2640-41, 2644-47.

77. *National Labor Tribune*, 15 June 1889.

78. Irwin Marcus, "The Duquesne Lockout of 1889: Prelude to Homestead in 1892," 1892 Homestead Strike Centennial Conference, Pittsburgh, PA, July 5-7, 1992, 2-9; Amalgamated Association, *Journal of Proceedings*, 1890, 2958-59; Amalgamated Association, *Journal of Proceedings*, 1891, 3362, 3364, 3382-85; Amalgamated Association, *Journal of Proceedings*, 1892, 3859.

79. Amalgamated Association, *Journal of Proceedings*, 1892, 3860, 3863; 3912; *Engineering and Mining Journal* 52, (1 August 1891): 129; Mark Reutter, *Sparrow's Point* (New York: Summit Books, 1988), 46-47; John Bodnar, *Immigration and Industrialization* (Pittsburgh: University of Pittsburgh Press, 1977), 41-42; *Iron Age* 49, 5 May 1892, 874.

80. Amalgamated Association, *Journal of Proceedings*, 1892, 3887-89; *Engineering and Mining Journal* 52 (4 July 1891): 13; Fitch, *The Steel Workers*, 118; James Holt, "Trade Unionism in the British and U.S. Steel Industries, 1880-1914: A Comparative Study," *Labor History* 18 (Winter 1977): 14; Bulletin of the American Iron and Steel Association 25, (26 August 1891): 251.

81. Hogg [pages 39-47] offers an entire chapter's worth of evidence on the worsening condition of the iron and steel industry between 1889 and 1892.

82. *Engineering and Mining Journal* 53, (5 March 1892).

83. *Iron Age* 49, (16 June 1892): 1182.

84. *National Labor Tribune*, 11 June 1892; Hogg 63; *Pittsburgh Post*, 15 July 1892 excerpted in *The River Ran Red*, 143. Both of these Carnegie mills struck in sympathy with the men at Homestead, and, like Homestead, management restarted them with nonunion labor.

85. *Bulletin of the American Iron and Steel Association* 26 (6 July 1892): 196.

86. *Iron Trade Review* 25, (23 June 1892): 5; *Iron Age* 50 (29 September 1892): 582.

87. George Harvey, *Henry Clay Frick: The Man* (New York: Charles Scribner's Sons, 1928), 16.

88. Harvey's book is a hagiography, useful only for extensive quotation from Frick and Carnegie's private correspondence. Kenneth Warren's *Triumphant Capitalism: Henry Clay Frick and the Industrial Transformation of America* (Pittsburgh: University of Pittsburgh Press, 1996) is vastly superior.

89. Andrew Carnegie forced this strike to a quick settlement because of his company's need to run at full capacity. Frick resigned the chairmanship of the H.C. Frick Coke Co. over the dispute. The two men presumably worked out their differences over labor relations because Frick returned to Carnegie Steel with more responsibilities by the end of 1887. See Warren, pages 43-49.

90. Harvey, 166.

91. United States House of Representatives, *Investigation of Homestead Troubles*, Report #2447, 52nd Cong., 2nd Sess., 1892-93, 22; Bridge, 203-05; Joseph Frazier Wall, "Andrew Carnegie's Responsibility for the Tragedy at Homestead," 1892 Homestead Strike Centennial Conference, Pittsburgh, PA, July 5-7, 1992, 71.

92. "Frick Explains," *Pittsburgh Commercial Gazette*, July 8, 1892, excerpted in *The River Ran Red*, 94-95.

93. Misa, *A Nation of Steel*, 270; Harvey, 166.

94. Wall, *Andrew Carnegie*, 577; Andrew Carnegie to William Gladstone, September 24, 1892, Andrew Carnegie Papers, Vol. 17.

95. For more on the break between Carnegie and Frick, see Warren, 240-68 and Wall, *Andrew Carnegie*, 714-64.

96. Stanley Committee Hearings, 2528; Wall, *Andrew Carnegie*, 575-76.

97. Carnegie quoted in *Bulletin of the American Iron and Steel Association* 32 (20 November 1898): 177.

98. Andrew Carnegie, *The Autobiography of Andrew Carnegie* (Boston: Northeastern University Press, 1986/Originally published by Houghton Mifflin, 1920), 225.

99. Paul Krause, "Patronage and Philanthropy in Industrial America: Andrew Carnegie and the Free Library in Braddock, Pa.," *The Western Pennsylvania Historical Magazine* 71, (April 1988): 128.

Chapter Two

The Decline of the Amalgamated Association of Iron, Steel and Tin Workers and the Rise of the Implied Contract

> So today the Amalgamated Association is again more than anything else an iron workers' organization. Its largest membership comes from the iron mills of Ohio, Indiana and Illinois. It still has a foothold in the sheet and tin mills, but it does not number in its jurisdiction one large steel mill where heavy material is handled.
>
> —John A. Fitch, *The Steel Workers*, 1910.[1]

Whereas the elimination of the Amalgamated Association at Homestead occurred over a few short months, the elimination of the union from the industry happened more gradually. Changes in technology that undercut the importance of skilled workers to the production process began long before the Homestead lockout; yet technological change did not eliminate the need for skilled workers. Jobs which required the craft-type manipulative skills that Amalgamated members possessed became increasingly rare as steel production took off during the 1890s. Ex-puddlers were often in the same position as common labor in the new labor market since both groups had to learn these new skills in order to get the better-paying jobs. Steel manufacturers did not de-skill craft workers in order to gain increased control over production, rather technological changes which increased production rendered old skills largely irrelevant. Most firms built entirely new facilities to produce steel when they entered this sector of the business and kept the Amalgamated Association from ever entering their mills. Because the rise of Bessemer steel production bypassed almost all of the places where skilled workers held sway, Amalgamated Association members could not even slow down production in order to extract concessions. Control had passed almost entirely into management's hands.

In order to understand the course of this transition from an industry with some unionized workers to a non-union industry, it is necessary to appreciate the differences in the production process for different sectors of the industry. The last chapter covered the differences in the production processes that made iron and steel. As steelmaking expanded during the 1890s, ironmaking, the sector of the industry over which the union held some sway, contracted because of the Panic of 1893. Between 1892 and 1903, the few major manufacturers in the steel sector and nearly all of the iron manufacturers in the Pittsburgh area that still recognized the union after Homestead gradually ceased to sign the scale.[2] Most of the firms which operated nonunion in the 1880s and 1890s were in what was known as the "basic steel" segment of the industry. These companies produced steel rails, structural shapes and other large items commonly sold to large manufacturers. But some firms within the steel sector still depended upon skilled workers to further refine the product into specialized goods like steel hoops, plates of sheet steel or other products with a less-lucrative market than structural shapes or rails. The various refinements made to steel in order to create these specialty products are outlined in the chart pictured in Figure 2.1. Many specialty firms continued to recognize the Amalgamated Association because they still depended upon the skills of its members to perform this extra step in the production process. Therefore, despite the devastating effect of technological change on skilled ironworkers, the transition from iron to steel did not destroy the union completely.

During the 1880s, when technological change first began to undercut the Amalgamated Association's power, the union's power base began to shift to those sectors of the industry where skill remained vital to the production process. In the 1890s, the union's presence in the sheet steel and tin plate sectors of the industry actually grew at the same time its traditional base in the basic steel sector faced a sharp decline. Yet a niche presence in a few sectors of the industry could not overcome the growing hostility of employers. Around the turn of the century, steelmakers began an all-out assault on the legitimacy of organized labor so as to justify

Figure 2.1. Courtesy of Hagley Museum and Library.

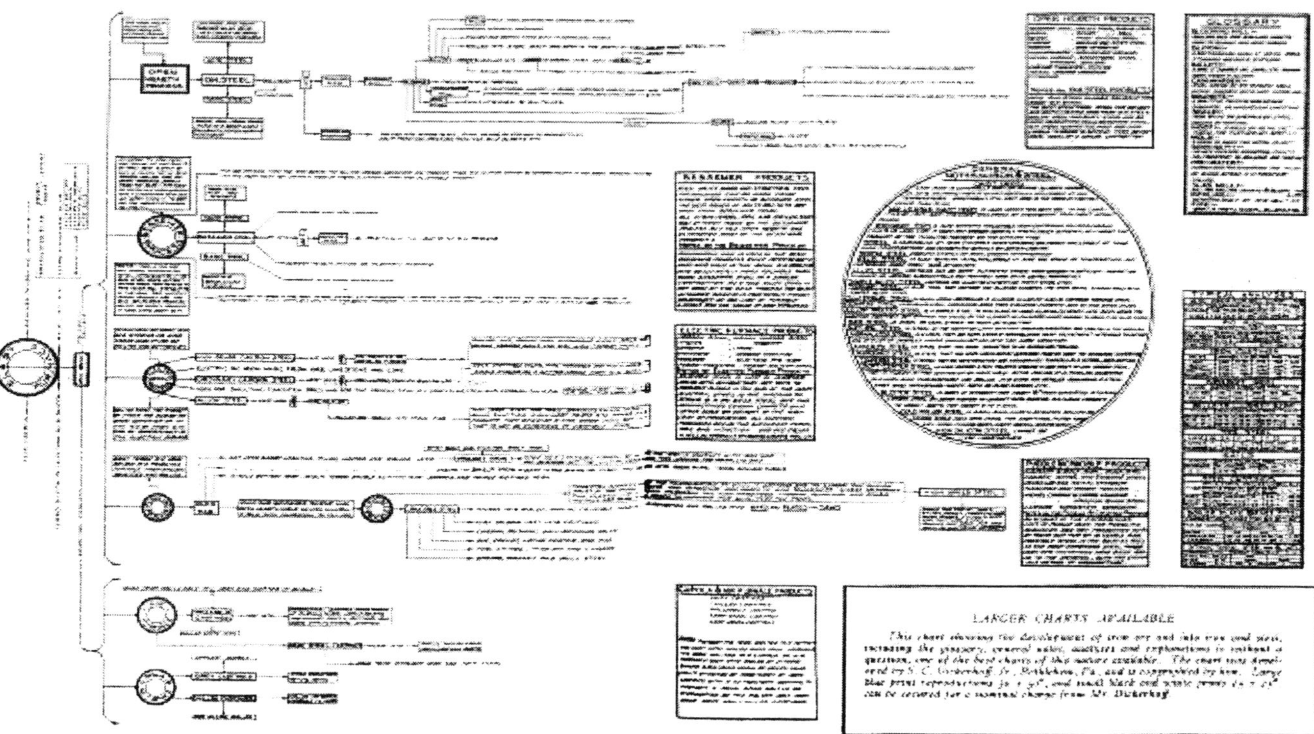

This chart illustrates the wide variety of products produced by iron and steel producers in the early 1900s. Because of this variety, to speak of a single iron and steel industry without recognizing its different segments is a mistake.

remaining nonunion. Led by the example of U.S. Steel, the industry began to redefine the relationship between labor and management. Relying on an emerging conception of labor contracts shaped by courts hostile to trade unions, steelmakers tried to establish a direct relationship between employers and each individual employee. By doing this, steel industry executives and other like-minded manufacturers made the ethos of individual achievement the philosophical basis of all employer/employee relations.

Management's ability to impose its worldview upon its workers increased as the power of the Amalgamated Association declined. As the steel industry's control over its workforce grew, it began to force employees to accept difficult labor conditions. In the wake of the Homestead lockout, employers made the twelve-hour day and the seven-day week the accepted industry norm. The highly-skilled workers who had once been the backbone of the union suffered the most during the 1890s. The demand for skilled puddlers began to decline in the years before Homestead because buyers preferred steel to iron. The Panic of 1893 proved particularly harmful to workers in the iron industry. As the economy grew worse and more iron mills closed their doors, the few highly-skilled jobs in the steel industry had more and more applicants. This change in the labor market, combined with the collapse of the union, meant wages for skilled workers dropped precipitously. "Before 1892, I made $10 to $12 a day," declared one longtime Homestead employee in 1908. "After the strike wages went down to $7 and by 1903 they were $3. At the same time, the work load increased and my hours of work were increased."[3] Even Illinois Steel, which continued to sign the Amalgamated scale for years after the Homestead lockout, cut the wages of its unionized workers 33% in 1893. The core of the Amalgamated Association's membership faced a concerted, industry-wide effort to equalize wages across skill levels because the skills they possessed had become expendable.[4]

Contrary to the experience of skilled workers, the desire of employers to equalize wages brought the earnings of less-skilled workers up during these same years (although nowhere near the level that unionized skilled workers once received). Common labor faced the same longer hours and increased workloads, but it often received the opportunity to learn new skills needed in the emerging sectors of the industry. These chances allowed less-skilled workers to move to better-paying jobs. This explains why the average wage of steel plants that ceased to recognize the union tended to increase in the years after the union disappeared; however, the drop in employment because of new production processes meant the total wage bills of these firms still tended to drop.[5] This rise in wages also shows that even nonunion firms had to pay to maintain control over their workers. Steelmakers imposed a nonunion industrial relations system on their workers, but it was never as stable as David Brody suggests in *Steelworkers in America*.[6] Manufacturers had to deal with frequent strife within their workforce throughout the Nonunion Era, and even in peaceful times steelmakers remained constantly alert for signs of trouble. Nevertheless, changes in technology throughout the industry and attacks on the legitimacy of trade unionism made the possibility of rebuilding a union during these years very difficult.

The Amalgamated Association Confronts Changes in Technology

Former Amalgamated Association president William Weihe told the Congressional committee investigating the Homestead lockout that his union "never objects to improvements and makes allowances in every particular where there are improvements . . . [W]henever there is an improvement made by which certain men will be done away with, then their jobs will be done away with. There is no objection."[7] Certainly this statement accurately describes the transition from iron to Bessemer steel. As a matter of policy, the Amalgamated Association accepted lower rates for workers whose jobs became easier as a result of technological change. After 1892, it offered special scales to steel manufacturers throughout the industry in order to maintain its presence in an increasingly hostile environment. For this reason, Jones and Laughlins (later called Jones & Laughlin) completed its conversion from iron to steel during the 1890s without eliminating the union from its mills. This organization's attitude toward technological change was not uncommon among unions in the late nineteenth century. Indeed, few labor organizations directly opposed management's right to use new machines during this period. Most simply sought to contain the pace of change and to preserve jobs in the process.[8]

However, to see the Amalgamated Association's response to the introduction of Bessemer steelmaking as evidence of its acquiescence to all technological change would be a serious mistake. Most ironmakers became steelmakers by building new facilities and keeping unions out, not by forcing unionized workers to accept new terms and conditions of employment. By doing this, they avoided confronting skilled workers over issues concerning the production process. The Amalgamated Association could not prevent or even slow the transition from iron to steel because it had little success in these new mills. It had better luck in mills that began in iron and converted to steel, but the majority of steel workers were employed elsewhere (Of the eleven Bessemer works in the United States operating in 1896 which had an annual production capacity of at least 300,000 tons, only two had made puddled iron when they first opened).[9]

In these few places where it did organize steel workers, the union made numerous concessions out of necessity. If the Amalgamated Association had fought technological change, employers might have felt the need to destroy it, and in basic steel, union leaders knew the organization could not win such a fight. Furthermore, Weihe's statement about accepting technological change does not apply as well to the sectors of the industry outside of basic steel. When changes in production had an obvious adverse impact on the union's membership in important sectors that the Amalgamated Association dominated, union members fought to stem the tide of change. Two sectors, nailmaking and tin plate production, can stand for all the products created. One started its decline before the initial collapse of the union, the other afterwards.

From the early-1870s to the mid-1880s, Wheeling, West Virginia, led the United States in nail production. Skilled labor controlled the production process in Wheeling's nail mills during this period, and most of these workers belonged to the Amalgamated Association. Like other iron or steel products, the nailmaking process began in blast furnaces that produced raw iron. Puddlers (called boilers in the nail mills) refined the iron until it reached the desired consistency. The iron then moved to rolling mills, where it passed back and forth through large rolls until it reached the optimum thickness and width. Those plates then went to nail mills where skilled nailers supervised the feeding of the sheets into machines which produced cut nails. Under this labor system, skilled craftsmen received high wages; many even entered the ranks of management through promotion or by starting their own mills. This organization of work dated from the 1840s and it survived through the mutual acceptance of management and labor alike.[10]

Two roughly simultaneous technological developments helped to change the labor system in this sector of the industry. First, manufacturers introduced a variety of new inventions to make the production process more efficient. This led directly to the second change, the switch from iron to steel. The most important technological innovation was the automatic nail-making machine, which increased the number of nails a manufacturer could produce, and cut the number of workers needed to oversee the production process. Continuous rolling devices, automatic nail feeders and other improvements made more of the skills used in nailing obsolete. During strikes, employers replaced many nailers with the less-skilled nail feeders whom they had once supervised. These technological changes increased the productive efficiency of rollers and feeders, but not of puddlers. The second development, the widespread use of steel nails, affected puddlers directly. Between 1884 and 1889 steel nails rose from 5% to 69% of all nails made in the United States. This change not only increased production, it also improved the quality of the product since steel nails held better and were easier to drive than nails made of iron. This development also eliminated puddlers from the production process, along with their constant demands for wage increases. The net result of all this was a large savings for nail manufacturers. At one West Virginia firm, labor costs dropped from $1.03 to 56 cents per keg over the two year span it took to switch over to steel. By 1886, it was estimated that across the industry manufacturers could save 10 cents per keg producing steel nails instead of iron.[11]

In 1884, the Amalgamated Association convention, which was dominated by puddlers, demanded a 20 percent premium for making steel nails because they claimed steel nails were harder to manufacture than the traditional iron kind. Fearing for their jobs, most Wheeling nailers did not collect the premium. Instead, the nailers dropped out of the organization and formed their own union. When nailers struck in 1885 along with other unionized workers, the employers hired less-skilled nail feeders to take their place along with armed guards to protect them. Almost a year after the strike began, the nailers accepted a settlement which strongly favored the Wheeling manufacturers. Wheeling nail mill workers lost their 1885 strike because new technology made them expendable. Many nailers were not rehired, and those who were never received as much in wages as they had before the strike. In fact, most Wheeling workers never returned to the Amalgamated. As more firms switched to steel, many lodges disbanded because the skills their members possessed became obsolete and there was nothing that could be done about it. Among the few firms that produced steel nails and still signed the scale, the union had trouble enforcing its provisions. By 1892, the advent of the wire nail drove those firms out of business, thereby eliminating unions from the nail-producing sector of the industry long before the Homestead lockout.[12]

By the time nailers disappeared from the Amalgamated Association, the union's membership numbers had already recovered because of an influx of tin plate workers from Wales. They came in response to the growth of the industry caused by the McKinley Tariff of 1890. Before the tariff took effect, most observers believed that Americans did not have the skills to make tin plate because of previous failures by entrepreneurs to build up this sector of the industry. After the tariff took effect, this belief quickly dissipated because production expanded quickly. "The [tin plate] industry has developed with satisfactory and, in view of attendant difficulties, with surprising rapidity," wrote a Special Agent for the Secretary of the Treasury in an 1892 report. "Capital, at first cautious, is now being freely invested in this branch of manufactures."[13] Nevertheless, American capital depended on Welsh labor during the early years of the industry. Up to that point in time, Wales had possessed a near monopoly on world production. Therefore, only Welshmen knew how to run tin plate machinery. Manufacturers encouraged Welsh tin plate workers to emigrate to the United States in the early 1890s by offering them high wages in exchange for their skills. Because Welsh tin workers had a long tradition of trade unionism, they became the core of the Amalgamated Association by the end of the 1890s. In fact, the Amalgamated Association of Iron and Steel Workers changed its name to the Amalgamated Association of Iron, Steel and Tin Workers around this time in order to reflect the switch in its constituency.[14]

Although the American tin plate industry had to use Welsh methods and Welsh labor to launch production, technological changes came fast and furious. No single innovation made the American tin plate industry successful. Instead, American manufacturers made numerous small changes which had a significant cumulative effect. For instance, American tin plate mills started using tin shears powered by electric motors rather than tin shears powered by steam. This decreased the skill needed to operate them because machines could rest while not in use. American tin plate makers also rearranged the position of the machines in their mills so as to resemble the continuous operations of Carnegie Steel's

Bessemer mills. This change increased throughput and decreased wasted motions by employees. 1891 saw the introduction of an automatic tin polishing machine. Observers estimated that this innovation alone eliminated the need for nine employees. As was the case with the nailers, these kinds of technological changes quickly made the skills possessed by the recent Welsh immigrants largely irrelevant. In fact, tin plate manufacturers deliberately cultivated technological changes in order to cut labor costs. As one manufacturer wrote in 1892, "Welchmen [sic] who have heretofore been working at different things through the country at normal wages, $1.50, $2, and sometimes $2.50; will not do anything in the tin industry less than $3.50 to $5 and $6 per day. . . . [U]ntil we get our own people used to it, there must necessarily be some waste in the cost of labor." The way to get Americans used to it was to invent methods that they could learn easily. The number of men needed to run a tin plate mill increased because of technological change, but so much more tin plate could be produced after these changes occurred that increased revenue more than compensated for the cost of hiring more less-skilled workers. By 1908, less than half of the tin plate workers in the country were Welsh nationals. At this point, tin plate manufacturers could eliminate their skilled union workers and not worry about their ability to continue producing efficiently.[15]

By the turn of the century, the benefits of technological change were so lucrative that employers in nearly every sector of the industry wanted to eliminate the union so they could keep the additional profit entirely to themselves. The transition from iron to Bessemer steel made the Nonunion Era possible, but the supplanting of Bessemer production by the open hearth process made operating on a nonunion basis even more profitable. Steelmakers began experimenting with the open hearth process in the 1880s because of their desire to produce large batches of high-quality steel for structural shapes. The idea behind open hearth steelmaking was to recycle the heat of spent exhaust gasses to raise the temperature within the furnace to levels impossible through other production processes. This way, the heat alone could remove carbon from the molten iron, rather than requiring further manipulation by workers. By controlling the amount of air allowed into the furnace, manufacturers could control the chemical composition of the steel and make a product that was more elastic and tougher than Bessemer, though less rigid. This quality made open hearth steel particularly well-suited for the emerging market in structural shapes and armor plate. Open hearth plants were also more efficient than Bessemer mills. They required fewer workers and had higher outputs.[16]

Because the builders of buildings, bridges, ships and subways all demanded steel produced by this new method, open hearth steel production took off fairly rapidly. In 1892, only 13.6% of all steel produced in the United States was made by the open hearth method. By 1901, that figure rose to 34.6%. By 1914, 73% of American steel was made through the open hearth method. Other than the Homestead Works (which completed the changeover to open hearth in 1888), most large plants converted to open hearth production with no union present.[17] The Amalgamated Association could not stop the transition from Bessemer to open hearth because it no longer had a discernible presence in the basic steel industry. Therefore, this important change in the steelmaking process did not affect industrial relations at all. The industry was already largely non-union and remained largely non-union as the transition to open hearth steelmaking took hold. By the end of World War I, the industry had adopted a fierce anti-union stance so as to guarantee that the additional profits generated by this technique would remain with the company. The firm most responsible for this industry-wide position was the United States Steel Corporation.

United States Steel Versus the Amalgamated Association

J.P. Morgan organized United States Steel, the world's first billion-dollar corporation, in 1901 in order to end the unbridled competition within the steel industry that had marked the 1890s. Since numerous pooling agreements had failed to maintain prices, consolidation became the only way to guarantee that rogue steel firms would not undercut their competitors. Eleven major mergers occurred in this industry during 1898 and 1899. The formation of U.S. Steel was the logical culmination of this trend because as long as the unpredictable and fiercely competitive Andrew Carnegie remained active in the market, any other firm in the industry could potentially be undersold. $1.4 billion in capital went into this new industrial giant, although modern estimates suggest that as much as half this figure represented nothing but the faith of stockholders in future earnings. This figure represented one sixty-seventh of the total wealth of the nation at that time. U.S. Steel controlled 72% of the country's

Bessemer steel production, 60% of open hearth steel, 59% of steel rails, and 85% of all wire, tubes and pipes. It produced more steel than either Great Britain or Germany and more than a quarter of the world's output. Its ten divisions also included companies with substantial interests in iron ore, coal, shipping and railroads. Although it would steadily lose market share over the course of its existence, U.S. Steel continued to dominate the industry (and industry labor policy) into the 1930s.[18]

Three of the ten companies that consolidated to form the Corporation had a substantial number of workers who belonged to the Amalgamated Association: the American Steel Hoop Company, the American Sheet Steel Company, and the American Tin Plate Company. Together the unionized workers of these three companies made up about 10% of U.S. Steel's workforce. At American Steel Hoop, 9 out of 14 mills were organized, at American Sheet Steel, 23 out of 28 mills, at American Tin Plate, all the mills were organized but one. The Corporation's other subsidiaries employed some union members, but for the most part organized labor was already relegated to the sectors of the industry that these three subsidiaries represented. It is no coincidence that these strongly organized subsidiaries were all in sectors of the industry where skilled labor remained a part of the production process longest.[19]

In 1901, the Amalgamated Association of Iron, Steel and Tin Workers still had almost 14,000 members. Although down from its highpoint in 1891, the size of the union's membership still compared favorably to other points in its history.[20] Therefore, U.S. Steel could not take the Amalgamated Association lightly. "I am certain that the new combination will recognize the Amalgamated Association," union president T.J. Shaffer told the *Pittsburgh Dispatch* shortly after U.S. Steel formed. Nevertheless, he acknowledged, "[I]t is only by experience that we can give a conclusive answer to the question, 'Will the new combination be a benefit to organized labor?'"[21] By 1909, the union had more than enough evidence to answer that question in the negative. Not only did U.S. Steel prevent any of its unorganized mills from unionizing, the Corporation eliminated the union from its already-organized mills by winning two large strikes in 1901 and 1909. "The United States Steel Corporation has declared war on labor," proclaimed the American Federation of Labor after this second major strike began. "In its secret councils this corporation has decreed that the only obstacle to its complete sway—organized labor—shall be crushed."[22] And crushed it was. By 1912, the Amalgamated Association had split into two distinct unions, yet the combined membership of both these organizations amounted to only 5,730 out of a potential 275,000 employees in the entire industry.[23]

Elbert Gary, the Chairman of U.S. Steel from its inception, led the fight against trade unionism during the Corporation's early years as well as the fight to keep the firm nonunion until his death in 1927. Gary controlled every aspect of U.S. Steel's policies. Following interviews with lower-level executives about U.S. Steel's labor policies, the journalist Ray Stannard Baker reported, "[T]o a remarkable degree these men I talked with . . . echoed Judge Gary's views. They would give facts, but would express no opinions whatever of their own. It is a wonderfully disciplined organization that Judge Gary has created. It speaks as one man."[24]

Although Gary did not come from humble origins, he promoted the idea of pulling oneself up by the bootstraps as much as Andrew Carnegie himself. Elbert's father Erastus Gary was a successful farmer and land speculator in Illinois. The Galena and Chicago Railroad went right through his property when built in 1846. The sale of the land made Gary's family rich. Erastus Gary also served as a magistrate in DuPage County Illinois for over twenty years. Well-placed friends of the elder Gary got Elbert his first job in law. Gary began his involvement with the steel industry in 1892 when he arranged the consolidation of five firms into the Consolidated Steel and Wire Company and began to serve on the board of directors of this concern. In 1898, he became president of the Federal Steel Company, a new conglomeration of plants in the Midwest that was the largest firm in the industry save for Carnegie Steel. Because Federal steel had been backed by J.P. Morgan, Morgan picked him to lead U.S. Steel when it formed in 1901 because he could count on Gary's loyalty.[25]

Despite the advantages in his life, Chairman Gary adopted all the trappings of a self-made man. Gary often compared the work of his employees unfavorably to the manual labor he performed while growing up, claiming, "I do not believe any one of them works more hours or harder than I did as a lad on my father's farm."[26] According to one biographer, Gary kept an electric sign on his desk that read "It can be done" because "He believed that hard work and determination could accomplish the seemingly impossible."[27] His role as president of the American Iron and Steel Institute, which began in 1910, made him the most single important person in the entire industry. Publicity surrounding his leadership role during the 1919 strike made Gary one of the best-known union opponents in the United States.

Following the lead of Ida Tarbell, who published a surprisingly laudatory biography of Gary in 1925, historians have treated U.S. Steel's early labor policy as a product of a philosophical division within the Executive Committee, the body that controlled the Corporation. In these accounts, bankers and lawyers from the Morgan wing of the business supported policies that helped the Corporation maintain its long-term profitability while so-called "practical steel men," took a short-run view of most problems.[28] The steel producers were mostly the former Carnegie partners. Many (but certainly not all) had been picked from relative obscurity and worked their way up to the top tier of the company. Because of their life experience, they were more likely to cite the ethos of individual achievement in order to oppose any concessions to unions. The following exchange recounted in Tarbell's biography illustrates the significance of this distinction with regard to labor policy in the traditional account:

> "I have always had one rule," said [one member of the Executive Committee]. "If a workman sticks up his head, hit it." It was the Carnegie rule, born of war. "So long as I am here," said Judge Gary, "no workman's head shall be hit! You can get another chairman, but I shall never recognize that policy."[29]

In other words, the men from outside the steel industry had an enlightened labor policy while the former Carnegie officers believed in unyielding repression.

Half this equation is right. The ex-Carnegie officers hated unions. However, even though U.S. Steel directors who came from the Morgan interests would go on to pioneer seemingly enlightened labor policies, they also hated unions. For example, William Edenborn, who came to the Corporation from Morgan's Consolidated Steel and Wire Company and who was a hard-liner in labor matters, stated he "would not give way one inch" when U.S. Steel faced a strike by the Amalgamated Association in 1901 because "a concern operating with a union is pretty badly handicapped."[30] More tellingly, George W. Perkins, the Morgan partner and U.S. Steel director most responsible for the Corporation's program of welfare capitalism, wrote, "[W]e certainly cannot afford to have the Miners' Association get control of our men," when the Western Miners Association organized a strike at U.S. Steel's Minnesota iron ore fields in 1907.[31] In short, United States Steel officials never accepted organized labor before the late-1930s, no matter how committed to long-term thinking they happened to be.

In the first months of the Corporation's existence, the Executive Committee's distaste for organized labor was tempered by circumstances. Both the bankers and the practical steel men on the Executive Committee believed they had no choice but to sign the scale for their previously unionized plants. They feared the bad publicity and adverse financial consequences that a showdown with the union might have brought. "[W]hile it is very humiliating," admitted Gary, "nevertheless it is a critical period and we had better temporize if it can be done." However, this did not mean that U.S. Steel was an easy mark. Even before the Amalgamated presented the Corporation its scales for the first time, the Executive Committee had already passed a resolution which stated, "That we are unalterably opposed to any extension of union labor and advise subsidiary companies to take [a] firm position when these questions come up and say that they are not going to recognize it, that is, any extension of unions in mills where they do not now exist."[32] Although not entirely anti-union, this strategy gave management more time to pursue its ultimate goal of eliminating the Amalgamated from its facilities. By fighting the union on a plant-by-plant basis, the process attracted less public attention than it would have otherwise.[33]

The Amalgamated Association, on the other hand, actively sought confrontation. Ultimately, the union wanted to organize the entire corporation. Since it perceived U.S. Steel as vulnerable in large part because of the Corporation's debts on its initially overvalued securities, Amalgamated Association leaders believed the union had to strike quickly. Before the old contract expired, the leadership rejected two compromises offered by U.S. Steel's sheet and hoop mill divisions (one of which actually would have increased the number of organized plants in the Corporation by four). On July 1st, 1901, Amalgamated President T.J. Shaffer called these workers out on strike, along with tin plate workers who had already agreed to a contract. Later, union members at U.S. Steel's few remaining organized steel mills hit the picket lines as well. Approximately 20,000 men answered the strike call, but it soon became clear that the Amalgamated overestimated the difficulty that management would have replacing its skilled members. The Corporation restarted many organized plants with nonunion labor and transferred work from closed union mills to operating nonunion mills. When the parties reached a final settlement in September, the union lost six tin plate mills, two hoop mills, and five sheet metal works. It also lost eight steel mills.[34] "We might have exacted harsher terms with reference to the number of nonunion mills," explained the company's negotiators in a post-strike report to U.S. Steel's Board of Directors, "but it was not thought wise by your Management to take the position of openly oppressing organized labor."[35] Ironically, the strike proved to be a public relations windfall for the Corporation because it allowed management to portray the Amalgamated Association as an organization that did not honor its contracts.[36]

U.S. Steel gradually eliminated the union from its remaining plants with little difficulty. In the years following the 1901 strike, lodges in the organized sectors of the Corporation either lost their charters after losing short strikes or gave them up voluntarily. By 1908, only fourteen of U.S. Steel's mills remained organized. The final showdown between the Amalgamated Association and the Corporation occurred in 1909. On June 1st of that year, one month before the scale expired, the company posted a notice at the plants of its last unionized division which read, in part, as follows: "After careful consideration of the interests of both the company and its employees, the American Sheet and Tin Plate Co. has decided that all its plants after June 30th, 1909, will be operated as 'open' plants." Because the Corporation refused even to meet with union leaders, the Amalgamated Association had no choice but to call a strike for the day this order took effect. Every organized mill but one in the Corporation's sheet and tin plate division responded to the call. The strike even shut down eight unorganized mills. U.S. Steel countered by shifting work to open, nonunion plants and importing strikebreakers to open those closed by the lockout. By mid-September, management claimed sixty-nine percent of production had been restored. With organized labor gone from its tin plate mills, U.S. Steel's entire operation now ran nonunion.[37] The fact that it took eight years for the Corporation to eliminate trade unionism from its mills should not be interpreted as a lack of commitment to anti-union principles. Because U.S. Steel started with so many employees in well-organized sectors of the industry, it had more unionized employees to eliminate than its major competitors.

When faced with strike activity, the Corporation's competitors displayed the same uncompromising attitude and tactics that U.S. Steel did. In 1909, the largely immigrant workforce of the Pressed Steel Car Company in McKees Rocks, Pennsylvania, struck in protest over poor wages.

Even though the Industrial Workers of the World (IWW) aided the unskilled strikers, nobody could mend the differences between unskilled immigrant employees and skilled American-born workers. Seeing the strike as a cause for foreigners, the skilled workers returned to work shortly after the struggle began. Later, President F.N. Hoffstot's decision to introduce trainloads of strikebreakers rounded up by New York's Pearl Berghoff Detective Bureau resulted in violence that left twelve dead and forty injured, but the company still won the strike. Unorganized machinists inaugurated a strike which shut down Bethlehem Steel's flagship South Bethlehem, Pennsylvania, plant in 1910. That strike ended after 108 days with minimal violence. The settlement hardly changed the working conditions that existed before the strike, did not raise wages and recognized no union. On December 20th, 1915, a small group of unorganized, mostly unskilled laborers walked off their jobs at a Republic Steel plant in the Youngstown, Ohio, area. By January 5th, 1916, the total number of strikers grew to 2,500, both skilled and unskilled. About this time, the strike spread to the Brier Hill plant of Youngstown Sheet and Tube, raising the total number of strikers to between 8,000 and 10,000. The employees of both companies demanded higher wages. On January 7th, a clash between strikers and mill guards led to rioting which resulted in $500,000 worth of property damage in the immigrant neighborhoods of East Youngstown. After the Ohio National Guard arrived to keep order, the strike ended within a few days.[38] Other firms in the industry that did not face strikes often cited U.S. Steel's labor policy as their reason for not recognizing the Amalgamated Association, claiming they would be unable to compete if forced to absorb the higher labor costs that inevitably followed union recognition.

Even U.S. Steel faced similar impromptu uprisings in the years after 1909. In 1912, unskilled workers shut down the Corporation's National Tube Company plant in Pittsburgh for about a month by conducting a spontaneous walkout. Although U.S. Steel refused to grant their demand of a two and one-half cent per hour wage increase, management did make minor improvements in working conditions in order to encourage strikers to come back to work. That same year, a spontaneous strike in response to the discharge of three men in the Homestead mill's transportation department closed that mill and the Edgar Thomson Works. The Corporation made no concessions and both mills restarted within two weeks. In May 1916, striking unionized machinists from the Westinghouse East Pittsburgh electric plant convinced workers at Edgar Thomson to join them on strike. The company brought guards in overnight, and violence that erupted the next day resulted in four dead and twenty wounded. The strike quickly collapsed. In 1918, skilled maintenance workers at three U.S. Steel plants in Birmingham, Alabama, walked off their jobs as part of a citywide strike to win the eight-hour day. The mills operated with less-skilled workers in their place. After the federal government declined to intervene, the strike collapsed. Such incidents highlighted the impossibility of the industry's quest for absolute control over its employees. Despite the collapse of the Amalgamated Association, there were 14 strikes in the iron and steel industry in 1914, 30 in 1915, 72 in 1916 and 56 in 1917. Even though employers appeared to be completely "in the saddle" after U.S. Steel's 1909 victory, these conflicts demonstrate that management had to remain vigilant because its labor policies could never completely quash dissent.[39]

In 1918 and 1919, a new grass-roots campaign breathed life into trade unionism in the iron and steel industry. The leaders of this organizing effort were John Fitzpatrick of the Chicago Federation of Labor and William Z. Foster, a former member of the IWW and future chairman of the American Communist Party.[40] Fresh from success at organizing Chicago's packinghouse workers, these two men convinced the American Federation of Labor to form the National Committee for Organizing Iron and Steel Workers in August 1918. The twenty-four unions which had jurisdiction over some segment of steel employees agreed to work together and fund this massive effort. Foster, serving as Secretary -Treasurer of the National Committee, had operational control of the campaign. While World War I continued, the campaign was very successful. Buoyed by rapid progress in Chicago, the leadership extended organizing efforts to other cities in October 1918. Yet, ultimately, employers defeated this effort too by using the same methods of control they had been honing since 1892.[41]

When the war ended in November of that year and manufacturers no longer faced production obligations, they began to mount serious resistance. For example, employers fired union sympathizers. Harassment by local governments made it impossible for organizers to find places to hold their meetings. Under pressure from the rank and file, who had already staged many unsuccessful small-scale strikes for recognition since the war ended, Foster called a strike for September 22nd, 1919. Even though only 100,000 workers had joined the union at that point, approximately 250,000 heeded the strike call that day, approximately half the industry's workforce. However, aggregate figures do not give an accurate picture of what the strike was like everywhere. As the journalist Mary Heaton Vorse pointed out, "There was not one steel strike but fifty. There were strikes in fifty different communities. Through ten states the steel workers struck." The response to the strike varied from place to place. At plants in eastern Pennsylvania and the South, production either continued despite the strike or resumed within days. The strike was more effective in the Pittsburgh area, where it stopped production entirely at many mills.[42]

Although the response to the strike was better than organizers had hoped, Foster's organization faced an uphill battle in keeping the works it shut down from resuming operations. The men on the picket lines were mostly unskilled, foreign-born workers. The workers who stayed on the job tended to be American-born and better paid. Many firms restarted operations with the assistance of skilled workers who crossed the picket line and thousands of unskilled replacements (many of whom were African American). A friendly press corps assisted the industry in its efforts to convey the impression that production had resumed and therefore the strike was lost. Newspapers and business leaders also publicized Foster's radical past to discredit the strike in the eyes of the public. Local and state authorities frequently resorted to violence to force striking steelworkers back to work. The most important reason for the failure of the strike was management's determination to avoid union recognition at all costs. Because the strikers demanded recognition of their union rather than higher wages or better working conditions, the industry refused to compromise.[43]

Organized labor had counted on President Wilson's October 1919 Industrial Conference to provide the impetus for government arbitration of the strike. When this failed to materialize, union leaders recognized the futility of their situation. In early November, Amalgamated Association President Michael Tighe pulled his skilled constituents off the picket line in order to preserve the remaining power base of his now-inconsequential organization. With thousands of steelworkers following Amalgamated Association members back to work, the National Committee for Organizing Iron and Steel Workers declared the strike over on January 8, 1920. "The tradition of defeat in the steel industry was too strong," Foster later wrote, "thirty years of failure were not easily forgotten."[44]

The Ethos of Individual Achievement Enshrined

That tradition of failure began at the mills of Carnegie Steel during the late-1880s and 1890s. Although not the first producer to eliminate the Amalgamated Association from its mills, Carnegie Steel's tactics for keeping those mills nonunion influenced the entire industry. In the years before the Homestead lockout, as more of its mills began to operate on a nonunion basis, the firm created a spy network that helped it control its workforce and defeat repeated efforts to reorganize Homestead and other plants. Operatives in mill towns throughout the steel districts of western Pennsylvania and Ohio reported on everything from run-of-the-mill laziness to serious organizing efforts among employees. Such advance information made fighting organization much easier. For example, when workers at Homestead undertook the first steps toward collective action in 1899, Charles Schwab described Carnegie Steel's response to the firm's Board of Managers this way: "We have Agents in the Mills, and as fast as we learn the names of any men taking active part [in organizing a union] we discharge them." The company needed this system because its attempts to force steelworkers to accept increasingly unfavorable terms and conditions of employment met with considerable hostility from its employees. At Braddock, nonunion after 1888, the company used intelligence and brute force to defeat organizing campaigns there in both 1889 and 1890. During this second incident, a group described by plant manager Charles M. Schwab as a "posse" of about 250 Hungarians convinced employees in the Furnace Department to walk off their jobs. In response, Schwab organized approximately 100 armed workers sworn in as sheriff's deputies to protect employees from being influenced to join the strikers. When the strikers returned to the plant gates, there was some contained violence; but it was not widely reported and the works soon began full operations. The firm also beat back the union at Homestead in 1895 and at the Duquesne mill in 1901.[45]

Without a union in its mills, Carnegie Steel could exercise greater control over its labor costs. The company still paid its employees on a sliding scale, but this contractual arrangement became only one method by which the firm paid its workers. Faced with increased competition for labor in 1895, the firm instituted a wage increase, but at Andrew Carnegie's insistence it came in the form of a bonus rather than a change in the scale. The company benefited from the bonuses in two ways. First, the bonus could be targeted specifically to the kinds of labor that the company needed most. Second, and more importantly, the bonus could be rescinded if the labor market situation changed before the contract expired. By August 1896, company officials wanted to lower wages because the labor shortage had ended. "There is a very easy way to stop the bonus," wrote Carnegie to his management team. "When mills stop for a time, as they must, before starting them, let the men be told quietly that the firm regrets it cannot go on paying the bonus under present conditions. The men will agree to start without the bonus; if not, you can wait. No public notice need be given. When Duquesne starts without a bonus, it is easy to get it off at the other works." The company ended the bonus shortly thereafter.[46] The use of the bonus allowed Carnegie Steel to maintain the fiction that workers had entered into an agreement with management over their conditions of employment, even though the company retained the power to alter conditions of employment almost at will (as the rescinding of the bonus demonstrated).

After Homestead, Carnegie wanted to give the impression that his labor policy had not really changed from union days. The men who dominated the industry when Carnegie passed from the scene had no need to keep up appearances. Nearly the entire industry pursued an anti-union labor policy after 1900 because it made economic sense and fulfilled their beliefs about the social ills of organized labor. Since market power in the steel industry was concentrated in so few, like-minded hands, it is possible to let the views of a few well-placed men stand for those of all steelmakers. As time passed, their opposition became embedded in the practice of the industry, which reinforced the intensity of the manufacturers' opposition.

The ethos of individual achievement formed the ideological basis of the industry's labor policy. Steelmakers wanted to establish a one-to-one relationship with their employees because this would encourage employees to succeed. Even before the Nonunion Era began, firms that produced steel made a point of dealing with their workers on an individual basis, free from the influence of outside organizations. The justification for this policy was as much philosophical as economic. Among larger firms, this effort began at the close of the Homestead lockout. "We did not care whether they were union or non-union," explained Henry Clay Frick, President of the Carnegie Steel Company, before a Congressional committee investigating the dispute in 1892, "but we wanted men whom we could deal with individually."[47] By 1910, the Cambria Steel Company had enshrined this principle as part of its work rules: "The Company reserves the right under the Constitution and Laws of the Commonwealth of Pennsylvania and of the United States to deal with its employees respecting the nature and terms of their employment in their individual capacities." The firm assumed that all employees agreed to this arrangement and that they accepted management's justification for it.[48]

U.S. Steel's informal grievance system reflected its attachment to the ethos of individual achievement because it preserved the individuality of its workers. Despite their nonunion labor policy, Elbert Gary believed that the Corporation still practiced collective bargaining because employees knew "that any man, or number of men, whom they [selected] as a committee, [could] see the foremen, superintendent or head officer of the employing company and present any suggestion or claim with the full assurance, obtained by long and practical experience, that they [were] welcome and receive patient attention, full consideration and fair results."[49] U.S. Steel's workforce often reacted negatively to this principle. For example, investigators for the Interchurch World Movement who questioned workers during the 1919 strike about the value of petitioning their employer were greeted with jeers. One of the investigators concluded, "It is . . . probable that the corporation and its subsidiaries have never treated with a committee of employees, regardless of whether the employees were union representatives or not, concerning hours and wages."[50] When Ray Stannard Baker inquired about this grievance policy in 1920, the answer he received was:

> Say, Mister, you weren't born yesterday, were you? What chance do you suppose one "hunkie" or a bunch of "hunkies" would have getting to Judge Gary with a complaint, or even getting to the head man of the Illinois Steel Company? And what do you suppose would happen if they complained very often over the head of their foreman? Here's the pink slip for you guys.[51]

In short, employees did not take the idea of a direct relationship with their employer seriously. They recognized that true democracy could not exist as long as management remained in complete control of the terms and conditions of their employment. Therefore, there was no way that U.S. Steel's management could have had an accurate conception of the grievances their workers harbored.

The real goal of the Corporation's appeal policy was not to settle grievances, but to reinforce the principle of the open shop. It is tempting to view the idea of the open shop as public relations or self-serving propaganda that justified exploitative policies that made steel companies money. This is an oversimplification. Steel industry executives believed in the open shop because it fit with their preconceived ideas about society. They championed these notions both publicly and privately. To dismiss this as rhetoric is to ignore a considerable amount of evidence regarding their motivation. To do this would be materialism of the worst sort.

Elbert Gary defined the open shop as a labor system under which "every man may engage in any line of employment he selects and under such terms as he and the employer may agree upon; that he may arrange for the kind of and character of work which he believes will bring to him the largest compensation and the most satisfactory conditions depending upon his own merit and disposition."[52] Because it required a direct relationship between an employer and each employee, the open shop perpetuated management's freedom to control. Facing a giant corporation without the aid of a trade union, workers had to submit to their employer's authority or quit. They could never force management to change their terms and conditions of employment by themselves.

Men like Gary saw this industrial relations system as an exchange. Management offered workers competitive wages, as well as the opportunity to advance economically and socially if such advancement was deserved. In return, employees were expected to acknowledge without question management's freedom to control them. This arrangement formed the basis of an implied contractual relationship between an employer and each individual employee. U.S. Steel's formal policy was that workers had the right to join unions, but management possessed the freedom not to sign contracts with outside organizations. A few steel firms forced their workers to sign "yellow dog" contracts (which explicitly stated that workers could not join unions), but the vast majority of steel manufacturers signed no written contracts with their employees. The open shop protected the freedom of contract for workers in an industry where few contracts were ever signed.

In order to appreciate this apparent contradiction, it is necessary to understand the intellectual antecedents of the open shop. Many historians have written about the importance of republicanism to participants in the American Revolution and workers in the early-nineteenth century. Because working people succeeded in redirecting the political system towards protecting their position vis-a-vis their employers, employers began to look to the judicial system to protect their interests. Using common law as its basis, a conservative Supreme Court etched freedom of contract into the Constitution during the 1870s and 1880s. At the same time, explains William Forbath, American trade unions came to believe that "the promise of individual advancement out of hireling status was no way to ensure the worker's 'independence' and his republican citizenship." But with support from the legal system, the traditional interpretation of contractual relations easily overcame labor's opposition.[53]

In industries where the services of skilled workers became dispensable (like steel), written contracts fell out of favor because employers no longer needed legal agreements to meet their labor needs. Under the new paradigm, the law viewed labor as an individual commodity that each worker sold to his employer in the same manner that a manufacturer sold the product he produced. The provisions of the contract were assumed or legally established as the customs of the workplace when the employee began work at the employer's establishment. As industrialization progressed, this legal fiction became increasingly abstract. "The labor contract . . . is not a contract," wrote John R. Commons in 1924, explaining the established legal thinking at that time. "[I]t is a continuing implied *renewal* of contracts at every minute and hour, based on the continuance of what is deemed, on the employer's side, to be satisfactory service, and, on the laborer's side, what is deemed to be satisfactory conditions and compensation."[54] Legally, an employee's decision to work was considered consent to the contract, whether or not a written contract existed.

Under these circumstances, the terms of exchange reflected the unequal positions of employers and employees. In order to obtain employment, less-skilled labor had to accept a subservient role in the workplace, as well as the unfavorable terms and conditions of employment that went with it. This situation did not bother the legal system. In *Coppage v. Kansas*, decided in 1915, the U.S. Supreme Court observed, "No doubt, wherever the right of private property exists, there must and will be inequalities of fortune; and thus it naturally happens that parties negotiating about a contract are not equally hampered by circumstances."[55] According to the legal scholar John P. Roche, these words sound like "a caricature of the 'rugged individualist' viewpoint written by an enemy," but they do reflect the thinking of the legal establishment.[56]

Even without formal agreements, steel companies vociferously defended the freedom of contract. For example, in 1916, the Corporation's Carnegie Steel subsidiary argued before the Pennsylvania Supreme Court that that state's workmen's compensation law violated its employees' freedom of contract even though the company signed no contracts with its workers. Elbert Gary told the Senate Committee investigating the 1919 Steel Strike, "I think people ought to be allowed to make their own agreements, their own contracts with their men." He knew this was a relationship which the industry could easily dominate, acknowledging "that concentrated capital has the advantage over a single individual, if the concentrated capital is in the hands of dishonest and unfair men," but Gary and the other leaders of the steel industry did not believe this stipulation applied to themselves.[57] Since the opportunities for advancement they offered their employees were theoretically unlimited and since the wages they offered were higher than those in most other industries, steel manufacturers believed this arrangement was a fair one. Any advantage they accrued from this bargain result from having survived the social selection process described by both Herbert Spencer and Andrew Carnegie.

Because trade unions interfered with management's freedom to control the terms and conditions of employment in their mills, they interfered with the steel industry's implied contract. This is why employers viewed unions as a threat to management's intrinsic authority. After the turn of the century, the steel industry's belief in the freedom to control was incorporated into the nationwide campaign for the open shop. Laissez-faire economists, small business leaders and other anti-union crusaders cited the effect of trade unions on the possibility of individual achievement as a reason to oppose them. In fact, the evils of the closed shop played an equally important part to the benefits of the open shop in the anti-union movement's ideology. Elbert Gary became the most important industrial opponent of trade unionism in the entire country during the 1919 steel strike by passionately condemning the closed shop as a threat to the authority of American industry. He defined the closed shop as a system under which

> no man can obtain employment . . . except through and on the terms and conditions imposed by the labor unions. He is compelled to join the union and to submit to the dictation of its leader before he can enter the place of business. If he joins the union he is then restricted by its leader as to place of work, hours of work, (and therefore amount of compensation,) and advancement in position, regardless of merit; and sometimes, by the dictum of the union leader, called out and prevented

> from working for days or weeks, although he has no real grievance, and he and his family are suffering for want or necessities of life. In short, he is subjected to the arbitrary decision of the leader, and his personal independence is gone.[58]

Under this line of reasoning, compromise became impossible. Management feared that any recognition of the right of employees to organize could be the first step on the road to the closed shop. Because steel manufacturers consistently conceptualized their labor policies in such extreme terms, they seldom questioned their efforts to fight organized labor with every weapon in their arsenal.

Steelmakers not only contended that their policies protected their employees from the arbitrary control of union leaders; they insisted their policies protected every individual worker's possibility for advancement as understood in the implied contract. Charles Schwab (then president of U.S. Steel) expressed this sentiment well when testifying before the United States Industrial Commission in 1901:

> [I]f I were a workingman in one of these mills . . . I would not want to belong to a labor organization. It puts all men, no matter what their ability, in the same class of work, on exactly the same level. If I were a better workman—quicker, smarter—than the other men I would want to reap the benefit. . . . As a workingman I would not advance, and I would not be able to show superior ability over any other if I were in such an organization.[59]

In order to make sure that workers could continue to advance if they deserved it, steel manufacturers tried to maintain a policy of internal promotion so that workers would know that advancement was open to them. To Katherine Stone, internal promotion means that employers were creating job ladders that had no practical reason to exist since skills were becoming increasingly less important. She posits that employers created these ladders to promote competition for positions in order to undermine worker solidarity.[60] Sanford Jacoby counters this second argument by pointing out that rigid lines of promotion would actually lower the number of individuals competing for a particular position by making it more difficult to pick workers not on the immediate lower rung of the ladder or from outside the plant hierarchy.[61] No matter which of these arguments is correct, the existence of job ladders certainly embodies the principle of individual achievement.

Because it ostensibly put their employees' interests in front of their own, the ethos of individual achievement became a rhetorical position which steelmakers used to combat trade unionism throughout the Non-union Era. As late as 1934, the American Iron and Steel Institute complained about organized labor's desire "to bring all employees to the same level, independent of ability, energy or initiative. It inevitably discriminates against superior workmen."[62] Like the idea of the open shop, employers could make an idea that favored them sound like the best thing in the world for their employees. "Does any employer of labor," asked C.L. Patterson of the National Association of Sheet and Tin Plate Manufacturers, "possess the right to surrender to any labor leader, the rights of his employees to act as individuals, to contract for his services where he chooses, to exercise his ingenuity and his ability that his wage may be increased, that he may work where he chooses[?]"[63] The steel industry invariably answered "no" to this question since it believed that the interests of management and labor were the same.

The legal and moral reasoning that underlay the steel industry's anti-unionism was a product of nineteenth-century circumstances, specifically the possibility that individual workers could accumulate significant wealth in a newly-emerging industrial economy. The vast majority of steelmakers remained attached to this ideal long after possibilities for advancement into positions which could make their employees rich had dried up because of pride in their own success, moral objections to worker organization and concern about the economic costs of recognizing trade unions. As market conditions and government policies changed, this anti-union philosophy persisted. Because of this hostility to organized labor, industry leaders felt the necessity to fight unions by any means necessary. The tactics the industry used often took an enormous economic and social toll on both its employees and on the communities in which it operated. The details of these tactics suggest the extent of these costs (and therefore demonstrate the strength of this ideological imperative). These tactics are the subject of the next chapter.

Notes

1. John A. Fitch, *The Steel Workers* (Pittsburgh: University of Pittsburgh Press, 1989/Originally published by the Russell Sage Foundation, 1910), 135.

2. J. Bernard Hogg, "The Homestead Strike of 1892," Ph.D. Diss., University of Chicago, 1943, 196, n. 6; David Brody, *Steelworkers in America: The Nonunion Era* (Urbana: University of Illinois Press, 1998/ Originally published by Harvard University Press, 1960), 57-8.

3. Homestead employee Conn Strott quoted in Steven Cohen, "Reconciling Industrial Conflict and Democracy: The 'Pittsburgh Survey' and the Growth of Social Research in America," Ph.D. Diss., Columbia University, 1981, 98-99.

4. *Engineering and Mining Journal* 56 (21 October 1893): 428; Fitch, *The Steel Workers*, 157.

5. Talcott Williams, "The Steel Strike," *American Monthly Review of Reviews* 24 (September 1901): 331; United States Industrial Commission, *Report of the United States Industrial Commission*, Vol. 13 (Washington: U.S. Government Printing Office, 1902), 460; *Report of the United States Industrial Commission*, Vol. 7, 389; Michael Nuwer, "From Batch To Flow: Production, Technology and Work-Force Skills in the Steel Industry, 1880-1920," *Technology and Culture* 29 (October 1988): 811, 838.

6. Brody concluded that the nonunion industrial relations system in steelmaking gradually stabilized over the first decades of the century, became unglued during World War I on into 1919 and that manufacturers restored order during the 1920s. See, for example, Brody, *Steelworkers in America*, 263.

7. United States House of Representatives, *Investigation of Homestead Troubles*, Report #2447, 52nd Cong., 2nd Sess., 1892-93, 29, 74.

8. Jesse Robinson, *The Amalgamated Association of Iron, Steel and Tin Workers* (Baltimore: Johns Hopkins University Press, 1920), 126-28; David Jardini, "From Iron to Steel: The Recasting of the Jones and Laughlins Workforce between 1885 and 1896," *Technology and Culture* 36 (April 1995): 294, n. 31; Melvyn Dubofsky, "Technological Change and Workers Movements, 1870-1970," in *Technology, the Economy and Society*, Joel Colton and Stuart Bruchey, eds. (New York: Columbia University Press, 1987), 173.

9. Jardini, 278, n. 13.

10. Amos J. Loveday, Jr., *The Rise and Decline of the American Cut Nail Industry* (Westport, CT: Greenwood Press, 1983), 65, 78, 102-04.

11. Robinson, 126-27; Loveday, 113-16; Amalgamated Association of Iron and Steel Workers, *Journal of Proceedings*, 1890, 3026; Victor S. Clark, *History of Manufactures in the United States,* Vol. 2 (New York: McGraw Hill, 1929), 352.

12. Amalgamated Association, *Journal of Proceedings*, 1885, 1555-59; Loveday, 121-25; Amalgamated Association, *Journal of Proceedings*, 1889, 2641; Amalgamated Association, *Journal of Proceedings*, 1891, 3406. On the success of the wire nail, see Loveday, 135-46.

13. Carroll W. Pursell, Jr., "Tariff and Technology: The Foundation and Development of the American Tin-Plate Industry, 1872-1900," *Technology and*

Culture 3 (Summer 1962): 272-3; Ira Ayer, "Special Report to the Secretary of the Treasury . . . Relative to the Manufacture of Tin and Terne Plate," Government Printing Office, April 26, 1892, 17.

14. Robinson, 7.

15. Pursell, 277-79, 274; Ayer, 34. David Brody (*Steelworkers in America*, 14) incorrectly suggests that tin plate manufacture was "technologically backward." In fact, because innovations in tin plate making did not follow the pattern of other sectors of the industry, this made it harder for observers to appreciate their cumulative effect.

16. Thomas J. Misa, *A Nation of Steel* (Baltimore: Johns Hopkins University Press, 1995), 74-82; Charles Reitell, Machinery and Its Benefits to Workers in the Crude Iron and Steel Industries," Ph.D. Diss., University of Pennsylvania, (Menasha, WI, The Collegiate Press, 1917), 26, 33. For a step-by-step description of the open hearth production process, see Michael John Nuwer, "Labor Market Structures in Historical Perspective: A Case Study of Technology and Labor Relations in the United States Iron and Steel Industry," Ph.D. Diss., University of Utah, 1985, 52-57.

17. Misa, *A Nation of Steel*, 82-83; Thomas J. Misa, "Science, Technology and Industrial Structure: Steelmaking in America, 1870-1925," Ph.D. Dissertation, University of Pennsylvania, 1987, 363-64.

18. William T. Hogan, *Economic History of the Iron and Steel Industry in the United States* (Lexington, MA: D.C. Heath and Company, 1971), 463-68; Victor S. Clark, *History of Manufactures in the United States*, Vol. 3 (New York: McGraw-Hill, 1929), 54; Horace Wilgus, *A Study of the United States Steel Corporation in its Industrial and Legal Aspects* (Chicago: Callaghan and Company, 1901), 2; Gertrude D. Schroeder, *The Growth of Major Steel Companies, 1900-1950* (Baltimore: The Johns Hopkins Press, 1952), 38; Ray Stannard Baker, "What the U.S. Steel Corporation Really Is and How It Works," *McClure's Magazine* 18 (November 1901): 7; Merideth Givens, "Iron and Steel Industry: History and Present Organization," in *Encyclopaedia of the Social Sciences*, Vols. 7 and 8, Edwin R.A. Seligman, ed. (New York: Macmillan Company, 1937), 306.

19. United States House of Representatives, *Hearings Before the Committee on Investigation of United States Steel Corporation* [Stanley Committee Hearings], 62nd Cong., 2nd Sess., 1911-12, 1350; Ernest Ludlow Bogart, "The Steel Strike," *Bibliotecha Sacra* 59 (January 1902): 112-13, 120.
Tin plate is sheet steel dipped in tin. Therefore, the process for creating both these products was essentially the same, minus the dipping.

20. Fitch, *The Steel Workers*, 297.

21. T.J. Shaffer quoted in *Amalgamated Journal*, 28 February 1901; *American Federationist* 17 (January 1910): 35; United States Commissioner of Labor, *Report on Conditions of Employment in the Iron and Steel Industry*, Vol. 3, Senate Document No. 110, 62nd Cong., 1st Sess., 1913, 136.

22. *American Federationist* 17 (January 1910): 35.

23. United States Commissioner of Labor, *Report on Conditions of Employment in the Iron and Steel Industry*, Vol. 3, Senate Document No. 110, 62nd Cong., 1st Sess., 1913, 136.

24. Ray Stannard Baker, *The New Industrial Unrest* (Garden City, NY: Doubleday, Page & Company, 1920), 17.

25. Ida Tarbell, *The Life of Elbert Gary: A Story of Steel* (New York: D. Appleton-Century, 1925), 1-42; Stephen H. Cutcliffe, "Elbert H. Gary," in *Iron and Steel in the Twentieth Century*, Bruce E. Seely, ed. (Bruccoli Clark Layman, 1994), 145-57. Elbert Gary was commonly referred to as Judge Gary because he had once served two four-year terms as a judge in DuPage County Illinois.

26. Elbert Gary, "Extracts from minutes of steel manufacturers at Waldorf-Astoria, New York, Aug. 28, 1918," in U.S. Congress, Senate, Committee on Education and Labor, *Investigation of Strike in Steel Industries*, 66th Cong., 1st Sess., 1919, 240.

27. Arundel Cotter, *The Gary I Knew* (Boston: Stratford Company, 1928), 88-89.

28. John A. Garraty, "The United States Steel Corporation Versus Labor: The Early Years," *Labor History* 1 (Winter 1960): 5-6.

29. Tarbell, *Gary*, 156.

30. "Extracts from Minutes of the Executive Committee, United States Steel Corporation," in Stanley Committee Hearings, 3833.

31. George W. Perkins to J.P. Morgan, July 23, 1907, George W. Perkins Papers, Box 9, Rare Book and Manuscript Library, Columbia University, New York, NY.

32. "Extracts from Minutes of the Executive Committee," 3819, 3831.

33. Luke Grant, *The National Erectors' Association and the International Association of Bridge and Structural Ironworkers*, Report to the United States Commission on Industrial Relations (Washington, D.C.: U.S. Government Printing Office, 1915), 46.

34. Amalgamated Association, *Journal of Proceedings*, 1901, 6046; *New York Times*, 2 October 1901; *Iron Age* 68 (19 September 1901): 21.
For detailed accounts of the strike, see Bogart, 108-28 and Brody, *Steelworkers in America*, 62-68.
The Amalgamated Association's strategy during this strike proved to be very controversial. One result was a public feud between Shaffer and American Federation of Labor President Samuel Gompers. See Philip Taft, *The A.F. of L. in the Time of Gompers* (New York: Harper and Brothers, 1957), 24-42.

35. Report to Board of Directors of United States Steel quoted in Tarbell, *Gary*, 160.

36. Tarbell, *Gary*, 161.

37. Brody, *Steelworkers in America*, 69-73; Selig Perlman and Philip Taft, *History of Labour in the United States, 1896-1932* (New York: Macmillan Company, 1935), 139-43.
Those subsidiaries of United States Steel which did not make steel fought organized labor with the same intensity shown in the Corporation's campaign against the Amalgamated Association. For example, American Bridge Company, the U.S. Steel subsidiary which fabricated and erected iron and steel structures, was the driving force behind that industry's campaign against the International Association of Bridge and Structural Ironworkers. In 1907, the Oliver Mining Corporation spent $255,000 to employ "special deputies" and strikebreakers to protect them in order to prevent the Western Federation of Miners from organizing U.S. Steel's iron ore mining operations. The Pittsburgh Steamship Company, which controlled U.S. Steel's fleet of iron ore barges, led the efforts of the Lake Carriers Association against the organized sailors on the Great Lakes during the first decade of this century. See Sidney Fine, *"Without Blare of Trumpets"* (Ann Arbor, University of Michigan Press, 1995), 48, 62; on American Bridge; Donald G. Sofchalk, "Organized Labor and the Iron Ore Miners of Northern Minnesota, 1907-1936," *Labor History* 12 (Spring 1971): 221; on Oliver Mining Corporation, Paul F. Brissenden, "Employment System of the Lake Carriers' Association," *Bulletin of the United States Bureau of Labor Statistics*, No. 235, January 1918, 11 and Perlman and Taft,147-49 on the Pittsburgh Steamship Company.

38. Melvyn Dubofsky, *We Shall Be All* (New York: Quadrangle/New York Times, 1969), 199-209; Edward Levinson, *I Break Strikes!* (New York: Arno and the New York Times, 1969/Originally published by Robert M. McBride & Company, 1935), 70-88; Federal Council of Churches of Christ in America, "Report of Special Committee Concerning the Industrial Situation at South Bethlehem, PA.," June 14, 1910, 3; Robert Hessen, "The Bethlehem Steel Strike of 1910," *Labor History* 15 (Winter 1974): 3-18; Horace B. Davis, "The metal workers strike in East Youngstown and Campbell in 1916," May 1932, Harvey O'Connor Collection, Box 41, Archives of Labor and Urban Affairs, Walter P. Reuther Library, Wayne State University, Detroit, MI.

39. *The Survey* 28 (6 July 1912): 487-88; *The Survey* 28 (3 August 1912): 595-96; *Iron Age* 90 (5 December 1912): 1339; [George] Soule, "Preliminary Survey of Steel Strike For Use of the Commission," Mary Heaton Vorse Collection, Box 121, Archives of Labor and Urban Affairs, Walter P. Reuther Library, Wayne State University, Detroit, MI; Joseph Anthony McCartin, "Labor's 'Great War': American Workers, Unions, and the State, 1916-1929," Ph.D. Diss., State University of New York at Binghamton, 1990,159, 175-77; Alexander M. Bing, *War-Time Strikes and Their Adjustment* (New York: E.P. Dutton & Company, 1921), 295; Fitch, *The Steel Workers*, 137.

40. For more on Foster see, Edward P. Johanningsmeier, *Forging American Communism* (Princeton: Princeton University Press, 1994).

41. David Brody, *Labor in Crisis: The Steel Strike of 1919*, 2nd ed. (Urbana: University of Illinois Press, 1987), 63-77.

42. Brody, *Labor in Crisis*, 113; Mary Heaton Vorse, *Men and Steel* (New York: Boni and Liveright, 1920), 57.

43. Brody, *Labor in Crisis*, 108, 147-64.

44. Brody, *Labor in Crisis*, 115-24, 167-68; William Z. Foster, *The Great Steel Strike and Its Lessons* (New York: B.W. Huebsch, 1920), 26.

45. Paul Krause, "Commentary," in Brody, *Steelworkers in America*, 324; Kenneth Warren, *Triumphant Capitalism: Henry Clay Frick and the Industrial Transformation of America* (Pittsburgh: University of Pittsburgh Press, 1996), 68-73; Minutes of the Carnegie Steel Board of Managers Meeting, June 13, 1899, 5, Andrew Carnegie Papers, Vol. 66, Library of Congress, Washington, D.C.; Brody, *Steelworkers in America*, 81-82.

46. Wall, *Andrew Carnegie*, 626-27; Andrew Carnegie to J.A. Leishmann, August 21, 1896, Andrew Carnegie-Charles M. Schwab Collection, Historical Collections & Labor Archives, Pattee Library, Pennsylvania State University, State College, PA.

47. *Investigation of Homestead Troubles*, 33.

48. "Rules of Cambria Steel Company for Government of its Employees at the Works," April 21, 1910, excerpted in Sharon A. Brown, "Historic Resource Study: Cambria Iron Company," United States Department of Interior/National Parks Service, September 1989, 380.

49. Elbert Gary to Woodrow Wilson, August 31, 1919, Woodrow Wilson Papers, Series 2, Library of Congress, Washington, D.C. [Microfilm Reel 104, Frame 111224].

50. Interchurch World Movement, *Report on Steel Strike of 1919* (New York: Harcourt, Brace and Howe, 1920), 122-23; George Soule, "Preliminary Survey of Steel Strike for Use of the Commission," 2, Mary Heaton Vorse Collection, Box 121.

51. Baker, *The New Industrial Unrest*, 38.

52. Elbert Gary, Letter to Presidents of Subsidiary Companies, *Open Shop Review* 16, (September 1919): 404-05.

53. David Montgomery, *Citizen Worker* (New York: Cambridge University Press, 1993), 13-42; William E. Forbath, "The Ambiguities of Free Labor: Labor and the Law in the Gilded Age," *Wisconsin Law Review* (1985): 767-817. On the historiography of republicanism, see Daniel T. Rodgers, "Republicanism: The Career of a Concept," *Journal of American History* 79 (June 1992): 11-38.

54. Montgomery, *Citizen Worker*, 43-44; John R. Commons, *Legal Foundations of Capitalism* (New York: Macmillan Company, 1924), 285.

55. *Coppage v. Kansas*, 236 U.S. 17 (1915).

56. John P. Roche, "Entrepreneurial Liberty and the Fourteenth Amendment," *Labor History* 4 (Winter 1963): 12. I first became familiar with *Coopage v. Kansas* by reading Roche's article.
This situation is a perfect example of what Emile Durkheim describes in a famous passage from *The Division of Labor in Society*: "If one class of society is obliged, in order to live, to take any price for its services, while another can abstain from such actions thanks to resources at its disposal which, however, are not necessarily due to any social superiority, the second has an unjust advantage over the first in law. In other words, there cannot be rich and poor at birth without there being unjust contracts." Emile Durkheim, *The Division of Labor in Society*, translated by George Simpson (New York: Free Press, 1969), 384.

57. *Anderson v. Carnegie Steel Company*, 255 PA 33 (1916); *Investigation of Strike in Steel Industries*, 216, 217.

58. Sidney Fine, *Laissez-Faire and the General Welfare State* (Ann Arbor: University of Michigan Press, 1956), 61; Gary, Letter to Presidents of Subsidiary Companies, 405.

59. *Report of the United States Industrial Commission*, Vol. 13, 461-62.

60. Katherine Stone, "The Origins of Job Structures in the Steel Industry," *Review of Radical Political Economics* 6 (Summer 1974): 73-75.

61. Sanford M. Jacoby, *Employing Bureaucracy* (New York, Columbia University Press, 1985), 95.

62. American Iron and Steel Institute, "Collective Bargaining in the Steel Industry," June 1934, 11.

63. C.L. Patterson, "Independent Steel Companies Report on Interchurch Report," December 1, 1920, 41, Typescript, Firestone Library, Princeton University, Princeton, NJ.

Chapter Three

The Methods of Control: The Steel Industry Versus Unorganized Labor

> The story of union suppression in the steel industry will some day be adequately told, and it will furnish a unique page in the records of a dark past on which our successors will look back in wonder.
>
> —*The Public: A Journal of Democracy*, August 10, 1918.[1]

Businessmen tend to oppose trade unionism. After all, these organizations, almost by definition, cost employers money (at least in the short term). Few businessmen, however, hated organized labor as much as steel manufacturers did during the Nonunion Era. The intensity of their dislike comes through in the manner in which they put forward their ideals. Unions were not just a threat to profitability, they were an affront to the industry's worldview. Because of this hatred, no other industry spread its anti-union philosophy further and succeeded at keeping organized labor out of its shops for so long as steel manufacturers did. Since employers could dictate wages and working conditions to their employees for approximately forty-five years, this industry is the best example available of how American businessmen impeded the development of working class organization during the late-nineteenth and early-twentieth centuries. This does not mean that steelmakers could force employees to submit to their will unconditionally, but these employers did succeed in dictating the terms and conditions of employment to their workforce unilaterally. The presence of a union would have made it impossible for steelmakers to gain this prerogative, a prerogative which managers associated with their own self-worth. Therefore, their opposition to labor organizations was almost visceral.

Had the men who ran the steel industry tried to weigh the costs and benefits of operating nonunion, they would have had a difficult task on their hands. The immediate financial savings would have been the difference between paying union and nonunion wages, but because many steel companies deliberately mimicked union wages to decrease the appeal of organized labor to their employees, the size of this gap might have been very small. At first glance, the financial savings of operating nonunion might seem worth fighting for, but what if adverse conditions of employment decreased the efficiency of the operation? As the writer Herbert Casson asked in 1906, "[W]ill it pay in the long run to tear out the lives of men—to burn them up like coke and toss them on the cinder-pile at forty?"[2] Most steelmakers thought it would because they imagined that the long-term financial costs of union recognition would be even greater. Beside the financial costs, the ideological cost of operating nonunion would have been impossible for steelmakers to quantify. Nevertheless, the anti-union tactics pioneered by steel manufacturers in the late-nineteenth and early-twentieth centuries hurt the public image of the industry and created distrust between management and workers which, quite literally, affected profitability for decades.

A seemingly rational employer might have chosen to minimize his wage bill and ignored the possibility that socially destructive policies, which kept workers nonunion, hurt the bonds of steel-making communities or might have destroyed the long-term economic health of his business. Another rational response to the labor question might have been to try to keep one's workforce nonunion by cultivating ties with employees through the high wages and welfare capitalism. Steel manufacturers adopted both strategies at different times and at the same time. The harsher methods of control (described in the first sections of this chapter) suggest the industry's reflexive hostility to organized labor since their use shows that manufacturers believed the evils of unions justified even the most costly and disruptive anti-union tactics. The more benevolent policies (such as high wages and housing, described at the end of this chapter, and the welfare capitalist policies detailed in the next chapter) show the industry's paternalism and its desire to offer workers a means to improve themselves. Each of these policies illuminate different parts of the industry's anti-union belief system.

Spies, Detectives and Other Forms of Espionage

No anti-union labor policy carried greater economic and social costs for steelmakers than espionage. Whether a firm hired a detective agency or created its own in-house spy network, these systems cost money and bred cynicism in the minds of workers. U.S. Steel inherited Carnegie Steel's spy network when it took over the firm in 1901. Because of this system, John A. Fitch wrote in 1911, "I doubt whether you could find a more suspicious body of men than the employes of the United States Steel Corporation. They are suspicious of one another, of their neighbors, and their friends." Fitch contended that, "No corporation has a better system of espionage [than U.S. Steel]."[3] The Corporation kept detailed files on the lives of its workers and could supply weekly summaries of labor activities in any vicinity in which it operated. It also employed private strike-breaking detective agencies when needed. Questioned by the Senate Committee investigating the 1919 strike, Chairman Gary acknowledged the existence of U.S. Steel's espionage activities. "I cannot be very specific," he said, "but I am quite sure that at times some of our people have used secret-service men to ascertain facts and conditions."[4] In fact, when interviewed by representatives of the Interchurch World Movement (IWM), an organization of civic-minded religious leaders investigating this same strike, Gary confronted the investigators with a spy report about them.[5]

Many other steel firms besides U.S. Steel spied on their employees. Large independent firms like Jones & Laughlin had their own spy systems that operated much like the one in the Carnegie mills. Smaller companies could buy the services of spies from outside detective agencies. A series of solicitations from the Railway Audit and Inspection Company are preserved in the papers of the Lukens Iron and Steel Company, a small firm in eastern Pennsylvania. "Our Representative, Mr. E.W. Stull," wrote the Vice President and General Manager of this agency

> advises that he called at your offices on the 13th inst., in reference to placing secret operatives in your plant, for the purpose of making daily reports concerning any agitation that may be going on among your employees, loafing and other violations.
>
> If you should feel in need of service of this kind any time in the near future, would be pleased to furnish you with one or more men suited to work as regular employee and to render you daily reports covering his observations.[6]

Since these letters span five years with no reply, it seems doubtful that Lukens ever retained this agency's services. However, an executive at a different firm was so cavalier about the use of espionage that he gave a file of spy reports to investigators from the IWM. The correspondence in that file demonstrates that steel companies throughout western Pennsylvania commonly exchanged information gathered from their far-flung espionage networks. It also shows that steelmakers considered espionage part of everyday business.[7]

Detective agencies offered many other services to their clients in the steel industry besides information gathering. In a book written in 1917 for potential clients, the Sherman Detective Agency described what it did for one U.S. Steel subsidiary when hired to help win an unnamed strike.[8] First, the agency recruited six spies to gather intelligence, two from each nationality prevalent among the strikers. Two of these operatives assumed leadership roles within the local union from which they encouraged the strikers back to work and sowed dissension among other leaders. It also enlisted strikebreakers, importing between fifty and seventy-five a day into the plant. Then the agency hired trucks to bring the new men in, armed guards for their protection and cots for them to sleep on. Within eight weeks, the strike was declared off and the local union folded. Concluding its description of this incident, the agency wrote, "Appreciative of the good service rendered, and of the value of Sherman Preventive Strike Service, the client [i.e. U.S. Steel] has adopted it as a continuous privilege. Sherman Service is his insurance upon maximum continuous production."[9] Of all the services available from detective agencies, the steel industry probably utilized replacement workers most often. During the 1919 strike, "[p]robably half the strike-breaking agencies in the country were engaged in recruiting," claimed William Z. Foster. Thirty-thousand African Americans alone entered the steel mills as replacements at this time, most of them recruited by professional labor agents.[10]

Although detective agencies often supplied armed guards to protect steel mills during strikes, some firms also kept their own guards on permanent retainer. U.S. Steel employed, by one estimate, 3,000 private police to protect just its Pittsburgh facilities in the years before the 1919 strike. "Every time you turned around," recalled one former employee of the Corporation's Clairton, Pennsylvania, mill, "you saw a coal and iron policemen with a blackjack and a gun on his hip walking through the plant surveilling [sic] everything going on."[11] Like the Pinkerton agents used at Homestead, these men often created controversy. In 1913, when private detectives employed at the American Steel and Wire Company plant in Rankin, Pennsylvania, fired at a crowd of strikers who had been taunting them, the *Amalgamated Journal* held the guards responsible for doing "whatever inciting to riot that they deem so necessary on such occasions."[12] During the 1919 strike, the size of the Corporation's private army vastly increased because state and local governments armed and deputized many replacement workers under special laws. The use of private police at other steel companies increased as well. In Woodlawn, Pennsylvania, special deputies from Jones & Laughlin searched trains arriving at the local station and ordered suspicious persons to go back to where they came. If these people returned to Woodlawn, they were arrested, beaten and run out of town. In response to such tactics, Governor Pinchot of Pennsylvania revoked all industrial police licenses, including those of Jones & Laughlin, Bethlehem Steel, Carnegie Steel and other steel or steel-related firms. But despite the governor's action, manufacturers still maintained large police forces to help institute their labor policies during ordinary times. According to a 1928 report, three of the five largest private police forces in the state of Pennsylvania belonged to steel companies (Carnegie Steel and Bethlehem Steel) or a related U.S. Steel subsidiary (H.C. Frick Coal and Coke).[13] Steel producers accepted the stigma of employing this unpopular antiunion tactic because they recognized that maintaining a pliant, nonunion workforce required a strong element of force.

In instances when local trouble got out of hand, government forces assumed the same role as private guards. The Pennsylvania State Militia did this at Homestead in 1892 when labor sympathizers took control of the town after the violence of July 6th, 1892. In 1905, the Pennsylvania legislature created the State Police to deal with similar disturbances associated with labor disputes. In a statement made to the federal official investigating the 1910 strike at Bethlehem Steel's South Bethlehem plant, the local commander wrote that, "The troopers are nonpartisan inasmuch as strikes are concerned, and take no part either for or against the strikers or corporations," yet critics often charged the State Police with helping the steel industry enforce its labor policies.[14] At Bethlehem, for example, one local newspaper reported, "[S]quads of the State police were entering the houses of foreigners near the works and dragging them to work in the mills."[15] In 1919, state troopers, called "Cossacks" by the strikers, assumed a central role in the industrial relations of this industry. The investigation of this strike by the U.S. Senate Committee on Education and Labor includes many detailed descriptions of how the Pennsylvania State Police mistreated striking steelworkers. One organizer told the Committee, "We have evidence [of men] being corralled by the State troopers and [driven] to the mill gates and the bosses would congregate them, and those who would sign up to go to work were let go, and the others were cast into jail."[16] Many immigrants, unaware of American institutions, assumed that the presence of local or state troops meant that the federal government opposed their cause. For this reason, most were too scared to stay off the job for long.[17]

The combination of spies and strikebreakers served to discourage strikes and made those strikes that did occur very difficult for steelworkers to win. Employers did not hide the fact that workers who showed even the least inclination towards collective action would be fired. As the head of a Pittsburgh steel company told John Fitch, "If I knew that the men in our works had held a meeting . . . I would discharge every one of the men who were active in bringing the meeting about."[18] Therefore, dissident employees often chose to acquiesce rather than act on their displeasure because the potential consequences were so severe. The industry's use of blacklists compounded the punishment because it meant that dismissed workers faced the prospect of never working in the steel industry again. Despite the difficulties, employees in this industry still tried to organize because they did not want to accept the difficult working conditions that they faced. If the consequences of organizing were not so severe, undoubtedly employees would have tried it more often.

Because of the value of a subservient workforce, steelmakers used espionage despite the financial costs and the distrust it fostered among their employees. Conducting industrial relations in what the authors of the Interchurch World Movement report called the "atmosphere of war normal to the steel industry," invariably poisoned any efforts at goodwill that the steel companies offered their employees.[19] Steelmakers embraced espionage because they were constantly worried about losing the power they held over workers. Under such conditions, genuine partnership between workers and management was all but impossible. Espionage served as the only method of communication available between employees and employers. With no effective grievance system, spy reports were the only way for management to find out what workers were thinking and the only form of communication the steel companies believed they needed. The information gathered through spying played a vital role in keeping the steel industry nonunion. As one observer concluded after interviewing workers at Bethlehem Steel, "Remove the labor spies from the mills and the corporation would be faced with a real union tomorrow."[20]

Exploiting Ethnic Divisions

In 1911, the American Iron and Steel Institute (AISI) created a pamphlet on flies which was intended to teach cleanliness to the employees of its member steel companies. The AISI translated the pamphlet into ten languages: English, French, German, Italian, Hungarian, Polish, Croatian, Romanian, and two languages that the Secretary of the Institute's Welfare Committee called "Slavish and Slovenish." The pamphlet was so popular with the companies that received it, that they requested copies in seventeen additional languages, including Turkish, Armenian and Finnish.[21] Reaching steelworkers had not always been this complicated. Until the mid-1880s, English-speakers had constituted the vast majority of employees in this industry; but as the number of skilled workers decreased, immigration increased, and working conditions worsened, new ethnic groups like Poles, Italians, Hungarians and Bohemians began to displace groups like the English, Irish and Welsh. All these immigrant groups were considered "foreigners" by the workers they displaced, whether they were citizens or not. By 1911, nearly 60 percent of the steel industry's workforce was foreign-born. No wonder the American Federation of Labor complained, "So far as we have investigated there seems to be a preference given to foreigners."[22]

Many historians agree with this charge, alleging that steel companies deliberately exploited ethnic divisions among their employees as part of an effort to maintain a nonunion workforce. Two distinct methods of manipulation have been identified in the historical literature. The first was to mix different ethnic groups together in order to make it more difficult for employees to unite along ethnic lines. John Fitch and other authors cite a comment by William R. Jones, then Superintendent of Andrew Carnegie's Edgar Thomson Works, as proof of this contention. In 1875, Jones stated, "My experience has shown that Germans and Irish, Swedes and what I denominate 'Buckwheats'—young American country boys, judiciously mixed, make the most effective and tractable force you can find."[23] The other suggestion is that employers manipulated ethnic divisions by clumping workers of the same nationality in similar jobs. For example, historian Lizabeth Cohen writes:

> Up to 1919, employers had assumed that the best way to keep their semiskilled workforce from unifying politically was to divide it ethnically, each group doing a particular kind of work under the thumb of a foreign-speaking or at least foreign-comprehending foreman. In the steel mills of South Chicago, for example . . . Italians were the unskilled laborers in the bricklaying departments, Swedes manned the galvanizing departments, Poles provided the unskilled labor in the blast furnaces, and Croatians did the common labor in the finishing departments in the rail mills.[24]

Placing workers of many ethnicities side by side and clumping workers of the same ethnicity together in specific departments are mutually exclusive strategies. Although it is possible that different employers might have favored one strategy over the other, both could not have been practiced at the same time. Therefore, each of these potential methods of control should be considered separately in order to determine its prevalence and effectiveness.

The practical difficulties of mixing a multilingual workforce precluded the continuation of this strategy as an anti-union tactic. The foreign workers whom Jones mixed during the 1870s and 1880s were generally English speaking. By the turn of the century, the definition of "foreign" workmen had changed. "[I]t is well to explain," commented the *National Labor Tribune* in 1909, "that by this term is generally meant not English-speaking foreigners, such as the Irish, Scotch, and Welsh, but rather the foreigners from a particular region, especially the southern part of Europe."[25] In 1911, the United States Immigration Commission reported that 37.7% of the male immigrants in the steel towns it studied could not speak English. A 1915 study by the U.S. Bureau of Mines put the figure for non-English speakers at Pennsylvania blast-furnace plants at fifty percent.[26] Employees would have been even less likely to speak the languages of other ethnic groups in the mill. Operating complex machinery required teamwork, and teamwork was difficult when workers were unable to communicate with their foreman or with each other.

If workers had been mixed in such a way as to make communication between them impossible, bad things would likely have happened. For instance, inability to communicate was thought to be the main reason that immigrant employees had higher accident rates than employees who could speak English. "Never have a man in your employ to whom no one can talk," Bethlehem Steel instructed its foremen. "The greatest number of our more or less serious accidents are to foreigners, obviously because they do not realize the dangers of their new surroundings and cannot clearly comprehend the instructions of their superiors."[27] Immigrant steelworkers may have understood a few words of English or perhaps hand signals, but the possibility of them heeding a vocal warning or escaping hidden dangers was severely hampered by language barriers.[28] Mixing may have been an effective way to manipulate employees before the tide of new immigrants, but these kinds of problems meant that using this method of control on the polyglot workforce of the early twentieth century steel plant would have been considerably more difficult.

There is, however, considerable evidence that employers tended to clump workers of the same ethnicity together inside their mills. The United States Immigration Commission documented segregation by ethnicity in the departments of a typical plant in much the same way that Cohen describes pre-1919 Chicago: "Croatian laborers have secured a foothold and predominate in the blast-furnace, merchant-mill, and open-hearth department. . . . Magyars hold first place in the bridge and construction and general labor departments, while the Servians [sic] outnumber all other immigrants combined in the steel foundry and are also found in large numbers in the rail mill and the merchant mill."[29] It is worth noting that the employers who described this policy to the Immigration Commission did not cite labor control as their motivation. Some reported that they distributed their employees this way because they believed certain ethnic groups were best-suited for particular jobs; others allowed employees to distribute themselves and segregation resulted. It is also possible that this situation arose because foremen preferred to hire employees from their own ethnic group. But whatever the reason, this policy carried with it enormous economic risk. Letting employees of the same ethnic group accumulate in a specific area would have made it easier for a small group of workers to join together with others of their nationality and control part of the production process. And despite ethnic segregation by department throughout the industry, cultural barriers were overcome during many of the most important strikes of the Nonunion Era. As Paul U. Kellogg reported during the McKee's Rocks strike of 1909, "[N]ot the least wonderful element of the situation was the five or six men of the American committee, in the circle of foreign faces."[30]

Rather than favoring immigrants, many firms tried to avoid using foreign-born labor for cultural reasons—most notably, racism. As early as 1891, the *Bulletin of the American Iron and Steel Association* complained that Slavs (a blanket term applied to all East European immigrants) were "essentially a barbarous race, who have never been civilized. Like our North American Indians the savage in their nature is constantly asserting itself even when they are wholly surrounded by civilizing influences."[31] In 1906, Herbert Casson wrote, "I have found it to be the general opinion of practical steelmakers that the trade was being pulled down by the employment of such large numbers of unskilled immigrants, who can never be trained beyond a certain point."[32] The fear of collective action also created apprehension in the industry. Organized labor generally perceived immigrants as poor union material, but many employers thought otherwise. For example, East European immigrants were "a source of continuous concern" for management, particularly after the Homestead lockout.[33] This concern continued to dog employers well in the Nonunion Era. Steelmakers blamed immigrants for disruptions like the McKee's Rocks strike and the Youngstown strike of 1915-1916. The receptiveness of immigrant labor to the 1919 strike call only confirmed these earlier fears.

This apprehension translated into a strong preference for "American" labor among the industry's employers. "[I]n New York and some other cities," explained Andrew Carnegie in an 1892 interview with a Scottish newspaper, there were more strikes "because the labour we have to deal with there is mostly foreign, and therefore ignorant, but the intelligent native-born American workman gives no trouble."[34] In 1907, the *New York Times* reported:

> After having experimented with foreign labor for a number of years the big manufacturing concerns of the Pittsburgh districe [sic] have decided that they will not do.
>
> According to the manufacturers, one intelligent American, Englishman, German, or Irishman can do the work of two "foreigners."[35]

Not only manufacturers held this bias; foremen who hired their own labor also preferred Americans.[36] But if this preference really existed, why then did foreign-born labor supplant native labor in the steel mills of the United States?

The high number of immigrant steelworkers came about through supply and demand rather than as the product of any deliberate preference on the part of steel manufacturers because immigrants were often the only labor available to meet the industry's needs. Employers in the Pittsburgh District surveyed by the Immigration Commission cited the "rapid expansion of the industry and the inability to secure other labor" as the "principal reasons" for employing workers born in other countries.[37] This explains why the President of the Central Iron and Steel Company told the American Iron and Steel Institute in 1910, "I think we have got to get away from that idea of calling it foreign labor. It has come to stay. We can't get along without it."[38] Because single immigrants or married men living apart from their wives could survive on wages which families trying to maintain an American standard of living could not, immigrant workers provided the advantage of being less expensive than American workers and were easily replaceable.[39]

Only during the 1919 strike did steel manufacturers begin to explicitly inflame ethnic tensions in order to perpetuate their labor policies. By distributing William Z. Foster's syndicalist writings and claiming that "foreigners" controlled the strike, managers were making implicit appeals to American workers to remain loyal. Some firms and their sympathizers utilized more explicit methods as well. For example, a handbill circulated by foremen from the Corporation's National Tube Company subsidiary read:

> **WAKE UP AMERICANS!!**
>
> ITALIAN LABORERS, organized under the American Federation of Labor are going to strike Monday and are threatening workmen who want to continue working.
>
> These foreigners have been told by labor agitators that if they would join the union they would get Americans' jobs.
>
> They are being encouraged by ITALIAN MERCHANTS, who are in sympathy with them. ARE YOU GOING TO SLEEP AND LET MOB RULE THREATEN THE PEACE OF OUR TOWN?[40]

One spy working for an agency hired by U.S. Steel's Illinois Steel Company subsidiary received instructions "to stir up as much bad feeling as you possibly can between the Serbians and the Italians. Spread data among the Serbians that the Italians are going back to work. Call up every question you can in reference to racial hatred between these two nationalities; make them realize to the fullest extent that far better results would be accomplished if they would go back to work. Urge them to go back to work or the Italians will get their jobs."[41] The potential lasting effects of these words upon the community did not matter to these subsidiaries.

They cared more about short term gain than long term costs. The general distrust of immigrants that such propaganda played upon was an important reason why skilled workers generally did not join the picket lines in 1919. But afterwards, observed David J. Saposs, "[E]ven the Americans who did not strike have a greater respect for the "foreigners" than they did before the strike. . . . [N]ow they are convinced that the immigrant is a good striker."[42] The next time the industry faced labor trouble, manipulating the ethnic divisions within their workforce would prove more difficult.

Exploiting Racial Divisions

Unlike white Slavic Europeans, black workers seldom supported unions. African Americans first came to the mills of western Pennsylvania as strikebreakers in 1875. From that moment on, the Amalgamated Association did its best to prevent these migrants from challenging the privileged position of its skilled white membership. In the South, Tennessee Coal and Iron (TC&I) removed the union from its mills in 1902. The rest of the manufacturers in this region became nonunion by 1909. Even though they made up a substantial portion of the workforce, black workers occupied very few highly skilled positions in southern mills. In the North, strikebreaking was the only way African Americans could break into most facilities. The Amalgamated occasionally made statements expressing the importance of multi-racial organizing, but it never made any serious attempts to organize black workers. Because they often owed their jobs to the failure of unions, African Americans generally sided with their employers rather than with their white coworkers during labor disputes.[43]

Despite the manner in which African Americans first came to the iron industry, racial tensions did not play a major role in the labor relations of the steel industry between 1892 and 1914. The primary reason for this was the small number of black workers working in mills throughout the United States. In 1910, only five percent of steelworkers were African American, and over a third worked in Alabama.[44] In the North, the prevalence of Eastern and Southern European immigrants made it much harder for black workers to find jobs. Statistics obtained by John Fitch show that out of 23,337 employees working for Carnegie Steel in the Pittsburgh area in March 1907, only 331 were African American.

According to the 1910 *Pennsylvania Negro Business Directory*, the Cambria Steel Company employed few Negro laborers and out of 5,000 workers at Bethlehem Steel's South Bethlehem mill there were not "more than a round dozen of Negroes in any capacity whatever." In both the North and South, those African Americans who did find employment in the mills were usually relegated to the worst possible positions. Because there were relatively few of them and because of their lack of success at moving upward in the job hierarchy, white workers probably would not have perceived blacks as a threat to their livelihoods.[45] As R.R. Wright observed in his study of one hundred black steelworkers for the Pittsburgh Survey, "In all cases Negroes and whites seemed to work together without friction."[46]

The racist attitudes of employers and employees, reinforced by an especially high turnover rate among African Americans, explain why steel manufacturers did not hire them in greater numbers. However, firms in the Birmingham area, the only region of the country where black steelworkers were the majority before World War I, came to depend upon African American labor. Nevertheless, they generally had to keep from fifty to one hundred percent more employees on their payrolls than was necessary in order to operate their mills on any given day. "There are differences of opinion as to the capability of Negroes as a race to fit themselves for skilled positions," explained Fitch in 1912, "but whether capable or not, the unsteadiness at work of the Birmingham Negro of this generation acts as an effective check to the acquiring of a high degree of skill."[47] As a result of this "unsteadiness," a TC&I official described the black workers there as "shiftless, thriftless, sloppy, dirty . . . inefficient labor."[48] These kinds of racist beliefs contributed to African Americans always receiving the nastiest jobs in the mill and being paid less than their white counterparts, which made black labor even more unsteady, and thereby cost employers money by decreasing their firm's overall productive efficiency.

When European immigration dried up at the outset of World War I, the lure of higher wages convinced many African Americans to move north in what has come to be known as the Great Migration. The number of African Americans working at many plants doubled or even tripled. Between 1916 and 1917, the number of African Americans at Carnegie Steel increased from 1500 to 4000; at Jones & Laughlin the increase was from 400 to 1500. 220 African Americans were employed at U.S. Steel's Gary Works in 1914; by 1920 that figure rose to 2060. Several large

Pittsburgh employers, like Oliver Iron and Steel and Pittsburgh Forge and Iron went from having no African Americans to hiring hundreds during the war years. Yet even this groundswell did not satisfy the industry's wartime labor needs because the turnover rate of black workers in Northern steel mills during World War I may have been as high as 1000 percent. Companies like Carnegie Steel and Jones & Laughlin sent labor agents across the South to enlist African Americans for jobs in their mills in order to recruit all the black workers they could find. Overall, the percentage of African Americans working in the industry increased from 4.7 in 1908 to 12.4 percent in 1920.[49]

Black steelworkers aided employers in two ways: they assuaged the wartime labor shortage and they facilitated the use of a new anti-union weapon—racial prejudice. "If it hadn't been for the Negro [during the wartime labor shortage]," a U.S. Steel official said later, "we could hardly have carried on our operations." Black migrants traveled to the North because even the wages for the worst jobs in the mills, the only jobs they could get in most instances, were far better than those in the South. The magnitude of this migration fueled the racial prejudice of white workers, including those employed in the steel industry. Many western Pennsylvania steel towns were on the verge of race riots during the war years and the post-war reconstruction. "The strikers resent that negroes have been deputized, and are being used as strikebreakers," an investigator for the Interchurch World Movement reported. "The negroes fear trouble and are arming. Even if no trouble breaks out during the strike, there is a heritage of ill-will being built up here."[50] The steel industry deliberately cultivated this animosity, despite the social costs to the communities in which they operated.

At the beginning of the Great Migration, key steel manufacturers expressed concerns about racial conflict. "I have no unreasoning prejudice against the negro," explained William Brown Dickson of Midvale Steel in 1917. "I am ready to concede that he has the same right as myself to life, liberty and a reasonable opportunity for the attainment of happiness; but I also believe that no good can come to either race by an attempt to amalgamate them socially or economically, and that the sudden influx of negro labor into our Northern industrial centers is full of menace to all concerned."[51] But by the end of the war, companies deliberately moved black replacements from mill to mill in order to goad white employees into ending their strike rather than to actually produce steel. U.S. Steel paid African Americans in Gary to march through the streets there but not work, anticipating that this would be enough to convince white strikers to return. The steel industry's success at exploiting racial tensions was a major reason it won the strike. The issue of whether blacks should or even could be organized deeply divided the National Committee for Organizing Iron and Steelworkers.[52] Among the rank and file, the knowledge that their replacements had proven historically resistant to unionization increased the sense of hopelessness that strikers felt as the dispute dragged on for months. Likewise, increased isolation from other workers only served to draw black steelworkers closer to their employers even as employers were doing their best to tear communities apart.

Policies on employing African Americans in the steel industry differed upon a company by company basis in the 1920s and 1930s. African Americans in the steel industry suffered more from layoffs during the 1920-1921 depression than whites because many northern firms continued to view black workers as unreliable after the war. This affected black hiring throughout the decade. "In taking a job," explained W.P. Young of the Lockhart Iron and Steel Company in 1931, "it is a contract between two parties . . . but I have observed that many Negroes seem to feel the contract is one in which the employer is the only party; that he owes the employee everything and he, as the employee, owes the employer just as little as he can give him."[53] However, other steel manufacturers found African Americans to be a ready supply of labor to meet their needs after Congress restricted immigration from Europe in 1921 and 1924. The A.M. Byers Company of Pittsburgh retained its entire force of African American workers while firing enough white employees to reduce output by sixty percent. According to the firm's assistant superintendent, "they had retained the men upon whom they could rely the most."[54] No matter how a company viewed black labor, immigration restriction made them absolutely essential for filling the hottest, most-difficult positions in the mill. For this reason, the Bureau of Labor Statistics reported in 1926, "[T]he negro is in the steel industry to stay."[55] Nevertheless, management labor policies during the 1919 strike and later on created a legacy of distrust between black and white workers that poisoned labor relations in the steel industry for decades.[56]

Mill Towns and Employee Housing

Many steel companies had to offer their employees the chance to buy or rent a place to live. Workers in rural areas often faced severe housing shortages; skilled workers employed in urban mills had trouble finding homes that they really wanted. Critics charged that steel industry influence in the communities surrounding mills made steel towns into virtual fiefdoms. Members of management, employees or members of management's families often served as local government officials or civic leaders. In Clairton, for example, a burgess worked as the chief clerk at a steel plant. The Mayor of North Clairton served on the private police force of the local mill. The president of the Homestead Borough Council and a burgess in Munhall both held supervisory positions at the Homestead Works. The Mayor of Bethlehem was a vice-president at Bethlehem Steel. In 1935, the journalist Harvey O'Connor explained how U.S. Steel assumed control over the towns in which it operated:

> Since the turn of the century, the Steel Corporation . . . has held the political and social life of Pennsylvania in the hollow of its hands. . . . The mill superintendents ruled the boroughs through a Republican machine which derived its sustenance from political jobs and graft on liquor and prostitution. At election time a Republican banner floating across the main street from mill to Carnegie Steel office emphasized the dependence of Prosperity on Republicanism. Republican propagandists had the freedom of the mill for electioneering and the mill ticket usually won.[57]

Although critics like O'Connor assumed that the relationship between a steel firm and the local government served as a potent anti-union weapon, the relative importance of mill towns to the industrial relations system of the steel industry is less clear.

Consider the Cambria Steel Company (later bought by the Midvale Steel & Ordnance Company) which held great power in Johnstown, Pennsylvania. As the United States Immigration Commission observed:

> It owns the largest hotel and cafe, supervises the public library, owns a large and flourishing American residential suburb, which is situated on a mountain that rises directly from the city; owns and operates the railroad which carries all of the passengers and freight traffic between the city proper and this suburb; and owns the ground and a majority of

> the houses in two residential districts for its employes, and considerable land on which houses owned by its employes have been built.[58]

In 1910, over seventy percent of all male manual workers in Johnstown were Cambria employees. Despite such power, the National Committee for Organizing Iron and Steel workers met with great success organizing in Johnstown, eventually shutting down the mill there for over a month during the strike. Weirton, West Virginia, was the largest unincorporated enclave in the country. Here, the company was the local government. Nevertheless, violence occurred there too during the 1919 strike. In fact, William Z. Foster claimed the National Committee never "set up its organizing machinery in a steel town without ultimately putting substantial unions among the employees."[59] Therefore, the ability to dominate a community did not guarantee labor peace.

Company-owned employee housing remains closely associated with company towns in the popular mind. Yet in the years before the 1919 strike, steel companies made only minimal efforts to provide housing for employees. According to a report published by the U.S. Commissioner of Labor in 1913, fifty-six of seventy-four firms surveyed provided housing opportunities for their employees, but most involved only "the incidental ownership of a few houses." In October 1920, only 17.9% of employees in this industry were housed by their employers. Private real estate companies took care of this responsibility in most steel towns. U.S. Steel had no single policy on renting or selling employees homes until 1920.[60] In 1909, when the Corporation built Gary, Indiana, officials frankly admitted "that the building of the town was incidental, that their main concern was to construct a steel plant, and that city-making was a side issue into which necessity alone drove them."[61] Management rented some lots to highly skilled employees at a discount so they could erect their own houses, but unskilled workers had to fend for themselves. As an official of the Illinois Steel Company, the U.S. Steel subsidiary that ran the Corporation's Gary operations, suggested in 1917, "This Company should not undertake the housing of all of the Corporation employes, and many of them do not desire Company houses."[62] At Vandergrift, Pennsylvania, which was wholly owned by U.S. Steel's American Sheet and Tin Plate Company, the Corporation never engaged in the owning and renting of houses. On the other hand, in Morgan Park, Minnesota, owned and operated by U.S. Steel's Minnesota Steel Company subsidiary, even unskilled labor rented company-owned housing. By 1919, U.S. Steel had built a total of 25,965 dwellings nationwide. However, since most of these were in isolated coal towns, only 10,000 were available to the Corporation's approximately 200,000 steelworkers.[63]

The 1919 strike showed steel manufacturers just how effective a means of control the renting or selling of houses to employees could be. Since those workers who rented or had a mortgage from their employer did not want to risk eviction, they showed more loyalty during the strike than workers who rented from outside landlords. "At the commencement of the strike," observed the manager of Youngstown Sheet and Tube's land company, "almost without exception our foreign renting tenants stayed away from work, but after a few days, on finding their homes and families were being protected, they began to filter back to the mill, and before long the best of them had returned."[64] Because a tenant or debtor relationship with their employer bound workers to their jobs, rental agreements, mortgage loan plans and the like became more popular throughout the industry in the wake of the strike. In January 1920, the same month the strike formally ended, U.S. Steel implemented a company-wide home-owning plan which allowed employees to purchase homes from the Corporation by paying in installments or by taking out a company-backed mortgage. Bethlehem Steel began a similar program in 1923. This is the first evidence of steel manufacturers deliberately cultivating home-ownership among workers in order to control labor.[65]

Before steel manufacturers stumbled upon the use of employee housing as an anti-union tactic, they saw it as a way to express their cultural ideals. If they had to build towns for workers to live in, why not use them as a way to spread their values to their employees? In Morgan Park, U.S. Steel built a school used by children during the day and employees learning subjects like English at night. In Gary, the Corporation subsidized the building of churches and kept the community dry. Elbert Gary himself donated the money to build the local YMCA. When U.S. Steel began a home-owning plan for employees of all its subsidiaries in 1920, it permitted its employees to pay for company-owned housing in installments, build their own house or take out a mortgage with the firm on any other house of their choice. No matter which way they chose to carry out their purchase, the plan was supposed to encourage workers to became stable, loyal employees.[66]

Wages and the Regularity of Employment

The most important positive incentive which steel manufacturers provided to employees to encourage them to remain nonunion was high wages. Wages for skilled men fell sharply at the beginning of the Nonunion Era, but increases for less-skilled workers more than made up for this loss because there were so many more of them. These gains are why steelmaking can be considered a high wage industry during this period. Albert Rees' estimates of real hourly wages in fourteen manufacturing industries between 1890 and 1914 are the best figures available to show that steelmaking was a high wage industry.[67] His results for the years 1901 to 1914 are reproduced in Table 3.1. Each year, average real wages in the iron and steel industry are at the top or near the top of the fourteen industries surveyed.[68] With respect to the period after 1914, a 1919 study by the Bureau of Labor Statistics found that average hourly wages in the steel industry were the highest of 29 industries surveyed.[69]

How should these relatively high wages for an industry where worker skill was becoming increasingly less important be explained? There are many good economic explanations that could be factored in when answering this question. First, the vast majority of the workers in the industry were adult males who inevitably received higher wages than other industries with many women and children among their employees. Second is the possibility that steelmakers had to pay workers a premium to work in mills full of heat and smoke where the risk of accident was high. There is also the possibility that employers were paying efficiency wages: greater compensation because they found that their often-impoverished employees were more productive when paid more. This last explanation is least likely because most of the gains in production during the 1890s and the first decades of the Twentieth Century came from improvements in technology, not improvements in the quality of workers using that technology. As David Brody explains, "[N]o connection existed between earnings and productivity." To steelmakers, "[T]he labor market, not productivity, determined wages." And technological changes during this era put employers in a position to dominate the labor market. Table 3.2 illustrates the effect of these changes on wages and employment at two Pennsylvania blast furnaces and two open hearth furnaces operating in 1916. In each instance, one of the facilities had the newest mechanical improvements, the other used processes that dated from the late-nineteenth century. In both types of facility, the total labor force decreased

Table 3.1: Real Hourly Earnings in Fourteen Manufacturing Industries, 1890-1914 (1914 Dollars)

	Iron and Steel	Cotton	Wool	Silk	Hosiery and Knit Goods	Dyeing and Finishing Textiles	All Textiles
1901	$ 0.230	$ 0.119	$ 0.154	$ 0.127	$ 0.120	$ 0.175	$ 0.131
1902	$ 0.235	$ 0.121	$ 0.156	$ 0.135	$ 0.120	$ 0.182	$ 0.135
1903	$ 0.230	$ 0.124	$ 0.158	$ 0.140	$ 0.125	$ 0.178	$ 0.138
1904	$ 0.216	$ 0.120	$ 0.154	$ 0.135	$ 0.121	$ 0.174	$ 0.133
1905	$ 0.219	$ 0.116	$ 0.157	$ 0.147	$ 0.127	$ 0.186	$ 0.134
1906	$ 0.225	$ 0.121	$ 0.165	$ 0.143	$ 0.141	$ 0.186	$ 0.140
1907	$ 0.229	$ 0.132	$ 0.164	$ 0.146	$ 0.131	$ 0.177	$ 0.142
1908	$ 0.233	$ 0.132	$ 0.169	$ 0.136	$ 0.133	$ 0.183	$ 0.144
1909	$ 0.241	$ 0.130	$ 0.171	$ 0.151	$ 0.136	$ 0.190	$ 0.146
1910	$ 0.245	$ 0.137	$ 0.170	$ 0.151	$ 0.138	$ 0.190	$ 0.149
1911	$ 0.260	$ 0.137	$ 0.169	$ 0.158	$ 0.139	$ 0.184	$ 0.150
1912	$ 0.255	$ 0.140	$ 0.176	$ 0.160	$ 0.144	$ 0.187	$ 0.155
1913	$ 0.277	$ 0.142	$ 0.175	$ 0.181	$ 0.147	$ 0.194	$ 0.161
1914	$ 0.266	$ 0.141	$ 0.190	$ 0.169	$ 0.160	$ 0.201	$ 0.160

	Leather	Electrical Machinery	Paper and Paper Products	Rubber	Glass	Foundries and Machine Shops	Boots and Shoes
1901	$ 0.180	$ 0.214	$ 0.152	$ 0.191	$ 0.239	$ 0.214	$ 0.177
1902	$ 0.179	$ 0.216	$ 0.158	$ 0.185	$ 0.243	$ 0.225	$ 0.178
1903	$ 0.179	$ 0.233	$ 0.151	$ 0.183	$ 0.226	$ 0.229	$ 0.188
1904	$ 0.182	$ 0.220	$ 0.159	$ 0.184	$ 0.241	$ 0.225	$ 0.183
1905	$ 0.180	$ 0.224	$ 0.160	$ 0.188	$ 0.254	$ 0.228	$ 0.194
1906	$ 0.191	$ 0.228	$ 0.158	$ 0.200	$ 0.244	$ 0.236	$ 0.194
1907	$ 0.190	$ 0.222	$ 0.169	$ 0.191	$ 0.242	$ 0.233	$ 0.197
1908	$ 0.195	$ 0.229	$ 0.193	$ 0.214	$ 0.256	$ 0.239	$ 0.201
1909	$ 0.200	$ 0.228	$ 0.183	$ 0.214	$ 0.245	$ 0.241	$ 0.201
1910	$ 0.198	$ 0.233	$ 0.183	$ 0.220	$ 0.253	$ 0.243	$ 0.205
1911	$ 0.204	$ 0.235	$ 0.190	$ 0.220	$ 0.257	$ 0.246	$ 0.208
1912	$ 0.195	$ 0.242	$ 0.195	$ 0.224	$ 0.257	$ 0.248	$ 0.210
1913	$ 0.226	$ 0.244	$ 0.197	$ 0.225	$ 0.265	$ 0.254	$ 0.212
1914	$ 0.214	$ 0.240	$ 0.205	$ 0.239	$ 0.263	$ 0.253	$ 0.212

Source:

Rees, Albert. *Real Wages in Manufacturing, 1890-1914*. Princeton: Princeton University Press, 1961, p. 124.

Table 3.2: Comparison of Labor in Older and Modern Steelmaking Facilities

Blast Furnaces:	Old	New
Number of Men	88	51
Hourly Wage Rate	$.2242	$.2396
Total Daily Wages	$233.18	$146.26
Daily Output (Tons)	303	409

Open Hearth:

Type of Labor	Old	New
Unskilled*	132	30
Skilled	10	28

* Defined as work requiring "physical power."

Source:

Reitell, Charles, "Machinery and Its Benefits to Labor in the Crude Iron and Steel Industries," University of Pennsylvania Ph.D. Dissertation, (Menasha, WI: The Collegiate Press, 1917), pp. 19, 33.

substantially because new technology replaced what skilled men had once done. In the blast furnaces, the employer at the modern facility could afford a higher hourly wage because fewer men and a substantial increase in product more than compensated for the extra cost per laborer.[70] Although less-skilled workers needed more skill than before, an employer could always fire them and train others to do the same job relatively quickly. Under these circumstances, an employer concerned only with the bottom line could have assured that workers received no benefits from improvements in technology at all and not suffered from decreased productivity. Yet less-skilled workers' wages increased during the period covered by Rees' figures, even as the pool of possible recruits increased over time. How could this be?

Even though supply and demand in these years favored management, not all employers played their advantage in this market to the hilt. For example, in ordinary times the Corporation paid the highest wages for common labor in the entire steel industry. Because other manufacturers generally patterned their wages after those at U.S. Steel, their compensation rates were never more than a few cents per hour behind. Nevertheless, the Corporation consistently outbid its competition for labor in markets across the United States.[71] This suggests a deliberate decision by U.S. Steel to pay higher wages than their competitors regardless of market conditions. And even other steel firms outbid by U.S. Steel in turn outbid other manufacturing firms for less-skilled labor outside of times of need. Although economic concerns undoubtedly played a role in wage policy, steelmakers often justified these policies in cultural terms. They claimed that high wages were the price for obtaining their desired degree of control over their operations. In order to guarantee continued production in the event of a strike, firms liked to have more than enough labor to meet their needs. Employers paid their unskilled labor higher wages than unskilled labor in other European and American industries to secure this excess labor. Although higher compensation increased costs, employers believed this policy would pay off in the long run because a large labor pool acted as leverage. Testifying before Congress in 1910, Andrew Carnegie explained:

> When labor is plentiful, men do a great deal more work; at least 30 per cent more by my estimate. When wages are high and men are scarce, they do not do the work. The reason is this (I am not blaming the men for it; it is human nature): When labor is plentiful, a man is zealous to keep his job. When labor is very scarce, and you can not get other men, the man will be a great deal less attentive to his duties. That is my experience, and it is that of every employer of labor, I think.[72]

As Carnegie's statement indicates, this policy reflects an assumption about the nature of wage work: lack of competition in the labor market destroys the incentive to work hard. Therefore, in order to ensure performance, employers would pay a premium even if new technology muted the effect of individual effort. While a company that needed labor would have been willing to pay a high price for labor in a tight market to improve its production capacity, Carnegie's desire to keep wages high to guarantee surplus labor undercut his devotion to the immediate bottom line. His desire for control trumped his desire to keep costs down.

Steel manufacturers also believed high wages directly combated the influence of unions. "The way to keep out of trouble with your employees," remarked J.A. Campbell of Youngstown Sheet and Tube before a gathering of steel executives in 1911, "in my opinion, is to treat them fairly and not try to take advantage of them . . . by reducing their wages when they cannot afford to have them reduced."[73] Privately, one Corporation executive admitted that management supported high wages in order to prevent worker unrest. In a 1916 letter to the president of International Harvester, George W. Perkins drew a direct connection between U.S. Steel's high wage policy and labor peace. "[O]n more than one occasion," he explained:

> the presidents of subsidiary companies [of U.S. Steel] have been dead against wage increases, but they have been overruled by the finance committee and allowed no discretion practically as to the carrying out

> of the policy laid down by Judge Gary and his associates. I think the way wages have not been raised, the way the heads of departments have sort of tried to make believe they had raised them without raising them, you will find is more largely responsible for your labor troubles [at International Harvester] than anything else.[74]

Elbert Gary was quite open about using high wages to combat organized labor. As he told the presidents of U.S. Steel's subsidiaries in 1911, "Make it certain that the men in your employ are treated as well, if not a little better, than other men who are working for people who deal and contract with unions; make it certain you pay as liberal wages."[75] On this score, U.S. Steel practiced what Gary preached. U.S Steel's decision to grant its tin plate workers a wage increase in 1910, the same year those workers lost their union representation, was an illustration of this policy; so was the decision to raise wages three times over the course of a year in response to worker unrest at its Pittsburgh facilities during 1916. The entire industry maintained inflated wartime wage rates in order to combat the nationwide organizing drive of 1918 and 1919.[76] Industry leaders paid the price of high wages because their opposition to unions was based on more than just economic concerns.

Despite the efforts of steelmakers to keep wages high, critics of the industry often denounced compensation in the steel industry as inadequate because workers did not earn enough money to maintain an "American" standard of living. Employers countered that steelworkers were satisfied with their wages. In fact, many were. When reformers like Margaret Byington of the Pittsburgh Survey defined the American standard of living as a family wage, they were suggesting a new way of measuring the wages of unskilled workers. Most immigrants compared their standard of living not to that of established Americans but to the standard of living they had experienced in their country of origin. As one former steelworker told Ewa Morawska in 1981, "It was terribly hard work, and we lived poorly . . . But we ate good, broth with meat . . . while at home [in Europe] only borsht and potatoes, borscht and potatoes." According to Morawska, comments like these, highlighting the differences between America and Europe, "are repeated over and over again in immigrant letters and memoirs."[77] Another industry response to criticism over wages was to play up a worker's potential for upward mobility. In 1912, for example, the U.S. Steel's Assistant General Solicitor insisted, "The way out of their difficulty in supporting their families according to American standards is simply to rise out of the ranks of unskilled labor and into the semi-skilled and finally [into the ranks] of skilled labor."[78] Nevertheless, the vast majority of steelworkers could not advance in this manner. Skill and reward differentials were disappearing during this era, and because there were far fewer skilled positions than unskilled ones, only a few steelworkers (usually American-born and English-speaking) could make it into the ranks of skilled workers. Since steelmakers hired less-skilled labor at periods of peak demand and laid them off when demand ebbed, few less-skilled workers got a chance to prove their worth.

Many steelmakers preferred to run their mills full-tilt in good times and decrease capacity when times turned lean, even if this meant suspending operations in entire departments or entire plants. Assessing the extent of this practice, the United States Commissioner of Labor's 1913 *Report on Conditions of Employment in the Iron and Steel Industry* argued that the iron and steel industry experienced "greater fluctuations in its labor force during the course of the year than any of the large manufacturing industries whose demand is not seasonal." Employers chose to run "a department at top speed under the heaviest pressure while there [was] an active demand for its particular products and then [shut] it down as soon as the market [became] weak." Table 3.3 supports this point, showing the fluctuations in 21 different industries in 1908-1909. Many of the industries with similar turnover rates were seasonal industries.[79]

Until World War I, American steelmakers operated on an irregular basis, running full at times of peak demand and then shutting down. Unlike a seasonal industry such as canning, it did not have to be that way. Irregular operation was another social choice made by management rather than an economic necessity. As the economists Jett Lauck and Edgar Sydenstricker pointed out in 1917, "The steel industry furnishes an excellent example of . . . industrial practise that results in irregular employment," as opposed to seasonal needs.[80] The steel industry did not keep comprehensive turnover statistics until the 1930s. However, anecdotal evidence suggests the severity of the problem. Table 3.4 shows the intensity of the fluctuations in employment caused by irregular operation during years when the Census Bureau conducted its Census of Manufactures, but this is not the same as turnover because it gives no idea of how many different people filled the jobs available. The *Report on Conditions of Employment* includes figures on turnover at a typical steel plant between 1905 and 1910, gathered by a close examination of the records of

Table 3.3: Regularity of Employment in 21 Industries

	Percent Working:			
Industry	**12 Months**	**9 Months or Over**	**6 Months or Over**	**3 Months or Over**
Iron and Steel	20	44.1	75	94.2
Agricultural Implements and Vehicles	42.6	83	94.1	98
Cigars and Tobacco	73.2	90.9	97	99.4
Clothing	37.8	73.7	95.4	98.9
Coal Mining (anthracite)	9	76.1	96.4	99.3
Coal Mining (bituminous)	16.8	46.9	88.1	99
Collars and Cuffs	63.5	92.8	97.3	99.2
Copper Mining and Smelting	93.5	98.7	99.9	99.9
Cotton Goods	42.9	79.1	92.3	97.9
Furniture	54.5	88.8	98	99.3
Glass	53.8	77.7	90.8	99
Gloves	80.4	92.6	98.8	100
Iron-Ore Mining	60.3	83.7	95.6	99.3
Leather	38.6	65.2	87.1	96.6
Oil Refining	62.7	79.6	97.3	99.4
Shoes	29.9	64.1	90.9	98.3
Silk Goods	38.3	61.7	91.3	98.1
Slaughtering and Meat Packing	54.7	80.1	96.8	99.4
Sugar Refining	61.1	82.4	96.2	99.2
Woolen and Worsted Goods	37.3	67	89.8	97.7
Diversified Manufactures	41.4	76.4	95.5	98.9

Source: Stanley Committee Hearings, 2915.

a mutual benefit association set up by the company in question. Those numbers are displayed in Table 3.5.

The lack of good turnover statistics aside, it is certain that irregular operation had a devastating effect on ordinary steelworkers. Like high wages, this policy created a large pool of excess labor, floating from job to job. Less skilled, lower-paid workers tended to suffer the most from irregular operation because they were the ones let go most often. Employees interviewed by the United States Commissioner of Labor hated this policy because they found it "impossible in times of prosperity to tell upon what scale expenditures should be made in order to provide a fund

Table 3.4: Wage Earners, Per Month, in the Steel Works and Rolling Mill Industry

	1904	1909	1914	1919	1921
January	191,219	216,349	257,651	441,560	293,284
February	205,136	215,650	262,418	416,541	276,255
March	215,054	215,076	271,531	392,803	252,257
April	219,645	217,307	270,941	367,514	233,428
May	220,229	218,424	254,443	354,721	221,961
June	212,304	235,533	254,827	360,584	211,203
July	190,526	234,151	252,680	383,212	183,084
August	196,170	242,077	247,953	387,965	205,446
September	200,425	258,925	249,635	377,275	219,116
October	208,716	269,255	233,338	292,465	239,051
November	212,299	274,525	210,279	343,312	252,481
December	219,021	283,629	218,896	383,100	248,673
% Minimum Forms of Maximum	86.50%	75.80%	77.40%	66.20%	62.40%

Sources:

United States Bureau of the Census. *Biennial Census of Manufactures*, 1921. Washington, D.C.: Government Printing Office, 1924, 378.

Bureau of the Census. *Census of Manufactures, 1914*, vol. 2. Washington, D.C.: Government Printing Office, 1919, 221.

Table 3.5: Shifting of Labor Force in a Large Steel Plant, 1905-1910

	1905	1906	1907	1908	1909	1910
Employees, January 1	11,631	15,661	16,608	13,578	13,731	16,997
New Employees During Year	14,023	13,983	11,705	4,169	10,792	13,043
Total Employees	25,654	29,644	28,313	17,747	24,523	30,040
Employees Leaving Plant and Not Returning	9,874	12,909	14,570	3,907	7,387	14,374
% of Employees Leaving and Not Returning	38%	44%	51%	22%	30%	48%
Employees Leaving Work but Reemployed During Year	6,649	6,733	6,689	6,934	8,162	6,135
% of Employees Leaving Work but Reemployed	26%	23%	24%	39%	33%	20%

Source:

United States Commissioner of Labor. *Report on Conditions of Employment in the Iron and Steel Industry*, vol. 3. United States Senate Document No. 110, 62d Cong., 1st Sess., 1913, 381.

out of which a family can be supported during periods of idleness."[81] Many less-skilled workers would quit whenever they detected a risk of shutdown and look for work at other plants.[82] After all, high wage rates meant nothing to the unemployed. Irregular operation helped limit the cost of high wages in the steel industry. If employers offered workers fewer hours, their total wage bills would not be as high as if every employee worked full time, all year around.

Irregular operation also served as a potent weapon against organized labor because even displaced union loyalists poured into nonunion plants during lean times. Unable to support their families when working only six or eight months per year, a reduction in wages in exchange for the prospect of an entire year's work would have seemed like a bargain. U.S. Steel suspended operations at thirty-three union mills in 1901 to eliminate excess capacity at its disparate facilities, while no nonunion mills were idled. Obviously, this was not a coincidence. During negotiations with unionized workers at U.S. Steel's American Tin Plate Company subsidiary in 1903, management admitted to using this strategy in order to extract concessions. "[D]on't you realize," one official asked Amalgamated President T.J. Shaffer, "that if we go to the non-union mills and ask them to make these plates and run all the year around . . . the union mills will get less work than they otherwise would? After the friendly relations our company has had with your Association, is it wise to make it appear to us, that the only people to whom we can go with a business proposition and run any chance of having it considered are the workmen in the non-union mills?" Bowing to pressure, the union agreed to rebate the company 25% of its scale rates, even though its members still had a year left on the three-year contract they had signed in 1901.[83]

Because immigration created a large number of potential employees in the years leading up to World War I, high turnover did not have serious economic costs for the steel industry at this time. Therefore, employers could maintain their artificial production schedules without suffering a large economic cost. By operating their mills in this manner, industry leaders elevated Andrew Carnegie's example of hard-driving to what Thomas Misa calls "reckless mass production," a fixation on output so great that problems in the quality of steel created by this method were ignored.[84] Steel manufacturers might have run their mills at a more even pace (the way the British did or the way they themselves would run them during the depression of the 1930s), but this did not fit their distinct production-oriented mentality.

Even though irregular operation encouraged high turnover among steelworkers, steelmakers did not recognize the deleterious effects of this policy until World War One had begun. In fact, nobody in American business "discovered" the labor turnover problem until Magnus W. Alexander of General Electric began to examine it in 1913. Alexander began to assess this issue by asking several large employers how many employees they had to hire each year in order to maintain their average employment. None of them could provide quantitative answers. When he tried to piece together numbers, he found that many manufacturing firms faced turnover rates of over 100%. Subsequent research by other investigators found rates that were even higher. Managers in many industries suspected that turnover was inefficient because of the costs of training and replacing workers, but only now did they recognize the extent of this problem. Since many of these studies involved businesses in the metal trades, steel producers undoubtedly encountered this research; yet only when faced with costly wartime labor shortages did steelmakers begin to develop strategies to keep less-skilled workers on the job.[85]

Conditions of Labor in a Nonunion Industry

The methods by which management kept the steel industry nonunion show the overwhelming power which employers held over their employees. Without unions to oppose them, steel manufacturers could dictate the terms and conditions of employment that their employees faced. No other result of the decline of organized labor had a greater effect on the lives of the men who labored in this industry than long hours. "[T]he conclusion is unescapable [sic] that a real cause of the persistence of the twelve-hour day and the seven-[day] week is the defenselessness of the unorganized immigrant worker," argued the authors of the Interchurch World Movement report.[86] Over half of the industry's employees worked a twelve-hour day in 1910. Despite protests inside and outside the industry, that figure increased during the 1910s because of the demands of World War I. Industry leaders frequently claimed workers preferred longer hours, yet opposition to the twelve-hour day was a major motivation for the 1919 strike. The reason for the twelve-hour day's unpopularity was the way it dominated the lives of employees. "I don't live," one worker told Ray Stannard Baker, "I just exist—work and sleep. I don't get any time to see my family. I can't go to any entertainments without taking it out of my sleep, and I am too tired to go to church on Sunday or to do anything else but lie around."[87] The long turn, a twenty-four hour day that occurred in most mills once every two weeks when workers rotated between the day and night shift, only heightened the fatigue that steelworkers felt anyway. Such policies not only invited harsh public criticism, but inevitably hurt the productivity of steel labor. Nevertheless, employers fiercely defended the twelve-hour day because they equated this with their right to manage their workers without interference, and they feared the additional up-front costs that shorter hours would impose upon them (since workers moving from the twelve to eight hour day were unlikely to accept a one third cut in pay).

Numerous critics attacked these and other aspects of the industry's labor conditions during the Nonunion Era. According to John A. Fitch, these conditions made, "the overwhelming majority of [steelworkers], in both Corporation and independent mills . . . resentful and bitter toward their employers."[88] Elbert Gary repeatedly denied that his employees resented management because of the conditions under which they labored. In 1921, he argued, "During the twenty years of our existence there has not been material hostility shown or serious complaint made to the management by our workmen."[89] The fact that this claim came two years after the largest strike in the Corporation's history to that point shows the absurdity of this position. However, the question of whether Gary actually believed this claim cannot be answered this easily. Undoubtedly, Elbert Gary discounted the labor trouble at U.S. Steel as the work of outside agitators. Nevertheless, the Corporation often changed aspects of its labor policy to mitigate its harsher aspects because its leadership believed that complete domination without concessions would not pay. Rather than compromise on the question of unionization, U.S. Steel depended on welfare capitalism to offer worthy employees an alternative to organization that embodied management's cultural ideals.

Notes

1. *The Public* 21, 10 August 1918, 1007.

2. Herbert N. Casson, *The Romance of Steel* (New York: A.S. Barnes & Company, 1907), 363-63

3. John A. Fitch, *The Steel Workers* (Pittsburgh: University of Pittsburgh Press, 1989/Originally published by Russell Sage Foundation, 1911), 214.

4. U.S. Congress, Senate, Committee on Education and Labor, *Investigation of Strike in Steel Industries*, 66th Cong., 1st Sess., 1919, 177.

5. Interchurch World Movement, *Public Opinion and the Steel Strike* (New York: Harcourt, Brace and Howe, 1921), 74-75.

6. Fitch, *The Steel Workers*, 219; H.N. Brown to Charles Lukens Huston, May 15 1911, Lukens Iron and Steel Company Papers, Box 1998, Hagley Museum and Library, Wilmington, DE.

7. Interchurch World Movement, *Report on the Steel Strike of 1919* (New York: Harcourt, Brace and Howe, 1920), 27.

8. Neither the subsidiary nor U.S. Steel are named in the publication, but references to "mills," the client being "in the great majority" of a "national industry," and that industry being nonunion clearly suggest the firm in question is a Corporation subsidiary.

9. Sherman Detective Service, *A Few True Detective Stories That Are Interesting and Instructive* (Boston: Sherman Detective Service, 1917), 30-34. Portions of the Sherman publication are reproduced in *Public Opinion and the Steel Strike*, 65-68.

10. William Z. Foster, *The Great Steel Strike and Its Lessons* (New York: B.W. Huebsch, 1920), 176.

11. Strike Fund Committee of New York Alumni Chapter, Intercollegiate Socialist Society, "Steel," November 1919, 4, David J. Saposs Papers, Box 27, State Historical Society of Wisconsin, Madison, WI; John J. Mullen Oral History Interview, 1966, 1, Historical Collections & Labor Archives, Pattee Library, Pennsylvania State University, State College, PA.

12. *Amalgamated Journal* (6 February 1913).

13. *International Juridical Association Monthly Bulletin* 5, (October 1936): 47; Jeremiah P. Shalloo, "The Private Police of Pennsylvania," *Annals of the American Academy of Political and Social Science* 146 (November 1929): 59.

14. J.F. Robinson, "Statement of Captain in Charge of State Police," March 21, 1910, in United States Commissioner of Labor, *Report on Strike at Bethlehem Steel Works*, Senate Document No. 521, 61st Cong., 2d Sess., 1910, 47.

15. *Allentown Democrat* quoted in United States Commission on Industrial Relations, *Final Report and Testimony Submitted to Congress By the Commission on Industrial Relations* (in 11 Vols.), Senate Document No. 415, 64th Cong., 1st Sess., 1916, 10950.

16. *Investigation of Strike in Steel Industries*, 539.

17. Ray Stannard Baker, *The New Industrial Unrest* (Garden City, NY: Doubleday, Page & Company, 1920), 36.

18. John A. Fitch, "Old Age at Forty," *The American Magazine* 71 (March 1911): 659. For evidence that steel manufacturers used blacklists see Charles A. Gulick, *Labor Policy of the United States Steel Corporation*, Columbia University Studies in History Economics and Public Law, Vol. 106, No. 1, 1924, 125-27; Stanley Committee Hearings, 3078.

19. *Report on the Steel Strike of 1919*, 29.

20. Robert W. Dunn, *Company Unions* (New York: Vanguard Press, 1927), 87-88.

21. Thomas Darlington to E.A.S. Clarke of Lackawanna Iron and Steel, September 22, 1911, American Iron and Steel Institute Papers (filed in Board of Directors Minutes), Hagley Museum and Library, Wilmington, DE.

22. Fitch, *The Steel Workers*, 10-11; United States Commissioner of Labor, *Report on Conditions of Employment in the Iron and Steel Industry*, Senate Document No. 110, 62d Cong., 1st Sess., 1913, Vol. 1, XVI; American Federation of Labor, "Statement and Evidence in Support of Petition and Charges Presented to the President of the United States Against the U.S. Steel Corporation," Washington, D.C., 1910, 19.

23. Fitch, *The Steel Workers*, 147. The entire statement by Jones is in James Howard Bridge, *The Inside History of the Carnegie Steel Company* (Pittsburgh: University of Pittsburgh Press, 1991/Originally published by Aldine Book Company, 1903), 81.

24. Lizabeth Cohen, *Making a New Deal* (New York: Cambridge University Press, 1990), 163.

25. *National Labor Tribune*, 29 July 1909.

26. United States Immigration Commission, *Immigrants in Industries Part 2: Iron and Steel Manufacturing*, Reports of the United States Immigration Commission, Senate Document No. 633, 61st Cong., 2d Sess, 1911, Vol. 1, 176; Frederick H. Willcox, "Occupational Hazards at Blast-Furnace Plants and Accident Prevention," *United States Bureau of Mines Bulletin*, No. 140, November 1917,10.

27. *Investigation of Strike in Steel Industries*, 479; Bethlehem Steel Company, "Timely Hints for the Safety & Welfare of Our Employees," South Bethlehem, PA, January, 1916, 11; Willcox,10.

28. Willcox,10.

29. *Immigrants in Industries*, Vol. 1, 646-51; *Immigrants in Industries*, Vol. 2, 66. For other examples of employers clumping ethnic groups in specific departments, see Elmer Maloy Oral History Interview, November 7, 1967, 4 and Bernie Capozza Oral History Interview, May 4, 1974, 5, Historical Collections & Labor Archives, Pattee Library, Pennsylvania State University, State College, PA; John Bodnar, *Immigration and Industrialization* (Pittsburgh, University of Pittsburgh Press, 1977), 36-37.

30. Paul U. Kellogg, "The McKee's Rocks Strike," *The Survey* 22 (7 August 1909): 665.

31. *Bulletin of the American Iron and Steel Association* 25 (7 January 1891):5.

32. Casson, 252.

33. Paul Krause, "Commentary," in David Brody, *Steelworkers in America: The Nonunion Era* (Urbana: University of Illinois Press, 1998/Originally published by Harvard University Press, 1960), 324.

34. Andrew Carnegie, "Mr. Andrew Carnegie on Socialism, Labour and Home Rule," Aberdeen, Scotland, 1892, 21.

35. *New York Times*, 21 November 1907.

36. Fitch, *The Steel Workers*, 146.

37. *Immigrants in Industries*, Vol. 1, 279.

38. Edward Bailey of the Central Iron and Steel Company quoted in *Proceedings of the American Iron and Steel Institute 1910*, 74.

39. Isaac A. Hourwich, *Immigration and Labor*, 2nd ed. (New York: B.W. Huebsch, 1922), 408-09.

40. Foster, 199.

41. Interchurch World Movement, *Report on the Steel Strike of 1919*, 230.

42. David J. Saposs, Untitled Report on the 1919 Steel Strike, 3, David J. Saposs Papers, Box 26.

43. Dennis Dickerson, *Out of the Crucible* (Albany: State University of New York Press, 1986), 7-26; Herbert R. Northrop, "The Negro and Unionism in the Birmingham, Ala., Iron and Steel Industry," *Southern Economics Journal* 10 (July 1943): 32; Sterling D. Spero and Abram L. Harris, *The Black Worker* (New York: Columbia University Press, 1931), 246-52.

44. Northrop, 28. In the South, 39.1% of all steelworkers were African-American compared to 1.1% in the East and .5% of steelworkers in the Midwest (*Immigrants in Industries*, Vol. 1, 17).

45. John Bodnar, "The Impact of the 'New Immigration' on the Black Worker: Steelton, Pennsylvania, 1880-1920," *Labor History* 17 (Spring 1976): 214-15; Horace R. Cayton and George S. Mitchell, *Black Workers and the New Unions* (Chapel Hill: University of North Carolina Press, 1939), 76; Fitch, *The Steel Workers*, 349; *Pennsylvania Negro Business Directory 1910* (Harrisburg: Jas. H.W. Howard & Son, 1910), 58, 119.

46. R.R. Wright, Jr. "One Hundred Negro Steel Workers," in *Wage-Earning Pittsburgh*, Paul U. Kellogg, ed. (New York: Russell Sage Foundation, 1914), 105.

47. John A. Fitch, "Birmingham District: Labor Conservation," *The Survey* 27 (6 January 1912): 1528.

48. Spero and Harris, 246;

49. Abraham Epstein, *The Negro Migrant in Pittsburgh* (New York: Arno & The New York Times, 1969/Originally published by the University of Pittsburgh, 1918), 31; Elizabeth Balanoff, "A History of the Black Community of Gary, Indiana, 1906-1940," unpublished Ph.D. Dissertation, University of Chicago, 1974, 33; Peter Gottlieb, "Rethinking the Great Migration," in *The Great Migration in Historical Perspective*, Joe William Trotter, Jr., ed. (Bloomington: Indiana University Press, 1991), 70; Professor Francis D. Tyson, University of Pittsburgh, in "Testimony Before the Interchurch World Movement Commission," 138, David J. Saposs Papers, Box 26; Dickerson, 33; William T. Hogan, *Economic History of the Iron and Steel Industry in the United States* (Lexington, MA: D.C. Heath and Company, 1971), 455-56.

50. Spero and Harris, 257; Dickerson, 50, 62-64; [George] Soule, "Preliminary Survey of Steel Strike for Use of the Commission," Mary Heaton Vorse Collection, Box 121, Archives of Labor and Urban Affairs, Wayne State University, Detroit, MI.

51. *Iron Age* 99 (18 January 1917).

52. Interchurch World Movement, *Report on the Steel Strike of 1919,* 177; Balanoff, 153; David J. Saposs, "National Committee History," 1920, 85, Saposs Papers, Box 10.

53. Dickerson, 95; W.P. Young, "The Negro Worker Past and Present," October 26, 1931, National Urban League Papers, Industrial Relations Department, Box 34, Library of Congress, Washington, D.C.

54. United States Bureau of Labor Statistics, "Handbook of Labor Statistics 1924-1926," *Bulletin of the United States Bureau of Labor Statistics*, No. 439 (June 1927): 403.

55. United States Bureau of Labor Statistics, "Employment of Negroes in the Steel Industry of Pennsylvania," *Monthly Labor Review* 22 (June 1926): 1227.

56. For more on race relations in the steel industry in recent decades, see Judith Stein, *Running Steel, Running America* (Chapel Hill: University of North Carolina Press), 1998.

57. *International Juridical Association Monthly Bulletin* 5 (October 1936): 41; Harvey O'Connor, *Steel-Dictator* (New York: John Day Company, 1935), 247-48.
The literature on how steel manufacturers influenced local politics is voluminous. For other examples, see Fitch, *The Steel Workers*, 229-31; Brody, *Steelworkers in America,* 123.

58. *Immigrants in Industries*, Vol. 1, 329.
In the Immigration Commission report, the firm in question is identified only as "Company I." John A. Fitch ["The Labor Policies of Unrestricted Capital, *The Survey* 28, 6 April 1912, 21-22] identifies the company as Cambria and the town as Johnstown.

59. Ewa Morawska, *For Bread With Butter: The Life-Worlds of East-Central Europeans in Johnstown, Pennsylvania, 1890-1940* (New York: Cambridge University Press, 1985), 85; Gerald G. Eggert, *Steelmasters and Labor Reform, 1886-1923* (Pittsburgh: University of Pittsburgh Press, 1981), 134; Teresa Lynn Ankney, "The Pendulum of Control: The Evolution of the Weirton Steel Company, 1909-1951," Ph.D. Diss., Catholic University of America, 1993, 46-49; Foster, 41-44.

60. *Conditions of Employment in the Iron and Steel Industry*, Vol. 3, 418; Leifur Magnusson, "Housing by Employers in the United States," *Bulletin of the U.S. Bureau of Labor Statistics*, No. 263, October 1920, 11.

61. Graham Romeyn Taylor, "Creating the Newest Steel City," *The Survey* 22 (3 April 1909): 24.

62. E.C. Brown to J.H. Grose, "Questions by Carnegie Steel Company Addressed to Several Subsidiary Companies of the United States Steel Corporation Having Recent Housing or Town Site Developments," March 2, 1917,

Carnegie-Illinois Steel Corporation Collection, File 81.64.54, Mahoning Valley Historical Society, Youngstown, OH.

63. Leifur Magnusson, "A Modern Industrial Suburb," *Monthly Review of the U.S. Bureau of Labor Statistics* 6 (April 1918): 747-49; Samuel Yellen, *American Labor Struggles* (New York: S.A. Russell, 1936), 257.

64. *Year Book of the American Iron and Steel Institute*, 1922, 113-14.

65. United States Steel Corporation, *Bureau of Safety Sanitation and Welfare Bulletin*, No. 9, 30; Bethlehem Steel Company, "Ten Years' Progress in Human Relations," 1928,15-16.

66. Williams, File 81.64.54; United States Steel Corporation, The Committee on Housing, "Home Owning Plan," 1920.

67. There are two important studies of real wages in manufacturing during this era. One is by Albert Rees [*Real Wages in Manufacturing 1890-1914* (Princeton: Princeton University Press, 1961)]; the other is by Paul Douglas [*Real Wages in the United States, 1890-1926* (New York: Augustus M. Kelley, 1966/originally published in 1930)]. There are two reasons why Rees' figures are more reliable. First, Rees uses more information to determine cost-of-living. According to him, the cost-of-living did not rise as much as Douglas suggests. Therefore, he concludes that the real earnings of manufacturing workers were generally higher. Second, the information Rees uses to determine wages in the steel industry is better. The study upon which Douglas bases his steelworker earnings estimates omits Bethlehem Steel, as well as those sectors of the industry producing sheet steel, tin plate, terne plate, wire, nails and bolts. See Rees, *Real Wages in Manufacturing*, 74-119, 62. Rees, by the way, was my father so I am biased in this matter.

68. Rees, *Real Wages in Manufacturing*, 60-64, 143-44.

69. United States Bureau of Labor Statistics, "Industrial Survey in Selected Industries in the United States, 1919," *Bulletin of the U.S. Bureau of Labor Statistics*, No. 265, May 1920, 37.

70. Brody, *Steelworkers in America*, 41, 43-45; Charles Reitell, Machinery and Its Benefits to Workers in the Crude Iron and Steel Industries," Ph.D. Diss., University of Pennsylvania (Menasha, WI, The Collegiate Press, 1917), 9-17, 23-31.

71. John A. Fitch, "Arson and Citizenship," *The Survey* 35 (22 January 1916): 479.

72. U.S. Congress, House, Committee on Ways and Means, "Tariff Hearings," Vol. 2, Document No. 1505, 60th Cong., 2nd Sess., 1909,1848.

73. "Remarks Made at Dinner given at Waldorf-Astoria Hotel," May 4, 1911, 12.

74. George W. Perkins to Cyrus McCormick, May 4, 1916, George W. Perkins Papers, Box 14.

75. Elbert H. Gary, "Remarks to the Presidents of the Subsidiary Companies, United States Steel Corporation," October 19, 1911, 9.

76. Brody, *Steelworkers in America*, 73; Robert Ozanne, *A Century of Labor-Management Relations at McCormick and International Harvester* (Madison: University of Wisconsin Press, 1967), 109; Hogan, 457.
Paying union wages to nonunion employees remains a popular anti-union tactic in modern times See Richard B. Freeman and James L. Medoff, *What Do Unions Do?* (New York: Basic Books, 1984), 150-61.

77. Margo Anderson, "Does the Evidence Support the Argument?: Margaret Byington's Cost of Living Survey of Homestead," in *Pittsburgh Surveyed* (Pittsburgh: University of Pittsburgh Press, 1996), Maurine W. Greenwald and Margo Anderson, eds., 119-20; Morawska, 136.
For critiques of wage rates in the steel industry during this period, see, Margaret Byington, *Homestead: The Houses of a Mill Town* (New York: Arno & The New York Times, 1969/Originally published by the Russell Sage Foundation, 1910),180-84 and Interchurch World Movement, *Report on the Steel Strike of 1919*, 85.

78. Raynal Bolling, "The United States Steel Corporation and Labor Conditions," *Annals of the American Academy of Political and Social Science* 42 (July 1912): 46.

79. *Conditions of Employment in the Iron and Steel Industry*, Vol. 3, 21, 205.

80. W. Jett Lauck and Edgar Sydenstricker, *Conditions of Labor in American Industries* (New York: Funk & Wagnalls), 152.

81. *Conditions of Employment in the Iron and Steel Industry*, Vol. 3, 380, 205.

82. E.C. Ramage, "The Foreman in Relation to Employment," *Bulletin of the Pennsylvania Department of Labor and Industry* 7 (1920), 135-36.

83. Amalgamated Association, *Journal of Proceedings* 1901, 6046, 6050; J.R. Phillips of the American Tin Plate Company quoted in Amalgamated Association, *Journal of Proceedings* 1903, 6577.

84. Thomas N. Misa, *A Nation of Steel* (Baltimore: The Johns Hopkins University Press, 1995), 15.

85. Evan Metcalf, "Economic Stabilization by American Business in the Twentieth Century," Ph.D. Dissertation, University of Wisconsin, 1972, 82-87.

86. Interchurch World Movement, *Report on the Steel Strike of 1919*, 81.

87. Baker, 29.

88. Fitch, *The Steel Workers*, 233.

89. Elbert Gary, "Principles and Policies of the United States Steel Corporation," April 18, 1921, 9.

Chapter Four

A Kind Face on a Cold Policy: Welfare Capitalism in the Steel Industry

> Unless the services rendered to employes develop a loyal, contented working force and furnish proper incentives to stimulate wholehearted cooperation from the employe, they are wasted.
>
> —*Blast Furnace and Steel Plant*, February 1920.[1]

Andrew Carnegie considered the money he spent to improve the working and living conditions of his employees to be philanthropy. During the opening decades of this century, a wide variety of employers in all types of industries turned what Carnegie thought of as philanthropy into an important part of the way they did business. They used the term "welfare work" to describe the opportunities they provided for the betterment or increased comfort of their employees, but historians now prefer the term "welfare capitalism." Welfare capitalism was particularly important to the leaders of the steel industry. "With the fuller realization and necessity of welfare work in our industrial establishments," the manager of the U.S. Steel's Bureau of Safety, Sanitation and Welfare told the American Iron and Steel Institute in 1920, "these activities have gained such earnest recognition from employers of labor that today welfare work may be classified as one of the essential features in successful and efficient plant management."[2] Even though steel manufacturers often used economic justifications to explain the existence of their welfare policies, many of the most ambitious and expensive welfare programs reached only a limited number of employees. In these instances, the men who ran the steel firms kept these policies in place because such programs embodied values like the ethos of individual achievement and the desire for the freedom to control the terms and conditions under which their employees worked.

Welfare capitalism in the steel industry consisted of everything from old-age pensions and accident prevention to providing workers spaces to plant gardens. David Brody, in *Steelworkers in America*, argues that these efforts "added the measure of betterment needed to win the steelworker's consent to the terms of his employment. It insured the stability of the labor system that had developed along with the industry."[3] Brody's book paints welfare capitalism as an essential tool for maintaining the steel industry's profitable nonunion labor policy. This policy attached workers to the company at a time when its harshest anti-union strategies might have driven employees away. Using data released by U.S. Steel,[4] this chapter reconstructs key welfare programs at the Corporation so as to put Brody's argument to the test. In theory, expensive efforts at generating goodwill could have bought the loyalty of the workers who stood to benefit from them. In fact, they did not because many of U.S. Steel's most important welfare efforts attracted few participants and stimulated little genuine cooperation. The costliest welfare programs, such as the stock purchase plan and the pension program, reached only a tiny portion of the Corporation's workforce; certainly nowhere near enough people to ensure the stability of the entire labor system.

Furthermore, management's explanation of low participation rates suggests that U.S. Steel never intended welfare capitalism to operate in the manner Brody conceived it. Consider the Corporation's standard of success for two smaller kinds of efforts. Bathing facilities for employees were one of many smaller touches within U.S. Steel's overall welfare capitalist agenda. However, faced with a choice between a hot shower in the plant after a long day and more time at home with their families, many workers chose the latter. "It is not our fault if the men don't use the baths," the president of one U.S. Steel subsidiary told John Fitch, "but it is our fault if the baths are not there to be used, and if they are there, the men will learn after a while to use them." [5] This indicates patience with a not-insignificant expense that no mere economizer would have. According to the Director of Welfare at Carnegie Steel, A.H. Wyman, between 1917 and 1919, twelve percent of all employees participated in athletic and recreation programs under direct supervision, and a third of all employees used company equipment during their own leisure time. Wyman cited these figures as proof that such efforts were "extremely well-patronized."[6]

Why was management happy about programs with such lame participation rates? Why didn't the Corporation pull the plug on a particular scheme if it seemed unpopular with employees and therefore unlikely to be worth the expense? Brody argues that the steel industry aimed welfare work primarily at skilled workers because they already enjoyed "peaceful relations with their common laborers."[7] The problem with this point is that key strikes of the Nonunion Era, most notably the one in 1919, began among less-skilled labor, and even those that did not start with less-skilled workers often included them eventually (such as the strike at Bethlehem Steel in 1910). Furthermore, the limited number of employees who did participate in activities such as the stock subscription program came from all skill levels.

U.S. Steel stuck with its welfare efforts despite limited participation rates because it cared about more than simply the bottom line. Management used welfare capitalism to promote ideas like the ethos of individual achievement. In his famous "Gospel of Wealth," Andrew Carnegie wrote, "In bestowing charity, the main consideration should be to help those who will help themselves; to provide part of the means by which those who desire to improve may do so; to give those who desire to rise the aids by which they may rise."[8] After Carnegie retired from the industry, the officers of U.S. Steel (and later other firms) created expensive but often under-utilized welfare programs that embodied this principle. Many of these schemes, large and small, served as one way for employers to introduce their ideals to their workforce. Therefore, they didn't have to be accepted by employees in order to be justified.

Low participation rates for particular programs did not mean welfare capitalism failed to improve some employees' lives. Consider the example of Tennessee Coal and Iron (TC&I). After U.S. Steel bought this southern company, it poured millions of dollars into the area in and around the company's facilities. The Corporation built towns, hospitals and schools all for the use of its new subsidiary's mostly African-American workforce. It drained swamps and sent nurses to employees' homes to teach domestic hygiene. As a result of these efforts, malaria cases in the Birmingham district fell from 6000 each year to approximately 200. "[U.S. Steel] is doing more for humanity than is the United States," proclaimed one employee at the 1914 annual meeting. "[T]his company keeps men from being paupers."[9] Despite such positive developments, management had no guarantee that the workers it helped would credit management for these successes.

Perhaps the most obvious explanation for the persistence of unpopular programs was the paternalism that permeated the Steel Corporation's entire welfare structure. That paternalism began at the top. As Elbert Gary explained in 1919:

> Above everything else . . . satisfy your men if you can that your treatment is fair and reasonable and generous. Make the Steel Corporation a good place for them to work and live. Don't let the families go hungry or cold; give them playgrounds and parks and schools and churches, pure water to drink, every opportunity to keep clean, places of enjoyment, rest and recreation, treating the whole thing as a business proposition, drawing the line to be just and generous and *yet at the same time . . . retaining the control and management of your affairs, keeping the whole thing in your hands.* [emphasis added].[10]

The Corporation often pointed to its welfare work as evidence of a partnership between labor and capital, but the alliance which management offered workers was always a partnership between vastly unequal partners. Because of this skewed power relationship, welfare reinforced the autocratic nature of steel industry employers. U.S. Steel stuck with these paternalist programs even though this attitude undercut the effectiveness of its welfare efforts, since many workers did not participate in welfare capitalist programs at U.S. Steel because they were suspicious of the Corporation's motives. Other steel companies that practiced welfare capitalism patterned their efforts closely on those of U.S. Steel and faced similar problems as a result.

A "friendly critic" of U.S. Steel once described the Corporation's labor policy as being stuck in the stage of "detectives and toilets." This juxtaposition was probably intended to be humorous, but it was not far from the truth. Both parts of the steel industry's labor relations system that David Brody writes about—repression and welfare capitalism—were intimately related. Welfare capitalism drew attention away from the heavy-handed tactics that the industry used to fight organization, and made the Corporation's unswerving devotion to the open shop more palatable to the public. However, for employees, repression and welfare capitalism worked at cross-purposes. The cumulative effect of these programs on steelworkers of all skill levels was so slight that it could never outweigh the economic impact of the Corporation's aggressive anti-union policies. Even taking into account the enormous diversity of efforts under the rubric of welfare capitalism, participation in these programs was too limited to change the dynamics of industrial relations by convincing employees to willingly accept the difficult terms and conditions of employment that management imposed upon them.

What Was Welfare Capitalism?

In a 1923 book devoted to this subject, the industrial relations expert Louis Boettiger defines welfare work as any "effort of the employer to establish and maintain certain standards in respect to hours, wages, working and living conditions of his employees which are neither required by law nor by the conditions of the market."[11] During the 1890s, reformers called such efforts "industrial betterment" or "uplift work." In the first decade of the 1900s, reformers chose to refer to these activities as welfare work in order to distinguish them from charitable giving on the part of employers. The term welfare work became popular with industry because businessmen thought it suggested the "independent spirit" of the American working class. In other words, it meshed with the ethos of individual achievement that so many employers prized. Because welfare work encompassed an enormous number of endeavors, even the practitioners of this policy were not entirely certain what it entailed. "In recent years," a TC&I official remarked in 1915, "the term 'welfare work' has become familiar to every one, and activities under this head have multiplied at an amazing rate. An exact definition of the term is difficult, and it is hard to determine its limitations."[12] There were indeed few limitations as to what constituted welfare work in the iron and steel industry. One analysis undertaken in 1914 divided this phenomenon into thirty-two different "general subjects," some of which included a broad range of distinct activities.[13]

How can historians analyze such an amorphous concept? Welfare capitalism as an historical phenomenon should be bounded by both time and context. Employers have always provided goods or services for their employees that were not required by the law or the market. Only in the late-nineteenth century did reformers begin to tout such activities as a way to prevent the labor unrest that plagued the nation. Spurred on by groups like the National Civic Federation, welfare capitalism exploded onto the American economic scene around the turn of the century. National Cash Register, International Harvester, General Electric, H.J. Heinz and U.S. Steel were just a few of the large American corporations that created elaborate welfare programs between 1890 and 1910. Welfare capitalism expanded into nearly every sector of the American economy after World War I, but many firms severely curtailed or ended these activities during the Depression of the 1930s.[14]

Welfare capitalism should also be viewed in the context of the entire range of possible welfare policies. Although hundreds of businesses might fit the literal definition of welfare capitalist, some practitioners were more important than others. According to Daniel Nelson, approximately 40 large manufacturers introduced extensive programs in the decade before World War I. These firms introduced such a wide range of ambitious activities that they can rightfully be considered the unofficial leaders of what might be deemed the welfare movement. Smaller companies widely imitated the policies of these leaders when the welfare capitalist ideal took off in the late-1910s and early-1920s. Of these 40 firms, none was larger or more influential than United States Steel.[15]

Describing all of the Corporation's welfare activities would be a Herculean task. U.S. Steel built clubhouses and sponsored baseball teams, installed lockers and ran civics classes; the scope was simply enormous. Nevertheless, the Corporation often quantified its munificence towards its employees for use in its publicity efforts. As of January 1, 1920, by its own account, U.S. Steel had provided its workforce with all of the following:

Number of dwellings and boarding houses constructed and leased to employees at low rental rates	27,553
Churches	25
Schools	45
Clubs	19
Restaurants and lunch rooms	64
Rest and waiting rooms	210
Playgrounds	131
Swimming pools	11
Athletic Fields	96
Tennis Courts	107

Band stands	19
Practical housekeeping centers	18
Piped systems for drinking water	369
Sanitary drinking fountains	3,077
Wells and springs protected against pollution	647
Comfort stations (complete units, either bath or dry houses, closets, wash or locker rooms, in separate buildings or within enclosures in the building)	1,495
Water closet bowls	7,307
Urinals	2,551
Washing faucets or basins	17,369
Showers	2,672
Clothes lockers	116,749
Base hospitals	25
Emergency stations	286
Training stations (first aid and rescue)	62
Company surgeons, physicians and interns	167
Outside surgeons (on a salary)	107
Nurses (including nurses in training)	189
Orderlies and other attendants	115
Visiting nurses	68
Teachers and instructors	222
Sanitary inspectors	30
Safety inspectors (spending entire time on work)	101
Employees who have served on safety committees	25,948
Employees now serving on safety committees	5,500
Employees who have been trained in first aid and rescue work	16,881
Employees now in training	801[16]

Such a list provides some idea of the scope of welfare capitalism at U.S. Steel, but it offers no insight into how employees perceived these activities. Although the precise reaction which steelworkers had to welfare capitalism is impossible to assess, the effectiveness of welfare capitalism as an industrial relations strategy cannot be assumed.

Once again, consider the underpaid, predominately African American employees of TC&I. They lived and worked under perhaps the worst conditions of the entire industry. Despite U.S. Steel's many successful welfare capitalist policies here, strikes continually plagued TC&I after the Corporation took the company over in 1907. As late as 1923, labor turnover there was 57.4 percent.[17] So even here, within the one subsidiary of the Corporation where it was most needed, welfare capitalism did little to solve the fundamental problem of labor-management relations. If this policy was designed to keep these workers satisfied, it failed. Although the labor situation was never this bad in the rest of the Corporation, welfare capitalism did not prevent labor unrest at other Corporation subsidiaries either. The best explanation for the limited participation (and hence limited effectiveness) of individual welfare programs at TC&I, the rest of U.S. Steel and other steel firms, is the paternalism built into so many of these efforts.

Stock Subscription, Pensions and Safety

In 1913, a group of employees at the Anderson Tin Plate Works in Anderson, Indiana, sent the United States House of Representatives a petition concerning an antitrust suit filed by the Attorney General of the United States against their employer. That document read, in part:

> The signers hereto, employes owning stock of the United States Steel Corporation, and subsidiary companies, take this method of entering our vigorous protest against dissolution of said Corporation.
>
> Most of us have spent our lives in the steel industry and are in position to judge by comparison the benefits to all classes of employees resulting from the generous and humane treatment shown [by U.S. Steel] to its employes.
>
> By its stock subscription plan it has enabled many of us to start a savings fund. . . .
>
> By its pension plan it has prepared to take care of the aged and crippled employes, thus insuring their future comfort.
>
> In many other ways it has shown thoughtfulness, interest and willingness to help in uplifting its employes to an extent which compels our appreciation, and we earnestly appeal to you to exert your strongest effort and influence to prevent any change in these conditions, as we feel sure that interference with the Steel Corporation cannot result in any other way than prejudicial to our interest.

According to *Iron Trade Review*, approximately 50,000 employees from all parts of the Corporation signed petitions similar to the one originating in Anderson. "That the men who earn their wages largely by manual labor should voluntarily come forward on so gigantic a scale as they are now doing with an implied endorsement of their employer is worthy of much attention," the journal editorialized. "It indicates at least contentment at the prospects for future betterment that are being created for them by their superiors. No other state of mind could induce them voluntarily to undertake and complete their present purpose."[18]

Iron Trade Review acknowledged that the Justice Department received letters charging that the petition drive occurred only because management coerced workers into signing. Whether or not this was true, the publicity accorded to these petitions still shows how the steel industry wanted its welfare programs to be perceived by the public.[19] Ambitious and expensive programs like stock subscription and pensions showed the world that the Corporation was looking out for its employees' best interests by giving them a chance to help themselves. The manner in which U.S. Steel implemented these programs, along with its pioneering safety campaign, also reflected the Corporation's paternalism and its desire to control its employees. The apparent success of these activities provided the impetus for many other firms in and out of the steel industry to start similar programs. Although U.S. Steel was not the first company in the United States to institute this kind of welfare capitalism, it implemented these programs in a particularly clever manner. The attention these programs received was also new.

United States Steel introduced its stock subscription plan on the last day of 1902. Reaction was immediate, and very positive. The *Philadelphia Press* called the profit sharing plan "the most important event that has happened in the industrial world in a generation."[20] A writer for the magazine *The World's Work* hoped, "Success might be the beginning of a new industrial era in which cooperation might take the place of dissension, organized construction the place of organized destruction, an era in which the American industrial armies might move forward shoulder to shoulder into the markets of the world."[21] The reasons for this spate of public interest in the plan were twofold. First, because of the Corporation's unprecedented size, whatever it did in the first years after its formation in 1901 attracted considerable attention. Second, commentators thought the specifics of the plan were particularly effective. As the *Wall Street*

Journal suggested, "While the Steel Company's plan is not startlingly original in any of its details, it yet strikes us as excellently devised."[22]

The profit sharing plan had two parts: a bonus system, and a stock subscription plan. Profit sharing and stock ownership programs were often referred to interchangeably by employers of the time, but they were two distinct programs at U.S. Steel. The bonus system provided that between one and two and one half percent of all profits above $80 million would be divided between all levels of management, including foremen and superintendents. Half of that sum was distributed in stock and the other half in cash. The reason for the plan was to encourage supervisory personnel to push for greater production from their employees. The directors of the Corporation recognized that the bonus system would be unpopular with employees because incentives for foremen were supposed to speed up production. Therefore, management introduced additional profit-sharing to counter the negative effects of the bonus plan. "Because of the fact that the Steel Corporation is so much in the public eye," wrote George W. Perkins, the author of the profit sharing plan, to his colleagues on the board of directors, "we have felt that any profit sharing plan that did not, in some way, include every employee, would be subject to public criticism."[23] For this reason, the Corporation created its stock subscription program at the same time it implemented its bonus system. Although the common origins of the two at U.S. Steel provide important clues to the motivations the Corporation, the stock subscription plan received the lion's share of attention after their introduction, as well as in subsequent decades.

The stock subscription plan made it possible for employees "from the President of the Corporation itself to the men working by the day" to buy stock at a reduced price in installments over a three year period. The number of shares available to each employee depended on his salary. Management encouraged unskilled employees to participate in the program, but they were not permitted to subscribe for the same amount of stock as better-paid employees who presumably could afford to buy more. Employees who subscribed had their payments removed from their paycheck on a monthly basis. In return, they received the same dividends as other stockholders, a five dollar bonus for each share at the end of the year, and a portion of a special fund at the end of five years. Having the reward come two years after the stock was supposed to be paid off indicates that U.S. Steel wanted to encourage workers who participated in the program to stay with the firm. The bonus came from a special fund made up of the unpaid five dollar yearly bonuses of those who were unable to keep up their subscription payments. Those employees who defaulted on their stock subscriptions nevertheless had their initial investment and payments already made returned to them, along with 5% interest.[24]

The plan is a perfect reflection of the Corporation's interest in promoting individual initiative at the expense of collective action. Presumably, employee-stockholders would be more likely to align themselves with management rather than an outside union since they stood to benefit when the company made money. Nevertheless, Perkins denied that the plan was directed against organized labor. Shortly after its introduction, he told *The World's Work*, "We are not offering anything to the union or against [it]. The plan is for our own employees as individuals."[25] This sentiment coincides with the Corporation's desire to promote capitalist values. Worthy employees would benefit from the stock subscription program because it encouraged thrift.

Although the program did not make employees independently wealthy, it could be very lucrative to those workers who participated and held onto their stock. For example, an employee who bought a share of stock when the plan was inaugurated in 1903 received $65.04 from the special fund at the end of five years. Besides the $35 in regular dividends and $25 in special bonuses he had already received, this amounted to a $125.04 return on an investment of $82.50. Over the first five years of the plan, the return on the investment of one share of stock was 21.7% annually.[26] What deserves the most attention, however, is not how much those who kept their stock netted, but how few steelworkers ever made it that far.

Low participation rates limited the effect of the stock purchase plan on most employees from the plan's inception. As Table 4.1 demonstrates, seldom did any more than one in four employees buy stock under the subscription plan in any given year. Since it took five years to complete the program, the overall percentage of employees participating would have been higher than those percentages listed here because they refer only to a single year's offering. Yet an employee who bought one share a year for five years would be counted on Table 4.1 five times. Because of this possible confusion, perhaps the best indicator both of the Corporation's expectations and the plan's impact on employees can be seen in 1903, the first year of the program. Since the total number of employees subscribing constituted the total number of workers partici-

Table 4.1: U.S. Steel Stock Subscription Rates

	Number of Employees Subscribing	Average Number of Employees	Subscription Rate
1903	26,399	167,709	16%
1904	9,912	147,343	7%
1905	8,494	180,158	5%
1906	12,192	202,457	6%
1907	14,163	210,180	7%
1908	24,527	165,211	15%
1909	19,116	195,500	1%
1910	17,381	218,345	8%
1911	26,305	196,888	13%
1912	36,575	221,025	17%
1913	35,687	228,906	16%
1914	45,928	179,353	26%
1915	No Offer	No Offer	No Offer
1916	24,631	252,668	1%
1917	38,326	268,058	14%
1918	41,991	268,710	16%
1919	59,792	252,106	24%

In 1909, shares of less expensive common stock were first made available for subscription, thereby making the program affordable for a greater number of employees.

Sources:

Cotter, Arundel. United States Steel: Corporation With a Soul. Garden City, NY: Doubleday, Page & Co., 1921.

United States Steel Corporation. Annual Report of the United States Steel Corporation, 1903-1919.

The figures on the number of employees subscribing are taken from Cotter. They "differ slightly from those given in annual reports, a few employees having failed each year to go through with their subscriptions [Cotter, 47]".

pating in the program, the subscription for that year constitutes every employee enrolled. Slightly more than fifteen percent of the workforce participated that year. Privately, George W. Perkins complained, "We have had to make almost a man to man canvass to get [employees] to understand what the stock was and what the benefits from its purchase would be."[27] Nevertheless, the Corporation's annual report claimed, "The plan was most favorably received by the employes, the subscription exceeding by about one hundred per cent, the amount it was anticipated would be taken."[28] For this statement to be true, the anticipated response rate must have been terrible. By way of comparison, 63% of International Harvester's workforce signed up for that company's first offering under its 1915 stock subscription plan. U.S. Steel's participation rate never came close to that number, even in its best years. If welfare capitalism was really supposed to convince workers to accept their employer's terms and conditions of employment, it would have had to have reached a much larger proportion of the Corporation's workforce each year than the percentages listed in Table 4.1. Even in its best year during the pre-World War I era, 74% of workers remained unaffected. Compare this to the profit-sharing plan implemented at Kodak in 1912. That firm's policy automatically applied to all employees and the benefits were given out in yearly cash payments rather than making workers wait for a dividend.[29] If U.S. Steel had wanted to use the stock purchase plan to maintain productive efficiency or prevent union organization, the plan would have been more like Kodak's. At the very least, the anemic response to U.S. Steel's stock purchase plan severely limited its potential economic benefit to the Corporation as an industrial relations policy.

Not only did few workers sign up for stock, even fewer ever managed to make all their payments and receive a portion of the bonus fund after their subscriptions were completed. U.S. Steel always published the statistics of employees who signed up for stock each year, but it stopped figuring the number of employees who stayed enrolled long enough to receive their five year bonus after five years. The available statistics appear in the United States Commissioner of Labor's report on *Conditions of Employment in the Iron and Steel Industry*, published in 1913 and are reported in Table 4.2. More than half of the employees who signed up for the program over these five years never made it to the end. Estimates of the number of workers receiving a portion of the five year bonus in later years, based on the number of employees enrolled in the program, suggest that the failure rate was closer to three out of four

Table 4.2: U.S. Steel Stock Subscription Failure Rates

	Initial Subscribers	Remaining After 5 Years	Failure Rate
1903	26,399	5,409	80%
1904	9,912	4,085	59%
1905	8,494	3,731	57%
1906	12,192	4,792	61%
1907	14,163	5,588	61%

Sources:

Cotter, Arundel. *United States Steel: Corporation With a Soul*. Garden City, NY: Doubleday, Page & Co., 1921.

United States Commissioner of Labor. *Report on Conditions of Employment in the Iron and Steel* Industry, vol. 3. Document No. 110, 62d Cong., 1st Sess., 1913

most years during the 1910s.[30] This is probably why employees nicknamed the funds distributed to those who completed payment the "jackpot bonus."[31]

Most assessments of the stock purchase plan assume U.S. Steel meant for it to benefit the few skilled workers who had the resources to take advantage of the plan and who were most vulnerable to the temptations of unionization. For example, the American Federation of Labor wrote in a 1910 pamphlet, "We have good reason for believing that not one of the Corporation's employees in five earning under $1500 a year ever owned a share of its stock. It is doubted that the ratio now reaches one in ten."[32] Available evidence does not support this critique. The plan allowed those employees who made the least money to buy stock first, and they bought a significant percentage of the stock during the plan's early history. In other words, the few employees who actually participated in the stock subscription program included the skilled and unskilled alike. Table 4.3 shows that workers who earned less than $800/year made up more than one in three of the employees who chose to participate in the stock subscription program until 1919. The percentage of workers below $800/year subscribing decreased substantially only after the outbreak of

Table 4.3: Number of U.S. Steel Employees Subscribing

Employees subscribing for stock whose annual salary was:				
	Under $800	**$800-$2500**	**Above $2500**	**Percentage Under $800**
1903	11,373	13,845	1,181	43%
1904	4,126	5,094	692	41%
1905	3,531	4,297	666	41%
1906	5,070	6,277	845	42%
1907	5,276	7,915	979	37%
1908	9,094	14,277	1,156	37%
1909	6,948	11,134	1,034	36%
1910	5,858	10,426	1,097	34%
1911	9,196	15,835	1,274	35%
1912	14,999	20,076	1,503	41%
1913	12,322	21,687	1,678	35%
1914	14,901	29,090	1,937	32%
1915	No Offer	No Offer	No Offer	No Offer
1916	7,015	16,011	1,605	28%
1917	3,127	32,654	2,545	8%
1918	1,774	35,635	4,581	4%
1919	1,404	45,232	13,156	2%

Source:

Gulick, Charles A. *Labor Policy of the United States Steel Corporation*. Columbia University Studies in History, Economics and Public Law, vol. 116, 1924.

World War I, when increased turnover and across-the-board wage increases made that group's overall percentage among the employees of the Corporation significantly lower. Similarly, Table 4.4 shows that many workers bought only one share during the plan's first five years, presumably because they could not afford to buy more. Another problem with the skilled workers argument is that it assumes that U.S. Steel needed to keep the services of a particular class of employees. If this were true, they would not have regularly shut down their mills in times of peak demand, driving skilled and less-skilled workers alike into unemployment. Furthermore, even if U.S. Steel had intended the stock purchase

Table 4.4: Number of Subscribers Per Number of Shares at U.S. Steel

	1 Share	2 Shares	3-5 Shares	6-10 Shares	More Than 10 Shares
1903	12,934	10,300	3,896	244	5
1904	1,624	2,930	4,641	872	194
1905	3,032	3,590	1,582	192	60
1906	5,467	4,165	2,384	205	35
1907	6,023	5,962	1,925	233	36

Source:

"Memorandum For Mr. Filbert," April 17th, 1907. George W. Perkins Papers, Rare Book and Manuscript Library, Columbia University, New York, NY.

plan to appeal to the most-skilled workers, the ability to keep the few well-paid workers who participated hardly justifies the enormous cost of the entire program.

Critics of the plan also argued that owning one share of stock would have little effect on an employee's behavior. Industry leaders claimed otherwise. They believed even small stock purchases promoted the ethos of individual achievement among employees. "The men who can only afford to buy one share of stock a year are the laborers," argued George W. Perkins before the United States Commission on Industrial Relations. Yet Perkins still thought these men benefited from the program. "[T]he greatest thing they can render is their best efforts every day in their work [because the stock purchase plan] rewards [every worker] for the best interest he could give, whatever his job might be."[33] Because men like Perkins believed the stock purchase plan improved every employee's work ethic, it survived, even though the tepid response it received from employees meant it never could have stopped employees from organizing. Despite these claims and the industry's fears of organized labor, owning stock did not necessarily promote loyalty. "I have stock in the Steel Corporation," a gardener at the Braddock plant told an interviewer with the Interchurch World Movement. "If I saw Steel selling at a higher price than it ought, do you think I'd want to bring the price down. Not much. It's each man for himself. I'll beat you and you'll beat me if you can."[34] A woman interviewed by Margaret Byington for the Pittsburgh Survey pointed out that the twenty percent reduction in wages she and her husband, a U.S. Steel employee, had experienced over fifteen years greatly overshadowed the small dividend provided by her husband's shares.[35] Overall, despite the fact that the directors of the Corporation frequently claimed that owning one share of stock was enough to make an employee a "partner" in the business, the vast majority of workers, skilled and unskilled alike, chose not to get involved in the program. And since an appreciable number of low-paid employees did subscribe for small amounts of stock, lack of funds is not an adequate explanation for failure to participate.

The rejection of the stock subscription program by most workers suggests significant distrust of management on the part of U.S. Steel's employees. After all, the plan was affordable and potentially lucrative. Furthermore, the plan had few risks since payments already made were refunded with interest if an employee could not keep up with his installments. In 1903, when the price of the stock dipped temporarily, U.S. Steel even offered to buy back employees' shares at the original purchase price if the stock lost value. Nevertheless, most workers were unwilling to make a five-year commitment to their employer, perhaps because their employer never made a five-year commitment to them. Whatever positive benefit this financial opportunity provided for employees had to be weighed against the knowledge that layoffs and full scale downsizing of the permanent workforce could strike any employee at any time. If layoffs came, more pressing needs might not be met if funds were tied up paying installments on stock. Suspicions among employees could not have been helped by another clause in the plan which stated that only those employees who had "shown a proper interest in the welfare and progress" of the Corporation would receive their five dollar bonus each year (although there is no evidence that the clause was ever invoked to deny anybody money). Critics have cited this as proof that the purpose of the plan was behavior modification, but it seems more likely to have served as another reason to avoid enrolling in the first place.[36]

Even though the stock subscription plan failed to reach the bulk of its employees, the Steel Corporation still bragged that it was a smashing success. For example, in a carefully worded statement issued during the 1909 strike, U.S. Steel claimed, "Practically every frugal man in the employ of the corporation is the owner of several shares of stock. They are accumulating more and more each day."[37] In 1910, George W. Perkins called the stock purchase plan "Socialism of the highest, best and most ideal sort, a Socialism that makes real partners of the employer and the employe" (The echoes of Andrew Carnegie here were probably unintentional).[38] Even though the plan never approached this ideal, Perkins went on to become "the chief national advocate for profit sharing" and through his work with the National Civic Federation "influenced many large business organizations to adopt it in one form or another."[39] Five companies even copied the U.S. Steel plan word-for-word.[40] Such influence shows that when it came to welfare capitalism, firms cared more about implementing policies that reflected their core values than they did about pleasing their employees.

Like the stock subscription plan, United States Steel's pension program grew from the first years of the Corporation's existence. Andrew Carnegie's retired from business in 1901, after the buyout of Carnegie Steel by the House of Morgan and the subsequent creation of U.S. Steel had just made him the richest man in the world. Carnegie decided to use $4 million of the proceeds to establish a pension fund for his former employees. "I make the first use of surplus wealth upon retiring from business," Carnegie wrote at that time, "as an acknowledgment of the deep debt I owe to the workmen who have contributed so greatly to my success."[41] It was the first enduring pension fund established at any American manufacturing company. In 1911, United States Steel assumed the obligations of the Carnegie Pension Fund, added $8 million to the fund's assets, renamed it the United States Steel and Carnegie Pension Fund and made pensions available to the employees of all its subsidiary companies. The possibility of receiving pensions was supposed to demonstrate that workers who showed loyalty to the company over a long period of time would be rewarded. As U.S. Steel boasted to visitors of its exhibit at the Panama-Pacific Exposition in 1914, because of this program, "[W]hen old age comes after years of service, [employees] are ensured an income that will help to maintain them in comfort to the end of their days."[42] Like the stock subscription plan, the Corporation designed the pension plan in part to give employees a reason to stay with the firm over the long haul. What had been the gift of a grateful philanthropist became the gift of a paternalistic business enterprise determined to fulfill what its leaders saw as their obligation to their charges.

Despite U.S. Steel's professed benevolence, the Corporation implemented the pension program in a manner that severely limited the program's impact on most employees. Over time, management constantly tightened the eligibility requirements of the plan in order to limit the number of workers who would qualify, and thereby save money. Under the original Carnegie pension plan, workers became eligible to receive money upon retirement at sixty years of age, assuming they had at least fifteen years of service. The American Steel and Wire Company, the only other subsidiary of U.S. Steel which had a pension plan before 1911, allowed employees as young as 55 to collect benefits after ten years of service. When the United States Steel and Carnegie Pension Fund began, voluntary retirement came at the age of 60 provided the employee had served 20 years or longer at the company.[43] For the employees who had been anticipating pensions under earlier eligibility requirements, this was the first of many rule changes by U.S. Steel. Like most other pension programs of this era, U.S. Steel's system was non-contributory, meaning employees provided no money towards its operation. Therefore, the Corporation could alter the rules of its program whenever and however it saw fit. The most significant of many changes came in 1915, when U.S. Steel raised the retirement age to 65 and the required length of service to 25 years.

The breadth of the pension program at U.S. Steel and the effect of the 1915 rule change can be seen in Tables 4.5 and 4.6. Table 4.5 shows how pensioners as a percentage of the workforce grew steadily until the 1915 rule change caused a leveling off of this figure at slightly more than one percent. By way of comparison, in 1919, the International Typographers Union had over twice the percentage of those workers eligible for pensions receiving them. Table 4.6 shows that the number of new pensioners dropped by more than half when the 1915 rule change took effect; and perhaps more important, that after the eligibility requirements were tightened the percentage of workers receiving pensions after voluntary and compulsory retirement dropped off significantly. Although seldom utilized before 1915, over three-fifths of all retirements after the rule change occurred because of permanent disability (for which eligibility was left to the discretion of the pension fund's directors). The extra five years required by the 1915 rule change put voluntary retirement out of reach for many employees.[44]

U.S. Steel tightened its pension requirements over time in order to limit the cost of the plan. Private pension providers at this time did this sort of thing frequently. Large companies often faced unanticipated costs as their plans grew older, but employers with non-contributory pensions could limit their costs by tightening eligibility requirements. Indeed, corporate pensions in the 1920s tended to have very few beneficiaries. In

Table 4.5: U.S. Steel Pensioners as a Percentage of Employees

	Number of Pensioners	Average # of Employees	Percentage
1911	1,606	196,888	.01
1912	1,843	221,025	.01
1913	2,092	228,906	.01
1914	2,521	179,353	.01
1915	3,002	191,126	.02
1916	3,013	252,668	.01
1917	2,933	268,058	.01
1918	2,861	268,710	.01
1919	2,940	252,106	.01

Source:

Conant, Jr., Luther. A Critical Analysis of Industrial Pension Plans. New York, MacMillan, 1922.

United States Steel Corporation, Annual Report of the United States Steel Corporation, 1912-1920.

Table 4.6: Classifications of New Pensions at U.S. Steel

	New Pensions	Compulsory Retirement	By Request of Employee	By Request of Employer	Permanent Incapacity
1911	549	178 (32.4%)	298 (54.3%)	49 (8.9%)	24 (4.4%)
1912	363	45 (12.4%)	257 (70.8%)	27 (7.4%)	34 (9.4%)
1913	425	54 (12.7%)	259 (61.0%)	37 (8.7%)	75 (17.6%)
1914	612	74 (12.1%)	360 (58.8%)	75 (12.3%)	103 (16.8%)
1915	697	60 (8.6%)	467 (67.0%)	48 (6.9%)	122 (17.5%)
1916	275	37 (13.5%)	63 (22.9%)	5 (1.8%)	170 (61.8%)
1917	225	21 (9.3%)	39 (17.4%)	3 (1.3%)	162 (72.0%)
1918	201	27 (13.4%)	38 (18.9%)	10 (5.0%)	126 (62.7%)
1919	310	44 (14.2%)	57 (18.4%)	11 (3.5%)	198 (63.9%)

Source:

United States Steel Corporation, United States Steel and Carnegie Pension

1925, the approximately 500 private pension plans in the United States had only 36,000 employees enrolled in them. As one contemporary commentator wrote when considering this situation, "So small a percentage of pensioners to employees indicates clearly that while such pension systems may accomplish a measure of benefit, even collectively they make only a pitiable approach toward solving the problem of superannuation among industrial workers."[45] This encouraged the workers at these companies to devalue this kind of deferred compensation.

Not only was the number of pensioners small for a large firm like U.S. Steel, the monetary amount of pensions was hardly generous. The size of individual pensions at the Corporation could vary from $12 to $100 per month between 1911 and 1919, but the average individual pension amounted to $21.55 per month. In contrast, the minimum pension at International Harvester in 1919 was $30 per month. Many U.S. Steel employees received less than the $21.55 average because the highest disbursements went to management retirees who constituted seventeen percent of the pensioners enrolled at the beginning of 1918. Working class retirees were often forced to hold down jobs while collecting pensions (which was specifically allowed under the plan's rules as long as the job was unrelated to the steel industry). Out of nine industries surveyed by the Bureau of Labor Statistics in 1919, pensioners in the iron and steel industry (the vast majority of whom worked for U.S. Steel) took home $250.20 per year, the lowest sum in any industrial category. The Corporation's pension program kept the dollar value of disbursements down by basing their value on average salary earned over the last ten years of service, during which time most employees were likely to have worked substantially fewer hours and collected smaller paychecks than they had earlier in their careers. In 1931, the Steel Corporation changed its pension rules again, acknowledging "that compensation provided under the [previous] pension rules was inadequate, and that many who had come under the Pension Plan and were receiving compensation through it, found it difficult to subsist with any degree of comfort on the rates provided."[46]

As with the stock subscription program, U.S. Steel's critics argued that the Corporation created the pension plan in order to prevent unionization. However, this assumes that employees saw pensions as a benefit that was both obtainable to them and worth the wait. For many it was neither. Few workers spent their entire careers working in the mills. The work was irregular, dangerous and unpleasant.[47] Consider the complaint that a 50 year-old worker voiced to an interviewer in 1920. He noted that he would have to work 20 more years with U.S. Steel to be eligible for a pension but, as he explained, "What does a pension amount to? $40 or $50 in my case. How could I live on it? People think these big corporations are very kind with their pensions, etc., but they are dead wrong."[48] Once again, the existence of this plan was more important than the effect that it had on workers. Tiny pensions for a small number of workers satisfied management's desire to reward loyalty, but it didn't change the behavior of at least this one longtime employee. Although it is impossible to quantify these concerns, the existence of doubts surrounding U.S. Steel's promises of corporate welfare is important. Fact or fiction; if workers believed they would never obtain pensions and other benefits, this calls into question whether welfare programs could ever modify worker behavior.

U.S. Steel's brand of welfare capitalism involved more than just monetary compensation. The Corporation's championing of safety and accident prevention work in 1906 "marked a turning point in the history of the industrial accident situation in American industry."[49] Prior to 1906, steel companies refused to reveal the frequency and severity of accidents in their facilities "largely on the ground that any other policy would result in unintelligent hysterical outcry and clamor on the part of the public;" but the 195 fatalities in one city , which Crystal Eastman documented during her year investigating accidents for the Pittsburgh Survey, suggests the severity of the problem throughout the industry.[50] Before then, some of United States Steel's subsidiaries had safety programs in operation at their plants. A few of those programs predated the 1901 merger that created the Corporation. Nevertheless, Elbert Gary's 1906 statement on safety marked the first time that a firm the size of U.S. Steel tried to standardize safety activities in its disparate facilities. It read, in part:

> The United States Steel Corporation expects its subsidiary companies to make every effort practicable to prevent injury to employees. Much can be done by designing new construction and machinery with all practicable safeguards. Expenditures necessary for such purchases will be authorized. Nothing which will add to the protection of the workmen should be neglected. The safety and welfare of the workmen are of the greatest concern.[51]

By 1908, U.S. Steel's safety bureaucracy was in place. At the top of the hierarchy, the company created a permanent Committee on Safety. It consisted of a director of the Corporation and the presidents of five subsidiary companies. That committee appointed inspectors who traveled to all corporation facilities and made recommendations as to how unsafe conditions and practices should be changed. Each U.S. Steel facility had its own Plant Committee on safety, which included superintendents, assistant superintendents, master mechanics and safety inspectors. These bodies held weekly (or sometimes daily) meetings to discuss safety matters, and investigated all serious accidents that occurred in their jurisdiction. Workmen's Committees had three members who came from the rank and file of the mill. These employees inspected their plants once or twice a month for defects in equipment or unsafe practices by workmen, and sent regular reports to the plant committees. Employees who served on these committees received their regular rate of pay while undertaking their duties.[52]

Working in a steel mill had always been dangerous. With stories of careless disregard for human life on the part of corporations becoming a staple of muckraking journalism, it was only a matter of time before steelmakers felt the heat. For instance, William Hard's November 1907 expose in *Everybody's* magazine, "Making Steel and Killing Men," described how 46 men were killed at the Corporation's south Chicago plant during 1906:

> Twelve of them were killed in the neighborhood of blast-furnaces. One was hurled out of life by a stick of dynamite. Three of them were electrocuted. Three of them were killed by falls from high places. Four of them were struck on their heads by falling objects. Four of them were burned to death by hot metal in the Bessemer Converter Department. . . . Three of them were crushed to death. One was suffocated by the gas from a gas-producer. One of them was thrown from an ore bridge by a high wind. One of them was hit by a red-hot rail. One of them . . . was scorched to death by slag. And ten of them were killed by railroad cars or by railroad locomotives.

The rate of serious injuries in the industry was also alarming. Based on estimates from area doctors employed by U.S. Steel, Hard reported that as many as 2,000 workers were "merely burned, crushed, maimed or disabled" during the same period. Hard attributed the decision to tolerate these conditions to the prevalence of managers who worked their way up through the ranks.[53] Because they had risked their lives and succeeded, these men expected others to endure the same dangers they had.

Organized efforts to bring down accident rates in the steel industry began only when public criticism of unsafe conditions escalated. U.S. Steel pioneered many ideas, devices and practices that promoted safety in part as a response to articles like Hard's. For example, the Corporation made many changes in and around its mills after 1906 in order to make them safer. It improved the safety of cranes by constructing footwalks for repairers and operators. It enclosed gears, belts and shafts, so that hands and legs would no longer get caught in them. It built railroad viaducts, thereby allowing employees to cross railroad tracks inside steel plant grounds more safely. Safety undoubtedly improved at U.S. Steel after this campaign began. Statistics compiled by Mark Aldrich and presented in Table 4.7 show that fatality rates at the Corporation dropped by more than two thirds between 1907 and 1930. Injury rates dropped even more dramatically over this same period. "Roughly speaking," the President of U.S. Steel testified during a government antitrust suit, "the works are a paradise today compared with what they were in the old days."[54]

Despite improvements, legal considerations as well as management's belief in its own superiority undercut the effectiveness of this important program. Before state workmen's compensation laws took effect in the 1910s, the legal doctrines known as "contributory negligence" and the "fellow servant rule" meant that if an injured worker or a co-worker could be blamed for an accident the employer did not have to pay. Therefore, steelmakers tended to blame their workers for accidents. U.S. Steel's employees were bombarded with messages like, "You are responsible for the safety of others as well as yourself"; and "[T]he prevention of accidents and injuries, by all possible means, is a personal duty which EVERYONE owes not to himself alone but also to his fellow workers."[55] Slogans like these, which put the blame for accidents squarely on individual workers, appeared everywhere: the employment office, plant newspapers, countless safety bulletin boards, even the back of employees' pay envelopes. As early as 1913, U.S. Steel claimed that, "to a large extent, those accidents for which the employer is responsible have been eliminated."[56]

The safety movement began as a cover to avoid legal liability. In 1910, around the time accident rates began to drop, U.S. Steel created a voluntary accident relief program that paid as much as eighteen months worth of wages to injured employees or $3000 to the relatives of deceased wage-earners regardless of liability, on the condition that the injured party or the family did not file suit.[57] To Brody, the safety program was primarily the result of these practical economic motives.[58] Yet the way U.S. Steel implemented its safety program undercut its effectiveness. If the Corporation cared only about profits, it would not have created a policy that tried absolve the company from all blame (It

Table 4.7: Steel Industry Injury, Fatality, and Severity

	U.S. Steel:	Steel Industry:		
	Injury Rate	**Fatality Rate**	**Injury Rate**	**Severity Rate**
1907	*	0.7	80.8	7.2
1908	*	*	*	*
1909	*	*	*	*
1910	*	0.5	74.7	5.2
1911	*	0.3	51.5	3.5
1912	*	0.4	62.2	4.2
1913	60.3	0.4	59.6	4.3
1914	43.5	0.3	50	3.2
1915	41.5	0.2	40	2.7
1916	44.5	0.3	43	3.5
1917	34.5	0.4	47.7	4
1918	28.8	0.4	39.4	3.6
1919	26.1	0.4	41.6	3.6
1920	22.9	0.2	38.3	3.7
1921	13.2	0.2	30.8	2.5
1922	13	0.2	33	2.7
1923	12.7	0.2	33.2	2.7
1924	10.2	0.3	30.8	3
1925	8.2	0.2	28.3	2.5
1926	6.8	0.2	20.9	2.3
1927	5.3	0.2	18.8	2.2
1928	*	0.2	20.6	2.4
1929	*	0.2	20	2
1930	7.7	0.2	17.8	2.3
1931	7.8	0.2	17.5	2.3
1932	8.1	0.2	16.8	2.1
1933	9.1	0.2	19.5	2.3
1934	8.1	0.2	19.7	2.5
1935	6.3	0.2	14.9	2.2
1936	7.2	0.2	15.8	2.1
1937	6.8	0.2	15.4	2.2

Rates for fatalities and all injuries are per million manhours. Severity rates are lost workdays per thousand manhours.

*= No Data

Source:

Aldrich, Mark. *Safety Firs* t. Baltimore: The Johns Hopkins University Press, 1997, 310-11.

would have found the reason for an accident, whatever the cause, and fixed the problem so as to avoid expensive accidents in the future). It also would have avoided antagonizing workers by creating a safety program that treated them like children.

Looking at the actual content of the safety program reveals the influence of the ethos of individual achievement on the way management implemented it. U.S. Steel and other steelmakers consistently emphasized worker education over much more expensive structural improvements, even after the advent of workers compensation eliminated the financial incentives for doing so. For example, when investigating accidents, firms like U.S. Steel downplayed factors which they could control. In cases where an investigation offered no definitive proof of responsibility, many employers would classify it as workers' negligence automatically because "if the worker had not been negligent the accident could not have happened, therefore he must have been careless."[59] An investigation by the U.S. Bureau of Mines into all accidents at blast-furnace plants in Pennsylvania during 1915 found otherwise. Although the author concluded, "The classification of accidents according to responsibility is unsatisfactory," he estimated that only 21.8% of the accidents he investigated were the fault of workmen. He classified 16.8% as the fault of the employer, 29.8% as unavoidable hazards of the industry and 31.6% as "miscellaneous."[60] Had firms accepted blame when blame was due, this might have improved profitability by eliminating costly accidents in the future but accepting blame would have threatened management's feelings of superiority over employees.

This tendency to blame employees for accidents might explain why steelworkers often responded to safety programs in a hostile manner. Ida Tarbell, for example, found that U.S. Steel employees still mutilated illuminated signs bearing safety programs ten years after the Corporation first introduced its safety program. This response may also have derived from the manner in which employers carried these safety efforts out. Worker education efforts reflected the Corporation's paternalism. Officials delivered them in the manner of a Sunday School teacher instructing children on morals. For example, "The Fourteen Points of Accident Prevention," published in the newspaper of U.S. Steel's Joliet Steel Works, all began with the word "I" ("I will do everything possible to assist the Safety First Movement as my family and myself are the chief beneficiaries.").[61] Other safety programs emphasized the ethos of individual achievement so prevalent in the Corporation's overall labor policy.

A paper given by an official of the Illinois Steel Company subsidiary at the First Co-Operative Safety Congress in 1912 was called, "Our Foreigner: What We Are Doing to Help Him Help Himself." The speaker argued that safety work was essential to self-improvement because workers had to be kept alive in order to benefit from other aspects of the Corporation's labor policies.[62]

U.S. Steel's insistence on maintaining the twelve-hour day also undercut the effectiveness of its safety program. Long hours were a major cause of accidents. Working in a steel mill required the undivided attention of all employees because mishaps could occur anywhere around the plant at any time. "Sometimes a chain breaks and a ladder tips over," remarked one steelworker to a reporter from *McClure's Magazine*. "If everything is working all smooth a man watches out and everything is alright. But you take it after they've been on duty twelve hours without sleep and running like hell and everybody's tired and it's all a different story."[63] The United States Commissioner of Labor found a strong correlation between accidents and the long turn, the period when steelworkers were most tired, thereby providing proof for these kinds of anecdotes. Steel manufacturers tried to obscure the relationship between fatigue and accidents by overemphasizing the importance of human error. "In blaming their employes for lapses of attention which have resulted in accidents," observed John Fitch, "manufacturers may often be demanding a self-control and mental alertness such as few men can sustain throughout practically their entire waking hours."[64] The employees who had to suffer through the twelve-hour day recognized the link between the twelve-hour day and safety long before their employers acknowledged it. For this reason, U.S. Steel's program to improve safety in its mills must have seemed empty to those for whom it was designed to help.

Until its implementation, the eight-hour day was always the most obvious untried safety reform at U.S. Steel's disposal, but this would have been expensive. Historian Gerald Eggert estimates that it would have raised the cost of wages at U.S. Steel from 26.1% to 29.1% of the Corporation's total receipts. U.S. Steel rejected this kind of expense for safety because its cultural values blinded it to the possibility that shorter hours increased labor efficiency and hence saved money in the long run. Instead, the Corporation emphasized the impact of worker education because it cost comparatively little and reinforced management's belief in the ethos of individual achievement. In 1923, after considerable public pressure (culminating in the direct intervention of President Warren

Harding), the Corporation and the rest of the steel industry finally agreed to give its workforce an eight-hour day. The substantial decrease in the number and severity of accidents across the industry that followed this change made the link between the long working-day and accidents obvious, thereby demonstrating the inadequacy of previous safety efforts.[65] Accident rates did drop significantly in the years following the Corporation's initial safety campaign, but the reduction in accidents it achieved undoubtedly would have come earlier had U.S. Steel agreed to change the length of its working day before 1923.

Welfare Capitalism at Other Steel Firms

When questioned about the Corporation's stock purchase plan while testifying before the House Committee investigating U.S. Steel in 1911, Director Percival Roberts responded, "[W]e are feeling our way in all these things. It is a good deal of an exploration. We are getting into grounds that have not been trodden before. We do not know where we are going."[66] Replying to a survey from the National Civic Federation in 1906, the President of Youngstown Sheet and Tube admitted, "[W]e have given very little attention to the welfare of our employes."[67] Considering the pioneering nature of the U.S. Steel's welfare work, it is not surprising that other steel companies that enacted welfare programs waited until the Corporation's efforts had been tested. Those steel firms that did introduce elaborate welfare capitalist programs generally did not do so until the 1920s.

Welfare capitalism proved very popular in many industries during this decade because of the post-war Red Scare and general business prosperity. The Red Scare convinced many employers that they should do something to take the harsh edge off of capitalism so as to make socialism less appealing. The prosperity of the 1920s meant employers could afford to spend more on their employees and employees could afford to spend more on things like stock. U.S. Steel employees responded better to the stock subscription and pension plans after 1919. Some steel firms got better results than the Corporation did, but others were not as successful. For example, Youngstown Sheet and Tube had a full-time safety director, and an extensive program of welfare work by 1914. Nevertheless, the company cut back on nearly every aspect of its welfare program in 1920 due to lack of interest among employees. "Officials have come to the conclusion," reported *Iron Age*, "that many of the workers, perhaps the majority, do not want such assistance and are ungrateful for it."[68] And even though welfare capitalism was more popular than ever before among steel manufacturers during the 1920s, small firms never practiced welfare capitalism to the same extent that U.S. Steel did.[69]

The American Iron and Steel Institute (AISI) served as the main instrument for spreading welfare capitalism throughout the industry. In 1911, the AISI formed a permanent committee on welfare work. One of the committee's first acts was to hire Dr. Thomas Darlington as its permanent secretary. From 1904-1909, Darlington had been New York City's Commissioner of Health, but when hired for this job he was employed by U.S. Steel to investigate and report on the success of its welfare program. Under the aegis of the AISI, Darlington worked tirelessly to spread the ideal of welfare capitalism throughout the industry. Members of the Institute had free access to his advice, and he published often in the AISI's *Monthly Bulletin*. Articles, pictures and reports about welfare work throughout the steel industry were the bulletin's mainstay. For instance, it described Charles Close's discussion of the Steel Corporation's Welfare Bureau as "full of suggestion to other companies working on the same problems."[70] Many issues showed how different companies handled one particular kind of welfare activity. The Institute sent out surveys requesting firms to describe their activities in that particular area, and the *Bulletin* would publish extensive excerpts from the replies. A typical response to the AISI's efforts came from the works manager of the Interstate Iron and Steel Company one month when the subject was plant restaurants. "The August issue of the Institute BULLETIN will be highly interesting to us," he reported, "as the matter is pending at our works now, and we will be glad to learn of others' experience in this class of welfare work."[71]

Many other firms took up the same three welfare programs that formed the core of U.S. Steel's efforts. Stock purchase plans only spread into the rest of the steel industry after World War I. During the 1920s, thirteen steel companies (including the eight largest firms in the industry) had made some kind of stock purchase arrangement available to their employees. Most of these were modeled after U.S. Steel's program, with payments being drawn out of salary over an extended period of time. Many of them surpassed U.S. Steel's purchase plan in popularity. While an average of 22.5% of U.S. Steel's workforce subscribed for stock each year between 1920 and 1930, by the late twenties 38% of

Bethlehem Steel's employees signed up for its plan and 77% of Inland Steel's employees subscribed under that firm's program. These companies implemented their stock purchase plans during the 1920s, with business booming and wages rising. Nevertheless, other plans put into effect during this decade proved far less successful. Jones & Laughlin discontinued its stock subscription program after one year of operation because of an anemic response from its employees. Many smaller companies never implemented a stock purchase plan at all. "We have not found stock distribution to employees advisable because of the fluctuating character of our business," declared Charles Lukens Huston of Lukens Steel in 1925. "We do not need it in order to gain the interest and cooperation of our men, and we think that it holds more of danger than of good. . . . No careful man would recommend that an investor of small means put all his money into any single security."[72] This principle might help to explain why so many stock purchase plans failed when market conditions turned sour during the next decade.

By the late 1920s, the list of companies offering pensions included some of the industry's largest firms (like Bethlehem Steel, Colorado Fuel & Iron, and Armco). However, like U.S. Steel, most of these firms had trouble coping with their ever-expanding pension obligations. John A. Roebling's Sons of Trenton, New Jersey, raised the eligibility requirements for retirement by worker request from 60 years old and 20 years of service in 1922, to 65 years old and 25 years of service in 1929. At Colorado Fuel and Iron, the company imposed an explicit 45 year age limit on new hires at the time the pension program was instituted in order to limit the number of workers who would eventually qualify for pensions. Despite this step, the company still had trouble keeping the fund on a sound actuarial basis. International Harvester (the parent company of Wisconsin Steel) also had trouble keeping its pension fund solvent, even though eligibility requirements were raised throughout the 1920s.[73] As the Depression worsened during the 1930s, the relative generosity of all pension plans would prove meaningless for the thousands of workers laid off to keep these companies in business.

Of all kinds of welfare work in the steel industry, the safety movement spread the fastest and the furthest for two reasons. First, United States Steel tried to convince other companies in and out of the steel industry to adopt their reforms. Spokesmen for the company utilized every conceivable outlet to get their message of "Safety First" across to whomever would listen. U.S. Steel even maintained a safety museum at its headquarters in New York. The results of these public relations efforts were visible as early as 1910, when John Fitch, perhaps the harshest critic the steel industry ever had, wrote "No large corporation is manifesting a more intelligent determination in regard to accidents than the United States Steel Corporation."[74] Sometimes U.S. Steel safety officers addressed employees at other firms. Furthermore, the Corporation never patented the safety devices it developed, and even went so far as to invite executives at other firms to visit their plants in order to inspect them. Safety directors at various U.S. Steel subsidiaries published extensively in trade journals describing their activities. Because U.S. Steel's safety program was applicable to many different kinds of industrial plants, all kinds of firms copied the Corporation's system of shop committees. By the 1930s, the safety campaign developed by the Steel Corporation became the model for similar campaigns run by public and private institutions throughout the United States and Europe.[75] Since the good will created by these efforts did not help the immediate bottom line, these efforts are another example of management making policy for reasons other than the immediate bottom line. Even though this kind of positive public relations may have benefited U.S. Steel in the long run, its potential advantages could not be measured on a balance sheet.

There were, however, some immediate economic advantages to companies that followed U.S. Steel into the safety movement. This is the second reason that the safety program spread so far so fast among steel firms. State workmen's compensation laws encouraged employers to adopt safety programs in the 1910s and early 1920s because the safer the workplace, the lower a firm's contribution to a state workman's compensation fund. These same laws also raised the short-term costs of injuries and fatalities significantly. By the early-1920s, the expense of fatalities to companies rose from a few hundred dollars to one to three thousand dollars. The loss of limbs or eyes could cost employers almost as much under these new laws. The long-term financial impact of these kinds of injuries was potentially more significant if they led to increased contributions from a company to its state's workmen's compensation pool. As the Director of Labor and Safety at Bethlehem Steel's flagship plant in South Bethlehem, Pennsylvania, acknowledged in 1918, "[C]ompensation laws in general have been responsible for the national movement which has become a general propaganda and which perhaps otherwise might not have occurred at such an early date."[76]

Despite the benefits of improving safety, years after the Corporation first enacted its reforms and they had spread to other companies, much remained to be done. Investigators who examined the 1919 steel strike for the Interchurch World Movement were surprised to hear "so large a number of strikers complaining about hazards. [Workers] described with specificness menaces to life and limb, concerning which they had complained to foremen and superintendents month in and month out without avail."[77] According to the National Safety Council, as late as 1931 the steel industry still had an accident rate 29% above the national average. The fact that U.S. Steel's injury rate that year was less than half that of the rest of the industry shows just how much other companies could have done to improve the safety of their mills.[78]

Other kinds of welfare capitalism popular during the first decades of this century never found a permanent home in the steel industry. Before the passage of the National Industrial Recovery Act in 1933, only one third of steel firms ran plant restaurants, only 20% offered their employees outdoor recreation, only 15% offered indoor recreation and social facilities. By the early 1930s, the more elaborate forms of welfare capitalism had also disappeared. Only 6% of steel companies had stock purchase plans and only 6% had pension plans. The Depression even forced U.S. Steel to cut back on welfare capitalism. The Corporation discontinued its stock purchase in 1935 because the few employees lucky to be working could no longer afford such an extravagance. By the end of the 1930s, the Corporation made its pension program contributory because this made it significantly less expensive for U.S. Steel to maintain. Other kinds of welfare capitalism, like recreation and education, also ceased in favor of relief payments for wage workers unable to live on fewer hours of work at substantially lower compensation rates. When economic distress squeezed both employment rolls and profits, welfare capitalism became an unnecessary expense.[79]

"The Real Spirit of the Steel Companies of America"

U.S. Steel not only quantified its welfare activities, tracking the number of tennis courts it built or the number of pickle barrels it bought for a plant picnic, the firm paid close attention to its welfare expenditures and took every opportunity to publicize the amount it spent in its own publications or in press releases to other media. According to a summary done for its 25th anniversary in 1926, between the beginning of 1912 and the end of 1925, welfare capitalism had cost the Corporation $158,188,043. The stock subscription program alone cost $22,564,858. $13,014,343 had been paid out in pensions to employees over this same period. The lack of participation problem also applied to less expensive efforts that made up much of the remainder of the welfare budget. For example, out of 4,000 immigrant employees at Carnegie Steel's Youngstown, Ohio, facility, only 300 signed up for night school Americanization classes when this program was first offered, and that number soon dwindled to 27 because of the difficulty of balancing classes with domestic concerns and the rigors of the twelve-hour day. Total expenditures for welfare work at the Corporation amounted to over 8% of its total profits in the decade after 1912.[80] Critics have primarily concerned themselves with the supposed financial returns for spending this money. However, in a strictly utilitarian sense, it was irrational for U.S. Steel to pay these staggering sums for programs that benefited comparatively few workers.

Why would U.S. Steel and other companies spend so much money on welfare capitalism if these kinds of programs were not effective? The answer to that question depends on what standard of effectiveness is used to evaluate these efforts. A few of these programs, most notably accident prevention, did pay for themselves in the long run. But if the purpose of welfare capitalism was to buy the loyalty of employees, it failed. The massive defections among U.S. Steel's workforce during the 1919 strike demonstrated the discontent among the intended beneficiaries of the Corporation's largesse. As Horace Drury explained diplomatically in 1922:

> [T]he Steel Corporation has of its own accord, though perhaps not always fully consciously, been developing a labor policy, which both contains a lot of substantial and practical benefit to the worker in the way of earnings and conditions, and, in part at least, has back of it a very rich idea of extending the corporate organization so as to consolidate the interests of stockholders, managers and workers. . . . The trouble is no such unity has developed. Though some of the ideas have promise, and though much attention and expense have been devoted to special phases of the betterment program, the Corporation edifice, on the whole, is more like a house of sand than of stones solidly cemented together. . . .

> The weakness in the present system is, therefore, in the failure actually to reach the men.[81]

In other words, welfare capitalism did not improve the lives and working conditions of most employees enough to affect the attitude of the average worker toward his employer or his employment. On purely economic terms then, the cost of this policy did not justify the expense.

In the long run, welfare capitalism in the steel industry proved inadequate at co-opting workers because workers had little or no say in determining what was done on their behalf. After all, management did not poll employees in order to determine what changes in their living and working conditions would be most beneficial to them; changes were imposed unilaterally. The most common sentiment about welfare capitalism voiced to Ray Stannard Baker by the U.S. Steel employees he interviewed was, "Give us a chance to organize and decent wages and we will do our own welfare work and do it on a real democratic basis."[82] Yet steel manufacturers were reluctant to give up control over the conditions of employment faced by their employees because they considered this power to be their inherent prerogative as employers. Because the industry was more concerned with giving employees the opportunity to improve themselves in ways and through means chosen by management than with actually changing workers' behavior, using welfare capitalism to stabilize a nonunion industrial relations system was ultimately impossible.

Historians of welfare capitalism such as Stuart Brandes and Andrea Tone view welfare capitalism as an isolated phenomenon—distinct programs which can be considered and evaluated independent of the rest of a company's labor policy.[83] However, to properly assess this policy it is necessary to abandon the narrow perspective of previous scholarship and look at welfare capitalism in the context of management's overall experience with industrial relations. As John Fitch reported in *The Steel Workers*, his subjects saw their employers "giving with one hand and taking away with the other [and connected] the two in their minds."[84] Observations like this led Fitch to conclude that, "In spite of welfare work, pensions, sociological departments and Sunday Schools, the real spirit of the steel companies of America is one of arrogance and contempt for the rights both of their employees and the public . . . [The industry] indicates a desire to provide physical conditions that approach excellence; but it indicates on the other hand, a determination to rule at any cost."[85] In other words, welfare capitalism represented management's determination to control labor in the same way that it controlled every other factor of production. And to business leaders obsessed with the ethos of individual achievement, the limited impact of a stock subscription program or pension plan did not necessarily mean the program failed. The worthy benefited; the undeserving did not.

Welfare capitalism also gave anti-union employers like U.S. Steel a chance to put a kind face on a cold policy. The development of an elaborate spy system, the closure of previously unionized plants, and the employment of scabs during labor disputes were just some of the less charitable aspects of the industry's activities, which show the lengths that management was willing to go in order to prevent its employees from organizing. If welfare capitalism was a rational attempt to buy workers' love, these policies worked at cross purposes to it. Harsh anti-union tactics made it more likely that steelworkers would reject their employer's largesse because they still had no control over the conditions under which they labored. Nevertheless, welfare capitalism still satisfied the paternal instincts that formed an important part of the typical steel manufacturer's philosophy of industrial relations.

The profound effect that the worker's lack of control had on conditions of employment explains why the stock subscription, pension and safety programs could elicit such a tepid response from employees. While the inability to organize adversely affected workers' wages, working conditions, and even their home lives, welfare capitalism at its most effective could do little to alleviate the harsh conditions of employment which steel companies were largely responsible for perpetuating anyway. As long as welfare capitalist programs were imposed from above, the people who worked for the Corporation could not be fooled by the rhetoric because they lived through the harsh reality of life in the steel mills every day. Applying the old cliché about the carrot and the stick, steelworkers always experienced a lot more stick than carrot.

Two other reforms—shorter hours and the creation of the first employee representation plans in the industry—were popular with employees because they allowed employees to exert greater control over their own lives. Each one of these changes had an enormous effect on how industrial relations in this industry were conducted. But steel manufacturers did not embrace these reforms voluntarily. In fact, the majority of the industry, especially U.S. Steel, offered considerable resistance to both because they considered these reforms a threat to their freedom to control labor. The struggle over these changes, and the outside forces that contributed to their implementation, are considered in the next chapter.

Notes

1. *Blast Furnace and Steel Plant* 5 (February 1920): 161.

2. Charles L. Close, "Welfare Work in the Steel Industry," *Year Book of the American Iron and Steel Institute*, 1920, 37.

3. David Brody, *Steelworkers in America: The Nonunion Era* (Urbana: University of Illinois Press, 1998/Originally published by Harvard University Press, 1960), 179.

4. Because the Corporation had an interest in presenting its welfare programs in the best possible light, using U.S. Steel's own statistics to illustrate the ineffectiveness of these efforts makes this argument even more credible.

5. John A. Fitch, "Illinois: Boosting for Safety," *The Survey* 27 (4 November 1911): 1154.

6. A.H. Wyman, "The Value and Trend of Welfare Work Among Negroes in Industry," 1923, National Urban League Papers, Industrial Relations Department, Box 34, Library of Congress, Washington, D.C.

7. Brody, *Steelworkers in America*, 108-09.

8. Andrew Carnegie, "The Gospel of Wealth," in *The Andrew Carnegie Reader*, Wall, ed. (Pittsburgh: University of Pittsburgh Press, 1992), 139.

9. *Fortune* 13 (May 1936): 134; United States Steel Corporation, "Proceedings at Annual Meeting of Stockholders," April 20, 1914, 15.

10. United States Steel Corporation, "Proceedings of Meeting of Subsidiary Companies," January 21, 1919, 38.

11. Louis A. Boettiger, *Employee Welfare Work* (New York: Ronald Press Company, 1923),19.

12. Andrea Tone, *The Business of Benevolence* (Ithaca: Cornell University Press, 1997), 37-38; Lloyd Noland, "Welfare Work of the Tennessee Coal, Iron & Railroad Company," *Year Book of the American Iron and Steel Institute*, 1915, 257.

13. Thomas Darlington and Sidney McCurdy, "Present Scope of Welfare Work in the Iron and Steel Industry;" Papers read at the sixth general meeting of the American Iron and Steel Institute, New York, May 22, 1914.
These are the thirty-two different activities mentioned in the Darlington and McCurdy pamphlet: Prevention of accidents; Lighting; Drinking water supplies; First aid; Washing facilities; Hospitals; Laundries; Trained nurses and social workers; Lockers; Physical examination of employees; Toilet arrangements; Lunch buckets and lunch rooms; Drainage and sewage disposal; Com-

missaries; Care of stables and animals; Milk supplies; Heating workplaces in winter; Cooling workplaces in summer; Flies, mosquitoes and vermin; Clean mills and yards; Ventilation; Housing; Overcrowding; Gardens; Dust, gases and fumes; Rest and recreation; Education; Insurance; Relief funds; Pensions; Compensation; Saving and investing.

14. On the history of welfare capitalism across industries, see Daniel Nelson, *Managers and Workers: Origins of the New Factory System in the United States 1880-1920* (Madison: University of Wisconsin Press, 1975), 101-21; Stuart D. Brandes, *American Welfare Capitalism* (Chicago: University of Chicago Press, 1976); David Brody, "The Rise and Decline of Welfare Capitalism," in *Workers in Industrial America*, 2nd ed. (New York: Oxford University Press, 1993), 48-81; H.M. Gitelman, "Welfare Capitalism Reconsidered," *Labor History* 33 (Winter 1992): 5-31 and Tone, ibid. On the transformation of welfare capitalism during the 1930s and its modern manifestations, see Sanford Jacoby, *Modern Manors* (Princeton: Princeton University Press), 1997.

15. Nelson, 115-16. "The 40 firms," Nelson writes, "were concentrated in textiles, machinery, and, to a lesser degree, iron and steel. Nearly all were large, with more than 500 employees in 1905."

16. Close, "Welfare Work in the Steel Industry," 85-86.
The best place to find detailed descriptions of individual welfare capitalist endeavors is the *Bureau of Safety, Sanitation and Welfare Bulletin*. Eleven issues were published on an irregular basis from 1910 to 1926, and they can often be found bound together.

17. Marlene Hunt Rikard, "An Experiment in Welfare Capitalism: The Health Care Services of the Tennessee Coal, Iron and Railroad Company," Ph.D. Dissertation, University of Alabama, 1983, 3-4; W. David Lewis, *Sloss Furnaces and the Rise of the Birmingham District* (Tuscaloosa: University of Alabama Press, 1994), 384.

18. *Iron Trade Review* 53 (28 August 1913): 363.

19. *Iron Trade Review* 53 (28 August 1913): 394.

20. *Philadelphia Press*, 2 January 1903.

21. Arthur Goodrich, " The United States Steel Corporation's Profit-Sharing Plan," *The World's Work* 5 (February 1903): 3056.

22. *Wall Street Journal*, 2 January 1903.

23. George W. Perkins, "To the Officers and Employees of the United States Steel Corporation and of its Subsidiary Companies," December 31, 1902, George W. Perkins Papers, Box 27, Rare Book and Manuscript Library, Columbia University, New York, NY; *Iron Trade Review* 36 (8 January 1903): 29; George W. Perkins, "To the Board of Directors of the United States Steel Corporation," December 1, 1902, George W. Perkins Papers, Box 27.

24. Perkins, "To the Officers and Employees . . .".

25. Goodrich, 3058.

26. *Wall Street Journal*, 21 November 1913.

27. George W. Perkins to John D. Rockefeller, July 8, 1903, George W. Perkins Papers, Box 6.

28. United States Steel Corporation, *Annual Report of the United States Steel Corporation for 1902*, 20.

29. Robert Ozanne, *A Century of Labor-Management Relations at McCormick and International Harvester* (Madison: University of Wisconsin Press, 1967), 90; Jacoby, *Modern Manors*, 62.

30. These projections come from company-released snapshots of the number of workers participating in the program. For instance, in 1921 there were approximately 66,000 employees who were paying for stock in installments, or who had completed payment but were still collecting their annual bonus. Yet 285,000 employees had subscribed for at least one share of stock over the previous five years. This means only one in four was able to continue in the program until their five years of annual bonuses were exhausted.

31. Brandes, 90.

32. American Federation of Labor, "Statement and Evidence in Support of Petition and Charges Presented to the President of the United States," Washington, D.C., 1910, 30.

Similar critiques of the stock purchase plan are made by John A. Garraty [*Right-Hand Man: The Life of George W. Perkins* (New York: Harper & Brothers, 1960), 112-14] and John A. Fitch, [*The Steel Workers* (Pittsburgh: University of Pittsburgh Press, 1989/originally published by the Russell Sage Foundation, 1910), 208].

33. United States Commission on Industrial Relations, *Report of the United States Commission on Industrial Relations*, Vol. 8, Senate Document No. 415, 64th Cong., 1st Sess., 1916, 7604.

34. Mary Senior, "Interview with Mr. Snider," July 27, 1920, David J. Saposs Papers, Box 26, State Historical Society of Wisconsin, Madison, WI.

35. Margaret Byington, *Homestead: The Households of a Mill Town* (New York: Arno & The New York Times, 1969/Originally published by the Russell Sage Foundation, 1910), 177.

36. Brody, *Steelworkers in America*, 158; Perkins, "To the Officers and Employees of the United States Steel Corporation and of its Subsidiary Companies;" Garraty, *Right-Hand Man*, 113.

Those who contend that the plan had anti-union overtones forget that U.S. Steel did not need a stock subscription program to influence employee behavior. In the days before the National Labor Relations Act, when an employee could be fired for any reason, every employee feared being let go if he did not show a proper interest in the welfare and progress of the company whether he enrolled in the stock subscription program or not.

37. United States Steel Corporation Statement excerpted in *New York Times*, 16 December 1909.

38. *New York Call*, 27 May 1910.

39. *New York World*, 2 May 1915.

40. Brandes, 84.

41. Andrew Carnegie to the President and Board of Directors, The Carnegie Company, March 12, 1901, 4 in Carnegie Steel Company, "Regulations Governing the Carnegie Relief Fund," 1906.

42. Murray Webb Latimer, *Industrial Pension Systems* (in 2 Vols.) (New York: Industrial Relations Counselors Inc., 1932), 40; Charles A. Gulick, *Labor Policy of the United States Steel Corporation*, Columbia University Studies in History, Economics and Public Law, Vol. 116, 1924, 141;United States Steel Corporation, *Bureau of Safety, Sanitation and Welfare Bulletin,* No. 5, Dec. 1914, 101.

43. U.S. Steel employees faced compulsory retirement at age 70 under this plan, or they could retire because of permanent incapacity at any age provided they had twenty years of service. This and the other specifics of the pension plan which will be discussed below are included in United States Commissioner of Labor, *Report on Conditions of Employment in the Iron and Steel Industry*, Vol. 3, Senate Document No. 110, 62nd Cong., 1st Sess., 1913, 455-59.

44. U.S. Congress, Senate, Committee on Education and Labor, *Investigation of Strike in Steel Industries*, 66th Cong., 1st Sess., 1919, 433.

45. Don D. Lescohier, "Working Conditions," in *History of Labor in the United States*_(New York: Macmillan, 1935), 395; Anthony J. Badger, *The New Deal: The Depression Years, 1933-1940* (New York: Hill and Wang, 1989), 26; Luther Conant Jr., *A Critical Analysis of Industrial Pension Systems* (New York: Macmillan, 1922), 171.

46. United States Steel and Carnegie Pension Fund, *Ninth Annual Report*, December 31, 1919, 7; Ozanne, 84; Interchurch World Movement, *Public Opinion and the Steel Strike* (New York: Harcourt, Brace and Howe, 1920), 253; United States Bureau of Labor Statistics, "Welfare Work for Employees in Industrial Establishments in the United States," *Bulletin of the U.S. Bureau of Labor Statistics*, No. 150, February 1919, 108; Horace B. Davis, *Labor and Steel* (New York: International Publishers, 1933), 156; United States Steel Corporation, "Minutes of Annual Meeting of Stockholders," April 20, 1931, 9.

47. Gulick, 188.

48. John A. Fitch, "Interview with Lodeman," July 23, 1920, David J. Saposs Papers, Box 26.

49. Lescohier, 367.

50. Crystal Eastman, *Work-Accidents and the Law* (New York: Russell Sage Foundation, 1910). Eastman's observations were recorded between July 1, 1906 and June 30, 1907.

51. Gary quoted in Charles L. Close, "Safety in the Steel Industry," *The Annals of the American Academy of Political and Social Science* 123 (January 1926): 86.

52. Charles L. Close, "The Committees on Safety and Sanitation of the United States Steel Corporation," *Monthly Bulletin of the American Iron and Steel Institute* 1 (January 1913): 26-29.

53. William Hard, "Making Steel and Killing Men," *Everybody's Magazine* 17, November 1907, 580-81, 585-86, 588-89.

54. Mark Aldrich, *Safety First* (Baltimore: The Johns Hopkins University Press, 1997), 127; James A. Farrell quoted in District Court of the United States for the District of New Jersey, "United States of America v. United States Steel Corporation," October Term, 1914, Testimony, Vol. 10, 4104.

55. Anthony Bale, "America's First Compensation Crisis: Conflict over the Value and Meaning of Workplace Injuries under the Employer's Liability System," in *Dying for Work: Workers' Safety and Health in Twentieth Century America*, David Rosner and Gerald Markowitz, eds. (Bloomington, Indiana University Press, 1987), 36; David S. Beyer, "Safety Provisions in the United States Steel Corporation," excerpted in Eastman, 262; United States Steel Corporation, *Committee of Safety Bulletin* No. 2, 1 July 1911, cover.

56. United States Steel Corporation, *Bureau of Safety, Relief, Sanitation and Welfare Bulletin*, No. 4 (November 1913): 6.

57. For the details of U.S. Steel's accident relief plan, see Fitch, *The Steel Workers*, 330-35.

58. Brody, *Steelworkers in America*, 167-68.

59. Lucian W. Chaney and Hugh S. Hanna, "The Safety Movement in the Iron and Steel Industry, 1907-1917," *Bulletin of the United States Bureau of Labor Statistics*, No. 234, June 1918, 165; *Conditions of Employment in the Iron and Steel Industry*, Vol. 3, 172.

60. Frederick H. Willcox, "Occupation Hazards at Blast-Furnace Plants and Accident Prevention," *Bulletin of the United States Bureau of Mines*, No. 140, November 1917, 119.

61. Ida Tarbell, *New Ideals in Business* (New York: Macmillan, 1916), 62;*The Mixer*, No. 42 (April, May and June 1919): 6.

62. R.J. Young, "Our Foreigner: What Are We Doing To Help Him Help Himself," in Association of Iron and Steel Electrical Engineers, "Proceedings of the First Co-Operative Safety Council," Milwaukee, September 30 to October 12, 1912, 302-07.

63. *McClure's Magazine* quoted in Michael Nash, *Conflict and Accommodation* (Westport, CT: Greenwood Press, 1982), 105.

64. *Conditions of Employment in the Iron and Steel Industry*, Vol. 4, 151; Fitch, *The Steel Workers*, 67.

65. Gerald Eggert, *Steelmasters and Labor Reform, 1886-1923* (Pittsburgh: University of Pittsburgh Press, 1981), 95; Bradley Stoughton, *The Metallurgy of Iron and Steel*, 4th Ed. (New York: McGraw-Hill Book Company, 1934), 46.

For examples of how the introduction of the eight-hour day decreased accident rates at specific plants, see Curtis, Fosdick & Belknap, Attorneys and Counselors at Law, Industrial Relations Staff, "Report on Industrial Relations in the Colorado Fuel and Iron Company," [1924], Mark M. Jones Papers, Box 4, Record Group IV 3A 9, Rockefeller Archive Center, North Tarrytown, NY; Horace Drury, "The Three-Shift System in the Steel Industry," *Bulletin of the Taylor Society* 6 (February 1921): 19; S. Adele Shaw, "Now That Jerry Has Time to Live," *The Survey* 52 (1 September 1924): 570.

66. U.S. Congress, House, *Hearings Before the Committee on Investigation of United States Steel Corporation* (in 8 Vols.)" [The Stanley Committee], 62nd Cong., 2d Sess., 1911-12, 3396.

67. J.A. Campbell to H.H. Vreeland, January 17, 1906, National Civic Federation Papers, New York Public Library, New York, NY.

68. James M. Woltz, "Safety and Welfare Work as Carried on by the Youngstown Sheet & Tube Co., Youngstown O.," 1914; *Iron Age* 105 (17 June 1920): 1735.

69. This assessment of welfare capitalism in the steel industry affirms H.M. Gitelman's thesis that welfare capitalism was not as significant a phenomenon as most historians believe. According to Gitelman, the standard assessment of the prevalence of welfare capitalism is based on an "exaggeration of trends in a 'few highly visible firms.'" See Gitelman, 24-25.

70. American Iron and Steel Institute, "Minutes of the Board of Directors," April 26, 1911 and May 24, 1911; American Iron and Steel Institute Papers, Hagley Museum and Library, Wilmington, DE; *Monthly Bulletin of the American Iron and Steel Institute* 1, (January 1913):19.

71. *Monthly Bulletin of the American Iron and Steel Institute* 2 (August 1914): 219.

72. David H. Kelly, "Labor Relations in the Steel Industry: Management's Ideas, Proposals and Programs, 1920-1950," Ph.D. Diss., Indiana University, 1976, 87-89; Charles Lukens Huston, "Why We Could 'Carry On' in '93," *System* 47 (June 1925): 780.

73. Kelly, 90-91; E.D. McCallum, *The Iron and Steel Industry in the United States* (London: P.S. King & Sons, 1931), 290; John A. Roebling's Sons Company, Minutes of the Board of Directors, August 24, 1922 and August 6, 1929; John A. Roebling's Sons Company Papers, Alexander Library, Rutgers University, New Brunswick, NJ; Curtis, Fosdick & Belknap, 86-89; Ozanne, 84-85.

74. Aldrich, 92-93; Arundel Cotter, *United States Steel: "A Corporation With a Soul"* (Garden City, NY: Doubleday, Page and Company, 1921), 187; Fitch, *The Steel Workers*, 69; Brody, *Steelworkers in America*, 166-67.

75. Horace B. Davis, "Iron and Steel Industry: Other Countries," in *Encyclopaedia of the Social Sciences*, Vols. 7 and 8, Edwin R.A. Seligman, ed. (New York: Macmillan Company, 1932), 318.

76. Brody, *Steelworkers in America*, 167-68; Aldrich, 104; George T. Fonda, "The Relationship of the Workman's Compensation Laws to the Safety Movement," *Bulletin of the Pennsylvania Department of Labor and Industry* 5 (1918): 29; William B. Dickson, "Betterment of Labor Conditions in the Steel Industry," *Proceedings of the American Iron and Steel Institute 1910*, 60-61.

77. Interchurch World Movement, *Report on the Steel Strike of 1919* (New York: Harcourt, Brace and Howe), 1920, 66- 67.

78. "Steel Accident Rate High in 1931," n.d., Harvey O'Connor Collection, Box 22, Archives of Labor and Urban Affairs, Walter P. Reuther Library, Wayne State University, Detroit, MI.

79. Carroll R. Daugherty, Melvin G. De Chazeau and Samuel S. Stratton, *The Economics of the Iron and Steel Industry* (in 2 Vols.) (New York: McGraw Hill, 1937), 189-90; *Iron Age* 110, 21 September 1922, 737; United States Steel Corporation, "Remarks of Myron C. Taylor at Annual Meeting of Stockholders," April 5, 1937, 13-15.

80. United States Steel Corporation, "Twenty Fifth Anniversary," Bulletin No. 11, [1926]; *Iron Age* 105 (1 January 1920): 34; Richard Edwards, *Contested Terrain: The Transformation of the Workplace in the Twentieth Century* (New York: Basic Books, 1979), 95.

81. Horace Drury, "The Technique of Changing from the Two-Shift to the Three-Shift System in the Steel Industry," Report to the Cabot Fund, Boston, May 1922, 46-48.

82. Ray Stannard Baker, *The New Industrial Unrest* (Garden City, NY: Doubleday, Page & Company, 1920), 144.

83. Both Brandes' and Tone's work on welfare capitalism are footnoted earlier in this chapter.

84. Fitch, *The Steel Workers*, 211.

85. John A. Fitch, "The Labor Policies of Unrestricted Capital," *The Survey* 28 (6 April 1912): 27.

Chapter Five

Reluctant Reform: The Eight-Hour Day and Employee Representation

"Since the public-be-damned period has there been a change?"
"Yes, there's been a change."
"For the better?"
"Yes, there's been a change for the better. I think that in the walk and talk of business men there's been a change for the better."
He groped for a more emphatic word.
"There's been an awakening—a great awakening."
"The result of public agitation?"
The Judge shook his head slowly. He regretted once more, it seemed, the idea that nothing is good in the large corporation save what the public has made good.

—Interview with Elbert Gary,
as reported by the magazine, *The Outlook*, 1914.[1]

At the beginning of the Nonunion Era, the federal government helped steel companies in many ways. High tariffs protected American producers from low-priced imported steel; patent protection allowed firms like Carnegie Steel to prevent technological innovations from being copied by their competition; the armed forces bought large amounts of steel in the form of armor plate. During labor disputes, help from all levels of government often proved extremely useful. In 1919, the federal government helped the industry maintain the open shop by sending the U.S. Army into Gary, Indiana. Authorities in Pennsylvania sent troops to restore order during the Homestead lockout, the McKees Rocks strike of

1909, the 1919 strike and many less noteworthy instances. On occasion, local forces helped defeat smaller work stoppages throughout every sector of the industry.[2] This kind of assistance helped steelmakers maintain their one-sided implied contracts with employees.

However, as the Nonunion Era progressed, government action began to threaten the way steel manufacturers made labor policy more and more frequently. The numerous federal investigations of the industry symbolize this change. In 1892, a U.S. House of Representatives panel held hearings on the Homestead lockout. The Bureau of Corporations investigated the business practices of U.S. Steel in 1904 and 1905. In 1910, the House of Representatives studied a major strike at Bethlehem Steel. A special committee of the House of Representatives (known as the Stanley Committee) investigated U.S. Steel in 1911. The Commissioner of Corporations produced four volumes on the conditions of employment in the iron and steel industry between 1911 and 1913. A U.S. Senate Committee investigated the 1919 Steel Strike while it was still happening. Other investigations with broader mandates, which devoted considerable time and resources to steelmaking, include the United States Industrial Commission in 1901 and the United States Commission on Industrial Relations between 1914 and 1916. In order to forestall the proposed reform legislation that these government investigations tended to produce as well as to keep up their public image, steel companies often changed the way they did business.

The dissolution suit the Justice Department filed in 1911 against U.S. Steel under the Sherman Antitrust Act was the most significant potential threat to the way steelmakers did business.[3] From the inception of the Corporation, the threat of dissolution forced U.S. Steel to consider all of its actions with an eye towards how the public would perceive them. The Corporation remained concerned about the potential for government antitrust action throughout its first decade of existence, and Elbert Gary believed a good public image could help prevent the government from acting. After the dissolution suit finally came, it dragged on for almost ten years and generated considerable negative publicity for this publicity-conscious firm. Because U.S. Steel deliberately limited its anti-competitive behavior, it won the suit in 1920. The Corporation's most important antitrust protection device was its dominant firm pricing strategy. According to Thomas M. McCraw and Forest Reinhardt, the Corporation "decided at the end of each year what its prices were going to be during the coming year, then actually kept them at that level." This strategy encouraged U.S. Steel's competitors to undercut the Corporation's prices. As a result, the Corporation's market share declined from 66% in 1901 to 41% in 1930.[4] Elbert Gary encouraged this development because he believed that if U.S. Steel limited itself to less than 50% of the market (a figure he picked up from William Jennings Bryan), it would never be prosecuted as a monopoly since it would not be perceived as a threat to competition. Although this strategy did not prevent antitrust action, it encouraged U.S. Steel's competitors to take the side of the Corporation in the subsequent proceedings. Even before the final decision, consolidations in many other industries adopted this same strategy, taking advantage of the Court's tendency to distinguish between "good" and "bad" trusts.[5]

In the same way that U.S. Steel undercut its own market position to increase its popularity, the Corporation modified its labor policies to assuage public opinion and forestall government intervention in its industrial relations. As early as 1907, U.S. Steel Vice-President William Brown Dickson made a case for the end of Sunday labor as follows:

> In connection with the attacks being made on our companies by labor leaders, you have no doubt noticed the prominence which is being given the question of Sunday work in and about our mills.
>
> There is no question in my mind that this is the one weak point in our armor and that public sentiment, if thoroughly aroused by the publication of such facts . . . would condemn our present methods of operating.[6]

Dickson never stated what an aroused public could do to U.S. Steel; simply avoiding bad publicity was reason enough to act. The Corporation's Board of Directors passed a resolution that year recommending that Sunday labor "be reduced to a minimum," but the Corporation's subsidiaries generally ignored it. "[T]he resolution was adopted by the Finance Committee as a mere matter of form," Dickson later wrote, "taken to avoid further discussion."[7] This explains why the Sunday labor resolution did not stem the tide of criticism against U.S. Steel's labor policy. As public clamor over the Corporation's labor policies mounted, the possibility of government involvement spurred further calls for reform.

Faced with the possibility that federal legislation might help restore steel unionism to its prior strength, steel manufacturers increasingly began objecting to federal and state interference for the same reason they objected to trade unions: both phenomena prevented workers from exhibiting the individual initiative which management wanted to reward. As Elbert Gary put it in 1920, "Any concern, any organization, any government which seeks to promote, demote, or retain a man in position contrary to his just deserts, combats the public interest, the life and growth of the nation; and more than this, is perpetrating an incalculable injury to the man himself."[8] If workers did not get their just desserts, the outside forces that did the denying might impinge upon management's prerogative to control labor any way it saw fit.

Laisez-faire—the belief that business should be free from government intervention in its affairs—first became an important part of American political discourse during the Nineteenth Century. From then up until today, this idea has brought out the opportunistic side of American capitalists. Industry has regularly used laissez-faire as reason to reject regulations that threatened profitability; yet support for this philosophy has not stopped business from accepting government aid.[9] The steel industry would adopt this stance throughout the inter-war period as government became increasingly involved in operations that had once been the exclusive domain of management. The threat of government action played an important role in the two most significant labor reforms of the Nonunion Era: the eight-hour day and employee representation plans. Because these reforms occurred despite management resistance, they showed workers that steel manufacturers were not invincible. Although neither hours reform nor employee representation were in and of themselves fatal to the industrial relations system of the Nonunion Era, each one helped set the stage for the difficult struggle to come.

Defending the Twelve-Hour Day

For most of the Nineteenth Century, the majority of employees in the iron and steel industry worked twelve-hour shifts. Attempts to limit the hours of skilled ironworkers invariably failed because they did not have the support of employees. The reason for worker opposition had to do with total earnings. Ironworkers were usually paid by piece rates. This meant that the less time an employee worked, the less time he would have to produce, and the less money he could earn from his employer. Ironworkers also tended to view shorter hours as an unwarranted attempt to speed them up. As late as 1894, the Amalgamated Association of Iron and Steel Workers resisted attempts by manufacturers to put mills they represented on the eight-hour day. For decades, employers pointed to these experiences as proof that their employees supported the twelve-hour day, but these assertions were highly misleading. In iron production, skilled workers wanted longer hours because they had the ability to set their own pace. In steel production, no such control existed. Steelworkers paid hourly wages wanted higher wages and shorter hours, but employers drove their employees to ever-escalating heights of exertion. Steelworkers never supported the twelve-hour day, but since the vast majority of them never had a union to fight for their position, they had no choice but to accept the hours of labor imposed upon them. By 1910, approximately half of all employees in the iron and steel industry worked a twelve-hour day. By 1921, that figure had risen to somewhere between one half and two-thirds of employees.[10]

The first major attack on the twelve-hour day in the steel industry came from John Fitch in *The Steel Workers* and his subsequent writings. Fitch criticized long hours because of the physical and mental exhaustion they caused employees. He also decried the adverse effect of long hours on workers' families and on the cultural life of the communities in which they lived. "Old Age at Forty," an article Fitch wrote based on the preliminary findings for his contribution to the Pittsburgh Survey, caused a sensation when published in the March 1911 issue of *The American Magazine*. "Can you conceive of what it means to work twelve hours a day?," he asked:

> Twelve hours every day spent within the mill walls means thirteen or fourteen hours away from home, for the skilled men often live at least a half hour's ride from the mills. It means early hours for the wife, if breakfast is to be on time, and late hours too, if the supper dishes are to be washed. It doesn't leave much time for family either, when the husband begins to doze over his paper before the evening's work in the kitchen is done, and when necessity inevitably drives him early to bed so that he may get up for the next day's routine. It doesn't leave much chance to play with children when a man's job requires heavy toil, during ten or eleven hours of daylight, six or seven days, and then overturning of things and another week of night work, each shift thirteen or fourteen hours long, with the "mister" working while the children sleep, and sleeping while they play. But that is the regular round of events in the typical mill family while the weeks stretch to months and the months mount to years.

Charles M. Cabot, a U.S. Steel stockholder concerned by Fitch's stories, commissioned him to do a study of the twelve-hour day, which he then sent to every other owner of the Corporation's preferred stock. At U.S. Steel's annual stockholder's meeting in April 1911, Cabot proposed that a special committee be formed to investigate Fitch's findings. Elbert Gary, eager to get out in front of this potential public relations problem, readily agreed. This committee, chaired by the businessman Stuyvesant Fish, completed its work the next year. Although the Fish Committee report was supportive of most of U.S. Steel's labor policies, it agreed with Fitch that the twelve-hour day should be abolished. The Fish Committee also recommended that another committee be created to bring that about, but nothing came of this suggestion.[11]

William Brown Dickson staged a similar assault on long hours from within the industry. Dickson was one of the few steel executives of this era who began his career as a manual laborer. He started at Carnegie Steel in 1881. In 1886, Dickson became a clerk at the Homestead Works. In 1899, Carnegie brought him in as a junior partner. In 1901, he joined U.S. Steel with many of the other "Pittsburgh millionaires" made rich through the foundation of the Steel Trust. Like so many of his contemporaries, Dickson hated unions. His reasons were more personal than professional. When Dickson and his brother crossed picket lines during an 1882 strike, trade unionists beat up his brother and retaliated against him after the strike ended. Although anti-union, Dickson was sympathetic to efforts to improve working conditions because of his time in the mill—a perspective that few other steel executives shared. He opposed the twelve-hour day and the seven-day week because he knew firsthand what long hours did to the lives of employees. Because of tensions on the Board of Directors caused by his anti-Sunday labor campaign, Dickson resigned his position at U.S. Steel in 1911. After he became Chairman of Midvale Steel in 1915, Dickson instituted the eight-hour day there. However, Midvale was too small for its labor policies to have a noticeable impact on the rest of the industry. To add insult to injury, most steel companies, including U.S. Steel, brought back the seven-day week when demand skyrocketed during World War I.[12]

"Eight hours and the union" was the central slogan of the organizing campaign that led to the 1919 strike. The increased pace of production of the war years had made shorter hours more desirable than ever, but the defeat of the National Committee for Organizing Iron and Steel Workers seemed to end the possibility for reform. Yet thanks to the Interchurch

World Movement (IWM), the issue did not die. During the 1919 strike, the IWM attempted to mediate between labor and management. Although the National Committee was amenable to the idea, Gary and the rest of the industry refused the offer. Despite this rejection, the IWM still compiled a report of what they learned during the course of their investigation of the conflict. Released in July 1920, the report determined, "That the 12-hour day is a barbarism without valid excuse, penalizing the workers and the country."[13] Press coverage of the report, attacks on the patriotism of the IWM, and subsequent studies of the twelve-hour day kept this issue in the public eye, but the steel industry did not budge. When the American Iron and Steel Institute reaffirmed its support for the twelve-hour day in May 1923, John Fitch wrote this "clearly means that the major part of the steel industry has determined to do nothing in this matter, of its own accord."[14]

Industry leaders did not remain mute while their hours policy was under attack. Because of their concern for good public relations, management representatives vociferously defended the twelve-hour day, albeit often in a confusing and highly misleading manner. One tactic was to plead helplessness, to claim that external factors forced the twelve-hour day upon them. Even though less than a third of the departments in most mills required continuous operations, companies often argued that the twelve-hour day was a metallurgical necessity. As one unnamed steel company official explained during the 1919 strike, "I know the men work long hours, but one thing must be realized. Making steel is not making pies. From the time the raw ore is started until the steel is rolled out it is the trickiest, most exacting work in the world. Men cannot be changed. From the steel rollers and crane men to the puddlers every man is an indispensable cog. We can't change crews during operations. Lives depend on it, in the actual making and the fitness of the product."[15] Sometimes a firm deflected the responsibility for the twelve-hour day by blaming the market. "[T]hese conditions are not under the control of any one employer, however large, or of all the employers in any one industry," U.S. Steel argued in 1914. It also asserted it would lose its best employees to competitors who offered more hours because workers preferred the opportunity to earn as much salary as possible.[16]

Even though these arguments treated long hours as an unpleasant necessity, the industry sometimes claimed that its employees actually benefited from the twelve-hour day. As one U.S. Steel manager told Fitch, "A man is a lot better working those [extra] four hours than he is loafing."[17] Likewise, Chairman Gary told the Corporation's 1922 Annual Meeting, "I am not certain that in most cases it is a hardship rather than a benefit to a workman to refuse to allow him to work twelve hours a day when the work is not laborious and not injurious to him and when he desires to work longer and earn more money."[18] Conversely, a frequent defense of the twelve-hour day was that the work was intermittent, that employees spent much of their long shifts waiting between heats. For instance, Gary explained to the Senate committee investigating the 1919 strike, "[I]t is well known to anyone who is connected with the business that the men who work, these rollers who work 11 hours, the furnace men who work 12 hours, they are not actually working more than half the time." He then presented photographs to the committee showing steelworkers relaxing during their shift.[19] Both these arguments suggest that employees who complained about the twelve-hour day were really just lazy. This attitude was common among defenders of the industry's labor practices, who often considered the twelve-hour day a prerequisite for success rather than a hardship. A best-selling author sympathetic to the industry's point of view explained this perspective, "The man who has achieved, or is capable of achieving, under such circumstances is temperamentally prone to glorify hard work and to think of its results chiefly in terms of Lincolns and Schwabs and Edison. The man who himself has not, and probably could not, achieve under such conditions, inherently shrinks from the rigors of such a system and is temperamentally impelled to be most impressed with its failures."[20] Because the industry had little sympathy for employees who did not want to help themselves, most steel manufacturers did not take worker objections to the twelve-hour day seriously.

Management's most common explanation for its opposition the eight-hour day was cost, but only after agitation for reform took hold did the industry attempt to quantify it. A 1923 American Iron and Steel Institute report asserted that the eight-hour day would increase the cost of production by 15%, but its authors did not explain how they arrived at this figure.[21] In truth, nobody really knew exactly how much more it cost to run a steel plant on three shifts until a plant switched over to the new system. The actual expense depended on how much employees shared in the costs of the transition (by giving up a portion of their total earnings) and whether the additional number of employees necessary for three shift operation were available. Because most employees refused to have their total wages cut by a third, raises for existing employees were inevitable. Nevertheless, steelworkers often expressed a willingness to make wage concessions in order to get shorter hours. Yet employers still defended the twelve-hour day on the basis of allowing employees to make all the money they could. Steelmakers treated demands for shorter hours as an attempt by workers to get something for nothing. Workers did not even have the option to take a pay cut to achieve shorter hours because employers believed they had to determine the length of the working day unilaterally.

Ironically, the steel industry's insistence on keeping the twelve-hour day prevented companies from reaping the potential financial benefits of shorter hours. In almost every case of a steel firm making the transition to the eight-hour day before 1923, the increase in the productive efficiency of employees working fewer hours more than compensated for the increased costs of changing over to the new system. In 1881, William R. Jones of Carnegie Steel told the British Iron and Steel Institute that "it was entirely out of the question to expect human flesh and blood to labor incessantly for twelve hours." For this reason, some Carnegie Steel plants adopted the eight-hour day that same year. According to Jones, "This proved to be of immense advantage to both the company and the workmen, the latter now earning more in eight hours than they formerly did in twelve hours, while the men can work harder constantly for eight hours, having sixteen hours for rest."[22] In the intensely competitive environment of the late-1880s and 1890s, employers forgot Jones' experience. When other companies that entered the steel business during this era began their nonunion operations with the twelve-hour day, Carnegie Steel switched back too. It did this over the strong objections of the Knights of Labor, who had represented workers at the Edgar Thomson plant before losing a strike sparked in part because of this dispute.[23] Since the method of payment in Jones' era had been piecework, this experience may not even have been applicable to conditions after the turn of the century. New pioneers in labor reform had to demonstrate the value of shorter hours for wage laborers.

In 1911, the Commonwealth Steel Company became the first large firm to switch its furnaces to the eight-hour day during the Nonunion Era. Although it increased the hourly wages in its open-hearth department from 16% to 22% at the time the change took effect, the total labor cost per twenty-four hours actually dropped from $19.50 to $19.12 due to the increased efficiency of employees working under the new system. The Colorado Fuel & Iron Company (CF&I) switched to the eight-hour day in November 1918. Five years later, the firm's president, J.F. Welborn, reported:

> The trend of production per man-hour, with unimportant exceptions, has been upward since the adoption of the 8-hour day; and in every department of our steel manufacturing operations, from blast furnace to the wire mill, our production per man-hour is now greater than it was when all of these activities were operating on the 12-hour shift. Comparing these results of the last few months with periods of similar production when basic rates were 10 percent lower than current rates and the working time 12 hours per day, we find that almost without exception our labor cost per ton is lower than in the earlier periods.[24]

By 1921, at least nineteen firms scattered across the country had made the transition to the eight-hour day. Not all of them had positive results from shorter hours. Yet experts believed that if this transition did increase the cost of labor per hour, that increase would not be significant.[25]

Ironically, steel executives knew the potential economic advantages of the eight-hour day long before the industry completed its transition to shorter hours. When the prominent stockholders who made up the Fish Committee delivered their report in 1912, they told U.S. Steel that, "a 12-hour day of labor followed continuously by any group of men for any considerable number of years means a decreasing of the efficiency and lessening of the vigor and vitality of such men."[26] Further agreement with this position came from middle managers at U.S. Steel. In 1917, W.A. Field, the general superintendent at the Corporation's South Chicago plant requested permission to operate on a three-shift basis, but Corporation management denied the request for fear that it might set a precedent. Speaking to the engineer Horace Drury four years after he left the plant, Field argued that eight-hour day would have promoted efficiency because "anything which would clear away what the men might regard as a grievance would be of great value." Field also said that the change could have been made "without any increase in cost." The Assistant to the President of the Carnegie Steel Company, speaking confidentially, told Drury that his immediate superior thought that a majority of the Corporation's subsidiary presidents supported the eight-hour day.[27]

Conservative industry leaders refused to accept the idea that the twelve-hour day did more harm than good because this notion questioned the value of their own work experience and made it impossible for steelworkers to follow their example. As the twelve-hour day came under attack, they trumpeted the value of long hours despite available evidence that shorter hours would save their firms money. "It is hard work and long hours that has built up the west and America," declared Illinois Steel President E.J. Buffington in an interview with Drury. Buffington went on to tell Drury that he was "raised on a farm, and has himself worked 12 hours, and still works hard." In summary, he argued, "The important thing in the world is achievement. America is in danger of being ruined by prosperity and relaxation. Many nations have been ruined that way."[28] These views strongly resemble those of Elbert Gary, another former farmboy and three-shift opponent. This emphasis on the rigors of their early labor suggests a desire to contrast their own manliness against the laziness of their employees. This fascination with hard work to promote individual success blinded these executives to the potential economic gains from shorter hours, which had already been recognized by their subordinates.

Why then did the steel industry finally accept the eight-hour day? Concern about its public image alone did not lead to reform. Despite the public clamor over the twelve-hour day, the number of employees at U.S. Steel working a twelve-hour shift actually increased during the period when reformers like John Fitch escalated their campaign to change the industry's policy. Pressure applied by government authorities was the pivotal reason U.S. Steel and the other remaining twelve-hour firms finally shortened their hours. That pressure began during World War I. In response to demands by the Wilson administration's War Labor Policy Board, U.S. Steel enacted the basic eight-hour day (which meant the last four hours of the twelve-hour workday was paid at the overtime rate) on October 1st, 1918. The Corporation discontinued this measure when peace returned. After three years of criticism sparked by the 1919 strike, the government stepped back into the debate in May 1922. Inspired by his Secretary of Commerce, Herbert Hoover, President Warren Harding held a meeting of top steel executives to discuss this issue. The gathering resolved nothing. The only concession that the industry made was the creation of a five-man committee under the auspices of the American Iron and Steel Institute to investigate the issue and report back in a year. A year later, on May 25th, 1923, the committee came out in opposition to changing over to the eight-hour day. "Whatever will be said against the 12-hour day in the steel industry," its report concluded, "investigation has convinced this committee that it has not of itself been an injury to the employees physically, mentally, or morally."[29]

Harding sent Gary his response to the American Iron and Steel Institute report on June 18th. It contained this thinly veiled threat: "As I have stated before, I am, of course, disappointed that no conclusive arrangement was proposed for determination of what must be manifestly accepted as a practice that should be obsolete in American industry. I still entertain the hope that these questions of social importance should be solved by action inside the industries themselves, for it is only such solutions that are consonant with American life and institutions."[30] Rumors had already begun to circulate that Congress would determine a legislative remedy for this problem, and Harding's letter seemed to indicate that he would reluctantly support this solution. Privately, the President sent word to Gary that he was planning to speak on the twelve-hour day in the steel industry during a series of speeches on his way to Alaska; thus implying that he was willing to make this a campaign issue. On June 27th, 1923, only days after receiving Harding's letter, Gary, acting in his capacity as President of the American Iron and Steel Institute, announced that the industry had changed its mind. The twelve-hour day would be phased out beginning immediately.[31] Such a rapid turn of events strongly suggests that the President's threat to force the industry to act was the pivotal factor in this decision, much as Woodrow Wilson's intervention had been essential to forcing railroads to accept the eight-hour day seven years earlier. Otherwise, steelmakers would have bowed to public pressure stirred up by the IWM report. Yet this was not enough by itself. Although obviously concerned about public displeasure, Elbert Gary proved to be more concerned about the precedent of government interference in such an important labor policy.

Steel was the last major industry in America to formally end the twelve-hour day. Even as glass, papermaking and coal mining switched to eight-hour shifts in the years following World War I, the steel industry still resisted this national trend. Yet steelmakers in many other countries had already switched to the eight-hour shift before their American counterparts. In Great Britain, for example, shorter hours for blast furnace workers were implemented gradually beginning in 1898. Those producers who continued to hold out were required to change by law in March 1919. French steelworkers received the eight-hour day through bargaining with their employers that same year.[32] The American steel industry's resistance to shorter hours demonstrated the strength of management's desire to dictate the terms and conditions of employment. Even when employers in other industries relinquished this aspect of their freedom to control, steel manufacturers opposed change because they felt it could not be reconciled with their traditional prerogatives. By 1921, many American steel manufacturers prospered with their workers on the eight-hour shift.

Despite the experience of firms that shifted before 1923, the industry-wide increase in productivity following the change to shorter hours surprised many observers. According to a 1928 Bureau of Labor Statistics study of merchant blast furnaces, "Before [the move to the eight-hour day] took place, it was confidently expected by many that there would be a considerable increase in labor cost because of the increase in the number of men required to operate the furnace." In fact, the Bureau concluded, "[T]he actual results in the blast furnace industry following 1923 far exceeded anything that might have been expected. There are numerous cases of plants in which, within a year after the change was made, the total labor force was back again at the same number of men that had been employed under the 12-hour system."[33] "We went over without a ripple," explained an executive from an unnamed Pittsburgh steel company which had just started to change over:

> The striking thing about it was how easily it was done. There was no interference with production—nothing. It was a great surprise to us all. . . .
>
> We thought we would have to bring in thousands of new men, but we didn't. We changed over in August when things were dull. This gave us the opportunity to use many of our own men on the third shift who would otherwise have been out of work and that fact made the change go more smoothly.

This executive's firm had not finished the transition when *The Survey* published this interview in 1924, but he insisted that "the company will save money by putting all men on eight hours."[34] In 1934, eleven years after the iron and steel industry had first issued the proclamation ending the twelve-hour day, one expert concluded, "Shorter hours . . . have proved a boon to the industry both technically and financially. While not claiming that this is the sole reason for recent improvements, nevertheless the greatest advance in the technique and quality of production in the history of the industry has been coincident with the era of shorter hours of labor during the past few years."[35]

Many steelmakers had once opposed limiting workers to eight hours because they believed it would make it harder for employees to exhibit the initiative that led to success. Despite evidence that this policy hurt their economic interests, these steelmakers continued to use this justification to resist reform. The strength of management's belief in the value of long hours determined whether employers would fight shorter hours to save the cost in increased wages or go over to eight hours so as to save money by improving efficiency. Only pressure from the government convinced the militant core of steel industry leaders to change.

Employee Representation at Colorado Fuel & Iron

Throughout his administration, Woodrow Wilson tried to resolve labor disputes through mediation and collective bargaining. Employers threatened by this kind of intervention commonly responded by creating employee representation plans (ERPs), better known as company unions. The two most important company unions in the steel industry before the 1930s were those at Colorado Fuel & Iron and Bethlehem Steel. Both of these firms had large non-steel operations and both were among the first companies in America to start ERPs, yet CF&I was one of the few firms in any industry to create an ERP that inspired genuine reform. The driving force behind the ERP at CF&I was John D. Rockefeller, Jr., whose family was the company's primary stockholder for most of the first half of the Twentieth Century. Rockefeller created a labor policy different than those at other steel firms because he did not have the same value system as other steel manufacturers. The most obvious difference between him and other steelmakers was that he did not have to work his way up from anywhere since he was born at the top. Furthermore, CF&I was primarily a coal mining concern. CF&I created an ERP designed to compete with the United Mine Workers. It made concessions to keep the union out of its mines. CF&I extended its ERP to the steelworks out of fairness rather than necessity.

This explains its generosity and effectiveness compared to employee representation plans in the rest of the steel industry. At Bethlehem Steel, management's desire for the freedom to control and belief in the ethos of individual achievement severely undercut the effectiveness of this reform. When other steel companies created their own ERPs, they patterned them after Bethlehem's, not CF&I's.

Writing in 1926, Ernest Richmond Burton "broadly" defined employee representation as "any established arrangement whereby the working force of a business concern is represented by persons recognized by both the management and the employees as spokesman for the latter in conferences on matters of mutual interest." From their inception, critics dubbed these representation systems "company unions," and that term has persisted to this day because these employer-initiated arrangements are commonly associated with efforts to fight organized labor.[36] Daniel Nelson argues that company unions "reflected a variety of motives and objectives," but there is no question that their anti-union qualities were what made them attractive to most steel manufacturers.[37] During the Teens, most steel manufacturers resisted ceding any control over working conditions to employees and opposed employee representation for this reason. Those steel firms that did introduce employee representation plans did so only under pressure from the government and organized labor. They feared that these outside forces might lead to arrangements under which their freedom to control employees would grow even more limited.

The Colorado Fuel and Iron Company operated numerous mines throughout Colorado, Wyoming, Utah, New Mexico and Oklahoma. The coal, iron ore and other minerals produced at these properties provided the raw materials for its Minnequa Steel Works in Pueblo, Colorado, the only integrated iron and steel works in the western United States in the years before World War II. This mill manufactured two percent of all the steel products in the country, and it normally employed a workforce of 6,000 to 6,500 men.[38] Employee representation at CF&I grew out of the Colorado coal miners' strike of 1913 and 1914. Specifically, it was the product of the infamous Ludlow Massacre of April 20, 1914, during which the Colorado National Guard attacked a tent colony of strikers and their families, killing at least 25 people. Among the dead were two women and eleven small children.[39] Events at Ludlow severely damaged the reputation of the company and the reputation of the company's controlling shareholders, the Rockefeller family. The introduction of employee representation was part of an attempt to repair the damage.

John D. Rockefeller, Jr., by then the day-to-day manager of the Rockefeller fortune, introduced the plan to CF&I's workforce himself on October 2, 1915, during a widely publicized tour of the company's holdings in Colorado. Rockefeller told a meeting in Pueblo that:

> [O]nly after . . . careful and exhaustive personal study [was I] willing to go on with the plan of representation and undertake it for presentation to you. And, frankly, every waking moment since I left you men . . . last Saturday, practically every waking hour of this last week, has been spent with the officers of this company in constant, careful, earnest thought looking towards the development of such a plan as would serve our common interest in the best possible way.[40]

In truth, the plan had been under development for over a year, ever since the Ludlow Massacre. The primary author of the plan was Mackenzie King, an industrial relations expert then working for the Rockefeller Foundation who would go on to become Prime Minister of Canada. The company only expanded the plan into the steel works in May 1916.[41]

The Colorado Fuel and Iron employee representation plan was essentially the same in both parts of the business. It divided the steel works into nine divisions, each division serving as an election district for employee representatives. It mandated that one representative was to be elected for every 150 wage-earners, and spelled out detailed procedures for running those elections. The plan created four joint committees of labor and management devoted to specific issues of concern: Safety and Accidents; Recreation and Education; Sanitation, Health and Housing; and Industrial Cooperation and Conciliation. Joint conferences between all employee representatives and management could be called at any time by the order of the company president, but had to be called at least once every four months. Employee representatives could also call meetings on their own initiative in order to discuss grievances. The plan included certain privileges for employees such as the right to outside arbitration of grievances and the guarantee that they would not be discriminated against for belonging to labor unions. "The men seem to have reached a perfect agreement with their employers under this industrial plan," declared Rockefeller while touring the steel works in 1918. "As I walked thru the mills and yards, many men—plain day-laboring chaps—called me aside for a confidential word on conditions. They have suggestions to make and one thing or another. But all seemed satisfied."[42]

The most extraordinary clause in the plan acknowledged the right of CF&I employees to belong to trade unions: "There shall be no discrimination by the Company or by any of its employees on account of membership or non-membership in any society, fraternity or union."[43] The firm included the clause in the miners' plan first to suggest management's willingness to compete with the United Mine Workers (who had organized between fifty and ninety percent of its mine workforce) on the merits of their organization. Rockefeller's support for this clause of the plan differentiated him from nearly every other manager in both the steel and coal industry. "It seems to me," he wrote in 1916,

> that every man should have the right to decide for himself whether the Company is his best friend and champion or whether some outside organization is. If the company cannot convince the men that it is their best friend, that it will cooperate more zealously with them than any outside organization in safeguarding their interests and well-being and securing them the fullest protection and justice, then the men must and should ally themselves with any organization which they believe gives better assurances of such results.[44]

Even though it did not stop the growth of unions, management stuck to this principle to an extraordinary degree. For example, strikes rocked both CF&I's steel and mining divisions in 1919. Yet that same year Rockefeller reiterated to the president of CF&I his "profound conviction as to the justice and wisdom of the fullest adherence to" the clause in the Industrial Plan which said that there would be no discrimination against union workers, "both now and in the future."[45] In 1921, two years after one large strike and a year or so before another, Welborn wrote to all superintendents:

> It has been reported that within the last two months union organizers have been asked to leave three of the mining camps of the Colorado Fuel & Iron Company. A careful investigation has disclosed no reasonable foundation in fact for the alleged occurrence in two of the camps. In the third camp it appears that organizers were asked to leave. This action was taken without authority and contrary to explicit instructions. Adequate measures have since been taken to prevent the possibility of a repetition of this occurrence. . . .
>
> . . . This attitude will be maintained and this policy rigidly enforced in the future as in the past.[46]

While it might be tempting to denounce such statements as self-serving rhetoric, CF&I was on to something. Modern studies have shown that workers who have some say in their working conditions are more productive, quit their job less and are less likely to go on strike.[47] Although this research illustrates the economic benefits of dealing with outside trade unions, the CF&I Plan presumably would have allowed management to gain these benefits without the cost of an outside union. Although they did not use the same terminology that modern economists do, management recognized that these kinds of benefits existed. According to President Welborn, the plan produced "value . . . in the form of loyalty from the workers." A memorandum of agreement attached and published with the plan calls the "harmony and good-will" which this arrangement supposedly promoted "essential to the successful operation of the Company's industries in an enlightened and profitable manner."[48] Yet in order to gain such benefit, workers had to take the plan seriously. This meant that management had to make concessions, including concessions that originated from worker initiatives.

The introduction of the eight-hour day in November 1918 was the most important concession given to CF&I's steelworkers under the terms of the Employee Representation Plan because of the positive reaction to it from employees. As one steelworker told Ben Selekman of the Russell Sage Foundation, "The greatest thing that has ever resulted from the operation of the Industrial Representation Plan is the adoption of the actual eight-hour day. . . . Great credit is due the officers of the company for having worked it out so well and having applied it in every department." Workers also credited the plan with bringing about changes in the physical conditions of the plant and better safety work.[49] Because of changes like these the Colorado Fuel & Iron plan was the most popular ERP in the steel industry. Even after employees in the coal mines joined the United Mine Workers in 1933, CF&I's steelworkers stuck with their company union. In 1941, the National Labor Relations Board disbanded the plan after determining that it violated the National Labor Relations Act, yet it took three government-sponsored representation elections for an outside union to win recognition.[50] The ERP at Bethlehem steel showed this same kind of longevity. However, a close look at its history shows that management's determination to resist unions had more to do with its durability than did its popularity with employees.

Employee Representation at Bethlehem Steel

The Bethlehem employee representation plan was a modified version of the CF&I plan and the model for almost all subsequent ERPs in the iron and steel industry. The same forces that led to the creation of the employee representation plan at CF&I—successful organizing efforts by workers in non-steel operations and pressure from the federal government—were also key factors in Bethlehem Steel's decision to adopt this policy. The Bethlehem Steel ERP would never have existed if not for World War I. The company kept the plan after the emergency ended, but emasculated its provisions in order to use it as an anti-union weapon and public relations device.

Charles M. Schwab, born in 1862, took control of the Bethlehem Steel Corporation in 1904. Schwab's father ran a livery stable in Loretto, Pennsylvania. He started his business career at age seventeen, moving to Braddock, Pennsylvania, to work as a store clerk and bookeeper at grocery store. Bored by this kind of work, he took a job at the local steel mill—the Edgar Thomson Works of the Carnegie Steel Company—in the engineering corps as a surveyor's helper. In this capacity, he helped build blast furnaces, cranes and other equipment for the plant. At the age of nineteen, Schwab became chief engineer of the plant and assistant to the general manager. In 1886, Andrew Carnegie made him general superintendent of the Homestead works. In 1889, Schwab became general superintendent of the Edgar Thomson works in Braddock after his predecessor, Captain Bill Jones, died in a blast furnace accident. In 1893, Schwab returned to Homestead because Carnegie thought he was the right man to deal with the continuing labor problems there. In 1897, Schwab became president of Carnegie Steel and continued to serve in this capacity until the formation of U.S. Steel in 1901. Schwab was the first President of U.S. Steel, but he resigned that position in 1903 because of tensions on the Board of Directors.[51] From here, he went on to organize the Bethlehem Steel Corporation.

Before Schwab, Bethlehem Steel had been a small producer of specialty steel. Under Schwab's leadership, the firm diversified and grew quickly. In 1905, it controlled .2% of total steel production in the industry. By the end of World War I, Bethlehem's share of total steel production rose to 5.1%, thereby making it the second largest steel manufacturer in the world behind U.S. Steel. During the war years, earnings at Bethlehem Steel increased even faster than those at U.S. Steel because it did the best job in the industry of securing allied war orders. Schwab picked his partners the same way Andrew Carnegie did, trying to encourage self-made men. "There is not a man in power at our Bethlehem steel works to-day," wrote Schwab in 1917, "who did not begin at the bottom and work his way up, round by round, simply by using his head and his hands a little more effectively than the men beside him."[52] A 1915 article in the *New York Herald* introduced Schwab's protégés as "the Beth Boys" and explained "that for most of them the journey from their apprenticeship to their present high station has been so brief and the pace so rapid that they have had no time to show themselves or to inform the public of their existence. They have been engrossed with the work in hand to the exclusion of all other considerations."[53]

Due to its small number of plants, Bethlehem Steel was particularly vulnerable to strikes because each plant produced a high percentage of the company's total output. The 1910 strike by machinists and electricians at Bethlehem's flagship South Bethlehem, Pennsylvania, plant was the worst strike in the industry since 1901. In April and May 1918, these same employees conducted a series of strikes to protest the piece work system under which they were paid as well as the refusal of management to bargain collectively with them. Although only 440 striking electricians and 2,309 striking machinists out of a possible 7,000 walked off the job initially, operations at the plant ground to a halt, much as they did when many of the same workers had struck in 1910. Because the South Bethlehem plant did almost nothing but make ordnance for the Army and Navy at that time, the Wilson administration deemed the dispute a threat to vital war production and quickly turned it over to the National War Labor Board (NWLB), a government agency created to settle labor disputes in war industries. Work resumed at the plant pending the Board's decision.[54]

The NWLB's decision, rendered on July 31st, 1918, called for major changes in the company's labor policy. The Board mandated a guaranteed minimum wage and overtime pay for all the workers in the South Bethlehem facility. More importantly, this decision, like 226 other decisions handed down by the NWLB, required that collective bargaining under a shop committee system be established throughout the plant. Because this aspect of the decision also applied to the entire labor force, ordinary steelworkers in South Bethlehem would have some semblance of collective bargaining for the first time in their history. However, the nature of the new collective bargaining relationship became the subject of a sharp dispute between management and the government. It was the general policy of the National War Labor Board that "if an employer is to deal collectively with representative groups of his employees, it is essential that the desires of the employees should be known and be given at least equal weight with those of the employers." The plan that the board tried to implement in South Bethlehem took this idea seriously. It established a six member local mediation and conciliation board made up of three management and three worker representatives, with the right of employees to appeal decisions to the NWLB guaranteed. Furthermore, employees had the right to grieve compensation rates, which would be set by an NWLB examiner rather than management.[55]

Bethlehem Steel had no intention of letting outsiders wield so much power over its operations. Rather than openly defy the NWLB's decision, the firm decided to delay its implementation because it did not desire a direct confrontation with the government during wartime. When employees complained to the Board in September 1918 that its order was not being carried out, the NWLB cabled company president Eugene Grace for a response. In a face-to-face meeting with the Board two days later, Grace agreed to abide by the NWLB's order if the firm could get permission to increase prices. This would pay for the wage increases required by the decision. The Board accepted this arrangement because it feared that continued noncompliance by Bethlehem would result in other parties involved in future disputes not taking its decisions seriously. Bethlehem Steel wanted to undermine this arrangement from the outset. It began to design a new plan immediately after the Board's order. Management wanted this new representation scheme to satisfy the NWLB but prevent genuine collective bargaining from taking place.[56]

The firm employed Mackenzie King as a confidential advisor for this project. King accepted this assignment because he believed that the adoption of employee representation by a company the size of Bethlehem Steel would contribute to the popularity of this idea among other large companies. In the many employee representation schemes he helped create, King used suggestions from management to adapt each plan to a company's circumstances. In many cases, the structure and practices of each firm were tailored by individual managers in order for the plan to gain their support. The management of Bethlehem Steel was much more concerned about maintaining control of its human capital than management had been at CF&I. "We discuss matters, but we never vote," Charles M. Schwab once remarked. "I will not permit myself to be in the position of having the labor dictate to the management." This attitude created a conflict between King and his client. According to H.M. Gitelman, who examined Mackenzie King's papers for his study of CF&I, "By the time he left Bethlehem, King was sufficiently troubled not to want to return," probably because "he sensed Grace and his colleagues had no intention of seriously consulting with or listening to their employees."[57] This attitude violated the guiding principle of employee representation; namely, giving workers a voice over the conditions in which they labored.

On a superficial level, the employee representation plan King helped to create resembled the one at CF&I in many ways. The first sections of the plan outlined the election procedure and how representatives were to be allocated across the divisions of the plant. As was the case with CF&I, the plan mandated the appointment of a management representative to serve as a liaison between the representatives and management. The Bethlehem plan also included a similar committee structure and provisions for regular conferences between representatives and management. But there were also significant structural differences between the Colorado Fuel & Iron and Bethlehem plans. For example, although CF&I employees could bring grievances to outside arbitration (and actually did at least once), no higher authority than the president of the company existed under the Bethlehem plan. Furthermore, while CF&I allowed any employee to initiate a meeting at which he could present grievances, no Bethlehem Steel meeting could be held without the approval of management, and only employee representatives could address such a gathering. When finally presented with the company's version of employee representation in September 1918, the NWLB found the plan "undemocratic in principle, and likely to prove unsatisfactory in practice," citing, among other reasons, the traits of the plan described above. In October and November, NWLB examiners began conducting shop committee elections throughout the departments of the South Bethlehem plant. They did this under the arrangements designed by the Board with the full cooperation of Bethlehem's management. The trade union members at the plant "converted the NWLB shop committee into a *de facto* union." At the same time, however, Bethlehem Steel introduced its own plan at all of its steel plants outside the NWLB's jurisdiction, i.e. every facility *except* for South Bethlehem, in order to head off government efforts to institute NWLB-style plans in those facilities.[58]

After the Armistice was signed on November 11th, 1918, the company's attitude towards the NWLB-instituted representation plan changed dramatically. Management had tolerated it during the war; now it held only perfunctory meetings with the committees that were elected under the Board's supervision. In a conversation with the NWLB's examiner on November 17th, Grace declared the Board's authority "dead," and suggested that the committee system be supplanted by the collective bargaining scheme worked out by the company. On November 19th, NWLB examiners in the plant announced a finding in favor of the workers in the machine shop at South Bethlehem. Grace refused to implement it. On December 6th, he sent the Board a letter informing it that with the exception of distributing funds put up by the War and Navy Departments to laid off employees, Bethlehem Steel would no longer implement NWLB directives because its authority had expired with the cessation of hostilities. At the same time, Grace wrote the Board asking it to withdraw its examiners. The joint chairmen of the War Labor Board, one of whom was former President William Howard Taft, sent Grace an indignant response:

> You personally agreed to the installation of a system of collective bargaining satisfactory to the Board, and under the supervision of the Board's examiners. You now repudiate that system. . . .
>
> This is a question of the good faith of your company and of the Government itself. If the award of the Board should now be repudiated, your workmen would have every right to feel they had been deceived and grossly imposed upon by your company, by the War Labor Board, and by the other officials of the Government who prevailed upon them to remain at work on the assurance that they would be justly dealt with.

The NWLB's chairmen released these letters to the press in an effort to pressure Bethlehem Steel to reacknowledge the authority of the Board. However, the company accepted this temporary public relations setback because of the importance it attributed to maintaining control over its employees.[59]

The potential for government action during the war emergency had kept Bethlehem Steel from openly defying the administration. "Had the war continued," the former secretary to the NWLB later wrote, "and had the War Department been unable to carry out the decision of the

National War Labor Board through the agency of the Bethlehem Steel Corporation, the plants of the Bethlehem Company would have undoubtedly been commandeered."[60] After the war, Bethlehem Steel flouted the government with impunity (even though the NWLB still had legal standing) because the political will to enforce the Board's decisions had disappeared. The company started to lay off trade unionists elected as shop representatives under the Board's plan in the weeks following the Armistice. At an NWLB hearing in January 1919, a lawyer for Bethlehem Steel reiterated its position that the only obligation the company was willing to assume under the award was to distribute government funds as back wages. This was, in fact, the only part of the award that was ever implemented in full. After the NWLB dissolved, Bethlehem Steel introduced its version of employee representation to the South Bethlehem plant in January 1920, the same plan rejected by the Board during the war. Management introduced almost identical systems into all the various companies it acquired during the 1920s and 1930s.[61]

The company claimed that the plan was a great success everywhere. For instance, a booklet published by the company and distributed at its Sparrow's Point, Maryland, plant claimed:

> The Plan of Employees' Representation which was introduced voluntarily by Management at the Maryland Plant in October 1918, through the distribution of descriptive booklets was received enthusiastically by the employees. . . . The plan was accepted in good faith, the concensus [sic] of opinion being that it was a big step in the right direction to bring Management and Employees in closer relationship on matters of mutual interest.[62]

A 1921 press release, which described the details of the plan to the general public for the first time, tallied the number of cases settled and man-hours spent in meetings, asserting "earnest and sympathetic management and the confidence of employees are two factors that have contributed to the success of the plan."[63] In his introduction to "Ten Years of Progress in Human Relations," a company pamphlet celebrating the plan's tenth anniversary, President Grace declared, "The record of the intervening years is full of accomplishment. To recite all of the work done is obviously impossible, nor is it necessary, for its real worth as measured by its practical results is understood better by Bethlehem employees than it could possibly be described in these pages."[64]

Not all workers at Bethlehem Steel agreed with these assessments. Some longtime Bethlehem employees interviewed by Harvey O'Connor in 1935 claimed they had never heard of the company union until 1925 or 1926. Those workers who were aware of the plan distrusted management's motives for implementing it. An administrator for the National War Labor Board who interviewed employees at Bethlehem Steel's Lebanon, Pennsylvania, plant found that the few workers who actually understood how the plan operated "believed it was a method adopted by the Company for destroying the local union."[65] When the editor of the magazine *Labor Age* interviewed employees at the Bethlehem Steel's Lackawanna, New York, plant shortly after the firm implemented the plan there, employees offered comments like, "Put in to kid us," "Too much boss—not enough union," and "Real complaints can't be got across."[66] The leaders of the National Committee for Organizing Iron and Steel Workers, scared off by the existence of the plan, did not call Bethlehem out on strike when the great 1919 strike began. In response, they received an urgent plea from union representatives at every Bethlehem plant to extend the strike to their employer. After management refused to negotiate with the National Committee, citing the existence of the ERP as its main reason, the union quickly organized a walkout. When the 1919 strike finally reached Bethlehem Steel, 50,000 workers stayed away on the first day.[67]

After the employers put down the 1919 strike and government interest in the steel industry's labor relations waned, Bethlehem Steel used the employee representation plan to perpetuate the open shop at its facilities. According to one Bethlehem employee interviewed by investigators for the Interchurch World Movement, "on all questions of minor importance and of 'general welfare' the company was willing to agree, but on major issues the collective bargaining plan was a farce."[68] This tendency on the part of management applied particularly well to compensation issues. As an anonymous employee representative explained to the author Robert W. Dunn, "Wages are a thing you never hear discussed under the plan, although there is a subcommittee supposed to deal with that subject. You cannot bring them up at a general committee meeting. Motions for wage increases are passed along to subcommittees and as a rule die there, or are recommended back as impossible." The company initiated most of the actions actually taken under the plan, like the meeting called in 1932 to pass an "appropriate resolution" honoring Chairman Schwab on his seventieth birthday. By limiting substantive discussion, Dunn argued, "The workers of the more militant sort become disgusted with the plan. They cease to bring real grievances to the joint committee, knowing they will be sidetracked and meet with no satisfaction. The representatives become more 'constructive' and colorless."[69] In this manner, it would have been possible for the plan to have appeared successful in addressing grievances during the early years of its operation, even though the real demands of Bethlehem Steel employees were not being considered. The plan did, however, appear to help stop unions from gaining a foothold within Bethlehem Steel. This factor, above all else, made the plan popular when the remaining holdouts in the industry were forced by the passage of the National Industrial Recovery Act in 1933 to institute employee representation arrangements of their own.

Employee Representation at Other Steel Firms Before the New Deal

Many firms besides Bethlehem and Colorado Fuel & Iron faced employee strife during World War I. A few of them adapted employee representation schemes at that time, before they became a fixture in the industry during the New Deal. Like the firms described above, these companies did so largely under pressure from the government and successful organizing on the part of workers. The Midvale Steel & Ordnance Company became the object of a National War Labor Board case after a strike by machinists in June 1918. The question then, wrote William Brown Dickson, was "Shall we jump or wait to be pushed?" Midvale implemented an employee representation scheme (in consultation with officials at CF&I) over a two week period in late September 1918, before the National War Labor Board even rendered a decision.[70] "We recognize the right of wage-earners to bargain collectively with their employers," wrote A.C. Dinkey, the president of the firm, in a notice posted at each of Midvale's plants. He went on to invite employees to meet with management in order to formulate an employee representation plan "which shall be thoroughly democratic and entirely free from interference by the Companies, or any official or agent thereof." Midvale Steel took such decisive action in order to prevent the possible forced recognition of the machinists union in its mills. In a brief before the NWLB, the company made this attitude perfectly clear:

> We here and now express our willingness to perfect the present plan in any way that will secure fair bargaining directly with our own employees as such without regard to any organization, union or otherwise, that they may belong to. As we would not care to treat with such of them as belonged to the Presbyterian or Catholic churches through the church organization, or with such of them as are Eagles or Elks through those lodges, so we object to treating with union men through the Union organization. We dread the outside interests that would necessarily enter into such negotiations.

As at Bethlehem, important structural limitations on bargaining were written into the plan; grievances from non-representatives could only be submitted in writing, and arbitration could only occur if the company and the employees agreed on an arbitrator. Also like Bethlehem, Midvale used the ERP to justify the open shop, citing its presence as the reason not to meet with the National Committee for Organizing Iron and Steel Workers in the months preceding the 1919 strike.[71]

Unlike Bethlehem, Midvale's employee representation plan actually met with acceptance from the National War Labor Board. The underlying reason for the Board's approval was that Midvale Steel did not share Bethlehem's contempt for the idea of employee input. As an NWLB examiner sent to report on the operation of the Midvale plan observed, "The Committee seems to enjoy entire freedom of action in its dealings with the management. I have seen the Committee at work in conference with the General Manager of the plant and have noted its independence and persistency in presenting [the] claims of the men." Despite this relative freedom, workers did not respond enthusiastically to the Midvale plan. "All along, the men have been suspicious of it," reported one former employee. "They thought the company had to put it in because the war labor board said they had to get some sort of system started to keep the work going steadily during the war." Even management agreed with this assessment. "[M]any men viewed [the plan] with suspicion and some do yet, believing it a scheme to exclude unionism," explained H.D. Booth, the General Superintendent of Midvale's Nicetown, Pennsylvania, plant. "The union leaders ridicule the plan, but then we have had very little unionism in our plant—ours is an open shop." From management's perspective, as long as this condition was met, the plan was a success. But when the National Committee used the plan as a successful organizing tool at Johnstown before and during the 1919 strike, Midvale management lost interest in it.[72]

The Lukens Steel Company's experience with employee representation resembled that of Midvale Steel. The firm implemented its plan in September 1918 "under earnest pressure of President Wilson," but after the war both labor and management lost their enthusiasm for the scheme. In 1921, Charles Lukens Huston, the vice-president of the company, candidly informed the Manager of the Open Shop Department for the National Association of Manufacturers that "many of the men [do not wish] to be elected upon the Board of Representatives, and those who are elected [find] difficulty in arranging for constructive suggestions." Huston's frequent requests to industrial relations investigators not to publicize the existence of employee representation at the company's lone Coatesville, Pennsylvania, plant show that management never considered the plan anything more than an experiment. In 1923, Huston wrote that this experiment "has not resulted in anything satisfactory, or constructive . . . mostly . . . complaints and requests made by the men, most of which the representative committee, elected by secret ballot by the men themselves, found too unreasonable to submit, and the few that they did have to pass through and submit to save their face, were not of a character that commended themselves to the management." By 1924, Huston reported that the plan "was basically a dead letter."[73]

In order to evaluate the effectiveness of employee representation in the entire steel industry, it is necessary to broaden the discussion and consider these organizations in American industry overall. In 1921, Sherman Rogers, the industrial correspondent for *The Outlook* wrote an article entitled "Employee Representation: Success or Failure?" Citing anecdotal evidence from companies across the United States, he agreed with one manager who believed this new idea in industrial relations was "the greatest possible success." Still, he recognized a number of companies that had employee representation schemes forced on them by the War Labor Board during the war had already eliminated them and declared the idea a failure. According to Rogers, "These plants never tried it out fairly. Most of them did not hold a council meeting. Those that did entered into the arrangement with the enthusiasm of cold-storage oysters, and of course the results were very unfavorable. . . . It is quite natural that the system failed under those conditions."[74] Employee representation lasted longer in the steel industry than in some of the other industries subject to the War Labor Board's authority, but firms which stuck with the idea, like Bethlehem and Lukens, received an unenthusiastic response from their employees because they did not believe in the fundamental principle of employee representation: listening to their employees. These firms designed and implemented their ERPs in such a way so as to prevent their employees from exercising enough authority to encroach upon their control.

Colorado Fuel & Iron was an exception. As Ben Selekman concluded in his exhaustive study of the operation of this firm's ERP in its steel plant, "under the plan the men of the Minnequa Steel Works secured such important gains as the actual eight-hour day, an opportunity to participate in revising wage scales, a method of presenting and discussing grievances, and a greater degree of security in their jobs through enjoying the right of appeal to higher officials against the decisions of foremen and superintendents."[75] The company implemented most of these changes in order to compete with the United Mine Workers. CF&I extended these reforms to the steel plant as an afterthought. If it had no mining division, there would have been no Ludlow Massacre and Rockefeller never would have gotten involved in the steel plant's affairs. It would been run under nonunion principles similar to the rest of the industry. At other steel firms, management's desire for the freedom to control the effectiveness of their company unions prevented these organizations from bringing about real reform.

The juxtaposition of hours reform and employee representation demonstrates that steelworkers could not generate enough pressure on their own to bring about more than cosmetic changes in their terms and conditions of their employment. Hours reform became a reality only when the federal government inserted itself into the industrial relations system of the steel industry during World War I. With reference to employee representation, even wartime did not motivate the government to force steel companies like Bethlehem to make major changes in the way they managed their labor. Yet employee representation during the Teens and Twenties was not just another example of steel manufacturers getting the best of their employees. By creating employee representation plans, steel companies tacitly admitted that steelworkers should be consulted with regard to their working conditions, no matter how limited employee influence happened to be. Writing in 1927 in reference to the employees of Bethlehem Steel, a correspondent for *Labor Age* recognized the potential significance of company unions for the future:

> They are presented with this employer-created organization. It does not mean much. It gives them little. But it does this at least: It gives

> these poor deluded employees in very many instances the idea that organization is a needed thing, for the employers themselves have recognized that in forming these company groups. The employer has said, by his act, that there is value in organization. Even though it be his creature, as it always is, this organization is a standing proof of his fear of workers' real unionization. It shows a fear of an organization of their own choosing.[76]

In the late-1930s, steel workers would try to use these organizations as launching pads for the permanent unionization of the industry.

Because it had many other effective weapons with which to fight organized labor, U.S. Steel never faced serious pressure from organized labor during the war years. And even though U.S. Steel ceded to government demands to shorten its hours, the NWLB never threatened the firm's open shop policy because no labor disputes existed for the Board to mediate. This explains why the Corporation could safely reject employee representation at the same time firms like Colorado Fuel & Iron and Bethlehem Steel championed the idea. Always concerned with maintaining authority over employees, Elbert Gary believed employee representation was "only the beginning of a full and thorough unionization of the industry and that step by step it will lead up to the final and forcible control of the business and final division and distribution of the property."[77] U.S. Steel and most of the rest of the industry required additional government pressures brought on by the Depression before they embraced the idea of employee representation and made it a central part of their labor policies.

Notes

1. Donald Wilhelm, "'The Big Business' Man as a Social Worker," *The Outlook* 107 (22 August 1914): 1005.

2. Jonathan Rees, "Managing the Mills: Labor Policy in the American Steel Industry, 1892-1937," Ph.D. Diss., University of Wisconsin–Madison, 1997, 42-43.

3. The 55 volumes of testimony and exhibits generated by this suit are an excellent source of information on every aspect of U.S. Steel's business activities. See District Court of the United States for the District of New Jersey,

"United States of America v. United States Steel Corporation," October Term, 1914.

4. John A. Garraty, "The United States Steel Corporation Versus Labor: The Early Years," *Labor History* 1 (Winter 1960): 3; Thomas K. McCraw and Forest Reinhardt, "Losing to Win: U.S. Steel's Pricing Investment Decisions and Market Share, 1901-1938," *Journal of Economic History* 49, (September 1989): 598, 603, 610-13.

5. Naomi R. Lamoreaux, *The Great Merger Movement in American Business* (New York: Cambridge University Press, 1985), 180-81.

6. William Brown Dickson to W.E. Corey, January 26, 1910, William Brown Dickson Papers, Box 2, Historical Collections & Labor Archives, Pattee Library, Pennsylvania State University, State College, PA.

7. Dickson to Andrew Carnegie, April 2, 1914, William Brown Dickson Papers, Box 6.

8. Elbert Gary, "Address at Annual Meeting of the American Iron and Steel Institute," May 28, 1920, 9.

9. Sidney Fine, *Laissez Faire and the General-Welfare State* (Ann Arbor: University of Michigan Press, 1956), 30.

10. Jesse S. Robinson, *The Amalgamated Association of Iron, Steel and Tin Workers* (Baltimore: The Johns Hopkins Press, 1920), 106-07; United States Commissioner of Labor, *Report on Conditions of Employment in the Iron and Steel Industry in the United States*, Vol. 3, Senate Document No. 110, 62nd Cong., 1st Sess., 159; Horace B. Drury, "The Three-Shift System in the Steel Industry," *Bulletin of the Taylor Society* 6 (February 1921): 3.

11. Charles Hill, "Fighting the Twelve-Hour Day in the American Steel Industry," *Labor History* 15 (Winter 1974): 21-22; John A. Fitch, "Old Age at Forty," *The American Magazine* 71 (March 1911): 656.

12. Gerald Eggert, *Steelmasters and Labor Reform 1886-1923* (Pittsburgh: University of Pittsburgh Press, 1981), 24, 29, 17-18, 47-57; John A. Fitch, "The Long Day," *The Survey* 45 (5 March 1921): 796.

13. David R. Roediger and Philip S. Foner, *Our Own Time* (New York: Greenwood Press, 1989), 222; Hill, 24; Interchurch World Movement, *Report on the Steel Strike of 1919* (New York: Harcourt, Brace and Howe, 1920), 84.

14. John A. Fitch, "A Confession of Helplessness," *The Survey* 50, 15 June 1923, 321.

15. U.S. Congress, House, *Hearings Before the Committee on Investigation of United States Steel Corporation*, [Stanley Committee Hearings] (in 8 Vols.), 62nd Cong., 2nd Sess., 1911-12, 1307; *New York Call*, 24 September 1919.

16. United States Steel Corporation, "Statement as to Wages, Hours and Other Conditions of Labor Among Employees," 1914, 2.

17. John A. Fitch, "Hours of Labor in the Steel Industry," Boston, 1912, 17.

18. Elbert Gary, "Statement by Elbert H. Gary Chairman, United States Steel Corporation at Annual Meeting," United States Steel Corporation, April 17, 1922, 12.

19. U.S. Congress, Senate, Committee on Education and Labor, *Investigation of Strike in Steel Industries*, 66th Cong., 1st Sess., 1919, 160.

20. Marshall Olds, *Analysis of the Interchurch World Movement Report on the Steel Strike* (New York: G.P. Putnam's Son's, 1923), 231.

21. Elbert H. Gary, "Address of the President," *Year Book of the American Iron and Steel Institute*, 1923, 13.

22. William R. Jones quoted in James Howard Bridge, *The Inside History of the Carnegie Steel Company* (Pittsburgh: University of Pittsburgh Press, 1991/Originally published by the Aldine Book Company, 1903), 110.

23. John A. Fitch, *The Steel Workers* (Pittsburgh: University of Pittsburgh Press, 1989/Originally published by the Russell Sage Foundation, 1911), 95.

24. Horace Drury, "The Technique of Changing from the Two-Shift to the Three-Shift System in the Steel Industry," Report to the Cabot Fund, Boston, May, 1922, 17, 14; "Experience of Colorado Fuel & Iron Co. Under 8-Hour Day," *Monthly Labor Review* 17, August 1923, 405.

25. Bradley Stoughton, "Comparison of Two-Shift and Three-Shift Operations in the Iron and Steel Industry," *Journal of Personnel Research* 1 (September 1922): 235.

26. *Conditions of Employment in the Iron and Steel Industry*, Vol. 3, 161.

27. Horace Drury to Morris L. Cooke, January 15, 1921, Morris L. Cooke Papers, Box 179, Franklin D. Roosevelt Library, Hyde Park, NY; Drury to Cooke, January 6, 1921, Cooke Papers, Box 179.

28. Drury to Cooke, January 10, 1921, Cooke Papers, Box 179.

29. Charles A. Gulick, *Labor Policy of the United States Steel Corporation*, Columbia University Studies in History Economics and Public Law, Vol. 116, 1924, 40; Hill, 26-32; American Iron and Steel Institute, "Report of the American Iron and Steel Institute Committee on Proposed Total Elimination of the Twelve-Hour Day," May 25, 1923. "Wages and Hours of Labor," *Monthly Labor Review* 17 (July 1923): 92.

30. Harding to Gary, June 18, 1923 in American Iron and Steel Institute, "Twelve-Hour Day: Letters Between the President of the United States and American Iron and Steel Institute," July 6, 1923.

31. Paul U. Kellogg, "Shapers of Things," Remarks at Silver Anniversary Dinner of Survey Associates Inc., n.d., 10, William Brown Dickson Papers, Box 5; Hill, 32-34.

32. Drury, "The Three-Shift System in the Steel Industry," 10-12, 40.

33. United States Bureau of Labor Statistics, "Productivity of Labor in Merchant Blast Furnaces," *Bulletin of the U.S. Bureau of Labor Statistics*, No. 474, December 1928, 46-47.

34. S. Adele Shaw, "Now That Jerry Has Time to Live," *The Survey* 52 (1 September 1924): 568-70.

35. Bradley Stoughton, *The Metallurgy of Iron and Steel*, 4th Ed. (New York: McGraw-Hill Book Company, 1934), 46.

36. Ernest Richmond Burton, *Employee Representation* (Baltimore: The Williams & Wilkins Company, 1926), 19. For more on the origins of employee representation in America, see Burton, 25-44; Carroll E. French, "The Shop Committee in the United States," Ph.D. Diss., The Johns Hopkins University, 1922, (Baltimore: Johns Hopkins Press, 1923), 15-32.

37. Daniel Nelson, "The Company Union Movement, 1900-1937: A Reexamination," *Business History Review* 56 (Autumn, 1982): 336.

38. H. Lee Scamehorn, *Mill & Mine: The CF&I in the Twentieth Century* (Lincoln: University of Nebraska Press, 1992), 1-2; Ben M. Selekman, *Employes' Representation in Steel Works* (New York: Russell Sage Foundation, 1924), 37.

39. An enormous amount of material has been written on the Ludlow Massacre. Recent accounts include: Priscilla Long, "The Voice of the Gun," *Labor's Heritage* 1 (October 1989): 4-23; H.M. Gitelman, *Legacy of the Ludlow Massacre* (Philadelphia: University of Pennsylvania Press, 1988), 17-20; Scamehorn, 45-46.

40. *Colorado Fuel and Iron Industrial Bulletin*, October 1915.

41. CF&I consolidated the plan in the steel works with that of the mines in 1921. The old and new plans still remained essentially the same. See Selekman, 257-74.

42. Colorado Fuel and Iron Company, "Plan of Representation of Employes of the Colorado Fuel and Iron Company in the Company's Minnequa Steel Works," Rockefeller Family Archive, Office of the Messrs. Rockefeller, Rockefeller Archives Center, North Tarrytown, NY, Box 25 [Also see Selekman, 237-56]; *Denver Post*, 6 June 1918.

43. Plan of Representation of Employees," 3.

44. John A. Fitch, "Two Years of the Rockefeller Plan," *The Survey* 39 (6 October 1917): 18-20, 15; John D. Rockefeller Jr. to E.H. Weitzel, March 13, 1916, Rockefeller Family Archive, Office of the Messrs. Rockefeller, Box 15.

45. John D. Rockefeller, Jr. to J.H. Welborn, December 23, 1919, Office of the Messrs. Rockefeller, Box 15.

46. J.F. Welborn to All Superintendents, April 15, 1921, Industrial Representation Plan Collection, Colorado Fuel and Iron Archives, Pueblo, CO.

47. See Richard B. Freeman and James L. Medoff, *What Do Unions Do?* (New York: Basic Books, 1984), 7-11, 14-16.

48. Ben M. Selekman and Mary Van Kleeck, *Employes' Representation in Coal Mines*, (New York: Russell Sage Foundation, 1924), 37; "Memorandum of Agreement Respecting Employment, Living and Working Conditions," in Selekman and Van Kleeck, 414.

Selekman and Van Kleeck do not take these expressions of interest in making the plan work on behalf of employees seriously. Having seen many case reports for grievances growing out of the operation of the plan, I am more inclined to take Welborn and Rockefeller at their word.

49. Selekman, 85-86, 155-56.

50. Hogle, 330; In the Matter of the Colorado Fuel and Iron Corporation and the International Union of Mine Mill and Smelter Workers . . . and Steel Workers Organizing Committee, March 29, 1940, 22 N.L.R.B., No. 14.

51. Robert Hessen, "Charles M. Schwab," in *Iron and Steel in the Twentieth Century*, Bruce E. Seely, ed. (Brucolli Clark Layman, 1994), 378-88. For more on Schwab, see Robert Hessen, *Steel Titan: The Life of Charles M. Schwab* (New York: Oxford University Press, 1975).

52. Bethlehem Steel Corporation, "Review of the Commercial and Manufacturing Development of Bethlehem Steel Company, 1905-1940," July 26, 1941, Bethlehem Steel Corporation Papers, Box 17, Hagley Museum and Library, Wilmington, DE; Melvin I. Urofsky, *Big Steel and the Wilson Administration* (Columbus; Ohio State University Press, 1969), 229-30; Charles M. Schwab, *Succeeding With What You Have* (New York: The Century Company, 1917), 6-7.

53. *New York Herald*, 27 September 1915.

54. "Review of Testimony of Bethlehem Steel Case," June 26, 1918, Records of the National War Labor Board, Docket No. 22, Record Group 2, National Archives and Records Administration, Suitland, MD; In the Matter of Bethlehem Steel Corporation . . . and Steel Workers Organizing Committee, August 14, 1939, 14 N.L.R.B. No. 44, 547-48.

55. U.S. Congress, House, Committee on Claims, *Claims of Certain Employees of Bethlehem Steel Co.*, 67th Cong., 2nd Sess., 1922, 6; Joseph Anthony McCartin, "Labor's 'Great War': American Workers, Unions, and the State, 1916-1920," Ph.D. Diss., State University of New York at Binghamton, 1990, 102; William Leavitt Stoddard, *The Shop Committee* (New York: Macmillan, 1920), 29-30; John A. Henderson, "A statement to the workers . . . ," October 9, 1918, Records of the National War Labor Board, Docket No. 22; Lucian W. Chaney, "Methods of Procedure for Determining Classifications and Rates and Making Other Adjustments," November 1918, Records of the National War Labor Board, Docket No. 22.

56. *Claims*, 23-24, 37; McCartin, 338-40.

57. Gitelman, 189, 253-254; *They Told Barron*, Arthur Pound and Samuel Taylor Moore eds. (New York: Harper and Brothers, 1930), 82.

58. Bethlehem Steel Corporation, "Representation of Employees in the Plants of the Bethlehem Steel Corporation," October 1918; "Collective Bargaining," n.d., Records of the National War Labor Board, Docket No. 22; W.B. Woods, "Statement Regarding Administration of the Bethlehem Award," December

21, 1918, Records of the National War Labor Board, Docket No. 22, 2; McCartin, 346; 14 N.L.R.B. No. 44, 549-56.

59. *Claims*, 48; W.B. Woods, "Memo On Bethlehem Situation," November 17, 1918, Records of the National War Labor Board, Docket No. 22.

60. *Claims*, 111.

61. Dave Williams to Jett Lauck, March 3, 1919, Records of the National War Labor Board, Docket No. 22; McCartin, 355; "Employees vs. Bethlehem Steel Company," January 15, 1919, Records of the National War Labor Board, Docket No. 22; 14 N.L.R.B. No. 44, 558, 578.

62. Bethlehem Steel Corporation, "Employees Representation," 1919, 70.

63. Untitled Bethlehem Steel press release, January 28, 1921, Ivy Lee Papers, Box 47, Seeley G. Mudd Library, Princeton University, Princeton, NJ.

64. Bethlehem Steel Company, "Ten Years' Progress in Human Relations," 1928, 5.

65. Harvey O'Connor, "Notes From Bethlehem," May 17-18, 1935, Harvey O'Connor Collection, Box 22, Archives of Labor and Urban Affairs, Walter P. Reuther Library, Wayne State University, Detroit, MI; F.H. Bird, "Report on Shop Committee System Bethlehem Steel Company, Lebanon Plant, Lebanon, Pa.," February 13, 1919, 2, Records of the National War Labor Board, Docket No. 22.

66. Louis Francis Budenz, "Bethlehem Bunk at Lackawanna," *Labor Age* 15 (September 1926):16.

67. David J. Saposs, "History of the National Committee," 1-15, David J. Saposs Papers, Box 10, State Historical Society of Wisconsin, Madison, WI; *New York Call*, 30 September 1919.

68. Mary Senior, "Interview w/ J.W. Hendricks," Bethlehem, Pennsylvania, August 23, [1920], David J. Saposs Papers, Box 26.

69. Robert W. Dunn, *Company Unions* (New York: Vanguard Press, 1927), 86, 88; Norborne Berkeley, Assistant to the President, "To All Departments," February 8, 1932, Bethlehem Steel Corporation Papers, Box 1.

70. Dickson quoted in Raymond L. Hogler, "Worker Participation, Employer Anti-Unionism, and Labor Law: The Case of the Steel Industry, 1918-1937," *Hofstra Labor Law Journal* 7 (Fall 1989): 16; Eggert, 109-13.

71. Midvale Steel and Ordnance Company, "Plan of Representation of Employes," October 1, 1918, 4, 28-30; Midvale Steel and Ordinance Company, Brief Before a Section of the National War Labor Board, n.d., 16-17, Records of the National War Labor Board, Docket No. 129; Saposs, "History of the National Committee," 18-19.

72. Eggert, 121-24, 136-39; John O'Brien, "Machinists and Toolmakers vs. Midvale Steel and Ordnance Company, Nicetown (Philadelphia) Pa.," March 22, 1919, Records of the National War Labor Board, Docket No. 129; [John O'Brien], "Detailed Survey of Plan of Representation of the Midvale Steel & Ordnance Company," February 25, 1919, 11, 3, William Brown Dickson Pa-

pers, Box 7, Historical Collections & Labor Archives, Pattee Library, Pennsylvania State University, State College, PA.

The Midvale plan was reborn as the Bethlehem plan when Bethlehem Steel bought Midvale's Coatesville and Cambria plants in 1923.

73. Charles Lukens Huston to Burton R. Morley, March 15, 1924, Lukens Iron and Steel Company Papers, Box 1991, Hagley Museum and Library, Wilmington, DE; Charles Lukens Huston to Noel Sargent, November 22, 1921, Lukens Iron and Steel Company Papers, Box 1991; Charles Lukens Huston to Mary Smith, March 14, 1923, Lukens Iron and Steel Company Papers, Box 1991.

74. Sherman Rogers, "Industrial Representation: Success or Failure?," *The Outlook* 128 (31 August 1921): 691.

75. Selekman, 233.

76. William J. Griffiths, "The Silver Lining," *Labor Age* 16 (April 1927): 4.

77. United States Steel Corporation, "Remarks by Elbert H. Gary at Luncheon to Doctor Takuma Dan," December 9, 1921, 12.

Chapter Six

Fighting Organized Labor Under the Iron and Steel Code, 1933-1935

> What are we to do? Is section 7A being put into effect? Or is the steel industry not included? I have a vague feeling that the steel trust has plenty to do with it. Why? Because it seems that every time we organize we are attacked and dispersed like a bunch of whipped dogs.
>
> —Dominico Del Turco, steelworker,
> in a letter to Franklin D. Roosevelt, 1935.[1]

"In my long association with the steel industry," announced American Iron and Steel Institute President (and Bethlehem Steel Chairman) Charles M. Schwab on October 25th, 1929, "I have never known it to enjoy a greater stability or more promising outlook than it does today."[2] From August 1928 through July 1929, steel production surpassed that of any previous twelve-month period in the industry's history. Profits had not been so high since the boom years of World War I. Four days after Schwab's speech, the stock market crashed. Nevertheless, the titular leader of the steel industry remained optimistic. Addressing the Illinois Manufacturers Association in December 1929, Schwab argued "Steel's three biggest customers, the automobile, railroad and building industries, seem to me to justify a healthy outlook. We are a growing country and in addition to normal growth, which the Wall Street affair cannot seriously retard, the replacement factor alone in these industries furnishes a very substantial market for them and for ourselves."[3] At first, Schwab's continued optimism seemed justified. The year 1930 witnessed a mild recovery. Total production of finished steel was down over 25%

from the previous year, but this was still close to the average output for the industry over the previous ten years. Yet as the Depression deepened, steel production declined further. By 1932, total production had dropped from 40,597,000 gross tons of finished steel to 9,950,000. In late-1932 and early-1933, the industry operated at just 15% of its capacity. Total losses for steel companies that publicly reported profits amounted to $200 million in 1932. These losses occurred despite industry-wide efforts to cut operating expenses.[4]

Management made labor costs an important target when enacting austerity measures. Many workers faced layoffs as the Depression worsened. Table 6.1 shows the drop in employment throughout the industry. At U.S. Steel, the average number of employees shrunk from 254,495 in 1929 to 164,348 in 1932. The average number of employees at Bethlehem Steel, the second-largest firm in the industry, fell from 64,316 in 1929 to 50,807 in 1932. But Table 6.1 also demonstrates that those workers who kept their jobs suffered as well. The industry's workforce cuts would have been much more severe if it were not for a deliberate decision on the part of firms to impose work-sharing arrangements. Schwab, again in his capacity as President of the American Iron and Steel Institute, justified the practice by arguing, "The part time employment situation does not, of course, represent a normal or desirable condition, but it is a preferable alternative to wage reductions and large scale dismissals, and it guarantees food and shelter for many more than would be provided for if one group were sacrificed in order to keep others on a full-time basis."[5] Work-sharing remained a popular labor practice in the iron and steel industry even after the implementation of the New Deal's recovery program. Since this policy cut back on hours per worker, it decreased the take-home pay of employees in every sector of the industry. Despite this drop in wages, employees clung to their jobs as they never had before. Turnover for steelworkers dropped below the average of all manufacturing industries throughout the Depression.[6]

Steelmakers, exhibiting the same kind of paternalism apparent in their welfare capitalist programs, often asserted that their relief policies softened the impact of the depression for their employees. For example, Myron Taylor, who replaced Elbert Gary as Chairman of the United States Steel Corporation in 1927, told his stockholders in 1934, "There has been no brighter page in the history of any corporation than the treatment of U.S. Steel employees during the depression. So far as I know, no employee of the Steel Corporation has been in want."[7] U.S.

Table 6.1: Iron and Steel Industry Labor Statistics, 1929-1932

	Estimated Average # of Employees	Total Annual Wages (in millions of $)	Average Hourly Wage (in cents)	Average Hours Worked Per Week Per Employee
1929	421,000	733	65	49.5
1930	368,000	587	65	48.3
1931	279,000	359	63	35
1932	228,000	183	52.1	25.9

Source:

White, A.G. "Evidence Study No. 20 of the Iron and Steel Industry," National Recovery Administration Division of Review, June 1935, 10.

Steel did spend $577,000 in direct relief for its employees between 1932 and 1934 and $2,690,000 in "credits" for food, fuel, rent and medical services supplied by company-owned providers; but, all told, this amounted to approximately ten cents per week for every worker and family member dependent on a U.S. Steel paycheck, and much of the money spent on relief came directly from discontinued welfare capitalist programs. Furthermore, many large steel firms expected that their relief expenditures would eventually be paid back. When economic conditions started to improve in 1935, U.S. Steel began to deduct from the paychecks of its workers in order to compensate for its earlier "charity." Despite this practice, many steel companies forbade their employees from applying for relief from any other charitable organizations. As economic conditions worsened, the steel industry's private relief system broke down. Companies that had once prevented their charges from asking for outside help began to instruct the long-term unemployed to ask for federal assistance because they did not want to continue the expense of independent relief expenditures.[8]

The Roosevelt administration presented the National Industrial Recovery Act (NIRA) as its solution to the problems of both labor and management in all industries, including steelmaking. Passed during the legendary Hundred Days of 1933, the NIRA created the National Recovery Administration (NRA), an agency that brought leaders from nearly every industry in America together to compose codes of fair competition. The NRA also designated code authorities to enforce these codes. NRA codes regulated every aspect of the business: production, price, wages, etc. The NIRA also suspended federal antitrust laws.[9] NIRA proponents thought the codes would promote economic recovery in all industries by limiting competition, reducing working hours to increase overall employment, raising the wages of low-paid workers and encouraging collective bargaining. In reality, the law affected the economy in many ways that were impossible to predict at the time of its passage. According to a 1935 Brookings Institution study of the NIRA, "Though the general social objectives, and in particular the recovery objective, had widespread public support, the pursuit of them affected powerful groups whose special interests were necessarily sometimes in conflict with one another and sometimes in conflict with public ends. In some degree there developed a confusion between what were public objectives and what were the objectives of groups."[10] There is no better example of this conflict than the interaction between the NRA and the steel industry.

For decades, the industry had wanted to regulate itself so that companies could rise or fall based on their own skill in adapting to market conditions, but the industry feared government sanction if those policies ran afoul of federal antitrust laws. Now the government let the industry do what it had wanted to do. Charles Schwab, in the chairman's address to the Spring 1933 meeting of the American Iron and Steel Institute, applauded "the facilities and prestige of our government" being used to eliminate "unfair competitive practices with all of their ruinous effects upon prices, wages and profits."[11] Yet steelmakers objected to government involvement in the enforcement of this system. As the *New York Times* explained in 1933, the steel industry "would like to proceed in the new cooperative way as a self-governed industry and it freely says so."[12] Because most manufacturers benefited from the code, this attitude did not change over the course of the code period. The minutes of a 1935 meeting of the American Iron and Steel Institute Board of Directors summarize one executive's comments on this subject as, "Does not know where his company would have been without a code."[13] As was the case in previous decades, the industry did not object to regulation as long as it could maintain control over its operations.

Because of its desire for unfettered control, the industry's hatred of organized labor also continued into the Depression years. An incident that occurred in 1933 illustrates these feelings well. That summer, Secretary of Labor Frances Perkins invited the heads of all the major steel companies to Washington to prepare a statement on the Iron and Steel Code. When they entered her office, the steel men discovered to their surprise that American Federation of Labor President William Green was already in the room, at which point they "backed into a corner like frightened boys . . . their faces were long, their eyes were solemn." Perkins later called this "the most embarrassing social experience of my life."[14] The anti-union attitude of the steel industry had not changed, but new circumstances caused by the Depression opened up new fronts in the war between management and organized labor, most notably the enforcement of the collective bargaining provisions of the Iron and Steel Code.

Because of its importance to the economy, the Iron and Steel Code was the eleventh of the hundreds of codes approved by President Roosevelt, and the first for any heavy manufacturing industry. Steel manufacturers wrote their code entirely by themselves, with one notable exception. NIRA Section 7(a) required that employers give their employees the right to organize and bargain collectively through representatives of their own choosing, free from interference, restraint or coercion by their employers. The National Recovery Administration inserted the language of Section 7(a) into the Iron and Steel Code because the NIRA required that this language appear in every code. After the passage of the NIRA, the President issued an executive order that created the National Labor Board (NLB) in order to enforce the collective bargaining provisions of every code. The American Iron and Steel Institute (AISI) protested the collective bargaining provision of the Iron and Steel Code in the same terms it had used to oppose organized labor throughout the Nonunion Era, arguing, "The relations between the members of the Code and their employees are of so intimate a nature that they should and must be dealt with on the basis of individual merit. The matter is not one that can be properly dealt with in the Code."[15] Intense lobbying failed to remove the collective bargaining requirement. Although steelmakers intensely disliked the language of Section 7(a), they liked the order and stability that the code brought. How to take advantage of the economic benefits brought by the code while simultaneously avoiding the drawbacks of its labor provisions was the defining struggle of steel manufacturers during early New Deal years.

Bringing Order to a "Turkish Street Fair"

Since its formation in 1901, the United States Steel Corporation had been a steadying force upon the iron and steel market in America. A complicated system called Pittsburgh Plus also contributed to the industry's long-term price stability. Pittsburgh Plus dictated that all steel prices were to be based on the cost of production and transportation from Pittsburgh, no matter where the steel was originally produced. This allowed Pittsburgh manufacturers to compete for business with local producers in places like Chicago because transportation costs did not affect their price. At the same time, Pittsburgh Plus made it impossible for southern steel producers to take advantage of their lower production costs in order to break into northern markets. Although its origins are obscure, this system was firmly established by 1901. U.S. Steel worked to assure its continued existence. "No Soviet planner ever devised a more flagrantly artificial system than Comrade Gary's Pittsburgh Plus," quipped *Fortune* magazine in 1935. It broke down for short periods when price competition was particularly intense, but Pittsburgh Plus remained the single most influential determinant of national steel prices until 1924.[16]

In 1921, the Federal Trade Commission filed a successful lawsuit against U.S. Steel demanding that it abandon Pittsburgh Plus on the grounds that the arrangement restrained trade. In 1924, the federal court in which the government brought that suit issued a cease and desist order against this system. Despite this action, U.S. Steel agreed only to comply "in so far [sic] as it is practicable to do so."[17] Because the Coolidge administration was unwilling to enforce the cease and desist order to its fullest extent, Pittsburgh Plus continued after 1924 in a modified form. The new system had multiple basing points that reflected market conditions at steel centers other than Pittsburgh. Because of the increased competition brought by a more competitive price system, the price of all steel products declined steadily after 1924. The monthly average price of twelve iron and steel products dropped from $44.55 per ton in 1923 to $29.46 per ton in 1932. As a result of this decline, U.S. Steel stopped announcing its prices in 1929, thereby introducing even more competition into the pricing system. During the early years of the Depression, manufacturers sold most steel at cut rates in secret deals with concessions given to favored buyers. Companies constantly undercut each other's prices in order to retain a piece of the declining market. Eugene Grace, President of Bethlehem Steel, wrote in *Scribner's Magazine* that, "The selling of steel in 1932, and for the years preceding, had all the confusion of the selling of rugs in a Turkish Street Fair."[18]

The Iron and Steel Code maintained the multiple basing point system of the 1920s because the Roosevelt administration feared that changes in this system would hurt the competitive position of the industry. However, the code did include new provisions designed to enforce accepted prices and prevent "destructive" competition. Companies that signed the code had to file their lowest base prices for every product they produced with the code authority—the body charged by the government with enforcing the code—ten days in advance of a price change. This way, a competitor could meet any price decrease. However, rather than engage in competition, most steel firms posted identical prices. The code authority also had the power to fine any firm that signed the code $10 per ton if it sold under the going rate as well as the power to investigate the prices of any code members to determine if they were fair. If that code member did not change an unfair base price within ten days of an adverse decision by the authority, that body could fix a price for him. This power led directly to price collusion that increased the earnings of nearly every firm in the industry.[19]

Like the systems that came before it, the pricing structure used during the NRA years was so complicated that only experts and participants could follow it. By May 1934, steelmakers had filed 20,000 individual prices with the code authority that covered markets all across the country. In order to understand why this system was so complex, one need only look at the composition of the code authority. Whereas businessmen dominated the code authorities in many industries, not all members were businessmen and the government determined the composition of these groups. The NRA charged the Board of Directors of the American Iron and Steel Institute with enforcement of the Iron and Steel Code. In other words, business was quite literally regulating itself. During the code years, the AISI divided its board meetings between code business and trade association business.[20] Nevertheless, critics still charged that the group used its public functions to serve the private interests of its members. For example, after investigating the operation of the Iron and Steel Code, the Federal Trade Commission concluded:

> When highly organized groups of competitors establish and maintain an elaborate and complicated price formula, composed of numerous subordinate formulas that are themselves elaborate and complicated,

> when they incorporate in the master formula arbitrary factors such as common basing points and delivery charges other than the actual, thus arriving at identical delivered prices, it is a conservative conclusion that they have thereby simply arrived at the goal and object which motivated the initial step and each succeeding step in the process.[21]

The National Recovery Review Board (NRRB), headed by the famous trial lawyer Clarence Darrow, made the same point more succinctly, "The [Iron and Steel] code itself sanctions methods whereby competition in base prices is doubtless intended to be, and is in practice, eliminated."[22] In short, these government bodies believed that the AISI Board of Directors, acting as the code authority, used the Iron and Steel Code to suspend competition under the cover of the NRA.

As the administrator of the Iron and Steel Code, the AISI exercised its quasi-government authority in a totally unconstrained manner. "In agreeing to come under a code," wrote Edward A. Wieck of the Russell Sage Foundation, the industry "made plain at every stage what they wanted and what they would refuse to accept. They were entirely frank in their determination to have their way. If not by one road, then by another. They maintained this attitude throughout the NRA period, and succeeded in their efforts."[23] Because the AISI's Board of Directors claimed its powers derived entirely from the contractual power conferred on it by members of the code, it denied that government had any authority over its operations. Even though the code provided for NRA officials' access to meetings of the code authority, the directors discouraged outsiders from attending their meetings and refused to provide NRA officials with minutes from certain parts of its deliberations. The AISI denied access to investigators sent by the Federal Trade Commission and the National Recovery Review Board when these bodies examined the trade practices of the steel industry under the code. When the chief counsel of the code authority testified in defense of his client before the NRRB, he presented no evidence and called only one witness. When asked to proceed faster, the counsel left in protest. The NRRB charged that the authority's display was "play-acting for the purpose of creating the impression that the Board was unjust."[24] Such actions demonstrate the lengths to which the leaders of the AISI would go to protect their independence. In fact, steelmakers often praised the Roosevelt administration in the months following the passage of the NIRA for allowing it to implement the provisions of the steel code themselves. "Part of the uncertainty in industry during the past months," wrote Grace, who also served as the Chairmen of the AISI's Executive Committee

> has been occasioned by the fear in some quarters that the Recovery Act was merely a cloak for the aim of ultimate socialization. As time goes on this apprehension is lessening. The Administration has strongly asserted that it will not be the policy of the government to manage business, or to take control of business. . . . Even if the government were tempted into the paths of social dictatorship, American tradition is so strongly individualistic that public opinion would block any such effort.[25]

Of course, this tradition of individualism was the same prerogative the industry had been guarding since the beginning of the Nonunion Era.

The large firms that had dominated steelmaking in America for decades continued to do so under the Iron and Steel Code. Table 6.2 shows the extent to which industry leaders controlled the code authority through a weighted voting system that awarded the most votes to the companies which produced the most steel during the previous year. "It was a code by and for the proprietary interests in steel," wrote John Fitch shortly after its approval. "Prices were to be fixed . . . with no provision for the protection either of the consumer or the small producer." This dominance of large firms over small firms in the code authority was a common criticism of many NRA codes. Nevertheless, small steel firms seldom complained because they too benefited from the code's effects. The collusion sanctioned by the NRA led to a significant increase in prices of most iron and steel products over the life of the code. The price of pig iron increased 10.8%. The price of structural shapes and steel bars increased 12.5%. The price of tin plate increased 23.5%.[26] These increases are based entirely on the price directly from the mills. In reviewing the code, the Federal Trade Commission alleged that if transportation costs were factored into the equation, the price of some steel products increased by more than 100%. No matter what the size of the increases, steel manufacturers were not shy about expressing their approval for the code. "We don't have to go behind the barn any more to smoke the cigarette," quipped one anonymous steel man to the *New York Times*. "We have found that the code does for steel what steel has wanted to have done for it since the start of the century."[27] In essence, the NRA brought conditions in the steel industry back to the time before the era of

Table 6.2: Distribution of Voting Strength in the Iron and Steel Code Authority, 1935

	Number of Companies	Total Votes	Sales Value (in millions of $)
Companies with 1 vote	106	106	$53
Companies with 2 votes	20	40	$20
Companies with 3 votes	9	27	$13.50
Companies with 4 votes	13	52	$26
Companies with 5 votes	8	40	$20
Companies with 6 votes	9	54	$27
Companies with 7 votes	3	21	$10.50
Companies with 8 votes	4	32	$16
Companies with 9 votes	2	18	$9
Companies with 10-20 votes	9	116	$58
Companies with 20-30 votes	6	144	$72
Companies with over 30 votes	13	1,646	$823
Total	202	2,296	$1,148

Source:

White, A.G. "Evidence Study No. 20 of the Iron and Steel Industry." National Recovery Administration Division of Review, June 1935, 1.

antitrust laws. As long as the Iron and Steel Code was in effect, large steel companies could set prices without fear of government reprisal.

Even though the NRA eliminated price competition, the mandatory inclusion of the language of Section 7(a) in the Iron and Steel Code forced the government to take a stronger stand on labor issues. In anticipation of attempts to enforce collective bargaining, literally every large firm without an employee representation plan (ERP) established one in the weeks preceding the passage of the NIRA. To justify this action, the industry took the position that ERPs fulfilled the requirements of Section 7(a) during the hearings on the Iron and Steel Code. For example, the first draft of the code drawn up by the AISI and submitted for approval in July 1933 included language that legitimated these company unions:

> It is the belief of the industry that the method of collective bargaining set forth in [employee representation] plans provides for a day-to-day adjustment of all matters relating to employment of employes in the

> industry and at the same time insures to such employes an understanding of the conditions of the business of their employer which they would otherwise be unable to obtain; that such principles should be maintained; and that the rights of the employes and members of the industry to bargain collectively through representatives elected or appointed . . . should be preserved and protected.[28]

The principles of employee representation set forth in an addendum to the proposed code included clauses which stated that employees could only choose their representatives from a pool of employees selected by management and ensured that elections could only take place at a location designated by the employer. The addendum to the draft also stated that the final arbitrator on matters in dispute between labor and management was the employer. Organized labor staunchly opposed any acceptance of employee representation, a practice it considered in blatant violation of Section 7(a).[29] Because of the importance of this issue to both labor and capital, the viability of the entire code-making process rested on its resolution. Press reports foretold of a showdown between both sides of this issue at a public hearing on the proposed iron and steel code. That hearing occurred on July 31st, 1933.[30]

The first speaker was Robert Lamont, former Secretary of Commerce in the Hoover administration and president of the AISI. Lamont presented the entire code for discussion, but confined his remarks to the few points where the industry and the NRA disagreed.[31] When Lamont introduced the industry's language on employee representation, NRA Administrator Hugh Johnson objected, declaring that although this provision "was probably a border-line case, it seems to me inappropriate in that particular section of this Code, which contains the mandatory provisions of [NRA Section 7(a)]." Lamont responded that he would be willing to recommend to his organization that the proposed language be dropped. But before convening an on-the-spot meeting to get approval for this action, Lamont read a prepared statement:

> It should be distinctly understood, however, that the omission of this section does not imply any change in the attitude of the industry on the parts therein referred to; that the industry believes that the employee representation plans now in effect in its plants are desired by its employees; that the members of the industry will naturally do everything in their power to preserve a satisfactory relationships [sic] now existing with their employees, and that the section will be omitted for the

> sole purpose of avoiding the necessity of considering at this hearing any questions that are not fundamental to the code.[32]

When Lamont returned to the hearing, the industry withdrew the company union provision from the proposed code. Secretary of Labor Frances Perkins then shook hands with Lamont and thanked the industry for its "patriotic and far-sighted policy." American Federation of Labor (AFL) President William Green also testified at this hearing, but the Institute's tactical retreat forced him to confine his attacks to other provisions of the proposed code.[33] Later in the hearing, Secretary Perkins praised steelmakers for "removing the question of workers representation from the realm of controversy in this code."[34] In fact, the industry had done no such thing. After the hearing, it simply followed the same course that it would have if company unions had been authorized by the Iron and Steel Code.

Labor Organizing Under the NRA

In 1933, the largest union in the industry was still the Amalgamated Association of Iron, Steel and Tin Workers. By this point, this long-dormant organization was hardly even a shadow of its former self. Neither it nor any other union had made any concerted attempt to organize the steel industry since the great strike of 1919. Of the few labor disputes engaged in by the Amalgamated Association since 1919, every one resulted in the permanent loss of a once-unionized mill. The union organized no new locals between 1919 and 1933, and no disbanded locals revived. Amalgamated membership dropped from 31,500 in 1920 to approximately 4,700 in mid-1933. Nearly all of these union members were highly skilled employees working in sheet mills or at wrought iron furnaces. The President of the Amalgamated Association was Michael Tighe. Nicknamed "Grandmother" because of his conservatism, he had been the organization's leader since 1918. Tighe earned his nickname during the 1919 steel strike when he withdrew his members from the picket lines before the strike ended.[35] Writing in *The Nation*, Louis Adamic described Tighe as a "typical old-time trade-union bureaucrat . . . profoundly ignorant of the forces now operating in the world or in the country."[36] A union opponent of Tighe's once complained that he was "too damn conservative to be an Irishman."[37] For over a decade, Tighe had been content to attempt to preserve his union's small, highly skilled constituency and to do little else.

For this reason, the initiative for an organizing campaign after the passage of the NIRA came from American Federation of Labor President William Green. On June 17th, 1933, Green sent Tighe a telegram that read, in part:

> I urge you to launch an organizing campaign among the steel workers. Advise them that the law makes it possible for them to organize and to engage in collective bargaining. You have jurisdiction over steel workers and for that reason we hope and expect you will take advantage of the wonderful opportunity provided by the Industrial Recovery Act to organize steel workers. We are making a special drive in other mass production industries. Time is important, therefore I appeal to you to act quickly.[38]

Even though congressional debates over Section 7(a) and the Iron and Steel Code hearings had received an enormous amount of media attention, the Amalgamated Association had not planned to conduct an organizing campaign. Therefore, Tighe responded to Green's appeal this way:

> At the present time we are badly handicapped, we have five strikes on our hands at the present time for recognition of the union. . . . Have drained our finances along with closed banks. . . . Asked Secretary Morrison for some instructions as to what could be done in cases of this kind. Also told him to have the federation go ahead in the Steel Industry. Our yearly scales expire July 1st, which makes it imperative that we attend to that part of our work.[39]

Ignoring this protest, Green continued to press his case. Eventually, the Amalgamated leadership relented. The union sent 106 organizers into the field during that summer of 1933. Most of them had few qualifications for the job. Many were retired Amalgamated members who utilized outdated organizing techniques from decades past or friends of the central union office who went into the field without training.[40]

Despite the flaws in the Amalgamated Association's efforts, the union still gained membership in 1933. The reason for the campaign's success was the union's efforts to identify itself with the New Deal. In the same manner that the United Mine Workers used the slogan, "The President Wants You to Join the Union," the Amalgamated Association's literature made prominent mention of NIRA Section 7(a) and implied that joining them was a requirement of the act. In many instances, new union locals organized themselves. As the labor journalist Harvey O'Connor later remembered:

> So in 1933 along came the New Deal, and then came the NRA, and the effect was electric all up and down those valleys. The mills began reopening somewhat, and the steelworkers read in the newspapers about this NRA Section 7A that guaranteed you the right to organize. . . . All over the steel country union locals sprung up spontaneously. Not by virtue of the Amalgamated Association; they couldn't have cared less. . . . These people had never had any experience in unionism. All they knew was that, by golly, the time had come when they could organize and the Government guaranteed the right to organize!

Newly organized steelworkers gave their lodges names like New Deal, NRA and Blue Eagle, in commemoration of government's role in the creation of their organizations.[41]

All told, steelworkers organized 129 new Amalgamated Association lodges in 1933 and 1934. These lodges included approximately 50,000 new members, but perhaps as many as 150,000 steelworkers signed union cards without becoming active in their locals. Although these numbers show that the Amalgamated Association had some success, the failure of the Roosevelt Administration to fully enforce the collective bargaining provisions of the steel code and the success of company-dominated unions throughout the industry prevented the union from consolidating gains in its membership. As one anonymous activist explained, "[T]he old line lodges were refusing to take the unskilled and semiskilled workers. Many refused even the skilled craft maintenance men. And some wouldn't take skilled steel workers, just because they were new members." George Patterson worked as a roll turner for U.S. Steel at the South Works in Chicago. Unhappy with the Employee Representation Plan there, he contacted the Amalgamated: "They wouldn't have anything to do with us. [Louis Leonard, the secretary of the union] wrote me nice letters, but never came to see me or invited me to come down and talk over joining with them. The Amalgamated Association was lying there and wouldn't do a thing for us. . . . So we formed an independent union." Some locals unhappy with the Amalgamated joined the Communist-led Steel and Metal Workers Industrial Union (SMWIU), or formed federal locals directly affiliated with the American Federation of Labor.[42]

New members formed the base for a vigorous rank-and-file reform movement within a moribund organization. The leadership of the Amalgamated Association put protecting its base of skilled workers in front of any attempt to force employer recognition, but the men who ran the new lodges had opposing priorities. Unlike the old-time union leaders, the new activists were generally full-time steelworkers who took no salary for their union activities. They probably would not have been paid if they had been on salary, as thousands of workers who signed union cards refused to pay dues until the Amalgamated did something for them. This created tremendous pressure on the leaders of the new lodges to get their union to do something. Rank-and-file leaders led two major strikes during the fall of 1933: one of them at the Clairton Steel Works outside of Pittsburgh, the other at all the plants of Weirton Steel, based in Weirton, West Virginia. President Tighe denounced both walkouts as "outlaw."[43]

In March 1934, rank-and-file representatives from ninety-two lodges held a meeting to plot strategy for that year's Amalgamated Association convention. They returned to their locals to find out just how far the new Amalgamated members were willing to go to force the industry to recognize them. The representatives soon found that the membership overwhelmingly supported immediate action. Rank-and-file leaders developed a strategy to use their numerical strength at the convention to force the union to conduct a nationwide strike against the steel industry. Although Tighe tried various parliamentary maneuvers to prevent the insurgents from controlling the convention, the membership passed a seven-point program of concerted action to force union recognition by steel industry employers. The strike was set for June 20th. In a letter to a friend sent shortly after the meeting, Tighe complained that the new members that had come into the organization since the passage of the NRA were acting "against the best interests of the present organization." He charged that they had intentionally disrupted "the old A.A. as to form it into the Communistic class."[44]

Tighe's charge of communist influence had some basis in fact. In 1932, the communist-inspired Steel and Metal Workers Industrial Union formed and began organizing workers at the fringes of the industry. Before the SMWIU formed, its members had been part of the Steel and Metal Workers League, an affiliate of the Communist Party's Trade Union Unity League organized in 1929. Because of its small victories, the SMWIU may have had as many as 15,000 members at the beginning of the New Deal. In August 1933, the SMWIU won some concessions from the Pressed Steel Car Company at McKees Rocks after leading a strike there. This was the SMWIU's most notable achievement during the code years. Although a tumultuous November 1933 strike at U.S. Steel's Clairton, Pennsylvania, plant created headlines across the country, production continued without interruption. After the strikers started to apply for their old jobs back, the SMWIU organization there dissolved. By 1934, the SMWIU was down to about 7,500 members, most of them in small machine shops rather than steel mills.[45]

The SMWIU's priorities separated it from other communist-dominated unions. In general, its organizers put organization building before ideology. When Harvey O'Connor talked with strikers at U.S. Steel's structural steel works in Ambridge, Pennsylvania, he found "few of them knew much about the SMWIU. Didn't know it was communistic. Just a union, our own union."[46] In 1933, Communist Party leader Earl Browder denounced the SMWIU. He asserted, "It is . . . bunk when they say the SMWIU is controlled by the Communist Party. There are not enough Communists in it. There should be more."[47] The union's ideological open-mindedness made concerted action between communist steelworkers and the Amalgamated Association a real possibility, yet this never happened. On May 20th, 1934 rank-and-file leaders of the Amalgamated Association met with SMWIU representatives in the hopes of coordinating their activities. The talks bogged down over the communists' insistence that there be a joint statement by the leaders of the two groups on a local and national level. The Amalgamated insurgents feared being red-baited, and, since accepting communist members was illegal under the Amalgamated Association's constitution, a joint statement would have seriously threatened their cause. Nevertheless, both parties agreed to cooperate on a local basis wherever possible. As a result, Communist Party members gained influence in Amalgamated locals throughout the country during the early 1930s. "The policy must be flexible," argued one SMWIU official. "In those departments where the AA's strong [our members] must be INSIDE the AA: Wherever A.A. lodges exist, they must be inside." The SMWIU disbanded in November 1934 after the Communist Party abandoned dual unionism and returned to its previous philosophy of "boring from within." Its remaining members joined the Amalgamated as individuals in an attempt to keep the militancy of the rank and file alive. By that time, it was six months too late.[48]

The Amalgamated Association presented its demands to the steel industry in May 1934, in anticipation of a June 20th strike. The employers, speaking through the AISI, responded that under no circumstances would they recognize any outside unions. Therefore, the Amalgamated Association reconvened on June 14th in order to call the promised nationwide strike. The conservatives who controlled the platform managed to delay the discussion of the strike resolution until AFL President William Green came to the convention with a compromise proposal: a new, three-man, impartial panel to mediate disputes between steelworkers and their employers that would supersede the jurisdiction of the old National Labor Board in the steel industry. The idea had already been approved by the AISI, President Roosevelt, and the union's leadership, but it had to get through the rank and file. The group's leaders had already heard and rejected this proposal when Hugh Johnson first made it in the days leading up to the strike convention. Showing great political acumen, Tighe and his officers forced the compromise on the membership during a late-night session at which most of the rank-and-file leaders were absent. Demoralized by their failure to get the strike resolution passed, most of them were out getting drunk when Tighe's measure came up for a vote. The compromise approved, the Amalgamated called off the nationwide strike. When steelworkers across the country learned of developments at the Amalgamated convention, many tore up their union cards.[49]

President Roosevelt created the new government panel called for in the settlement by executive order on June 28, 1934. Its name was the National Steel Labor Relations Board (NSLRB). The President charged the NSLRB with the task of considering and determining the validity of allegations that steel companies were violating NIRA Section 7(a), mediating labor policy disputes, serving as a board of voluntary arbitration, and conducting elections for determining collective bargaining representatives. This may seem like an unprecedented intervention by government in the steel industry's industrial relations, but steelmakers knew that the NSLRB, like the NWLB before it, could not force them to change their labor policies because employers did not have to submit to the Board's authority. Despite this critical limitation on the power of the Board, conservative trade unionists like Green and Tighe counted on the NSLRB to help organize the industry. Tighe made this dependence clear in a circular letter to all Amalgamated Association lodges. "It is our purpose," he wrote, "through the opportunity now given us by the creation of this board under the new labor law to obtain the rights of organization and collective bargaining guaranteed us by section 7(a) of the Recovery Act, not by strikes, suspension of work, or violence, but by and within the framework of the law and procedure which will be worked out by us with this new governmental board."[50] The insurgents, on the other hand, had given up on government. "[T]o hell with all labor boards," declared one rank-and-file leader. "We can't live on Roosevelt's promises."[51]

Despite the hopes of some trade unionists, steel manufacturers quickly resolved not to let the new board change their labor policies. Hoyt A. Moore, counsel for the American Iron and Steel Institute, advised his client "that the Code does not cover any matters relating to labor relations of employers with employees . . . therefore . . . it would be very unwise for the Institute to have any direct communication with [the NSLRB] or the National Labor Relations Board."[52] When a steel company appeared before the NSLRB, it would start the proceeding with a brief statement attacking the constitutionality of the Board and denying that it had jurisdiction over the dispute in question. When a firm did not agree with an NSLRB decision, it would invariably ignore the Board's order or challenge it in court. In fact, no elections were ever carried out under NSLRB auspices. The reason the NSLRB proceeded so timidly was that the Roosevelt Administration did not wish to force a confrontation with the industry. If the industry publicly defied an NSLRB order, it was possible that the whole delicate balance of interests that kept the NIRA operating would collapse.[53]

In its short existence, the NSLRB heard a total of forty-two cases. The Board successfully mediated some of these disputes. Others led to decisions in favor of employers. Some small firms agreed to bargain with the Amalgamated Association after workers filed complaints with the Board; but of eight cases in which the NLB or NSLRB ordered a direct election at a major steel company, only one minor company ever recognized an outside union as a result. Legal challenges to seven of the Board's findings were still pending when the Supreme Court overturned the NIRA in May 1935, thereby rendering these disputes moot. When the NRA dissolved, the NSLRB dissolved along with it. After the Board's demise, a Brookings Institution study concluded, "It hardly can be said . . . that the National Steel Labor Relations Board had accomplished much in attempting to apply Section 7(a) to the industrial relations problems of the iron and steel industry."[54] In other words, the union's faith in the government board was misplaced.

The Amalgamated Association's lack of commitment to organizing also contributed to the collapse of the NIRA-era steel campaign. Between September 1933 and May 1934, the union reduced its organizing staff from 106 to 15. When new locals had trouble meeting their financial commitments to the international organization because of the high percentage of part-time and unemployed members, the Amalgamated expelled them. Internal conflict within the union did not improve the prospects of sustained organizing gains. In February 1935, Tighe revoked the charters of thirteen lodges that supported the use of more militant organizing tactics, claiming they "violated their charter . . . the Constitution . . . General Laws, and their Ritual Obligation . . . and committed acts of insubordination that would disrupt the organization and lead to destruction and finally jeopardize our present friendly relations with the employers that sign our agreements, making it practically impossible to obtain signed agreements with those who employ our membership."[55] The Amalgamated Association expelled seven more locals shortly thereafter on the basis of replies to a questionnaire sent out by the union's Executive Council. Together, all the expelled lodges represented approximately 75% of the union's membership. Although the leadership readmitted some locals in an October 1935 settlement, the Amalgamated Association's earlier membership gains had almost completely disappeared. Only 5,300 of the 100,000 to 150,000 recruits who had signed cards in the previous two years remained union members. Furthermore, new organizing had completely ceased. The Amalgamated gained only four new lodges during the entire 1935 calendar year.[56]

Labor historians who have studied the Amalgamated cite the internal discord and the extreme conservatism of the union's leadership as the reason for this loss in membership, but the success of employee representation as an anti-union tactic after the passage of the NIRA also played an important role. All the time steelworkers were fighting among themselves, steel companies used their employee representation plans to discourage the organization of their mills. By examining the manner in which steel companies implemented these arrangements, it is possible to see just how successful they were. Not all companies fought unions the same way. What follows are the experiences of two representative steel firms: U.S. Steel and Weirton Steel. Each company adopted different strategies to combat the Amalgamated Association. This disparity in strategy is indicative of a gradual break in the united front against organized labor that had existed since the start of the Nonunion Era. The changes in labor policy that resulted from this break greatly contributed to the upheaval in the labor relations that would come to the steel industry later in the decade.

Two Approaches to Employee Representation

There were seven firms operating employee representation plans in the iron and steel industry before the Roosevelt administration proposed the National Industrial Recovery Act in 1933. In the weeks leading up to and following the NIRA's passage, the number of steel firms with ERPs exploded. Of 67 plans studied by three researchers based at the University of Pittsburgh in 1937, 28 were inaugurated in June 1933, 12 in July, 6 in August and 3 in September. The sudden popularity of employee representation was a direct result of the NIRA. In a questionnaire for the study cited above, one anonymous steel executive admitted, "[W]e put in an employee representation plan because we were afraid our men would fall for this outside union stuff which we were sure would come right after the passage of the Recovery Act." The Pittsburgh researchers suggest that this attitude "was entirely typical of the views given by major executives of large companies during field trip interviews for this study."[57] Even companies like U.S. Steel and Weirton Steel, which had resisted employee representation in the past, started their own company unions after the passage of the NIRA. By the end of 1934, the number of employee representation plans in the iron and steel industry had grown to 93. These arrangements covered over 90% of the employees in the industry.[58]

Most steel companies modeled their ERPs on the one already operating at Bethlehem Steel.[59] By the time the NRA passed in 1933, the Bethlehem plan had prevented outside unions from gaining a foothold in that plant for fifteen years. Therefore, it was only natural that other steel firms looked to Bethlehem for guidance in this new experiment, which the government forced them to embark upon. Some executives simply obtained copies of the plan from Bethlehem's management and implemented it in full. Officials from some firms, including U.S. Steel, actually traveled to Bethlehem Steel facilities to observe how the plan operated. The Corporation copied the Bethlehem plan almost in full; it added two paragraphs near the beginning of its plan:

> The management of the works and the direction of the working forces, including the right to hire, suspend or discharge for proper cause, or transfer, and the right to relieve employees from duty because of lack of work, or for other legitimate reasons, is vested exclusively in the Management; and, except as expressly provided herein, these rights shall not be abridged by anything contained herein.

If this were not enough to make a U.S. Steel employee suspicious of management's intentions, the second additional paragraph suggested management's lack of commitment to employee representation as a permanent part of its labor policy:

> This plan shall be and remain in full force and effect *during the term of the National Recovery Act and thereafter may be terminated by the management* or by a majority of the duly elected employees' representatives upon three months' notice [emphasis added].[60]

Within days of its initial announcement, the plan took effect at nearly all of the Corporation's vast holdings.[61]

The manner in which U.S. Steel implemented its ERP clearly indicated that the initiative for the plan came entirely from management. For example, the National Steel Labor Relations Board later described how management implemented the plan at U.S. Steel's plant in Youngstown, Ohio. "[M]anagement selected and called in certain employees to whom they explained a plan of employee representation," the Board reported. "These men then formed their committees and arranged to elect employee representatives." Petitions with identical language attributed to ordinary steelworkers appeared throughout U.S. Steel's many facilities. This strongly suggests that the situation at Youngstown was typical of the circumstances at other plants. According to the Corporation, "As long as the plans are voluntarily chosen by employees and the plans are working effectively and satisfactorily to the employees, it is submitted that how the plans originated is immaterial."[62] The men who won the ERP elections tended to have close ties to management. At the Duquesne Works, five of the original fourteen winners later went on to become foremen or to assume other jobs with management responsibilities.[63]

U.S. Steel operated its employee representation plan the same way that Bethlehem Steel managed its plan during the 1920s. Management did its best to satisfy minor grievances in the hopes that this would forestall efforts for greater change, particularly demands for outside representation or large wage increases. "[U.S. Steel's] attitude on compliance with section 7(a)," explained Edward Kephart, head of the Amalgamated Association local at the Corporation's McDonald, Ohio, plant

> is to listen, lots of listening; but when you try to arrange a meeting for collective bargaining, to really get a basis of contractual relations with the company, that is different. Their attitude is, "We are willing to

> listen to grievances; we are willing to adjust grievances." There have been some adjustments made on grievances, but they draw the line between grievances and collective bargaining, and refuse to have anything whatever to do with you through collective bargaining, as controlled by labor organizations and their representatives.[64]

In the roll shop at the Illinois Steel Company's South Works in Chicago, management approved requests to place a stretcher and first aid equipment there, to bring in artesian water because of the poor quality of water from the city, and to provide employees with locks for their tool chests and bench drawers. As these examples indicate, the changes made through the plan were mostly inconsequential. "[T]he first year, you'd get another shower put in somewhere," remembered a representative from the Corporation's Clairton, Pennsylvania, plant, "you'd get some of the broken windows repaired, but no accomplishments of anything pertaining to our way of life."[65] The changes in working conditions enacted through employee representation and the desire to please, separate U.S. Steel's company union from those at many smaller companies, which did little or nothing for their employees under the auspices of their plans.

Over the course of 1934, management introduced amendments to the ERP. The President of the American Steel and Wire Company explained the changes to employees as a way to make the plan "more permanent, and to meet legal requirements"; in other words to make it more likely that the National Labor Board would recognize it as a valid vehicle for collective bargaining.[66] The changes included the end of length restrictions on eligibility for voting and serving as an ERP representative, the recognition of group grievances (rather than just those filed by individuals) and the right of employee representatives to discuss matters without a management representative present. The Board approved the amended plan in advance. As early as February 1934, three members of the NLB called U.S. Steel's newly-amended ERP, "the fairest plan yet to come before them."[67]

The author of these changes was U.S. Steel Vice-President Arthur H. Young. The son of a steelworker, Young began his career as a laborer at U.S. Steel's South Chicago plant. He worked his way up to safety and employment supervisor when International hired him to be its manager of industrial relations in 1918. There, Young authored International Harvester's influential employee representation plan. He left International Harvester in 1924 to work for Industrial Relations Counselors (a Rockefeller-sponsored consulting firm). U.S. Steel hired Young away from them in February 1934 to serve in a new position, Vice-President of Industrial Relations. Like so many of his colleagues, Young hated unions. He thought they disrupted the natural tendency of labor and management to act cooperatively. Young also praised the possibility of individual achievement, arguing that upward mobility bridged differences between labor and management. Because employee representation served as a vehicle for furthering cooperation and communication, it promoted "industrial mutual self-interest."[68] Young, therefore, was a transitional figure. His hatred of unionism did not foreclose the possibility of ceding some kind of control to employees for the good of the firm.

Because of the concessions sponsored by managers like Young, the Corporation's traditional role as the industry's leader in labor policy diminished during the code years. Other steel firms with new ERPs had much less tolerance for their workers asserting any control over working conditions or acting independently in any way. These manufacturers generally employed a mixture of modern industrial relations and traditional strong-arm techniques to maintain control over their labor force during the code period. The most important company to employ this strategy was Weirton Steel.

"I was born a commoner, have lived a commoner, and am still a commoner," wrote Ernest T. Weir, the founder of Weirton Steel, in 1936.[69] The son of a day laborer, Weir began his career in steel as a $3/week office boy. In 1899, he became chief clerk at the American Steel and Wire Company. He organized the Phillips Sheet and Tin Plate Company with two partners in 1905. In 1912, he formed his own steel firm and named it after himself. Weir merged Phillips with Weirton Steel in 1914 and assumed control of the whole company. In 1929, he merged Weirton Steel with the Great Lakes Steel Company of Detroit to form National Steel. This made Weirton Steel the most important subsidiary of the fifth largest steel producer in the United States.[70]

Weir was proud of the fact that most officials of National Steel had similar life stories, declaring: "[W]e made a survey of the higher executives in the National Steel Corporation. Their average age was low. We found that these men, with a single exception, had come from families of poor or average means; they had started at the bottom and they had made their own way."[71] To Weir, trade unions interfered with the justice that made this situation possible. Weir established his reputation as an implacable foe of organized labor during the 1919 steel strike. In Steubenville, Ohio, Weir had an armed mob force 185 Finnish employees he suspected of being IWW members to kiss the American flag before they were run out of town. He used uncompromising tactics to keep Weirton Steel's three plants (Weirton, West Virginia; Clarksburg, West Virginia; and Steubenville, Ohio) non-union in the face of the Amalgamated Association's post-NIRA push.[72] His challenge to the Roosevelt administration made the situation at these plants a test case for the entire New Deal labor policy.

Before the NIRA passed, Weir had already conferred with other steel executives about employee representation as a means to fulfill the requirements of Section 7(a). As a result of these conversations, Weir decided to adopt the Bethlehem Steel plan in all of National Steel's plants. Management's role in starting the plan was obvious from the beginning. On June 22nd, 1933, the company issued the following letter to its employees: "Beginning July 1st, the Employees' Representation Plan will be adopted by the Weirton Steel Company. This plan will provide for more effective communication and means of contact between the management and employees on matters pertaining to industrial relations and conditions under which the employees will work."[73] A group of workers at the Clarksburg, West Virginia plant described voting on the plan there as follows:

> During the early part of June 1933 notices, written on the Steel Company's letterheads, were posted in the Clarksburg mill signed the "Weirton Steel Company"; that the purport of this notice was that the company, in the near future, would hold an election *** about a week later the said Steel Company posted other notices announcing their plan of conducting said election, and the necessary qualifications making the employees eligible to vote; that the Company's officials appointed a committee to conduct and supervise the proposed election, and this committee of employees appointed by the Company's officials did conduct the election and were paid by the Company for their time the same as they would have been in performance of their regular duties; *** [ellipses in original].[74]

Weirton also hand-picked those employees who ran for employee representative. Once operating, the structure of Weirton Steel's employee representation plan discouraged independent gatherings by allowing a management representative to sit in on any meeting. This was not the case with U.S. Steel, where independent meetings occurred from the first days of the plan.[75]

Weirton Steel was also more aggressive than U.S. Steel in its use of traditional anti-union tactics to control its employees. In 1933, Weirton hired a detective agency to spy on its employees in search of union activity. Unlike U.S. Steel, where employees were only threatened with termination, Weirton fired at least 46 union members for participating in an October 1933 strike. In the days leading up to the aborted 1934 industry-wide steel strike, the *Pittsburgh Sun-Telegraph* wrote:

> [Weirton Steel] has machine guns, sawed-off shot guns, tear and sickening gas and other paraphernalia. They are prepared for a strike. It's unsafe for a union man to leave his home or go home unaccompanied. Thugs are walking along the streets with guns and black jacks in their back pockets. The mill police who have no right, no authority, are arresting and beating up union members on the street. The state police are patrolling the streets daily.[76]

At the same time, the firm installed spotlights at its plants and hired additional guards in anticipation of open warfare between labor and management.[77]

Despite these measures, the union organized locals at each Weirton Steel plant. When management refused to meet an Amalgamated delegation at the Weirton, West Virginia, facility, the local called a strike which successfully shut down all three Weirton plants for two weeks. Weir claimed that his decision not to meet with Amalgamated representatives was in compliance with Section 7(a). "Our duty under the NRA is clear," he wrote his employees during the strike. "We must recognize the committees which have been selected and cannot be expected to negotiate with any other committee that happens to present itself. Under the NRA, our employees are free to select committees of their own choosing, whether made up of employees or not, but once the committees have been selected, we must recognize those committees."[78] The Amalgamated, of course, was more concerned with whether the existence of the employee representation plan was legal in the first place. Therefore, in early October 1933, the union brought its case before the new National Labor Board. The strike ended on October 16th. The provisions of the settlement included the reemployment of strikers without prejudice, the right of employees to select their own representatives and an election to be held in mid-December under the supervision of the NLB, "the procedure and method of election to be prescribed by the Board."[79]

The election was to be the first test of Section 7(a) with a recalcitrant employer, but Weir backed out of the October agreement. In early December, Weirton announced that the company would run its own representation election, and that Amalgamated Association representatives would not be allowed on the ballot. Called again before the Board on December 7th, 1933, one member asked a delegate from the company union if his organization would flout the earlier agreement. "Yes," he replied. Asked further if it would ignore the wishes of the government, the delegate replied "if that's the way you take it, yes." Despite protests from many government officials, including Hugh Johnson of the NRA, Weirton went ahead on December 15th and held unsupervised elections in open defiance of the NLB. At a series of meetings held before that election, company President J.C. Williams and other Weirton officials exhorted their employees to vote for the union. At these meetings, President Williams exhibited copies of letters sent by customers threatening to withhold their business if the company's employees joined an outside union. He described negative experiences he had had with the Amalgamated Association earlier in his career. He stated repeatedly that he would make no contract with the Amalgamated even if employees voted them in. Other company practices during the weeks before the election included, "Unusual entertainment of employees; threatened discharge, lay-offs and transfers; offers of repayment of Amalgamated initiation fees; occasional physical forcing of employees to polls and marking of ballots; placing pay booth near voting boxes and suggesting voting before pay check offered." Not content to rely on such vigorous campaigning, the firm kept the names of Amalgamated Association officials off the ballot. The company union won in a landslide, even though many employees, fearing not to vote, marked their ballot with statements like "Forced to Vote" or with meaningless symbols.[80]

The NLB contended that Weir had agreed to supervised elections under the Board's rules as part of the October settlement, and that this election broke that earlier agreement. On January 15th, 1934, President Roosevelt called Weir in an attempt to mediate the dispute. According to the President, Weir "really believed that he carried out the spirit of the N.R.A. and the Labor Board because the election was conducted in accordance with the plan of 80 per cent of his employees, and the form of representation was also the one approved by 80 per cent of his employees." Weir's faith in the legitimacy of Weirton's ERP explains why he and the government never reached a compromise over collective bargaining rights. In March 1934, the government filed an equity suit in order to prevent these violations of the NIRA. By August 1934, the employees who had wanted to form an Amalgamated Association lodge dropped union recognition as a collective bargaining demand and stopped paying dues to the union. In February 1935, a federal judge made Weirton's victory complete, ruling that "in all respects [the Weirton ERP] complies with the provisions of Section 7(a) of the National Recovery Act."[81] With this victory, the company could extinguish all vestiges of Amalgamated Association support. But this was more than a victory over organized labor, it was a victory over the Roosevelt administration. The Weirton decision left the NLB, as well as its successor the NSLRB, unable to enforce its edicts.

Weir's resistance made him a hero among both steelmakers and anti-union businessmen across the nation. Ironically, Weir hurt the cause of anti-unionism in the long run because his actions encouraged calls for the government to exercise more power over labor. Most notably, the December 1933 election led directly to an Executive Order empowering the National Labor Board to hold elections. Eventually, the failure of the NLB to perform this function satisfactorily led Congress to replace it with a stronger overseer for industrial labor disputes—the National Labor Relations Board. The Weirton case was pending before the Supreme Court in May 1935 when the decision in *Schechter Poultry Corporation v. United States* overturned the entire NIRA, thereby deciding the matter in favor of management.[82] Weirton Steel's precedent-setting victory demonstrated to the world that U.S. Steel's role as the leader for labor policy throughout the industry was beginning to change. While men like Weir took up the mantle of Garyism, the Corporation began to moderate its policies. This split would grow wider when the challenge from organized labor grew stronger later in the decade.

"A Modern and Effective Method of Collective Bargaining"

Economic conditions in the steel industry improved greatly during the lifetime of the Iron and Steel Code. Between June 1933, the last month before the code took effect, and June 1934, the total number of wage earners in the industry increased 36.1%, the average hours worked per week increased 9.4% (a good thing during the Depression) and average earnings per hour increased 35.1%. Total annual production in the industry increased 12.3% from 1933 to 1934. Net earnings of the 154 companies that signed the code increased 68.4% over this same period. Wages and salaries increased 32%. The earnings of the top six firms in the industry, the ones with the most power under the code authority's system of proportional representation, increased by 91%under the code. Furthermore, the price-cutting restrictions in the code allowed these firms to make money while the industry produced at less than 50%of its total capacity. As a whole, the steel industry cut its total losses from $149 million in 1932 to $17 million in 1934. For that reason industry leaders wanted to retain the standards of fair competition dictated by the code after the Supreme Court overturned the NRA. An AISI resolution passed shortly after the Schechter decision urged "that the individual members of the iron and steel industry . . . maintain the present rates of pay and maximum hours of labor and the standards of fair competition which are set forth in the steel code, and . . . continue to protect the employees' rights of collective bargaining."[83] Since the provisions of the code had proven successful at reversing the decline of the industry, and its labor provisions were effectively emasculated, it is no wonder that the industry issued such a resolution. The stability of the code period would be sorely missed in the years followings its demise.

Publicly, the Roosevelt administration claimed the Iron and Steel Code was a great success. NRA Deputy Director Donald Richberg declared, "The code has been operating very well and we have had very good results in the way of maintaining employment and increasing wages despite ups and downs in the industry. . . . As a matter of fact, the code is operating without any friction. This code is rather exceptional as to compliance." And as J. Carroll Moody explains, "[T]he NRA most often pled with executives of AISI to 'play the game' or, at most, made veiled threats which were never carried out."[84] Despite poor compliance, particularly with its collective bargaining provisions, Richberg defended the code on the basis of the contribution it made to eventual recovery, "reducing unemployment, improving the standards of labor and increasing wage payments and the purchasing power of the workers."[85] The administration could do little to force greater compliance with the code because the failure to recruit such a key industry into the NRA fold might have threatened the viability of the entire program. This is especially true with regard to the collective bargaining provisions because steelmakers wanted to maintain the same control over their employees that had existed throughout the Nonunion Era.

The industry tried to prove that it had no labor problem in order to prevent government enforced collective bargaining. For instance, the AISI asserted that a turnout of eighty-five percent of eligible steelworkers in employee representation elections, held before the threatened June 1934 walkout, showed worker "opposition to a strike and . . . clear approval of such plans."[86] Another tactic was to provide statistics that tabulated the successful resolution of grievances. In 1934, the AISI reported that 4082 complaints were referred to ERPs throughout the industry between July and October 1933. Of these, employees' requests were granted 70% of the time. 18.3% were decided in favor of employers. Citing figures like these, the Institute concluded, "The Employee Representation Plan is a modern and effective method of collective bargaining. It operates in the best interests of all the workers, it eliminates misunderstanding and strife by promoting peace and harmony in industrial relations. It benefits the industry and the consuming public."[87] Privately, steel industry executives admitted that the great majority of disputes resolved by the ERP were minor grievances which management addressed as soon as it became aware of them.[88] Yet as long as the ERP kept worker demands for independent organization in check, steel manufacturers could reap the benefits of the NIRA code without serious consequences to their traditional prerogatives.

About the time the Supreme Court invalidated the NIRA, employee representatives throughout the industry began to make unprecedented demands on their employers, particularly employee representatives at U.S. Steel. Many began to organize interplant meetings so that they could compare and contrast their situations and make unified demands upon management. The passage of the National Labor Relations Act gave employees assurances that outside organizing activities would be protected by the government, and made it more difficult for employers to fire workers who caused trouble. However, the greatest catalyst for change in the steel industry was the formation of the Steel Workers Organizing Committee (SWOC) in June 1936. Its first target was United States Steel.

Notes

1. Dominico Del Turco to Franklin D. Roosevelt, February 27, 1935, Records of the National Steel Labor Relations Board, Box 12, Record Group 9, National Archives and Records Administration, Washington, D.C.

2. Fighting Organized Labor Under the Iron and Steel Code, 1933-1935Charles M. Schwab, "Address of the President," in *Year Book of the American Iron and Steel Institute,* 1929, 295.

3. *Iron Age* 124 (15 August 1929): 422; *Iron Age* 124 (12 December 1929): 1610.

4. *Iron Age* 151 (5 January 1933): 9; National Recovery Administration, "Code of Fair Competition for the Iron and Steel Industry," Washington, D.C.: U.S. Government Printing Office, August 19, 1933, 1.

5. Gertrude G. Schroeder, *The Growth of Major Steel Companies, 1900-1950* (Baltimore: Johns Hopkins Press, 1953), 216-17; Charles M. Schwab, "Address of the President," *Year Book of the American Iron and Steel Institute*, 1930, 255; "Code of Fair Competition for the Iron and Steel Industry," 11.

6. Thomas N. Maloney, "Degrees of Inequality," *Social Science History* 19 (Spring 1995): 51.

7. Taylor quoted in Harvey O'Connor, *Steel-Dictator* (New York: John Day Company, 1935), 283.

8. O'Connor, *Steel-Dictator*, 283-84; Carroll R. Daugherty, Melvin G. De Chazeau and Samuel S. Stratton, *The Economics of the Iron and Steel Industry* (in 2 Vols.) (New York: McGraw-Hill, 1937), 178, 906; David H. Kelly, "Labor Relations in the Steel Industry: Management's Ideas, Proposals and Programs, 1920-1950," Ph.D. Diss., Indiana University, 1976, 148.

9. A separate section of the NIRA allocated money for public works, but that did not affect the story at hand.

10. Leverett S. Lyon, et. al., *The National Recovery Administration: An Analysis and Appraisal* (Washington D.C.: The Brookings Institution, 1935), 881-82.

11. *Iron Age* 131 (1 June 1933): 851.

12. *New York Times*, 26 November 1933.

13. American Iron and Steel Institute, "Notes on Meeting of Members of Board of Directors," April 26, 1935, American Iron and Steel Institute Papers, Box 163, Hagley Museum and Library, Wilmington, DE.

14. Frances Perkins, *The Roosevelt I Knew*, (New York: Harper & Row, 1946), 221-223. Interestingly enough, William Irvin of U.S. Steel was the only executive who talked to Green that day. Perhaps this foreshadowed the flexibility of the Corporation's position towards labor later in the decade.

15. American Iron and Steel Institute, "Memorandum concerning the suggestions made by Secretary Perkins . . .," August 12, 1933, 11, American Iron and Steel Institute Papers, Box 183.

16. United States Steel Corporation, *United States Steel Corporation T.N.E.C. Papers*, Vol. II (United States Steel Corporation, 1940), 15-17; *Fortune* 12 (December 1935): 142.

17. Paul A. Tiffany, *The Decline of American Steel* (New York: Oxford University Press, 1988), 51-52; U.S. Steel quoted in Tiffany, 52. The steel industry would not fully abandon Pittsburgh Plus until the United States Supreme Court forced it to do so in 1948.

18. American Iron and Steel Institute, "Steel Facts and the Steel Code," April 1934, 8; Daugherty, et. al., 541; Eugene D. Grace, "Industry and the Recovery Act," *Scribner's Magazine* 95 (February 1934): 98.

19. Donald Richberg, "Commentary on the Report of the Federal Trade Commission on the Steel Code," n.d., p. 1, President's Official File 466e, Box 23, Franklin D. Roosevelt Library, Hyde Park, NY; "Code of Fair Competition for the Iron and Steel Industry," 25, 16, 28, 13.

20. "Report of the Board of Directors of the American Iron and Steel Institute on the operation of the Code of Fair Competition . . . ," [1934], Minute Book Steel Code, Vol. 1, American Iron and Steel Institute Papers, Hagley Museum and Library, Wilmington, DE.

On the dominance of large firms in other NRA Codes, see, for examples, Ellis Hawley, *The New Deal and the Problem of Monopoly: A Study in Economic Ambivalence* (Princeton: Princeton University Press, 1966), 19-146 and Colin Gordon, *New Deals: Business, Labor, and Politics in America, 1920-1935* (New York: Cambridge University Press, 1994), 166-203.

21. Federal Trade Commission, "Practices of the Steel Industry Under the Code," U.S. Senate Document No. 159, 73d Cong., 2nd Sess., 1934, 45.

22. National Recovery Review Board, "First Report to the President of the United States," [1934], 34.

23. Edward A. Wieck, "Steelworkers Under the NRA," August 3, 1936, 10, Edward A. Wieck Collection, Box 5, Archives of Labor and Urban Affairs, Walter P. Reuther Library, Wayne State University, Detroit, MI.

24. National Recovery Administration, "Digest of Excerpts Taken from the Iron and Steel Code History," 87, Records of the National Recovery Administration, Box 2976, Entry 25, Record Group 9, National Archives and Records Administration, Washington, D.C.; Jesse Carroll Moody, Jr., "The Steel Industry and the National Recovery Administration: An Experiment in Industrial Self-Government," Ph.D. Dissertation, University of Oklahoma, 1965, 159, 325-26; U.S. Congress, Senate, Committee on Finance, *Investigation of the National Recovery Administration*, 74th Cong., 1st Sess., 1935, 658; National Recovery Review Board, 12-13.

25. Grace, "Bringing Order . . . ," 96.

26. John A. Fitch, "Steel and the NRA," *Survey Graphic* 22 (October 1933): 497. An extensive list of price increases over the life of the code is in Daugherty, et. al., 599.

27. Federal Trade Commission, 53-56; *New York Times*, 26 November 1933.

28. Text of Proposed Iron and Steel Code in *New York Times*, 16 July 1933.

29. American Federation of Labor, "Statement by William Green, President, American Federation of Labor on the Code of the Iron and Steel Industry," July 31, 1933, 6-7.

The advance text of Green's speech includes his criticism of the provisions in the proposed code relating to employee representation. When the industry withdrew the provision, Green omitted the attack from his actual remarks. See Moody, 122.

30. O'Connor, *Steel-Dictator*, 135.

31. The points of disagreement ranged from limits on hours to the necessity of a lunch period. The important fact here is that all these points involved labor issues. See American Iron and Steel Institute, "Code of Fair Competition of the Iron and Steel Institute," American Iron and Steel Institute Papers.

32. Johnson and Lamont quoted in Moody, 121.

33. *New York Times*, 1 August 1933; Moody, 122.

34. Frances Perkins, "Analysis of the Steel Code," July 31, 1933, Records of the National Recovery Administration, Box 2975.

35. Horace B. Davis, *Labor and Steel* (New York: International Publishers, 1933), 251-54.

36. Louis Adamic, "The Steel Strike Collapses," *The Nation* 139 (4 July 1934): 9.

37. Robert R.R. Brooks, *As Steel Goes, . . .* (New Haven: Yale University Press, 1940), 50.

38. Green quoted in Harold Ruttenberg, "Steel Labor, the NIRA, and the Amalgamated Association," unpublished manuscript, Box 4, Harold Ruttenberg Papers, Historical Collections & Labor Archives, Pattee Library, Pennsylvania State University, State College, PA.

39. Tighe quoted in Daugherty, et. al., 951.

40. Daugherty, et. al., 953; Adamic, "The Steel Strike Collapses," 10.

41. Irving Bernstein, *Turbulent Years* (Boston: Houghton Mifflin, 1970), 454; Staughton Lynd, ed. "Personal Histories of the Early CIO," *Radical America* 5 (May-June 1971): 53; Harvey O'Connor, *Steel-Dictator* (New York: John Day Company, 1935), 187.

42. David Brody, "The Origins of Modern Steel Unionism: The SWOC Era," in *Forging a Union of Steel*, Paul F. Clark, Peter Gottlieb and Donald Kennedy, eds. (Ithaca, NY: ILR Press, 1987), 16; Lynd, "Personal Histories," 57; Brooks, *As Steel Goes . . .* , 49; Daugherty, et. al., 1035.

43. Adamic, "The Steel Strike Collapses," 10; Ruttenberg; Staughton Lynd, "The Possibility of Radicalism in the Early 1930s: The Case of Steel," *Radical America* 6 (November-December 1972): 41. The Weirton strike is discussed in greater detail below.

44. Ruttenberg; Tighe quoted in Moody, 249.

45. President, Carnegie Steel Company to Benedict Wolf, November 14, 1933, Records of the National Labor Relations Board, Pittsburgh Case Files, Box 2, Record Group 25, National Archives and Records Administration, College Park, MD; Edward A. Wieck, "Report on Steel & Metal Workers Industrial Convention," August 3-5, 1934, Edward A. Wieck Collection, Box 2; *Daily Worker*, 28 August 1933.

46. Harvey O'Connor, "Ambridge Trip," November 4-5, 1933, Harvey O'Connor Collection, Box 22, Archives of Labor and Urban Affairs, Walter P. Reuther Library.

47. Earl Browder quoted in Harvey Klehr, *The Heyday of American Communism* (New York: Basic Books, 1984), 122.

48. Brooks, *As Steel Goes . . .* , 55, 69; Wieck, "Steelworkers Under the NRA," 110; *Daily Worker*, 1 December 1933.

49. Ruttenberg; Adamic, "The Steel Strike Collpases," 12; Moody, 252.

50. *Steel* 95 (2 July 1934): 10; Michael Tighe, "Circular Letter . . . Regarding the National Steel Labor Relations Board," n.d., 2, American Federation of Labor Papers, Series 4, Box 66, State Historical Society of Wisconsin, Madison, WI.

51. James Douglas Rose, "The United States Steel Duquesne Works, 1886-1941: The Rise of Steel Unionism," Ph.D. Diss., University of California–Davis, 1997, 138.

52. Hoyt A. Moore to Grover C. Brown, September 10, 1934, American Iron and Steel Institute Papers, Box 180.

53. Rose M. Stein, "The Steel Barons 'Mediate'," *The Nation* 140 (2 January 1935): 20; Lewis L. Lorwin and Arthur Wubnig, *Labor Relations Boards* (Washington D.C.: The Brookings Institution, 1935), 342-50.
The NSLRB found several companies guilty of discriminating against unionized employees, but refused to acknowledge that such discrimination constituted a refusal to engage in collective bargaining.

54. National Steel Labor Relations Board, "Report of National Steel Labor Relations Board . . . ", [1935], Records of the National Steel Labor Relations Board, Box 19; "Second Report of the National Steel Labor Relations Board . . .", [1935], Records of the National Steel Labor Relations Board, Box 19; Kelly, 169; Lorwin and Wubnig, 350.

55. Rose, "The United States Steel Duquesne Works," 124; Amalgamated Association of Iron, Steel and Tin Workers, Minutes of Executive Board, February 5, 1935, Louis Leonard Papers, Box 10, Historical Collections & Labor Archives.

56. Daugherty, et. al., 966; Edward Levinson, *Labor on the March* (New York: Harper & Brothers, 1938), 71-72; Philip Taft, *The A.F. of L. From the Death of Gompers to the Merger* (New York: Harper & Brothers, 1959), 114;

Amalgamated Association of Iron, Steel and Tin Workers, *Annual Reports of International Officers*, 1935, 22.

57. Daugherty, et. al., 989.

58. Charles Cheape, "Trade, Innovation, and Expertise: Writing the Steel Code for the National Recovery Administration," *Business and Economic History* 25 (Winter 1996): 72; Brooks, *As Steel Goes . . .* , 79.

59. Exceptions included the American Rolling Mill Company and Youngstown Sheet and Tube, which had ERPs that predated the NIRA. Some firms modeled their employee representation plans directly on the one at U.S. Steel, but since this plan was modeled on Bethlehem Steel's the common ancestor was still the same.

60. U.S. Congress, Senate, Committee on Education and Labor, *To Create a National Labor Board*, 73nd Cong., 2d Sess., 1934, 89-90.

61. Brooks, *As Steel Goes . . .* , 4.

62. National Steel Labor Relations Board, "Earl W. Jenkins, Earl W. Hall, et. al. . . . v. National Steel Labor Relations Board," Brief for Respondent, n.d., 8, Records of the National Steel Labor Relations Board, Box 4; [Heber Blankenhorn], "Company Unions Formed by Detective Agencies," n.d., Heber Blankenhorn Papers, Box 1, Archives of Labor and Urban Affairs, Walter P. Reuther Library; United States Steel Corporation, "Statement in Opposition to the Proposed 'National Labor Relations Act,'" March 26, 1935, 4.
The origins of an ERP would be an important point when tested before the NSLRB or National Labor Relations Board, because initiating the plan was a sign of management endorsing the plan. The National Labor Board interpreted this as a violation of Section 7(a), just as the National Labor Relations Board would later interpret this practice as a violation of the National Labor Relations Act.

63. Rose, "The United States Steel Duquesne Works," 154.

64. U.S. Congress, House, Committee on Labor, *Labor Disputes Act*, 74th Cong., 1st Sess., 1935, 238; George A. Patterson to A.C. Rasch, July 21, 1934 and George A. Patterson to A.C. Rasch, December 26, 1934, George A. Patterson Papers, Box 2, Chicago Historical Society, Chicago, IL.

65. John J. Mullen Oral History Interview, 1966, 1, Historical Collections & Labor Archives, Pattee Library; Federated Press, "U.S. Steel's Company Union Bluff Called; It Wilts," n.d., Harvey O'Connor Papers, Box 23.

66. C.F. Blackmer, "To Employees of the American Steel and Wire Company," February 15, 1934, Records of the National Recovery Administration, Box 2977.

67. Rose, "The United States Steel Duquesne Works," 118; Federated Press, "U.S. Steel's Company Union Bluff Called; It Wilts," n.d., Harvey O'Connor Papers, Box 23.

68. Rose, "The United States Steel Duquesne Works," 185-87.

69. E.T. Weir, "I Am What Mr. Roosevelt Call an Economic Royalist," *Fortune* 14 (October 1936): 120.

70. Alec Kirby, "Ernest Tener Weir," in *Iron and Steel in the Twentieth Century*, Bruce E. Seely, ed. (Bruccoli Clark Layman, 1994), 466-69; Teresa Lynn Ankney, "The Pendulum of Control: The Evolution of the Weirton Steel Company, 1909-1951," Ph.D. Diss., Catholic University of America, 1993, 50.

71. Weir, 122.

72. Ankney, 47, 51.

73. In the Matter of Weirton Steel and Steel Workers Organizing Committee, 32 N.L.R.B., No. 179, June 25, 1941,1208-10.

74. In the District Court of the United States for the District of Delaware, "United States of America v. Weirton Steel Company," Equity No. 1060, Brief for the United States, [1934], 14.

75. John A. Fitch, "A Man Can Talk in Homestead," *Survey Graphic* 25 (February 1936): 76.

76. 32 N.L.R.B., No. 179, 1163; Kelly, 146; La Follette Committee Hearings, 7045-46; *Pittsburgh Sun Telegraph* quoted in Ankney, 132.

77. Alfred Romagnoli to Frances Perkins, June 9, 1934, Records of the Federal Mediation and Conciliation Service, Dispute Case Files, Case #176-1609, Record Group 280, National Archives and Records Administration, College Park, MD; *Amalgamated Journal*, 19 October 1933.

78. E.T. Weir to the Employees of the Weirton Steel Company, September 29, 1933, Records of the Federal Mediation and Conciliation Service, Dispute Case Files, Case #176-344.

79. Ankney, 95; "United States of America v. Weirton Steel Company," Brief for the United States, 26.

80. Ankney, 96-97; Lorwin and Lubnig, 103; "United States of America v. Weirton Steel Company," Opinion of the Court, February 27, 1935, 15-16, "Brief for the United States, 31, 36; Harold M. Stephens, "Memorandum for the President: United States v. Weirton Steel Company," August 21, 1934, Records of the National Steel Labor Relations Board, Box 21.

81. Franklin D. Roosevelt to the Attorney General and General Johnson, January 16, 1934, President's Official File #342, Box 1, Franklin D. Roosevelt Papers, Franklin D. Roosevelt Library, Hyde Park, NY; Harold M. Stephens, "Memorandum for the President," August 21, 1934, President's Official File #1164, Box 1, Roosevelt Papers; "United States of America v. Weirton Steel Company," Opinion of the Court, February 27, 1935, 73-74.

82. "Executive Order Strengthens Power of National Labor Board," February 1, 1934, Records of the National Recovery Administration, Box 2977; Irving Bernstein, *Turbulent Years* (Boston: Houghton Mifflin, 1970), 178.
The government lost this round with Weirton Steel because of general confusion as to what constituted a violation of Section 7(a), but the National Labor

Relations Board dissolved Weirton Steel's company union in 1941. Even a cursory review of the voluminous amount of evidence collected by the Justice Department strongly suggests that this decision might have been taken earlier if the Wagner Act had been in place when the first Weirton decision was made. See 32 N.L.R.B., No. 179.

83. National Recovery Administration, Press Release No. 6998, August 5, 1934, American Federation of Labor Papers, Series 4, Box 64; Daugherty, et. al., 441, 444; O'Connor, *Steel-Dictator*, 317, 328; *Iron Age* 135 (6 June 1935): 61.

84. *Steel* 45 (15 October 1934): 14; Moody, 325-26.

85. Richberg, "Commentary,"10.

86. American Iron and Steel Institute, "Steel Workers' Elections Show Overwhelming Majority Are Opposed to Strike—Present Employee Plans Favored," June 13, 1934, American Federation of Labor Papers, Series 4, Box 70.

87. "Steel Facts and the Steel Code," 4-5. 4.6% of the cases withdrawn and 7.1% of the cases were compromised.

88. Frederick Harbison, "Labor Relations in the Iron and Steel Industry, 1936 to 1939," Ph.D. Diss., Princeton University, 1940, 17.

Chapter Seven

The Steel Workers Organizing Committee Versus U.S. Steel

> Personally, I expect to see this movement extended. The plant representatives will reach out toward each other and we shall have company-wide bargaining agencies. After that the organization of employes at one company will seek affiliation with that of another, and we shall have an organization of employes at the United States Steel Corporation. And then, the organization in the independent steel companies will be brought in and the steel workers of the country regardless of the identity of the employer, will belong to a single organization.
>
> —Anonymous U.S. Steel Executive, February 1936.[1]

Myron C. Taylor was born into luxury in 1874. His father made his millions in leather and textiles. Taylor attended Cornell University for his undergraduate degree and for law school, during which time he studied with the future Supreme Court Justice Charles Evans Hughes. Upon completion, Taylor began his career in corporate finance. His first success came in the textile industry, where he invested and served as board chairman for numerous firms. Before World War I, he organized firms that made special fabrics for the growing auto industry. After the war, he reorganized the Goodyear Tire and Rubber Company so that it could escape its creditors. In 1925, he joined U.S. Steel's Board of Directors. Upon Elbert Gary's death in 1927, Taylor became chairman. Unlike the autocratic Gary, Taylor readily passed responsibilities to his subordinates, choosing to concentrate his attentions on the Corporation's finances. During Taylor's tenure as chairman, U.S. Steel rationalized its corporate structure, consolidated its plant operations and modernized its facilities.[2] This lawyer and financier also did something that the traditional steel men who had once run the company never would have considered. On March 2nd, 1937, after secret negotiations with Congress of Industrial Organizations President John L. Lewis, he signed a contract with an independent union, the Steel Workers Organizing Committee (SWOC).

In November 1937, eight months after his controversial decision on union recognition, Taylor announced his resignation as U.S. Steel's Chairman of the Board, effective the next April. When United States Steel held its annual dinner for its directors and top managers on January 11, 1938, it became a testimonial banquet for the retiring chairman. Numerous speakers reviewed many of the achievements of Taylor's ten-year tenure. About halfway through the speeches, the toastmaster asked Nathan L. Miller, the former Governor of New York and the Counsel for the Corporation, to speak about the factors that led to the contract with SWOC. Because his remarks were intended for "the members of the family within these walls," Miller felt comfortable "giving the lowdown" on aspects of the negotiations leading up to that agreement, which outsiders had "grossly misrepresented."[3]

Contrary to the popular wisdom on this subject, Miller focused on a November 1936 complaint filed by the union charging it with multiple violations of the National Labor Relations Act (NLRA). Also known as the Wagner Act (after its primary sponsor, Senator Robert F. Wagner of New York), it became law when President Roosevelt signed this legislation on July 5th, 1935. Congress intended for the Wagner Act to replace Section 7(a) of the recently declared unconstitutional National Industrial Recovery Act. It not only repeated Section 7(a)'s guarantee that workers could "organize and bargain collectively through representatives of their own choosing," but also outlined a series of unfair labor practices defined as violating this guarantee and created the National Labor Relations Board (NLRB) to enforce the law. The NLRB held hearings on the SWOC complaint in December 1936. A decision was pending on this matter at the time of the U.S. Steel/SWOC agreement.[4]

Naturally, the entire steel industry hated the Wagner Act. The editor of the journal *Steel* condemned it for being drafted "in an atmosphere of vindictiveness toward employers and of animosity to employe representation plans."[5] Before the law passed, Charles Hook of ARMCO steel complained in a nationwide radio address that it

> would place the Federal Government in the position of dictating the most intimate labor relationships between the employers and their employees in every city, town, and hamlet in the country. . . . It would deprive both the employers and the employees of their inherent rights as free American citizens to conduct their relations in a spirit of mutual respect and confidence, under local conditions and free from the interference or dictation of third parties.[6]

Employers in many industries, including steel, had refused to enforce the NLRA until it had undergone a test in the Supreme Court, but, according to Miller, the Corporation feared the risks that this strategy would have entailed. He told the dinner:

> I have not the slightest doubt that if we had gone to a conclusion [of the NLRB decision-making process] with the Wagner Act sustained, we would have had an order of the Board so drastic that without the slightest doubt we would have had a closed shop in the steel industry today and the C.I.O. would most certainly been recognized as the exclusive bargaining agent. . . . We did not get any order, and it is due to the fact that . . . Mr. Taylor concluded the famous "Taylor-Lewis Agreement."[7]

In other words, Taylor felt the primary threat to the open shop at U.S. Steel in March 1937 was not SWOC, but the NLRB.

The Corporation or any of its representatives never offered this explanation in public. At his final stockholder's meeting, Taylor claimed that he had signed the contract because of his "duty as a trustee for our stockholders and as a citizen to make any honorable settlement that would ensure a continuance of work, wages and profits." He argued that he wanted to avoid a costly strike at a time when business was beginning to enter a sustained recovery.[8] Rather than absorb the cost of fighting the union, this statement implies that Taylor wanted to pass that cost on to his competitors. This line of explanation was immediately adopted as the best explanation for U.S. Steel's change in policy by contemporary observers. Scholars have followed this line of reasoning too. Many have tended to see Taylor's explanation as an indication that the Corporation made a rational economic decision when it abandoned its open shop policy.[9] Labor historians pay particular attention to the role that steelworkers themselves played in Taylor's decision. For example, Melvyn Dubofsky and Warren Van Tine argue that U.S. Steel changed its labor policy "because workers and their labor movement had refashioned American economic and political reality."[10]

In fact, SWOC was much less successful at organizing workers at U.S. Steel in the weeks preceding the Taylor-Lewis agreement than most scholars recognize. Corporation executives believed that only government intervention through the NLRB could have forced U.S. Steel to accept the closed shop in its mills. The Taylor-Lewis agreement recognized the union as collective bargaining representative only for those employees who had explicitly joined. This seemed like a better alternative than the closed shop that management feared. This does not deny that the need to avoid a costly strike played a role in the Corporation's decision, but the firm's commitment to individual achievement and unfettered control over its labor relations outweighed whatever underlying economic rationale management had in making the agreement. In fact, the easier economic choice would have been to fight the union because the Corporation knew it was weak. Therefore, the cost of that fight would have been minimal. Instead, U.S. Steel recognized SWOC because it believed that eventual support from the U.S. government would soon make the union too strong to control. Yet the Corporation could not forsee the outcome of this policy decision. By taking this position, U.S. Steel brought about the union shop faster than it would have otherwise come.

A Different Approach to Organizing Steelworkers

Although more successful than any other steel industry organizing campaign during the Nonunion Era, SWOC was not successful enough to have forced the industry to recognize it without the threat of government intervention. SWOC built its campaign to organize the steel industry upon the ashes of the Amalgamated Association of Iron and Steel Workers' organizing efforts during the code years. Local leaders came out of efforts to use the ERPs to extract significant concessions from management. Those efforts predated SWOC. For example, on February 27th, 1934, the employee representatives at the National Tube Company subsidiary plant in Ellwood City, Pennsylvania, asked the National Labor Relations Board to settle a dispute over wages between the ERP's labor and management representatives. A U.S. Steel vice-president had to be dispatched to Pittsburgh in order to strike a compromise. When workers at the Corporation's Duquesne plant elected Elmer Maloy as an employee representative, the first thing he did was demand a wage increase. Maloy later proposed amendments to the employee representation plan that even a management representative supported.[11] The reason for all this unsanctioned initiative by employee representatives was, as one CIO official later recognized, that workers felt "safer and more secure by using the apparatus which the company has set up" than they would have by joining outside unions.[12]

The first moves towards complete independence among U.S. Steel's ERPs appeared shortly after the passage of the Wagner Act. Seeing the law as legal cover for collective action, employee representatives worked to turn the ERPs into outside unions. In August 1935, workers at U.S. Steel's South Works in Chicago voted to organize their own independent union. By the fall, it had a dues-paying membership of between 1300 and 1500 people. It would eventually grow to some 3,000 people before affiliating with SWOC in July 1936. In September 1935, all the employee representatives in the multi-plant American Sheet and Tin Plate subsidiary held a convention in New Castle, Pennsylvania. At first, U.S. Steel tried to stop the gathering, but when it became apparent that the convention would be held anyway, the Corporation paid for the entire gathering, including the travel expenses of the delegates. After hearing speeches from management on the first day, the representatives voted to exclude management from the two remaining days of the meeting. The convention passed resolutions asking for a 15% wage increase, an increase in the minimum monthly pension and vacations with pay.[13]

The convention idea spread throughout U.S. Steel's many subsidiaries. On January 26th, 1936, 80 delegates from the nine original Carnegie Steel plants met at the Fort Pitt Hotel in Pittsburgh. Management was informed of the gathering in advance, but when the company offered to pay the expenses for this meeting, the representatives turned them down, fearing acceptance might compromise their independence. The meeting voted to establish a permanent central committee of employee representatives from throughout U.S. Steel's plants in the Pittsburgh area. Representatives from five plants showed up at the Central Committee's first March meeting. That meeting demanded recognition of the Central Committee as the collective bargaining unit for the Pittsburgh area and compulsory arbitration. Around this same time, the company unions at Gary, Duquesne, and McKeesport, Pennsylvania, as well as the Edgar Thomson Works in Braddock, Pennsylvania made similar demands on management. In June 1936, the employees at Duquesne reelected their former employee representative, John J. Mullen, to his old position, even though he had left the employ of the company the previous January. Management opposed this action because it set a dangerous precedent with regard to outside representatives, but Mullen served in the post anyway.[14]

Encouraged by such actions and upset about the breakdown of the Amalgamated Association of Iron, Steel and Tin Workers' efforts to organize the steel industry, John L. Lewis, then just President of the United Mine Workers (UMW), brought the issue of a new steel organizing campaign to the October 1935 convention of the American Federation of Labor (AFL). "We are anxious to have collective bargaining established in the steel industry," he told the delegates, "and our interest in that is, to that degree, selfish because our people know that if the workers were organized in the steel industry and collective bargaining there was an actuality, it would remove the incentive of the great captains of the steel industry to destroy and punish and harass our people who work in the captive coal mines throughout this country, owned by the steel industry."[15] During this gathering, Lewis punched William L. Hutcheson of the carpenters' union, an act that led directly to the formation of the CIO a few weeks later.[16] Besides "selfish" reasons pertaining to the captive mines, the steel industry had to be organized if workers in other mass production industries were to have any hope of exercising their right to collective bargaining because steel remained the lead industry in the American anti-union movement. Therefore, CIO officials began to consider how to organize steel shortly after the group's formation that November.[17]

The AFL Executive Council charged the Amalgamated Association with the task of outlining a blueprint of its own during the 1935 convention. Under the plan drawn up a few months later, the Amalgamated asked the Executive Council "to sponsor, conduct and manage the campaign of organization," but under this proposal all new recruits would become members of the Amalgamated Association. Furthermore, the union insisted

> that as a preliminary to the actual campaign of organization an intensive publicity campaign be conducted by the best experts in the American Labor Movement to bring the story of organization to the Iron and Steel Workers, to develop thereby a desire for organization on the part of the steel workers, and to completely enlist the support of all other branches of organized labor behind the campaign.

The Executive Council rejected this proposal because it lacked a cost estimate and because the Council wanted the campaign to be under the direct control of AFL President William Green. Green devised a new plan that put him in control, and sent it to all AFL affiliates along with a plea for funds to finance the drive. The response was tepid except for an offer of $500,000 from the unions in the Committee for Industrial Organization, the name of the CIO during the period before the AFL kicked out its member unions. The CIO's offer was conditioned on the steel campaign being organized along industrial lines rather than the craft stratifications that the AFL preferred. "The policy of the Executive Council," argued Lewis, "would preserve the leadership of the organizing campaign in the hands of men who through the years demonstrated their utter incapacity to establish stable organization and modern collective bargaining in the mass production industries." President Green, in turn, complained that the CIO has led, "the public to believe, as well as the members associated with the American Federation of Labor, that if the industrial form of organization is given to the steel workers they will come running in. . . . No one ever discusses the difficulties, the opposition, the discrimination, persecution or discharge. The power of entrenched privilege. The only thing that is discussed is the form of organization." The AFL proposed another organizing plan that respected traditional craft union lines, but the Amalgamated Association turned them down. On June 3rd, 1936, the Amalgamated agreed to accept the CIO's offer of funds and to affiliate with the CIO. As part of this deal, the CIO established the Steel Workers Organizing Committee on June 17th.[18]

Under the terms of this deal, the SWOC had complete control over the organizing campaign. "Messrs. Tighe and Leonard have almost literally nothing to say and not much more than that to do," wrote *Fortune* magazine a few months after the campaign began. "Technically the new members join the Amalgamated, but the Amalgamated has handed everything over to the Steel Workers' Organizing Committee except actual issuance of charters."[19] SWOC itself was a top-down organization. Lewis had the power to name every member of the Committee. His most important appointment was United Mine Workers Vice-President Philip Murray as SWOC's chairman. Like the UMW, the Committee divided the country into three regions: Pittsburgh (which included the Youngstown area), the Midwest (mainly Chicago and Gary) and the Birmingham region; and it established field offices in each one. SWOC relied on the experience of other CIO unions for organizers, most notably the UMW, because, as Murray later put it, "In an industry with so little history of successful organizing . . . it was well nigh impossible to recruit a competent staff from the ranks of steel workers." At first, SWOC hired approximately 150 organizers. Later that figure grew to as many as 328.[20]

"The objective of the Committee," declared Chairman Murray, reading a statement of policy at the group's organizational meeting, "is to establish a permanent organization for collective bargaining in the steel industry. We repeat:—To establish a permanent organization of the workers for the orderly and peaceful presentation and negotiation of their grievances and demands is the task to which we shall devote ourselves."[21] In order to achieve this goal, SWOC devised a strategy that differed greatly from that of every prior campaign to organize the steel industry during the Nonunion Era. The group's two overriding concerns were caution and secrecy. SWOC devoted the first months of the campaign to advertisement and education. It staged mass meetings where SWOC staff members, ministers, professors and congressmen touted unionism and its benefits for steelworkers. Unlike the National Committee during the disastrous 1919 strike, SWOC would not summon its members to the picket line before they were fully prepared. This stance had the added benefit of contradicting management accusations that SWOC only wanted to stir up trouble. The Committee needed secrecy in order to overcome employer resistance. In previous steel industry campaigns, the Amalgamated Association would usually organize a new lodge when ten or more workers applied for membership. Invariably, these leaders would be singled out for punishment, often discharged; then the lodge would collapse. SWOC adopted the policy that "a charter will be issued and the local union will begin to function as such only when a *sufficiently large number of employees* have signed up as to insure the greatest possible degree of strength and solidarity." Organizers sent signed membership cards directly to the national office to limit the chances that management spies would learn the names of new recruits.[22]

SWOC's first target was the employee representation plans at U.S. Steel's Carnegie-Illinois subsidiary (the two subsidiaries merged in 1935 as part of Taylor's corporate restructuring). Carnegie-Illinois alone employed about half of all the workers in the Corporation in 1937, and nearly one fourth of all the steelworkers in the industry. Besides its size and importance, the independence that Carnegie-Illinois employee representatives had already shown was an important reason why SWOC tried so hard to organize them. This policy was a sharp break with the traditional AFL method of calling ERP members names. As Murray later explained, "We realized that a great many of the employee representatives, perhaps the majority, were men honestly interested in doing a good job under The Plan which had been imposed on them and their fellow employees. Our job was to show these men what real unionism meant. To denounce them all as company agents or stooges would be untruthful and poor strategy."[23] Employee representatives who supported SWOC helped the campaign because they never thought their support would get them fired. If they did, this would have supported "the charges often made that the employee representation plans . . . are simply a creature of the employers and in no sense . . . an instrument for real collective bargaining purposes."[24] By turning the company's anti-union instrument against its maker, SWOC magnified the potential to disrupt management's efforts to quell the uprising as it had in previous years.

SWOC's use of communists as organizers was another sharp break with the past. The old leadership of the Amalgamated Association had not only denounced the communists within its ranks, they had made it a violation of the union's constitution for a communist to join. Although the key posts in SWOC belonged to loyal members of the UMW, communists held many important positions within the organization. For instance, the Committee placed a Communist Party official in charge of foreign language organizing. A communist also ran one of the district offices. The most important SWOC official with communist ties was Lee Pressman, a former party member who headed SWOC's legal department. National Chairman William Z. Foster later estimated that sixty of SWOC's full-time organizers were Communist Party members. Communists had been John L. Lewis' chief opponents in factional struggles within the UMW. Why then did SWOC tolerate their presence in its organizing campaign? In steel, more than in any other industry, the only experienced organizers were communists. The Steel and Metal Workers Industrial Union's limited success in the wake of the NRA had served as an important indicator that this citadel of the open shop was not invincible.[25] "Some of the mine workers put in charge said frankly they knew little about steel," reported Edward Wieck after a tour of the Pittsburgh-Youngstown district. "[I]t was very evident that others who did not say so were in the same fix—they leaned heavily on the radical workers who knew steel and its workers."[26] Although they never achieved enough power to influence major policy decisions, the experience and commitment which communists brought to the campaign undoubtedly helped it achieve success.[27]

The rank-and-file movement within the Amalgamated Association during the NRA had been the first time steelworkers made a serious effort to organize along interracial lines. SWOC exhibited this same commitment; in fact, it was a hallmark of the entire CIO. At the beginning, SWOC hired ten black organizers for its staff and assigned them specifically to African American communities. "We have found that the Negro has no confidence in white organizers," remarked one local union president. "He may sign up but it's no sign he's really organized. Individual contact from other Negroes is the best medium to keep the Negro organized." In the Birmingham district, every local with any black constituency named at least one African American Vice-President.[28] The best testament to the success of SWOC among black workers comes from the results of a survey sponsored by U.S. Steel. In the summer of 1936, the Industrial Relations Department of the Corporation's Illinois Steel subsidiary hired the African American journalist Claude Barnett to organize a survey of black steelworkers in Gary, Indiana, to determine their attitude toward SWOC. He found that 40% had joined or planned to join the union. Another 20% indicated that they knew about it, but had nothing more to say. Only 24% percent stated that they would not join.[29] The efforts made to win over this group indicate that SWOC had learned from organized labor's failure in 1919 that African American workers could not be ignored.

The Industry Responds

As soon as SWOC commenced its campaign, steelmakers offered a swift and clear reply. On July 1st, 1936, the American Iron and Steel Institute ran a full-page advertisement in newspapers throughout the country. After charging that the leadership of the campaign had no connection to the industry and that SWOC would use intimidation to achieve its goals, the AISI reiterated the same principles that it had championed since the beginning of the Nonunion Era: "No employee in the Steel Industry has to join any organization to get or hold a job. Employment in the industry does not depend on membership or non-membership in any organization. Advancement depends on individual merit and effort. These are fundamental American principles to which the industry will steadfastly adhere." The Institute went on to argue that existing company unions already satisfied workers' desire for collective bargaining, "The overwhelming majority of the employees in the Steel Industry recently participated in annual elections under their own representation plans and elected their representatives for collective bargaining. The elections were conducted by the employees themselves by secret ballot. One of the purposes of the [SWOC] campaign is to overthrow those plans and the representatives so elected." At the end of the text, the AISI promised that, "The Steel Industry will use its resources to the best of its ability to protect its employees and their families from intimidation, coercion and violence, and to aid them in maintaining collective bargaining free from interference from any source."[30]

The advertisement gave the impression that steel companies had united against organized labor, but this impression was misleading. Myron Taylor opposed this declaration, although he did not try to stop its publication. Taylor's firm took a different approach to fighting SWOC because its business circumstances were not the same as those of the rest of the industry and because it was the primary target of the campaign. With more to lose from a prolonged strike, the Corporation proved to be more willing to compromise. An emerging generation of leadership at U.S. Steel contributed to this new flexibility on labor matters. Upon taking over U.S. Steel in 1927, Myron Taylor slowly moved to bring in new blood. In 1931, Taylor set an age limit of 65 for the Corporation's board directors. As a result the age of the leaders at U.S. Steel dropped dramatically. In 1928, the average age of the members of the board of directors was 64 years old. By 1937, it had dropped to 59. The average age of the last six additions to the board in 1937 was 45. Taylor himself retired in late-1937, continuing this trend.[31]

The new generation had different career histories from the men who had once managed U.S. Steel. Like Taylor, many of the new directors started their careers outside the steel industry. And like Taylor, many of these new corporate leaders did not start their careers working in the mills at the bottom of the job ladder. Therefore, they were not wedded to the old leadership's core values. For example, Edward Stettinius, Jr., the vice-chair of the Corporation's Finance Committee and Taylor's successor as chairman, was the son of the president of the Diamond Match Company. Benjamin Fairless received an undergraduate degree in civil engineering from the College of Wooster. He began his career as a surveyor for the Wheeling and Lake Erie Railroad, and started work in the mills as an engineer. Fairless was also one of many executives hired away from other steel companies, something which seldom happened in the earlier days when working one's self up from the bottom of the heap was the Corporation's guiding employment philosophy.[32]

Chairman Taylor had spent most of his career outside the steel industry, so he did not have the same personal interest in the ethic of individual achievement that had been so important to the previous generation of the Corporation's executives. This held true for many of the other men running U.S. Steel by the late-1930s. John A. Fitch talked with a number of U.S. Steel executives in preparation for an article published in February 1936. He asked each of them why the troublemakers making demands of the company were not fired. This is his composite of their responses:

> Times have changed. New laws are on the statute books, many of them of a character that could never have been anticipated. We've had 7-a and now we have the Wagner law both of which in effect prohibit discharging men for joining unions. We are not law-breakers. We go along with the government. True enough, 7-a was unconstitutional. We think the Wagner law is unconstitutional too, but that isn't all there is to it. These laws and other things have created a great nationwide sentiment about the right of collective bargaining and the idea that a working man has a right to join a union has gained widespread currency.[33]

Had the management of U.S. Steel felt differently, it would have fought SWOC like its smaller competitors did rather than accede to its demand for recognition. This dichotomy of approaches represented a sea change in the history of labor relations in the steel industry. "The Steel Corporation dislikes unions as much as ever," wrote a writer for *The Nation* in August 1936, "but it is no longer the aggressive leader in the crusade. In this as in other fields leadership has passed to independents like National and Republic."[34] In other words, outside observers could already see the difference in approaches to labor relations between U.S. Steel and its smaller competitors seven months before the Corporation's March 1937 agreement with SWOC.

Not every leader at U.S. Steel saw labor in a new light. Consider the reaction to Taylor's 1935 order liquidating the Corporation's 40 year-old spy system. Despite Taylor's order, conservative forces in the Corporation management hierarchy continued to sponsor espionage. As J.M. Shields of the National Labor Relations Board explained in 1936, "plant officials have privately stated their helplessness 'to do anything about the spy stuff.' Presidents of subsidiaries had declared themselves helpless."[35] Two of the first witnesses before the Senate Committee of Violations of Free Speech and the Rights of Labor (better known as the La Follette Committee) were employee representatives who had been offered money to report on their colleagues. Nevertheless, the Corporation did not use espionage the same way it once did. In the past, U.S. Steel would have fired any worker who joined a union, but now it tolerated union organizers among its employees. "The company knew we were in the A.A.," one employee representative remembered. "I was even approached by a company official and asked if I knew which side my bread was buttered on. I told him I did. He told me I'd better tear that Amalgamated card up. I refused to do this."[36] And although it stockpiled tear gas and guns in the mid-1930s, U.S. Steel never used these munitions against its employees.

It helped those with a more liberal attitude toward labor matters that the SWOC drive did not appear to start well. A representative of the AISI who attended SWOC's first national meeting in Homestead on July 5, 1936 reported: "I am certain that there were not over a thousand persons in attendance, and a large percentage of these were spectators. . . . The lack of enthusiasm—which could not be credited to any fault of the two admittedly good speakers—was gratifying to me. Further, the many comments which I overheard would not indicate that there is any real danger at the drive being successful."[37] Because of its confidence in ultimate victory, U.S. Steel continued its policy of making limited concessions to combat worker efforts at organization. Yet rather than stifle organization, over time these concessions just led to more demands. For example, in response to calls from employees, the Corporation announced in May 1936 that workers with a service record of five years or more would be eligible for vacations with pay. But demands over vacation continued. Employee representatives wanted additional vacation time for employees with more seniority. Another important issue for employee representatives was the basic forty-hour week. This meant workers would be paid overtime for any work over that amount. In July, the Corporation announced that time-and-one-half would be paid to employees who worked over eight hours a day or forty-eight hours a week. Ironically, both SWOC and some employee representatives denounced this concession for being tantamount to the imposition of a forty-eight hour week. According to one anti-SWOC employee representative, "One hundred organizers for John L. Lewis could not have done as much good for an outside cause as this did."[38]

U.S. Steel's biggest mistake was its refusal to grant a wage increase to its employees. Before and after the CIO formed, employee representatives from all corners of the Corporation had been demanding a raise. But in mid-1936, U.S. Steel decided that all wage requests had to be decided in Pittsburgh rather than at the local plant. Yet because of engineering studies of whole mill departments being conducted at that time, responses to wage requests were sometimes blocked for as long as six months. The most common argument the Corporation made in response to such demands was to plead poverty. "[T]he management of this company wants very much to grant a wage increase," wrote Carnegie-Illinois President Fairless to the employee representatives of the Farrell–Mercer Works, but "a ten percent wage increase would take almost all of the profit that the U.S. Steel Corporation earned in the first six months of this year." This, Fairless concluded, would take money from the "rank and file of the people who constitute the backbone of this country," namely the Corporation's stockholders.[39] In response, Philip Murray issued a public statement attacking the company's position. He predicted, "The growing tide of the Steel Workers Organizing Committee's campaign compels a wage raise, and the steel industry, with U.S. Steel leading, will grant it."[40] With such arguments on their side, employee representatives continued to pass resolutions asking for raises even after management had already denied many raise demands.

The conflict over a wage increase provided an important impetus for continued interplant organization. "The only way we will get anywhere," noted Elmer Maloy, the same employee representative who had caused trouble in Duquesne before the SWOC campaign began, "is to bring a question up as one unit and not 28 individual plants." In keeping with this principle, employee representatives from both the Chicago and Pittsburgh districts of Carnegie-Illinois met in Pittsburgh on August 25th. They presented a list of demands such as a universal 40-hour week and a 25% wage increase to a Carnegie Steel vice-president in person, but only a few of them wanted to affiliate with SWOC at that time. At another meeting on September 9th, the joint committee of representatives issued a call both for employee representatives throughout the Corporation to join them, as well as for a national wage agreement. Once again, they attempted to present all their demands in person to a management representative. Carnegie-Illinois told them that no one would meet with them. In October, the Corporation created the Pittsburgh District General Council, the first official interplant body of employee representatives. Although the body was originally to consist of six hand-picked representatives, the size of the body was expanded to 18 after the Corporation's intentions became public. The progressives on the panel rejected amendments to the ERP that one representative claimed would make it "nothing but a plaything of management," and subsequently guided through another resolution calling for a wage increase. On November 6th, 1936, right after the presidential election, U.S. Steel finally agreed to grant its workers an across-the-board 10% wage increase, months after other large companies in the industry had already done so.[41]

Even this concession backfired. "SWOC forces Steel Barons to Grant Wage Increase," blared the headline of the Committee's newspaper, *Steel Labor*. Whether or not this claim was actually true, there is no doubt that the union was in front on this issue, putting pressure on U.S. Steel at a time when it was already having trouble controlling its employee representatives. SWOC's long-running campaign for higher wages at U.S. Steel gave it enormous legitimacy when the Corporation finally gave in on this issue. Management's decision to couch its wage proposal in a one-year "contract" with employee representatives was another source of trouble for the Corporation. This proposal was another break with past precedent in labor relations. It signified the first time since 1908 that U.S. Steel ever offered to sign a contract voluntarily. Under this agreement, future wage increases would have been tied to the cost of living. SWOC claimed management delayed the wage proposal only to stop President Roosevelt from taking credit for labor peace before the 1936 election. The Committee also argued that this precedent meant steelworkers' wages would never go up in real terms, even if there were increases in productivity. Many employee representatives refused to sign the contract; others signed reluctantly. The Corporation suffered further embarrassment when in response to the protests of two progressive employee representatives, Secretary of Labor Frances Perkins expressed the opinion that employee representatives had no legal standing to sign contracts. Furthermore, the wage concession did not stop employee representatives from joining together in interplant conferences and demanding further concessions. On November 22nd, employee representatives from the Cleveland-Youngstown area held their first joint conference.

Their demands included a five dollar per day minimum and a further $1.24 per day increase for some employees.[42]

On December 20th, 244 employee representatives from 42 different firms throughout the eastern United States met in Pittsburgh and joined SWOC en masse. At this point, these haphazard gatherings of employee representatives merged together to become the CIO Representative Council. The representatives elected Elmer Maloy as president of this new body. In its first resolution, the Representative Council condemned employee representation "as a farce, a sham, an insult to the intelligence of steel workers, and a Rip Van Winkle form of collective bargaining where the company union representatives try to bargain and the management actually does the collecting." [43] More defections by workers and employee representatives came in the weeks following this meeting, until the March 2nd, 1937, Taylor-Lewis agreement eliminated the risk of joining up and created a flood of applicants for the new union.

How Successful Was SWOC?

"[T]he S.W.O.C. was extraordinarily effective from the moment it was organized," wrote Benjamin Stolberg in 1938.[44] Such initial accounts of SWOC's early history have greatly influenced the subsequent historiography of this subject. Irving Bernstein, in an account only slightly less flattering than Stolberg's, wrote in 1970, "[B]y the end of 1936 it was evident that the steel organizing drive was a success, perhaps to be a great success, and that SWOC had made decisive gains among U.S. Steel's employees."[45] Recent work on this subject is more skeptical about SWOC's strength prior to the U.S. Steel accord. David Brody calls SWOC in early 1937, "essentially a paper organization, a mountain of membership cards plus an indefinable reservoir of goodwill."[46] Such skepticism is warranted. SWOC was not nearly as strong as it seemed in late-1936 and early-1937, not only in terms of commitment among its members, but also in sheer numbers. Had U.S. Steel decided to fight rather than concede, it probably would have won. However, Myron Taylor was more a compromiser than a fighter. Therefore, the Corporation recognized SWOC.

U.S. Steel's employee representatives, although an important and influential constituency, could not make up for the absence of SWOC members among the rest of the workers in the Corporation's mills. To believe that winning over an employee representative was like organizing rank-and-file steelworkers is the equivalent of believing that the company unions actually represented the constituency that elected him. "The company unions represented no one and there was scarcely a person in the organization who believed they did," explained SWOC staffer Meyer Bernstein to the economist Walter Galenson. "Our maneuverings with the ERP's were more feint than anything else. Once in a while ERP men would come over to us, but they didn't necessarily bring any men membership with them."[47] Nevertheless, SWOC still took credit for the actions of independent-minded employee representatives whether or not participants had joined the union. In this way, SWOC created an impression of strength that did not really exist.

Independent action by U.S. Steel's company union representatives began before SWOC ever formed, and would have continued had it never formed. SWOC's leaders recognized this; therefore, rather than demand that every representative they approached immediately join the union, organizers tried to establish a long-term relationship with them. By offering advice and encouragement, they tried to gain their confidence and good will. "The organizer is constantly ready with his arguments and proof," explained one internal CIO memo, "and in time the company union boys swing over." SWOC wanted to bring employee representatives to the gradual realization that they were never going to have their concerns fully addressed working through the ERP. It helped representatives reach out to one another by holding inter-plant conferences; sometimes the Committee even offered to foot the travel expenses of delegates. More importantly, SWOC encouraged employee representatives to continue to make demands on U.S. Steel. "Every time the company refused to give in or delayed its answer to the demands," explained Northeast Region Director Clinton Golden to Frederick Harbison, "we were able to demonstrate the futility and hypocrisy of the company unions."[48] Many employee representatives whom SWOC approached eventually joined the union, but others resisted. Some even continued to resist after the Corporation extended recognition to the Committee.

Despite its poor kickoff rally at Homestead, SWOC's public statements claimed it was making constant steady progress in enlisting recruits throughout the fall of 1936 and winter of 1937. According to *Steel Labor*, on August 20th, "[S]ome 40,000 workers, represented in company unions, are taking their inspiration from the SWOC."[49] In order to increase the size of its membership, SWOC suspended dues collection in

November 1936.[50] On the 20th of that month, the Committee claimed a membership of 82,315. On January 9th, 1937, *Steel Labor* claimed SWOC's membership passed 125,000. According to Robert R.R. Brooks, SWOC had approximately 200,000 members at the time of the U.S. Steel accord on March 2nd. Because the union kept its membership rolls secret, these claims were never verified. "How many men these tactics have so far succeeded in organizing is an utter mystery," wrote *Fortune* in October 1936. "Literally no one in the world knows, except the half-dozen men at the head of the S.W.O.C. and a few of the C.I.O. leaders."[51] Since their goal was to convince employers to recognize their union without a strike, these union leaders had every incentive in the world to exaggerate their strength.

Once-secret membership figures in the official papers of David M. McDonald, then Secretary Treasurer of SWOC, show the extent to which the Committee practiced this strategy. These numbers are displayed in Table 7.1. The McDonald figures show that actual SWOC membership was tens of thousands less than the organization claimed publicly. It claimed to have 82,000 members in late November, but had only 48,370 even after two weeks of potential growing time. It claimed 125,000 members on January 9, 1937, but had only 91,000. On February 6th, 1937, the last week before the Taylor-Lewis agreement for which U.S. Steel membership figures are available, only 23,475 Corporation employees had joined the union out of approximately 129,940 employees in the United States Steel Corporation. That amounts to only 18%.[52]

The poor national membership figures were the result of serious problems with organizing efforts at plants throughout the U.S. Steel organization. The local at the Edgar Thomson works had only 783 members. Despite a concentrated effort and the claims of 4000 members, the Homestead Works also remained largely unorganized. At Duquesne, the union had 1300 members out of a workforce of 6000, and only a handful of them paid their dues. The vast majority of the members were less-skilled, foreign-born workers. Therefore, SWOC's lack of success at places like Duquesne may demonstrate the ethnic divisions in the plant's workforce. Had there been an NLRB election on the question of union representation in late-February 1937, SWOC probably would have lost.[53]

If SWOC was trying to deceive the Corporation about the extent of its strength, the ruse failed. U.S. Steel had been keeping close watch of SWOC's progress since the Committee formed the previous summer, and the Corporation never saw the union as a serious threat. In July

Table 7.1: SWOC Membership, December 1936-March 1937

Week Ending:	Member at U.S. Steel	Total Enrollment in SWOC
12/5/1936	*	48,370
12/12/1936	*	60,101
12/19/1936	14,134	70,796
12/26/1936	15,875	76,373
12/31/1936	17,261	80,281
1/9/1937	19,067	91,023
1/16/1937	20,465	100,088
1/23/1937	21,602	*
1/30/1937	22,533	*
2/6/1937	23,475	117,426
2/13/1937	*	121,130
2/20/1937	*	128,533
2/27/1937	*	136,101
3/6/1937	*	143,059
3/10/1937	*	240,022

* = Information Unavailable

Source:

United Steelworkers of America, President's Office.David J. McDonald Papers, Box 156. Historical Collections & Labor Archives, Pattee Library,Pennsylvania State

1936, Arthur Young reported that "there is no indication our employees are taking any particular interest in the organizing campaign of the C.I.O."[54] In August 1936, Young told upper management that SWOC meetings were "not well attended" and that most of those present were members of the United Mine Workers.[55] In September, he estimated the strength of the union in the company's mills at 1600. In the same vein, a report from an outside consulting firm dated November 17th, 1936, concluded, "Efforts to organize the employees have met with little success."[56]

Because of its internal intelligence apparatus, the Corporation knew what SWOC did not make public: the union's membership figures were inflated and the employee representation plans were checking further growth. Even acknowledging gains in late 1936-1937, the Committee was not keeping up with the growth of the workforce brought about by increased employment to meet the demands of a rebounding market for steel. Therefore, the SWOC campaign alone could not have forced U.S. Steel to the bargaining table.

Philip Murray later claimed that SWOC "virtually 'captured' every company union in the steel industry," but the committee's strength among employee representatives has been exaggerated as much as its membership figures.[57] The Committee claimed credit for every demand that any body of employee representatives made on its employer, but this did not necessarily mean the representatives supported the union. In Duquesne, for example, SWOC had only won over five of the plant's fifteen representatives by the time of the March accord. One of those representatives, Joint General Conference Chairman Elmer Maloy, had to be paid "cold cash" for his support.[58] Many company union representatives remained loyal to management even after the signing of the SWOC contract. Because U.S. Steel knew of SWOC's weakness, only fear of a government-imposed closed shop arrangement can adequately explain Myron Taylor's decision to recognize the union.

U.S. Steel Breaks Ranks

The talks between Myron Taylor and John L. Lewis that culminated in the March accord began after a chance encounter in the dining room of the Mayflower Hotel in Washington, D.C., on January 9th, 1937. Taylor had been thinking about the wording of a possible compromise between U.S. Steel and the CIO since the previous summer. Therefore, when Lewis quietly suggested a meeting, Taylor offered to see him the next day. This led to a lengthy series of conferences that eventually resulted in a contract. Despite the fact that Lewis was making front page news every day because of the famous General Motors sitdown strike, the media did not know about these talks until after the two parties announced the initial agreement. Some directors were against recognizing the union in any way, but others offered encouragement. The leaders of the Corporation's competitors had been told about the talks early on in the negotiation process. They did not like this development, but could do little about it. Lewis told almost nobody about his talks with Taylor.[59]

The negotiations took place in strict secrecy. Had Lewis been seen at U.S. Steel's New York headquarters, his presence would not have been surprising because he had been elected a collective bargaining representative for some of the Corporation's "captive mines" in 1933. Nevertheless, to preserve their secrecy, most of the negotiations between the two men occurred at Taylor's Fifth Avenue townhouse. Their extended talks broke down at least once; but on March 2nd, 1937, U.S. Steel signed a preliminary agreement recognizing SWOC as a collective bargaining agent for its employees who belonged to the Amalgamated Association of Iron, Steel and Tin Workers. The press, the public and industry observers were all shocked. Observers had been expecting an all-out war between the Corporation and the Committee. Instead, the two parties signed a formal contract on March 17th. Walter Galenson calls this deal "one of the critical junctures in American economic history" because it not only assured the survival of trade unions in a critical industry, but also served as a catalyst for other industries to organize. Although the decision of General Motors to recognize the United Auto Workers a week earlier is remembered because of the dramatic sitdown strikes that preceded it, the U.S. Steel agreement was achieved without violence and with minimal government coercion.[60] This accord marked the beginning of the end of the steel industry's Nonunion Era. Large independent companies continued to resist SWOC, most notably during the Little Steel Strike of 1937, but the Committee's legal maneuvers to protect the rights guaranteed to its members in the National Labor Relations Act would eventually force most of these companies to recognize outside unions during the ensuing years.

The initial agreement between the Steel Workers Organizing Committee and U.S. Steel had five sections. The first section stated that the Carnegie-Illinois Steel Corporation recognized SWOC as the collective bargaining agent for its employees who belonged to the Amalgamated Association. Management also recognized and agreed not to interfere with the right of employees to join the union. In return, SWOC agreed not to intimidate or coerce employees to do the same. Section Two of the agreement increased wages by ten cents an hour for all Carnegie-Illinois employees. Section Three formally established an eight-hour day and a forty-hour week. It is also mandated time and one-half pay for all hours worked over that total. Section Four created a joint committee to establish a working committee to negotiate issues like working conditions and arbitration for disputes. The last section set the length of the contract. It ran for about a year, until February 28th, 1938. Other major U.S. Steel subsidiaries signed nearly identical contracts on March 17th.[61]

To U.S. Steel, the wording of Section One made the agreement palatable. SWOC's willingness to accept bargaining rights only for those employees who had joined the organization meant that, in principle, the new agreement did not alter the Corporation's labor policy at all. Workers who did not join SWOC would not be forced to do so. Interested employees could theoretically continue to bargain with U.S. Steel through the company union. The Corporation believed it could maintain its own ERPs as a counter to the union, as is illustrated by a notice from Carnegie-Illinois President Benjamin Fairless to the workers of his subsidiary:

> The policy of the Carnegie Illinois Steel Corporation remains unchanged. As previously stated on many occasions, the company recognizes the right of its employees to organize and to bargain collectively through representatives of their own choosing. The company will recognize any individual or group or organization as the spokesman for those employees whom they represent, but will not recognize any single organization or group as the exclusive bargaining agency for all the employees. Under this policy the status of the employee representation plans is likewise unchanged. It will continue to be the spokesman for those employees who prefer that method of collective bargaining that has proven so mutually satisfactory throughout its experience.[62]

For this reason, Governor Miller could still insist in 1938 that "there never has been a moment since N.I.R.A. was first inaugurated when the open shop principle was so firmly entrenched legally as it is at the present moment by force of [the Taylor-Lewis] agreement."[63] By then, management cared more about the principle of the open shop than it did the cost of actually bargaining with a union. The Corporation voluntarily recognized SWOC in order to maintain the principle of choice between an inside and outside union, even though at this point it could have probably fought the union and won.

Although the Taylor-Lewis agreement theoretically maintained the open shop at U.S. Steel, so many employees joined SWOC in the weeks following the agreement that in reality the open shop ceased to exist. "I don't know how many we had in U.S. Steel," wrote Meyer Bernstein days after the Corporation signed the preliminary agreement. "But now there is a stampede there. Literally. The office is a madhouse. By the time the details of the agreement are decided upon, we shall certainly have far above a majority in Big Steel, and possibly in all independents as well."[64] SWOC's official membership records show the extent of this stampede. The Committee practically doubled in the weeks following the agreement [See Table 7.1]. Undoubtedly, this marked increase in membership was a direct result of the agreement with U.S. Steel. SWOC did not have complete control over the Corporation's employees. As late as September 1937, only 44% of its workers were SWOC members. Nevertheless, the union did have enough members to become the only viable union in the Corporation's shops.[65]

The limited success of SWOC at U.S. Steel is a sign that the Corporation's fear of a government-imposed closed shop was irrational. The real threat to management's freedom to control in early 1937 came from the SWOC organizing drive. By recognizing the union in order to prevent government intervention, Taylor signaled to uncommitted steelworkers that SWOC was a viable collective bargaining agent. Therefore, the Taylor-Lewis agreement destroyed U.S. Steel's employee representation plan, even though it was supposed to save that organization by preventing the National Labor Relations Board from declaring it in violation of the Wagner Act. Upon reflection, it is easy to see why so many steelworkers joined the outside union in March 1937. The terms of SWOC's contract were superior to anything ever offered through U.S. Steel's ERP. It included the wage and hours clauses from the preliminary agreement, as well as other concessions. Management also agreed to consider seniority as a factor in promotions for the first time. The contract established a formal grievance procedure under which the final arbiter would be an impartial umpire picked with the mutual consent of both parties. The contract recognized July 4th, Labor Day and Christmas as official holidays. Perhaps most importantly, it set a formal date for labor and management to sit down and begin to negotiate the next contract.[66]

A few former employee representatives tried to create alternatives to SWOC. In January 1937, conservatives in the Chicago area created the Steel Employees Independent Labor Organization. By that summer, the thirty-five cents per month it charged in dues made this organization self-supporting. It even had offices, a lodge hall, a full-time president and an attorney. Nevertheless, the group eventually disappeared because it never won a contract. A group in the Pittsburgh area created the American

Union of Steel Workers in the days following the preliminary accord between SWOC and the U.S. Steel. This Pittsburgh group wanted to revive the company union. This organization attracted considerable media attention when it sent a letter to William Green asking for his assistance. The head of the AFL's Metal Trades department met with this organization, but the AFL eventually withheld recognition on the grounds that it was under "company influence." The final blow to the company union came after the U.S. Supreme Court handed down the famous Jones & Laughlin decision in April 1937. This ruling upheld the constitutionality of the National Labor Relations Act, including its provisions against company-dominated labor organization. In response to the decision, U.S. Steel withdrew all financial support for the ERP and stopped providing facilities for elections or other company union activities.[67] At that point SWOC had no rivals for the loyalty of the United States Steel Corporation's employees. This guaranteed the Committee a strong base of support for its campaign to organize the rest of the steel industry.

"The Tremendous Force of Government"

Like other pro-management observers in the days following the surprise announcement, the editors of the trade journal *Steel* felt the need to make sense of the Taylor-Lewis agreement. "Last week as the Carnegie-Illinois Steel Corp. signed up with the SWOC, the big question in the industry was "what was back of it?" They argued that it was "the tremendous force of government," embodied by 28 million labor votes for Franklin D. Roosevelt in the last election and the threat of further government intervention in other areas of labor relations.[68] During the 1936 election, John L. Lewis closely identified SWOC's cause with the President's cause. In the national radio broadcast that launched the steelworkers' organizing campaign, he linked American steelmakers with the "economic royalists" whom Roosevelt had denounced in his acceptance speech before the Democratic National Convention in Chicago earlier that summer. As the presidential campaign wore on, SWOC diverted considerable energy and resources to Roosevelt's reelection and to the election of local candidates who supported organized labor. Staff members addressed many Roosevelt rallies, and in turn the committee invited many candidates who supported the President for re-election to address its rallies. Not only did Roosevelt win SWOC strongholds throughout the country by large margins, voters removed long-standing Republican anti-labor regimes from seventeen western Pennsylvania steel towns. Since local governments had played an important role in restricting civil liberties during earlier organizing drives, this made SWOC's subsequent efforts significantly easier.[69]

Raymond L. Hogler, a legal scholar, argues that "labor law played at best a minor role in the SWOC organizing campaign" because the vast majority of steelmakers did not recognize workers' rights established by the Wagner Act.[70] This interpretation considers the effect of labor law too narrowly. Labor law embodied the moral force of government whether or not organizers needed to invoke it. The belief that government was on their side and would eventually support them if they asserted their rights inspired many steelworkers to join the union movement. As SWOC Subregional Director Philip Clowes explained to the House Labor Committee in 1939, "We could not organize without the Wagner Act; some protection for our civil rights, our guaranteed rights, our constitutional rights."[71] More importantly, as Philip Murray put it before the same body, the act convinced some steel manufacturers "that the shape of things had changed, that the rights of workers could no longer be denied without imperiling the entire democratic structure of our Government." The success of SWOC-backed candidates in the 1936 elections showed that the public supported politicians who championed collective bargaining.

During its long organizing campaign, SWOC tried to invoke the legal remedies of the Wagner Act only as a last resort. Rather than rely on the NLRB, it wanted to organize the industry itself. "All officers and organizers must understand that primary reliance must not be placed upon the Board for organizing work," wrote the CIO's Legal Department in a memo distributed to all SWOC lodges. "[T]he Board is to be used as an auxiliary weapon only."[72] SWOC first filed charges with the NLRB against U.S. Steel in November 1936, long after the campaign against the Corporation had begun. This case was never fully resolved because of the March accord between the two parties, but U.S. Steel feared this decision would be the mechanism by which the government would impose the closed shop on the entire corporation. "The case had already been decided," explained Nathan Miller to the attendees at the 1938 annual dinner. "It was a certainty that at its termination we would be confronted with the most drastic order that the Board could make."[73] Because of U.S. Steel's unwillingness to openly defy the government and its attachment to the open shop, the Corporation signed its first contract with the union. This is where the "tremendous power of government" benefited the Steel Workers Organizing Committee the most.

Despite its intention to do otherwise, SWOC came to depend upon government-imposed labor law in its organizing effort. The union established a large legal department and made contacts with attorneys in all the steel centers of the country. Their legal team looked into local ordinances on literature distribution, permits for meetings and other issues in order limit the obstacles organizers faced. These local attorneys came to the aid of any worker or organizer who happened to get arrested. This allowed organizers to constantly test the boundaries of the NLRA, thereby encouraging assistance from state and federal officials interested in enforcing the law. In December 1936, for example, a "flying squadron" of SWOC organizers descended on Weirton, West Virginia, accompanied by investigators from the La Follette Committee. The organizers distributed 5,000 copies of *Steel Labor* at the gate of the mill, and left town without incident. During instances where the rights of labor were impeded, SWOC lawyers would file a grievance before the NLRB.[74]

This conception of how government contributed to SWOC's success fits well within two common historiographic understandings of the relationship between the New Deal and the rise of the trade union movement. The traditional view of labor and the New Deal stresses Franklin Roosevelt's indifference to labor reform, rather than the usefulness of those reforms to trade unions. For example, writing in 1973, David Brody pointed out that, "One carries away a distinct impression of *inadvertency* in the role the New Deal played in the expansion of the labor movement."[75] Radical labor historians tend to stress the role of rank-and-file action over the importance of new laws. In the *World of the Worker*, James R. Green approvingly quotes one CIO organizer who said "industrial workers made 'their own labor history' during the Depression."[76] To Green and other New Left scholars, the structure of collective bargaining that the Wagner Act set up helped sap worker militancy by making them rely on a bureaucratic structure for redress.

The case of the steelworkers offers evidence for both these arguments. SWOC got no help from Franklin Roosevelt. In fact, the administration appeared even less sympathetic to the cause of trade unionism in the steel industry as time passed. Nevertheless, the laws that the administration approved, especially the Wagner Act were essential to the Committee's organizing activities. Yet for much of 1936 and 1937 SWOC wasn't really doing anything substantive to help steelworkers because independent-minded ERP representatives and other employees essentially organized themselves. The National Labor Relations Act was both a cause and a tool of this emerging mass movement. "[T]he new federal labor law reinforced . . . activism [among steelworkers]," writes Robert Zieger:

> Favorable decisions by the [NLRB] and in the appellate courts on these cases regularly buoyed SWOC's standing even in nonunion mills, providing proof that the old regime in the steelworks was gone forever. Discharged union activists often won substantial back pay awards and returned triumphantly to their jobs. Resort to the legal arena reinforced SWOC's and the CIO's status as the protector of workers' rights and as a substantial and vigorous actor in the industrial relations regime.[77]

If the bargaining structure of the NLRA proved to be the kiss of death for worker militancy, it also needs to be recognized that the mass movement among steelworkers may never have gotten off the ground without this legislation. It provided legal protection for the people engaged in the activities that made the mass movement possible, even if that protection was not always necessary. The pivotal role that the NLRB played in convincing U.S. Steel to recognize SWOC without a strike is another way that the law contributed to the enlargement of the rank-and-file.

U.S. Steel's largest competitors had no such fear of the NLRB, nor of any other part of government. Firms like Republic Steel and Bethlehem Steel used every tactic available to keep labor unions out of their plants. This is but one indication that the old ways remained strong among the smaller independent companies during the SWOC campaign. Men like Eugene Grace of Bethlehem Steel, Ernest T. Weir of Weirton Steel, and especially Tom Girdler of Republic Steel, who got their starts at U.S. Steel, maintained the same intense opposition to organized labor that the previous generation of leaders held. Unlike Taylor, they refused to compromise their anti-union beliefs, despite the threat of NLRB action and an enormous financial cost. Their recalcitrance sparked the infamous "Little Steel" strike of 1937. Although the management of these firms would win this showdown with SWOC, the fallout from the strike would eventually lead to government action that helped the union spread throughout the industry.

Notes

1. John A. Fitch, "A Man Can Talk in Homestead," *Survey Graphic* 25 (February 1936): 76.

2. Bruce E. Seely, "Myron C. Taylor," in *Iron and Steel in the Twentieth Century*, Bruce E. Seely, ed. (Bruccoli Layman Clark, 1994), 420-23; *Time* 30 (8 November 1937): 59; United States Steel, *Myron Taylor: An Appreciation*, privately published, c. 1956.

3. Nathan N. Miller, "The Thirty-Seventh Annual Dinner of the United States Steel Corporation," January 11, 1938, Edward R. Stettinius Papers, Box 36, The Albert and Shirley Small Special Collections Library, University of Virginia Library, Charlottesville, VA.

4. Miller, Stettinius Papers, Box 36.

5. *Steel* 97 (8 July 1935): 13.

6. Charles R. Hook, "The Effect of the Wagner Bill Upon Recovery," American Iron and Steel Institute, May 3, 1935, 2.

7. Miller, Stettinius Papers, Box 36.

8. Myron Taylor, "Ten Years of Steel," April 4, 1938, U.S. Congress, Senate, Committee on Education and Labor, *Violations of Free Speech and Assembly and Interference With Rights of Labor*, [La Follette Committee Hearings], 74th Cong., 2nd Sess., 1938, 10777.

9. See *Fortune* 15 (May 1937): 179; John David Lages, "The CIO-SWOC Attempt to Organize the Steel Industry, 1936-1942: A Restatement and Economic Analysis," Ph.D. Diss., Iowa State University, 1967, 77-91; Walter Galenson, *The CIO Challenge to the AFL* (Cambridge: Harvard University Press, 1960), 93-95; Irving Bernstein, *Turbulent Years* (Boston: Houghton Mifflin, 1970), 467-70; Richard A. Lauderbaugh, "Business, Labor, and Foreign Policy: U.S. Steel, the International Steel Cartel, and Recognition of the Steel Workers Organizing Committee," *Politics & Society* 6 (1976): 433-36; Melvyn Dubofsky and Warren Van Tine, *John L. Lewis*, (New York: Quadrangle/The New York Times, 1977), 275-76; David Brody, *Labor in Crisis*, 2nd ed. (Urbana: University of Illinois Press, 1987), 179-85; Colin Gordon, *New Deals: Business, Labor, and Politics in America, 1920-1935* (New York: Cambridge University Press, 1994), 226-30.
Few economists or historians have ever factored in the role of government intervention in U.S. Steel's decision before. One study that considers the possibility of NLRB intervention as one of many reasons for Taylor's decision is James Douglas Rose, "The United States Steel Duquesne Works, 1886-1941: The Rise of Steel Unionism," Ph.D. Diss., University of California–Davis, 1997, 261-62. While earlier explanations are based on informed speculation, mine is based on private information from a vital participant in the negotiations.

10. Dubofsky and Van Tine, 275.

11. A.C. Jewett, "Memorandum," October 27, 1934, Records of the National Labor Relations Board, Pittsburgh Case Files, Record Group 25, Box 8, National Archives and Records Administration, College Park, MD; Elmer Maloy Oral History Interview, November 7, 1967, 12, Historical Collections & Labor Archives, Pattee Library, Pennsylvania State University, State College, PA.

12. [John Brophy], "Summary of Situation in Steel," November 23, 1935, Katherine P. Ellickson Collection, Box 16, Archives of Labor and Urban Affairs, Walter P. Reuther Library, Wayne State University, Detroit, MI.

13. Fitch, "A Man Can Talk in Homestead," 73-74; Raymond L. Hogler, "Worker Participation, Employer Anti-Unionism, and Labor Law: The Case of the Steel Industry, 1918-1937," *Hofstra Labor Law Journal* 7 (Fall 1989): 29; Rose M. Stein, "Steel Robots That Came Alive," *The Nation* 142 (2 February 1936): 160-61.

14. Robert R.R. Brooks, *As Steel Goes . . .* (New Haven: Yale University Press, 1940), 13; Rose, "The United States Steel Duquesne Works," 194; U.S. Congress, House, Committee on Labor, *Proposed Amendments to the National Labor Relations Act*, 76th Cong., 1st Sess., 1939, 1698.

15. American Federation of Labor, *Report of Proceedings*, 1935, 539.

16. This story has been told many times. See, for example, Philip Taft, *The A. F. of L. from the Death of Gompers to the Merger* (New York: Harper and Brothers, 1959), 140-46; Bernstein, pp. 386-404 and Robert Zieger, *The CIO, 1935-1955* (Chapel Hill: University of North Carolina Press, 1995), 22-29.

17. Galenson, 79.

18. Amalgamated Association of Iron, Steel and Tin Workers, *Annual Reports of International Officers*, 1935, 132-37; American Federation of Labor, Minutes of the Executive Council, January 28, 1936, 179, George Meany Memorial Archives, Silver Spring, MD; Taft, 116-20; American Federation of Labor, *Report of Proceedings*, 1936, 90; American Federation of Labor, Minutes of the Executive Council, May 6, 1936, 48.

19. American Federation of Labor, *Report of Proceedings*, 1936, 92-93; *Fortune* 14, October 1936, 148.

20. Philip Murray, "The Problem Before SWOC on June 17, 1936," 1, CIO Papers, Box 33, Department of Archives and Manuscripts, The Catholic University of America, Washington, D.C.; La Follette Committee Hearings, 10418-19.

21. Steel Workers Organizing Committee, "Statement of Policy Adopted at Meeting, June 17, 1936," La Follette Committee Hearings, 10603-04.

22. Frederick Harbison, "Labor Relations in the Iron and Steel Industry, 1936 to 1939," Ph.D. Diss., Princeton University, 1940, 30-31; Clinton S. Golden, To All Staff Members, June 25, 1936, La Follette Committee Hearings, 10605.

23. Frederick Harbison, "Collective Bargaining in the Steel Industry: 1937," Industrial Relations Section, Princeton University, September 1937, 3-4; Steel

Workers Organizing Committee, "Proceedings of the First Wage and Policy Convention," December 14-16, 1937, 32.

Max Gordon suggests that it was Communists within SWOC who championed the idea of "capturing" the company unions while SWOC staff members opposed it. While this may have been true in the Youngstown area (the territory in which his two sources for this conclusion are based), SWOC's national leadership was committed to the idea of radicalizing employee representatives from the outset of the campaign. See Max Gordon, "The Communists and the Drive to Organize Steel, 1936," *Labor History* 22 (Spring 1982): 254-65.

24. Clinton Golden, "Company Unions," July 13, 1936, La Follette Committee Hearings, 10609.

25. Gordon, "The Communists and the Drive to Organize Steel," 254-56.

26. [Edward A. Wieck], "Summary of Observations . . ." September 23, 1936, Edward A. Wieck Collection, Box 10, Archives of Labor and Urban Affairs.

27. All the Communists in the organization were subsequently let go after SWOC established itself in the industry. See Gordon, "The Communists...," 259 and "Personal Histories of the Early CIO," Staughton Lynd, ed. *Radical America* 5 (May-June 1971): 69.

28. Wieck, "Summary of Observations . . .;" Horace R. Cayton and George S. Mitchell, *Black Workers and the New Unions* (Chapel Hill: University of North Carolina Press, 1939), 205, 207.

29. [Claude Barnett], "The Gary Project: Summary and Recommendations," Claude Barnett Papers, Box 280, Chicago Historical Society, Chicago, IL.

For more on Claude Barnett's Gary Project see Lizabeth Cohen, *Making a New Deal* (New York: Cambridge University Press, 1990), 335-36.

30. La Follette Committee Hearings, 10281.

31. *Fortune* 15 (May 1937): 94; *Fortune* 13 (March 1936):186, 188; Myron Taylor, "Remarks to the Annual Meeting of Stockholders," April 5, 1937, p. 10.

32. *Fortune* 13 (March 1936), 186, 188; Bruce E. Seely, "Edward Reilly Stettinius, Jr.," in *Iron and Steel in the Twentieth Century*, 415-17; "Benjamin Franklin Fairless," in *Iron and Steel in the Twentieth Century*, 120-23.

33. Fitch, "A Man Can Talk in Homestead," 75.

34. Dwight Macdonald, "Steelmasters: The Big Four," *The Nation* 143 (29 August 1936): 239.

35. *Fortune* 15 (May 1937): 94; J.M. Shields, "Spies in the Steel Industry," La Follette Committee Hearings, 95, 11-26.

36. Charles Bollinger Oral History Interview, July 1966, 2, Historical Collections & Labor Archives, Pattee Library.

37. Hoyt A. Moore to J.M. Larkin, July 7, 1936, American Iron and Steel Institute Papers, Box 177, Hagley Museum and Library, Wilmington, DE.

38. Brooks, 89; Carnegie-Illinois Steel Corporation Employee Representation Plan, Pittsburgh District Joint General Conference, August 12, 1936, 14, Harold Ruttenberg Papers, Box 4. Historical Collections & Labor Archives, Pattee Library; Harbison, "Labor Relations in the Iron and Steel Industry," 34.

39. Rose, "Shop Floor Divisions and the Making of Steel Unionism During the 1930s," unpublished paper in author's possession, 9; B.F. Fairless, "To the Employee Representatives of Farrell–Mercer Works," September 8, 1936, 1, 3, Ruttenberg Papers, Box 4.

40. Philip Murray to Sub-Regional Directors, September 11, 1936, Ruttenberg Papers, Box 3.

41. Carnegie-Illinois Steel Corporation Employee Representation Plan, Pittsburgh District Joint General Conference, August 12, 1936, 13; Hogler, 29-30; Philip Murray to Sub-Regional Directors, September 11, 1936; *Steel Labor*, 20 October 1936.

42. *Steel Labor*, 20 November 1936; Harbison, "Labor Relations in the Iron and Steel Industry," 40, 43; Brooks, p. 100; "Reps News Letter," December 1, 1936, Ruttenberg Papers, Box 4.

43. CIO Representatives Council, "Minutes," December 20, 1936, Ruttenberg Papers, Box 4.

44. Benjamin Stolberg, *The Story of the CIO* (New York: Viking Press, 1938), 71.

45. Bernstein, 467.

46. David Brody, "The Origins of Modern Steel Unionism: The SWOC Era," in *Forging a Union of Steel*, Paul F. Clark, Peter Gottlieb and Donald Kennedy, eds. (Ithaca, NY: ILR Press, 1987), 21.

47. Galenson, 656, n. 41.

48. Murray, "The Problem Before SWOC," 2-4; Congress of Industrial Organizations, "Answering Company Union Arguments," n.d., 5, Katherine P. Ellickson Collection, Box 15; Harbison, "Labor Relations in the Iron and Steel Industry," 33.

49. *Steel Labor*, 20 August 1936.

50. Harbison, "Labor Relations in the Iron and Steel Industry," 31, n. 1. Dues collection resumed in April 1937.

51. *Steel Labor*, 20 November 1936; *Steel Labor*, 9 January 1937; Brooks, *As Steel Goes . . .* , 120; *Fortune* 14 (October 1936): 148.

52. "Membership Enrollment in Large Steel Manufacturing Concerns," February 6, 1937 and "Summary of Membership Enrolled Week Ending 2-27-37," United Steel Workers of America, President's Office, David J. McDonald Papers, Box 156, Historical Collections & Labor Archives.

53. Rose, "The United States Steel Duquesne Works," 255-57.

54. Edward Stettinius Jr. to Myron Taylor, July 30, 1936, Stettinius Papers, Box 63.

55. Edward Stettinius Jr. to Myron Taylor, August 11, 1936, Stettinius Papers, Box 63.

56. Edward Stettinius Jr. to Myron Taylor, September 1, 1936, Stettinius Papers, Box 63; "Digest of Ford, Bacon & Davis Report No. 37 . . . ," February 2, 1937, Stettinius Papers, Box 45.

57. Philip Murray, untitled speech before the Carolina Political Union, 6.

58. Rose, "Shop Floor Divisions," 10; Rose, "The United States Steel Duquesne Works," 230-31.

59. *Fortune* 15, May 1937, 93-94, 176, 179-80; Miller, Stettinius Papers, Box 36.

60. William Serrin, *Homestead* (New York: Vintage Books, 1992), 211-12; Galenson, 93. On the captive mines agreement, see Dubofsky and Van Tine, 192-97 and Bernstein, 41-52, 56-60.

61. *Steel Labor*, 6 March 1937; *Steel Labor*, 20 March 1937.

62. Dubofsky and Van Tine, 275; B.F. Fairless, "Notice," March 3, 1937, Ruttenberg Papers, Box 4.

63. Miller, Stettinius Papers, Box 36.

64. Meyer Bernstein, unaddressed letter, March 6, 1937, Meyer Bernstein Papers, Box 1, Historical Collections & Labor Archives, Pattee Library.

65. "Summary of Membership Enrolled Week Ending 3-17-37," McDonald Papers, Box 156; "Steel Workers Organizing Committee Versus United States Steel Corporation," c. September 30, 1937, McDonald Papers, Box 156.

66. B.F. Fairless, "Notice," March 3, 1937, Ruttenberg Papers, Box 4; Dubofsky and Van Tine, 274-76.

67. Harbison, "Collective Bargaining in the Steel Industry," 33-34; John A. Fitch, "Steel and the C.I.O.," *Survey Graphic* 26, April 1937, 190; B.F. Fairless to the Employees of Carnegie-Illinois Steel Corporation, April 26, 1937, American Iron and Steel Institute Papers.

68. *Steel* 100 (8 March 1937): 19.

69. Dubofsky and Van Tine, 250; Murray, "The Problems Before the SWOC on June 17, 1936," 6; Eric Leif Davin, "The Littlest New Deal: How Democracy and the Union Came to Western Pennsylvania," paper presented before the conference, "Steel and Steelworkers, 1919 to the Present," June 24, 1995, Carnegie-Mellon University, 1-3.

70. Hogler, 67.

71. *Proposed Amendments to the National Labor Relations Act*, 2076, 1913.

72. David J. McDonald, "To All Lodges and Staff Members of the S.W.O.C.," October 5, 1938, Meyer Bernstein Papers, Box 1.

73. Rose, "The United States Steel Duquesne Works," 240; Miller, Stettinius Papers, Box 36.

74. Unnamed CIO Official "Pre-Contract Labor Day Speech, 1936, Canton, Ohio," n.d., La Follette Committee Hearings, 10630; *Steel Labor*, December 5, 1936.

75. David Brody, "The New Deal and the Labor Movement," in *Workers in Industrial America* (New York: Oxford University Press, 1980), 145.

76. James R. Green, *The World of the Worker* (New York: Hill and Wang, 1980), 172.

77. Zieger, 63-64.

Chapter Eight

The Little Steel Strike and Beyond

> In refusing to grant unions more than the barest minimum of recognition, management encourages the belief—which is widespread among union members in American industry—that it is still opposed to collective bargaining and unions and is only waiting for an opportunity to cast both aside.
>
> —Clinton S. Golden and Harold J. Ruttenberg [of the Steel Workers Organizing Committee], *The Dynamics of Industrial Democracy*, 1942.[1]

The impact of U.S. Steel's agreement with the Steel Workers Organizing Committee sent shock waves through the iron and steel industry. By April 10th, 1937, 51 companies had signed contracts with the Committee. By May 1st, this number had risen to 88. By May 19th, it had grown to 114. The March 17th agreement with U.S. Steel served as the model for all these subsequent contracts. The steel companies that signed contracts with SWOC did so for many different reasons. Some signed in order to stop strikes or head off threatened labor actions. Others signed after losing NLRB-sponsored representation elections. Some firms signed because their executives simply recognized that the union had come to stay and they needed to adjust their labor policies accordingly. All told, the firms that signed contracts with SWOC in the spring of 1937 employed approximately 300,000 workers.[2]

In the fall of 1937, the journalist Louis Adamic sat down to talk to an executive from one of these companies who had recognized SWOC in the months since the U.S. Steel agreement. Adamic gave him the pseudonym Richard Paynter and also kept the name of Paynter's company secret at his request. In the interview, Paynter told Adamic of the day early in the spring of that year when a CIO representative came to visit him:

> He told me right off who he was and what he wanted to talk about. I asked him to sit down, and he began to sell me the idea of us letting the C.I.O. start a union in our plant. He implied it would be to our advantage. Talking very calmly, persuasively he proceeded to tell me—quite accurately, by the way—about all the petty troubles and pains-in-the-neck we'd had in the mill the past few weeks, which in the long run, he hastened to point out to me, amounted to a lot of trouble and expense, which, he further lost no time in emphasizing, were bound to increase as the years went by, regardless of how good a personnel manager we had. Why? Because, he said, in shops where the union had fought and men belonged to it secretly all sorts of damned things happened all the time, which led to fear, nervousness, and jitters among the men, to secret sabotage and loafing on the job and so on. What he was saying was, to an extent, undoubtedly true, and he proceeded to tell me, too, that if we let the union come in, it would take care of our petty difficulties.

"[T]o fight Lewis—to fight the C.I.O.," Paynter told Adamic, "was not the constructive thing to do; and after . . . United States Steel entered into agreement with the C.I.O., when the C.I.O. man came to us, we said "O.K." and we're not sorry."[3] One might easily imagine the leaders of the one hundred thirteen other steel firms that signed contracts with SWOC before May 1937 following the same train of thought; perhaps after a visit from a CIO representative, perhaps not.

But there remained a small cadre of large firms who were unlikely to even speak to a SWOC representative, let alone recognize an outside union. For years, Bethlehem Steel, Republic Steel, Inland Steel, Jones & Laughlin and Youngstown Sheet and Tube were known collectively as "Little Steel."[4] Yet these firms were far from little. Apart from U.S. Steel, they constituted the largest firms in the industry. Unlike the Steel Corporation or Paynter's firm, Little Steel refused to give up its opposition to organized labor in 1937. To Paynter, the economical thing to do was to limit the strife and the fighting so as to save costs immediately and in the future. Little Steel chose to continue to fight organized labor at whatever the cost. Why did different firms choose different policies when faced with similar economic circumstances? Part of the answer is the intensity of the anti-union beliefs of the men who ran these companies. The leaders of U.S. Steel came out of the same ideological lineage as the men who ran the industry during the early decades of the century. As Frank Purnell, the President of Youngstown Sheet and Tube, explained in late-1937, "True labor relations, as I conceive them, involve that intimate relationship which should exist directly between employers and their employees. Such relations include full recognition of the legitimate ambitions of workers, the aims and aspirations of their lives, the conditions through which they seek to attain those aspirations and the maintenance of co-operation between employer and employed."[5] Yet ideology is not the only factor at work here.

Paynter, for example, told Adamic that his company underwent a "conversion" after it decided to recognize the CIO.[6] Market pressure put on by U.S. Steel's recognition of the union and the SWOC's growing numerical strength after the Corporation capitulated provided the impetus for this change in policy. Of 260 companies with SWOC contracts in 1942 for which data was available, over 90% showed declining production costs since the first month of collective bargaining.[7] Therefore, it is likely that many of these firms were as happy as Paynter's that they signed SWOC contracts. But for the leaders of Little Steel, the economic circumstances that convinced Paynter's company to recognize the union and these potential economic benefits were not enough to overcome their intense distaste for organized labor.

But despite their beliefs, even the most belligerent Little Steel executives had to make some changes to fit the changing economic and political climate of the late-1930s. They still spoke of the importance of allowing workers to succeed on their own, but the anti-union attitude and tactics of steelmakers leading up to and during the Little Steel Strike differed in subtle ways from what came before. One key difference was that industry executives in the late-1930s did not personalize the ethos of individual achievement as much as earlier steelmakers did. In the late-1930s, manufacturers still made much of the possibility of advancement for worthy employees, but the idea that workers might move to the very top of the industry disappeared. One reason for this may be the growth of employment in the industry. In 1936, in the depths of the Depression and despite years of new labor saving devices, the iron and steel industry employed 414,000 workers—almost three times as many people as it employed in 1879.[8] With more and more workers competing for better jobs, it would have been increasingly difficult to tell workers that they could make it to the top of the heap. Job hierarchies that made advancement possible continued to exist, but the days when employers could claim that anybody could rise to be the chairman of the board had passed. By the late-1930s, fewer steel leaders than ever before started at the bottom of the industry and rose to the top. Therefore, to make the Social Darwinist argument that merit differentiated them from their employees would have been disingenuous. It also would have run the risk of alienating the first steelworkers in decades who had the option of joining an outside union.

Because of competition with unions like SWOC for employee loyalty, the men who ran Little Steel stressed their affinity with workers and their needs, rather than their superiority. In management's view, organized labor and the government were outside forces that threatened employer and employee alike. Denouncing the Wagner Act in a 1936 speech before the American Iron and Steel Institute, Eugene Grace explained how these two threats worked together, "In case after case throughout the country we see the curious spectacle of employees and their employer, whose mutual relations are satisfactory, forced by a hastily conceived and discriminatory law to join together and fight for their independence against an irresponsible group of professional labor organizers."[9] In strike situations, Little Steel followed the so-called "Mohawk Valley" formula, a blueprint for non-union companies fighting organized labor written by the National Association of Manufacturers in 1936. Among other things, the plan recommended that firms form citizens' committees from the local community. Those committees would denounce the union as geographic and cultural outsiders.[10] In essence, steelmakers were asking their workers to side with familiarity over class.

What differentiated the methods of opposition that Little Steel used to fight unions from those utilized earlier in the era was the central role that employee representation plans played in these efforts. Managers used ERPs as vehicles to show their workers that the company cared about them. Throughout the late-1930s and into the 1940s, companies like Bethlehem Steel constantly reiterated support for their ERP and credited it for positive developments like wage increases and the continued existence of welfare capitalism. U.S. Steel had followed this same practice in the months preceding the March 1937 agreement, but used in conjunction with other anti-union tactics like spies and blacklists, these organizations could become even more effective at stamping out trade unions. During the SWOC campaign of 1936, only 200 employees joined the union at Bethlehem Steel's flagship South Bethlehem, Pennsylvania, plant. During the Little Steel strike only one Bethlehem Steel plant (in Johnstown) ceased operation. The success of management's anti-union tactics made it possible for the firm to keep all its other facilities open, even when other firms faced massive shutdowns.[11] To the leaders of Little Steel, company unions were the only acceptable form of collective bargaining. Both SWOC and the government threatened to interfere with these seemingly mutually beneficial arrangements.

The difference in impact caused by the Little Steel Strike demonstrates that the companies which made up Little Steel did not all use their ERPs to fight unions in the same way. At Bethlehem Steel, for example, management used its plan to grant numerous concessions to employees. For instance, in 1936, 592 of 722 grievances dealing with wages resulted in pay increases for workers. That same year, the ERP became the vehicle by which management gave its employees vacations with pay. Republic Steel adopted an ERP modeled on the one at Bethlehem Steel in June 1933. In April 1934, a company representative wrote, "We look upon the Plan, in short, as a method of coordinating efforts of the men and management to the mutual advantage of both."[12] It did not work out that way. Despite the existence of the ERP, Republic still faced numerous strikes before SWOC ever appeared on the scene. For this reason, management came to rely upon an elaborate network of spies and company policemen to keep their workers nonunion. A federal court, reviewing the NLRB's judgment against Republic Steel growing out of the SWOC campaign, described how the company fought organization:

> Almost immediately after SWOC commenced its organization campaign Republic in turn began a counter campaign to crush the Union. It announced to all its employes at once that "Republic stands for the 'Open Shop' principle', that "no employee has to join any organization to get or hold a job", and that "every employe owes a duty of loyalty to the Company so that its best interests may be served. Conduct detrimental to the interests of the Company and which may disrupt the satisfactory relations between employes and management will not be tolerated". The Union was denounced and vilified. From the beginning the organizers of the Union were followed and spied upon by Republic's company police. The latter also maintained surveillance over union meetings, thus discouraging employe attendance. Employees were threatened with discharge if they accepted Union literature outside plant gates. Union organizers were attacked and brutally beaten.[13]

The inspiration for Republic Steel's aggressive tactics was, of course, the system of repression in effect throughout the industry earlier in the century.

In much the same way that the 1919 strike made Elbert Gary's reputation as an anti-union zealot, the effectiveness of Republic Steel's espionage system during the 1937 Little Strike made that firm's president, Tom M. Girdler, famous. Girdler was born on a farm in Silver Creek Township, Indiana, in 1877. His father was the superintendent at the local cement mill, owned by Girdler's uncle. Growing up, he worked at the cement plant himself. For the rest of his life he would cite this experience as the root of his understanding of common labor. Girdler went on to attend Lehigh University. A wealthy aunt paid his tuition. He began his career in steel working after graduation as a foreman and superintendent at the Oliver Iron and Steel Company from 1902-1905. He got the job because a college roommate's uncle owned the firm. Girdler worked as an assistant superintendent at Colorado Fuel and Iron from 1905 to 1907 and as a superintendent at Atlantic Steel in Atlanta from 1907 to 1914. He moved to Jones and Laughlin in 1914 and worked his way up to President by 1928. In 1929, Girdler left Jones and Laughlin to head Republic Steel, a merger of smaller steel companies that began as the third-largest firm in the industry. Although the Depression hurt the firm, Girdler guided Republic Steel out of red ink by 1935. His election to the presidency of the American Iron and Steel Institute in 1937 demonstrates his influence in the industry.[14]

Girdler devoted much of his 1943 autobiography *Boot Straps* to labor issues. The defense of individual achievement in the book resembles the ideas expressed by steelmakers throughout the Nonunion Era. According to Girdler:

> There are few prominent in management who have not risen from the base of the pyramid, and the exceptions usually work under a handicap in competition with associates who have worked in overalls at the side of other men in overalls. Because this is an outstanding fact about large-scale industrial organizations in America, most of our labor "issues" have been invented by selfish people who only pretend to be interested in bettering the conditions under which men do their work.

Girdler went on to denounce trade unions as a threat to traditional management prerogatives, calling them "a terribly *disorganizing* influence . . .

at work at the base of all industry in America. The boss is no longer boss. Because organization is my forte this aspect of the intrusion of an outside influence horrifies me." [15] This quotation is indicative of the difference between the anti-unionism of Little Steel in the 1930s and the steelmakers of the previous generation. Girdler insists upon exercising control of his organization, but he justifies that prerogative by invoking his expertise instead of his biography. The leadership of Little Steel and many other firms used similar justifications for their freedom to control because, like Girdler, few began as common labor anymore.

Tom Girdler perfected the anti-union techniques used at Republic Steel while working for Jones & Laughlin during the 1910s and 1920s. However, after Girdler left Jones & Laughlin in 1929, the system ultimately failed to prevent organization. That company's flagship plant was in Aliquippa, Pennsylvania. When the Amalgamated Association began its post-NIRA organizing campaign, the town's nickname of "Little Siberia" seemed well-deserved. Jones & Laughlin responded to the first stirrings of union activity with what the NLRB later called "violent terroristic activity." In August 1933, for example, one of the few organizers ever to appear in town was beaten severely while walking the street, arrested, taken before a Justice of Police, fined $5 for disorderly conduct, and refused a transcript of record for purposes of appeal. Company-owned vehicles trailed him until he left town shortly thereafter. Within a month after the invalidation of the NIRA by the Supreme Court, Jones & Laughlin renewed its anti-union campaign, using more measured tactics to achieve its goals. Management pressured employees to participate in the ERP at the same time it discharged every union sympathizer in its ranks. The company learned which workers to fire and which to keep through its extensive spy system. The union supporters fired by Jones & Laughlin in 1935 filed a complaint with the National Labor Relations Board in January 1936, charging that this action violated the National Labor Relations Act. The NLRB's decision, issued in April of 1936, found in favor of the plaintiffs and ordered their reinstatement. Jones & Laughlin filed suit to block implementation of the decision. The firm challenged the NLRA as an unconstitutional abuse of the Commerce Clause. It also criticized the NLRA as a "constant threat" to the company's "normal right to manage its own business." Jones & Laughlin never denied that the discharges were for union activity.[16]

In a landmark decision that surprised many legal observers, the Supreme Court upheld the constitutionality of the NLRA in a 5-4 vote on

April 12th, 1937. Delivering the majority opinion, Chief Justice Charles Evans Hughes wrote:

> The steel industry is one of the great basic industries of the United States, with ramifying activities affecting interstate commerce at every point. The Government aptly refers to the steel strike of 1919-1920 with its far-reaching consequences. The fact that there appears to have been no major disturbance in that industry in the more recent period did not dispose of the possibilities of future and like dangers to interstate commerce which Congress was entitled to foresee and to exercise its protective power to forestall.[17]

Hughes also iterated the Court's support for the constitutionality of labor's right to organize and bargain collectively. After this decision, Jones & Laughlin disbanded its employee representation plan, although it quickly re-formed as the United Iron and Steel Workers of Aliquippa. The president of the new "independent" organization was the former head of the ERP. Management also began negotiations with SWOC, even though it was quite open about its refusal to sign a contract. With no hope of achieving a signed contract through negotiation, SWOC struck Jones & Laughlin on May 12th. There was minor violence in the first few days of the strike, and rumors that the company was deputizing men to break the picket line. However, Pennsylvania's Democratic Governor George Earle appeared on the scene to broker a settlement before anything else happened. The cornerstone of the agreement was a highly publicized NLRB election, pitting SWOC against the former ERP. The winner would be recognized as the exclusive bargaining agent representing Jones & Laughlin employees. Much to management's surprise, SWOC won by over a two-to-one margin, 17,028 to 7,207. The Committee became the sole collective bargaining representative for the employees of Jones & Laughlin.[18] It was SWOC's second major victory of the year, and (it hoped) its first of a string of victories against Little Steel.

The Little Steel Strike

Rather than dissolve their company unions after the Jones & Laughlin decision and allow the NLRB into their plants to conduct fair representation elections, the remaining holdouts in Little Steel clung to the belief that their employee representatives might pass amendments to their plans that would bring the ERPs into compliance with the NLRA. These amendments, written by company lawyers, turned the company unions into "independent" employee associations. These organizations lasted longer than the ones at U.S. Steel because they had the active support of management. Furthermore, Little Steel raised its employees' wages in April 1937, thereby continuing the industry's tradition of using wage increases to fight organization. Thanks to actions like this, conditions at most Little Steel companies compared favorably with those at U.S. Steel, except these firms lacked a union contract. Although the National Labor Relations Act required employers to bargain in good faith, the Jones & Laughlin decision did not require a company to sign an agreement with a trade union. Therefore, when SWOC sent letters to all the unorganized Little Steel firms in the spring of 1937 most of the companies agreed to meet with them even though they had no intention of bargaining in good faith.[19]

At the beginning of negotiations, SWOC proposed that each Little Steel company sign a contract similar to the one at U.S. Steel. As before, SWOC did not ask to be named the exclusive bargaining agent; it only wanted to represent those steelworkers who were already Amalgamated Association members. On May 11th, SWOC met with officials from Youngstown Sheet and Tube, who agreed in principle to the committee's terms, but refused to sign a contract. Republic Steel had the same reaction during a different meeting on the same day. After two meetings on May 14th and 25th, Inland Steel offered to sign a "statement of policy," but refused to sign a contract. There were no meetings between SWOC and Bethlehem Steel. Instead, the assistant to the general manager of that company's Cambria Works sent a letter to a local SWOC official stating that the company would not sign a contract. The failure of these negotiations led directly to the Little Steel strike.[20]

The Little Steel Strike was actually a series of separate strikes. It began when Tom Girdler locked his employees out of Republic Steel's Massilon, Ohio, mill on May 20th. SWOC retaliated by walking out of the rest of Republic's mills. Republic asserted that it was still operating at forty percent of its total corporate capacity and invited reporters into various mills to judge this claim for themselves. On May 26th, the Committee struck Inland Steel and Youngstown Sheet and Tube, shutting them down completely. The strike against Bethlehem Steel began on June 11th, when workers at the company's Cambria plant in Johnstown, Pennsylvania, walked out in sympathy with railroad workers who ran the track leading into the plant. It did not spread to any other plants in the

Bethlehem system. On June 21st, officials from each of these companies met with a specially appointed Federal Steel Mediation Board. Some of the executives expressed a willingness to talk to SWOC, but each participant reiterated his company's refusal to sign contracts with the Committee. After meeting with union leaders, the Board proposed a settlement based on recognition if SWOC won NLRB-sponsored representation elections. Little Steel rejected the proposal. "[I]n view of the attitude of the companies," explained the Board in its report to Secretary of Labor Frances Perkins, it "could not accomplish anything further by way of mediation."[21]

Today, people remember the Little Steel Strike primarily because of the events of May 30th, 1937, Memorial Day. That morning, a group consisting of between 1000 and 2500 strikers, workers from other plants, their wives and children, had attended a meeting at a union hall on the south side of Chicago, Illinois. At the close of that meeting, CIO organizers led the crowd on a march toward the gates of the local Republic Steel plant—the place where most of the strikers had worked before the walkout began. They intended to exercise their right to picket, a right assured to them by a recent order from the city's mayor. 50 Chicago policemen who had been stationed at the plant in response to previous unrest met the crowd. The police ordered the marchers to disperse. After a six or seven minute standoff, some people at the back of the crowd threw rocks and a crude club towards the police. They did not hit anyone. The police responded by throwing two tear gas bombs. Even though the demonstrators had already begun to take flight, the police began shooting. 10 marchers died of their wounds; 7 of them were shot in the back. 30 other marchers were injured by the gunfire; 9 of them would be permanently disabled. Scattered disturbances occurred at other strike centers throughout the Midwest, but nothing approaching the violence in Chicago.[22]

Interpretations of the Chicago incident by labor and management could not have been more different. "They were unarmed," noted John L. Lewis in the first official CIO statement on the tragedy. "The killing took place on an open prairie blocks from the gate of the sacred property of the Republic Steel Company. Not a single policeman was shot. Those who were injured suffered from the naked hands of men who were fighting for their lives." From these circumstances, Lewis concluded, "This company and the police force are guilty of planned murder."[23] Tom Girdler, on the other hand, defended the actions of local authorities. In a letter to Mayor Edward J. Kelly, he wrote, "Your prompt action to prevent threatened violence and destruction of life and property by an organized, armed and embittered mob, prepared and armed to attack our South Chicago plant, necessarily depended upon an official attitude toward obedience to law which showed itself to be both sincere and courageous."[24] The evidence uncovered by a Senate special committee to investigate violations of free speech and the rights of labor (better known as the La Follette Committee), which studied this incident extensively, suggests that labor's position was closer to the truth. Its investigation found that the police attacked without provocation and that the crowd was entirely within its legal rights picketing on the field near the plant.[25] The general acceptance of these findings has been an important reason that this incident is remembered as the "Memorial Day Massacre."

Despite the violence, the mills shut down by the strike all reopened as steelworkers gradually returned to work. National Guard troops reopened many of the closed mills in Ohio despite the fact that they had originally come to protect strikers. In some cities, special "citizen's committees," funded by the steel companies, encouraged striking workers to return to their jobs. The Governor of Indiana brokered a settlement between Inland Steel and SWOC on July 1st. The company agreed to recognize SWOC and institute the terms of the U.S. Steel agreement, but this arrangement did not force management to recognize the union. None of the other steel companies settled with the Committee as a result of the strike. By late June, SWOC called off the strikes against Bethlehem Steel and Youngstown Sheet and Tube, recognizing it had lost. Nevertheless, SWOC refused to call off its strike against Republic Steel. As late as October 1937, 12,850 men remained on strike against Tom Girdler's firm. However, the impact of the strike dwindled as management replaced most of these workers.[26]

As with the blame for events in Chicago, interpretations of the result of the strike varied depending on the perspective of the viewer. Although Tom Girdler acknowledged that SWOC had caused temporary problems, he told the *New York Times* in August 1937 that "the relations with our men are happy and there is a better understanding than ever before. . . . The C.I.O. presence is on the wane."[27] In a December 1937 speech, Girdler credited his workers with breaking the strike. "The men who wanted to work," he declared, "were threatened and beaten and their families were terrorized. Every form of violence was experienced from the tearing up to railroad tracks to dynamiting of plant entrances. . . .

Notwithstanding these tactics, the strike failed. It failed because these methods outraged whole communities and increased the determination of the majority of our men to return to their jobs."[28] Union supporters denied these charges. Despite the failure to organize most firms in Little Steel, the number of firms that signed SWOC contracts continued to grow in the months following the strike. Some union sympathizers even viewed the strike itself positively. "When history judges the steel strike," wrote Mary Heaton Vorse in 1938, "it will probably be rated as one of the most important battles of all industrial warfare in this country. It could be fairly said that neither side won. For, if workers suffered a defeat, the steel operators were not successful in their objectives. This was not 1919 and the workers were not crushed."[29]

Even if you accept the Little Steel strike as a clear victory for management, that victory proved costly. Defending itself cost the Little Steel firms an enormous amount of money in weapons and protection, as well as untold damage to their reputations. The monetary costs quickly appeared in Little Steel's bottom line. In his discussion of the SWOC campaign, Walter Galenson demonstrates that those steel firms that faced serious strikes in mid-1937 earned significantly lower profits that calendar year than those companies that signed contracts with the union.[30] Since collective bargaining actually increased efficiency and earnings, John Lages concludes that these companies "appear to have been so totally dedicated to keeping the union out of their firms that dollar cost and revenue considerations simply did not play an important role or were ignored in their decision to resist. To the extent that such economic information was ignored in their decision making, the leaders of Little Steel were *not* behaving rationally."[31] Like their predecessors, Little Steel let ideology trump profit. Anti-union employers like Girdler made guesses about increased profits in the future through preventing the organization of their mills, but in the Little Steel Strike that guess was wrong. The threat of government intervention did not get men like Girdler to change their minds about the profitability of unions because they had already defied the government with impunity. SWOC's legal strategy and the outbreak of World War II ended that possibility in the years following the strike.

Achieving Victory Off the Picket Line

Unable to beat Little Steel on the picket line, SWOC looked to the government for help. Even before the Memorial Day incident in Chicago, John Lewis made his desire for both state and federal intervention known, arguing, "Somewhere in this nation should be a force strong enough to bring these uniformed killers and co-conspirators to justice. Somewhere in this nation should be a force greater than a steel company. Somewhere in this nation should be enough earnest and honest citizens to compel action by the Federal and state authorities."[32] Despite such pleas, President Roosevelt did nothing—even after the massacre. To make matters worse, the President told a press conference, "The majority of people are saying just one thing, 'A plague on both your houses'."

To understand this famous remark, the context in which Roosevelt said it is important.

> "Is that your opinion?," the press asked Roosevelt.
> "It is what we agreed," he responded.
> "The majority of Americans?"
> "That is what Charlie Taft [of the Special Mediation Committee] and I agreed was the general feeling of the country."[33]

The papers quoted this line as if Roosevelt believed this sentiment himself, even though he intended it to be an expression of the opinion possessed by "the majority of Americans." This apparent lack of sympathy helped accentuate a split between Roosevelt and the most important labor leader in the country at the time. John L. Lewis attacked the President for his apparent callousness as soon as the remark hit the papers. The comment would contribute to an eventual full-blown feud between the two men. Because Roosevelt had offered SWOC little help up to that point and because of the lack of sympathy this comment suggested, the Committee would come to rely upon the National Labor Relations Board to help it organize the most recalcitrant employers.

In December 1937, SWOC General Counsel Lee Pressman explained the strategy of the Committee's Legal Department to the SWOC's First Wage and Policy Convention. "It is hoped," he told the delegates, "that the decisions of the Labor Board when issued in connection with the foregoing cases against the little steel producers, will so severely condemn the practices which have been carried on by these steel corporations and afford such protection to their employes, that the organization of steel workers may be completed in the steel plants."[34] The decisions in these cases eventually achieved Pressman's goal. During the late-1930s, SWOC established itself by winning representation elections held under NLRB auspices, despite management's vehement objections to elections, let alone the Committee. Through July 1939, SWOC won 81 of 122 NLRB elections. In 39 elections where its opponent was an independent union or former representation plan, SWOC won 22.[35]

All of Little Steel would eventually be organized through this method. On October 18th, 1938, the NLRB ruled that Republic Steel had to reinstate workers unlawfully discharged during the Little Steel Strike and pay them wages lost since the date of their termination. This decision would eventually affect 7000 employees and cost the company two million dollars in back pay. Republic Steel appealed the ruling through every legal channel. When the United States Supreme Court refused to take the case in April 1940, Girdler finally agreed to abide by the decision. Despite his long resistance to unionization, Girdler insisted at this time that "[Republic Steel] has always been friendly to organized labor. Some of my best friends are in organized labor." Organized labor thought otherwise. A SWOC spokesman called the Court's inaction "the greatest victory ever achieved by organized labor." Besides the legal costs of fighting the NLRB, Republic Steel paid an additional $350,000 in 1945 to settle claims filed by strikers and the families of strikers who were killed or injured during the 1937 melee. Add these penalties to other costs stemming from the dispute, like loss of business, the price of munitions and advertising expenses, and Republic's experience in the Little Steel strike takes on all the characteristics of a Pyrrhic victory.[36]

Although SWOC's Legal Department targeted Bethlehem Steel too, the threat of government action did not drive it to the bargaining table. Like Republic Steel, the company's President believed in the traditional prerogative of management to control its business and hated trade unions. Eugene Grace was born in 1876, the son of a ship captain. He graduated Lehigh University in 1895 with a degree in electrical engineering and started working at Bethlehem Steel as a crane operator in 1899. That position paid less than $1.80 per day. After six months, the company promoted him to the open hearth department. In 1902, he became he became superintendent of yards and transportation. In this position, he attracted the attention of Charles M. Schwab. Much the same way that Carnegie arranged Schwab's rise through the ranks, Schwab mentored Grace. In 1913, he became President of Bethlehem Steel Company

(Schwab's title was Chairman). In a 1935 statement designed to justify his executive bonus, Grace explained his work ethic, "There are . . . very few days in the year during which my business activities, which have been confined entirely to furthering the interests of the Corporation, have ended with my departure from my office. I have worked many nights until late in the night or early in the morning. My job has been a twenty-four hour job." Like others who came before him, Grace believed that he was worth every penny he got. In the area of labor relations, Grace tried to reward others who worked as hard as he did, putting employees of all grades on the incentive system so that they would be encouraged to work harder for the company. His dealings with the National War Labor Board show that his opposition to outside unions dated back to the World War I era. Out of these wartime disputes, Grace fashioned the Bethlehem Steel Employee Representation Plan into the most successful company union in the industry. It took a new series of strikes and more government intervention to force Grace to let his beloved company union die, and get him to bargain with strangers.[37]

In February 1941, Bethlehem management agreed to let employees at its Lackawanna, New York, plant vote on their collective bargaining agent after they won a 39-hour strike. This led to a four-day strike at South Bethlehem in March. When state and local police tried to disperse strikers, the dispute led to serious violence (but no casualties). As part of the settlement, the company agreed to let South Bethlehem workers vote for their bargaining agent as well. Between May and September of that year, SWOC won elections at all of Bethlehem Steel facilities. At this point, Bethlehem's ERP dissolved. SWOC's success against the rest of Little Steel was less dramatic than its victory over Bethlehem, but these NLRB decisions played an equally important role in the future of collective bargaining in this industry. SWOC won its case against Inland Steel on November 12th, 1938. It won its case against Youngstown Sheet and Tube on February 17th, 1941. On July 25th, 1941, Republic Steel, Inland Steel and Youngstown Sheet and Tube agreed to abide by the results of an NLRB cross-check of SWOC membership at their plants in order to avoid representation elections. The Board certified that SWOC held majorities at each company.[38]

SWOC had won recognition from all of Little Steel by mid- to late-1941, but the business of negotiating a specific contract remained. Collective bargaining between SWOC and all of Little Steel began in September 1941. During the course of these negotiations, the United States entered World War II. In January 1942, the government created a new National War Labor Board (NWLB) to prevent strikes at companies involved in the war effort. The World War I version of the board had to depend on the power of public opinion to force companies to comply with its decisions, but the new NWLB had the full backing of the U.S. Government. Furthermore, the new NWLB had the power to determine wages throughout the economy and to grant organized labor "union security." Union security consisted of two important contract provisions: maintenance-of-membership and dues check off. Both these devices appear in labor contracts today. Maintenance-of-membership means that new hires are automatically enrolled into the union. Dues check off means that union dues are automatically subtracted from an employee's paycheck (thereby saving union officials the time and expense of collecting dues from each member individually). SWOC believed it needed union security because it did not trust Little Steel. "For the past three or four decades," wrote the Committee in a brief submitted to the NWLB:

> the industrial relations policy of the basic American industries was fixed and established by the steel industry. The history of industrial relations for the steel industry reveals that (a) there was a determination on the part of employers to combat unions at every step and to prevent their coming into existence, and (b) this policy was maintained under the slogan of the "open shop".
>
> It is most interesting to note the second point because the four corporations involved in this proceeding attempt to deny the union shop on the same basis, namely, that they insist on maintaining the "open shop."

The Board's July 1942 Little Steel decision included both maintenance of membership, dues check off and a wage increase in exchange for limits on future wage increases. This became the basis of the of the Little Steel Formula, by which the NWLB guaranteed the security of unions at the same time it limited wages across many industries.[39]

Neither of the parties to the Little Steel case was completely happy with the decision. Still objecting to recognition on philosophical grounds, Little Steel abided by the decision only because of the war emergency. As Tom Girdler explained in his 1943 autobiography, "My associates and I are law-abiding citizens. . . . We made contracts with the C.I.O. for each Republic plant as fast as Labor Board certification established that a majority of our employees had signed up as members of the union.

Ever since we have done our conscious best to make the relationship work to the mutual advantage of our employees and the company. . . . But this does not mean my opinions have changed."[40] To defy an activist government at that point might have led to hostile publicity and an armed takeover of their facilities, much like what happened at Montgomery Ward in April 1944. Similarly, labor would spend the remainder of the war trying to achieve wage increases above the caps set by the Little Steel decision. Yet despite this problem, the maintenance-of-membership provision of the decision helped SWOC grow from 373,000 members in 1941 to 733,000 members in 1946. Thanks to the dues check off provision of the Little Steel decision, the union's net worth grew sevenfold between May 1942 (right before the Little Steel decision) and November 1943.[41] In June 1942, SWOC adopted its first constitution, thereby becoming the United Steel Workers of America (USWA). The advent of this new national organization, with a growing membership throughout the industry meant that the demise of the Nonunion Era was complete.[42]

A Legacy of Distrust

The government forced Little Steel to engage in collective bargaining with its workers because of World War II, but it could not force employers to treat their workers with respect. Likewise, it could not force employees and their unions to trust management. In the case of employers, cultural attitudes that underlay their fierce opposition to organized labor persisted into the New Union Era. In the case of employees, memories of the Nonunion Era encouraged them to keep up their guard. For this reason, the same conflict over the distribution of control in the workplace continued in a new context. Steel manufacturers still believed that they deserved the freedom to control every factor of production, especially labor. Unions still threatened that prerogative. Buoyed by the organizing victories of the late-1930s, steelworkers expected greater influence over both the conditions under which they labored and the production process itself. Instead, they were disturbed to find that their employers still wanted to treat them as nothing more than one of many factors of production.

Before the war began, SWOC leadership took the initiative to establish a better working relationship with the industry. Beginning in 1938, the union established cooperation programs at 40 or 50 small, financially troubled metal-fabricating firms that were willing to cede some shopfloor control to the union in order to increase productive efficiency. Two SWOC staffers, Harold Ruttenberg and Clinton Golden, were the intellectual force behind these efforts to get labor and management to confront the problems of the industry together. By early-1940, they had convinced the union to make cooperation a central tenet of the union. During its May 1940 convention, SWOC proposed special labor-management committees "designed to mobilize the resourcefulness and ingenuity of our members in the interest of increased and efficient production . . . provided of course management is willing to completely accept the Union." This idea spread to the higher ranks of the CIO. In a 1941 address to the CIO convention, Philip Murray proposed a series of "Industry Councils," so that labor could have a voice in planning for all defense areas. Although most industries rejected such arrangements outright, steel firms agreed to implement the plan under the strain of the wartime emergency and the threat of government intervention. By March 15th, 1944, there were 451 of these committees throughout the iron and steel industry, representing some 719,530 workers.[43]

Union officials tried to use these committees to show management ways that production might be improved, but little came from these recommendations because management never took the committees seriously. As one visitor from the government's War Production Board described the situation at U.S. Steel plants around Pittsburgh in October 1943, plant managers appointed "management representatives with no real authority, [refused] to allow meetings on company time, [and refused] in many instances to set up adequate subcommittee organization or well-planned suggestion systems with adequate cash rewards."[44] Although some of these bodies helped decrease absenteeism and raise productivity, they disappeared soon after peace returned. This reconfirmed to most employees that management would not cooperate with labor unless compelled to do so by outside forces. Stung by this rebuke, the USWA would become as enthusiastic about cooperating with management as management was about cooperating with the union. "[I]t became very apparent to me, and to Golden, that you have to have union-management cooperation," said Harold Ruttenberg in a 1986 interview with the author John Hoerr. "You had to tie the economic benefits that flow to workers to increased productivity in order to do it." According to Ruttenberg, he resigned from the USWA in 1946 because he was unable to find support for this philosophy within the union.[45]

In his impressive account of labor relations in the American Steel industry after World War II, *And the Wolf Finally Came*, Hoerr includes a description of Golden and Ruttenberg's philosophy to suggest what might have been. Labor and management might have cooperated together in a time of prosperity for their mutual benefit. Instead, the distrust between labor and management that began during the Nonunion Era persisted into the New Union Era and poisoned the collective bargaining process. Eventually, both sides eschewed cooperation, even as the industry's economic position became increasingly dire. In fact, the quotation from which the title of Hoerr's book derives suggests the relationship between this mutual suspicion and the eventual collapse of the industry. "One of the problems in the mills," said USWA vice-president Joseph Odorcich in a 1983 interview, "is no union man would trust any of the companies. To the average union man, they're always crying wolf. And the wolf finally came." Hoerr also documents that distrust from management's perspective, "The idea that labor should participate in any significant way in decision making on the shop floor, much less at higher levels in the steel plants and the corporation itself, did not fit in with U.S. Steel's management style and philosophy."[46] The fact that Hoerr is writing about the 1980s here rather than the 1910s shows just how important the Corporation's attachment to its freedom to control has been throughout its history.

In *The Decline of American Steel*, Paul Tiffany explains the relationship between labor management distrust and the eventual fate of the industry in a different way. Tiffany's book encompasses the period from 1946-1959, an era when the steel industry experienced five separate national strikes. To him, the rising wage and benefits bill, which the industry faced as a result of these strikes, helped create an opening for imported steel that would devastate the domestic industry a few decades later. Government, too, deserves part of the blame in Tiffany's account for its inability to work out an industrial policy with labor and management that might have helped save the steel industry from foreign competition. "Neither steel managers, union leaders, nor several administrations much distinguished themselves by their actions," he writes in his conclusion. "Instead, they provide a striking example of how embedded ideologies of suspicion and distrust could contribute to the decline of a major and vital sector of the national economy." Key aspects of these embedded ideologies date from the Nonunion Era. In 1949, for example, Harry Truman appointed a fact-finding board to try to head off what would become the second of these five postwar strikes. U.S. Steel rejected the board's proposed solution, in part, because of "the firm's usual reflex resistance into its "freedom" to do as it pleased. U.S. Steel and indeed the entire industry had never been well disposed to accept organized labor as a legitimate interest whose rights were to be taken seriously." The strike went on, and within a few weeks the Corporation accepted the board's proposal.[47] The reflex that led U.S. Steel to engage in this futile and costly resistance was another part of the cultural legacy from the Nonunion Era.

Mark Reutter, in his study of Bethlehem Steel's Sparrows Point plant, finds the same dynamic at work in labor relations during the Postwar Era as Hoerr and Tiffany. "What the men themselves wanted the union for," recalls one steelworker quoted in Reutter's book, "was to have everyone respect your seniority and ability, and not have these bosses' pets and brown nosers get the best jobs. We got more money, that was important sure, but we got respect more, that was number one." In return for this forced respect, a desire that stemmed from earlier labor-management relations in the industry, Bethlehem Steel made Sparrows Point the best mill in the industry for "[squeezing] the most out of men and machinery." Nevertheless, despite modernization and expansion, Sparrows Point still faced the problem of deindustrialization. Expanding his analysis at the end of his study in order to diagnose the problems facing the entire steel industry in the late-1980s, Reutter concludes:

> Labor relations have remained perversely counterproductive, with the union blaming management for lack of investment, management blaming labor for inefficient work rules, and both blaming the government when demand dried up. Had the USWA and management talked more constructively outside the context of wages and benefits, they might have helped the industry. But then they would have hurt themselves in an atmosphere where the division between supervision and labor was absolute.[48]

Other factors, in particular the failure of the industry to get behind new technologies like the basic oxygen furnace and continuous casting early, undoubtedly contributed to the decline of American steel, but the problem in labor-management relations compounded other difficulties by making changes designed to adapt to new circumstances more difficult.

"We appreciate that the union-management marriage, in the first instance, was frequently a shotgun affair, that one party went through the marriage ceremony against its will. It is only natural that the party forced into the marriage hesitates to embrace its unwanted partner enthusiastically. But respect—full and complete—can grow with the years as well as hate."[49] When Clinton Golden and Harold Ruttenberg published these words in 1942, they hoped that steelmakers would learn from successful cooperation during World War II and create a new industrial relations regime after the war that threw off the legacy of the past. This did not happen. "The United Steelworkers," writes Thomas Misa, "like unions in most mass-production industries, gave up their early vision of industrial democracy, in which workers would take a share of responsibility for shop-floor decision making. Instead, a bargain was struck that gave unions handsome contract settlements in exchange for management gaining absolute control over the shop floor. In effect, a fat paycheck was the price of labor management peace."[50] The marriage became a more stable relationship over time, even if the bride and groom were not completely happy together. Yet it was never a marriage between equals. If labor had received some kind of control over the production, it would not have felt the need for wage increases that helped price American steel out of the market. In the long run, cooperation would have been better for both parties. Instead, the bride and groom retained two distinctly different views of what a marriage should be, born out of the period before they were betrothed. The economic circumstances of the industry changed remarkably during the postwar period, but the attitude of management with regard to its employees and the resentment of labor at the way it was treated hardly changed at all.

Notes

1. Clinton S. Golden and Harold J. Ruttenberg, *The Dynamics of Industrial Democracy* (New York: Harper & Brothers, 1942), 220.

2. U.S. Congress, House, Committee on Labor, *Proposed Amendments to the National Labor Relations Act*, 76th Cong., 1st Sess., 1939, 1918; Frederick Harbison, "Collective Bargaining in the Steel Industry," Industrial Relations Section, Princeton University, 1937, 23-24; Robert R.R. Brooks, *As Steel Goes . . .* (New Haven: Yale University Press, 1940), 121.

3. Louis Adamic, "Talk with a C.I.O. Employer," in *My America* (New York: Harper & Brothers, 1938), 431-32.

4. Weirton Steel is sometimes included in pre-1937 lists of the Little Steel firms, but it did not face a strike that year. Therefore, to include it among these firms in this study would be needlessly confusing.

5. Frank Purnell, "Current Problems of Labor Relations," Address at the 200th Meeting of the National Industrial Conference Board, November 17, 1937, 5.

6. Adamic, *My America*, 430-32.

7. Golden and Ruttenberg, 263-64.

8. American Iron and Steel Institute, "The Men Who Make Steel," New York, May 1936, 28-29.

9. Eugene Grace, "Industry and the Public," American Iron and Steel Institute, May 28, 1936, 17.

10. Keith Sword, "The Johnstown Strike of 1937: A Case Study of Large-Scale Conflict," in *Industrial Conflict: A Psychological Interpretation*, George W. Hartmann and Theodore Newcomb, eds. (New York: The Cordon Company, 1939), 86-87.

11. In the Matter of Bethlehem Steel Corporation . . . and Steel Workers Organizing Committee, 14 N.L.R.B., No. 44, August 14, 1939, 576-77, 625-28; Kathleen Purcell Munley, "Shopfloor Memories of Organizing Bethlehem Steel 1936-1942," *Labor's Heritage* 9, (Spring 1998): 62-63.

12. *Bethlehem Review*, No. 31. March 1937, 6; J.A. Voss, "Our Employee Representatives," *Republic* (April 1934): 10.

13. U.S. Congress, Senate, Committee on Education and Labor, *Violations of Free Speech and Rights of Labor: Private Police Systems*, [La Follette Committee], Report No. 6, Part 2, 76th Cong., 1st Sess., 1939; *Republic Steel Corporation v. National Labor Relations Board*, 107 F.2d 474 (1939).

14. Tom M. Girdler, *Boot Straps* (New York: Charles Scribner's Sons, 1943); Carol Poh Miller, "Tom M. Girdler," in *Iron and Steel in the Twentieth Century*, Bruce E. Seely, ed. (Bruccoli, Clark, Layman: 1994), 161-67.

15. Tom M. Girdler, *Boot Straps*, 379, 449.

16. In the Matter of Jones & Laughlin Steel Corporation and Amalgamated Association of Iron, Steel & Tin Workers . . . , 1 N.L.R.B., No. 33, April 9, 1936, 503-04, 510, 516; *National Labor Relations Board v. Jones & Laughlin Steel Corp.*, 301 U.S. 21 (1937).

17. 301 U.S. 43.

18. James Green, "Democracy Comes to 'Little Siberia': Steelworkers Organize in Aliquippa, Pennsylvania, 1933-1937," *Labor's Heritage* 5 (Summer 1993): 19-22; Brooks, *As Steel Goes . . .* , 122-28; *Proposed Amendments to the National Labor Relations Act*, 1944-46.

19. Harbison, "Collective Bargaining in the Steel Industry," 31-34.

20. Donald Sofchalk, "The Little Steel Strike of 1937," Ph.D. Dissertation, Ohio State University, 1961, 17; Irving Bernstein, *Turbulent Years*, (Boston: Houghton Mifflin, 1970), 482-83.

21. Brooks, *As Steel Goes...*, 136-38; Sofchalk, 139-42; Federal Steel Mediation Board to Frances Perkins, June 30, 1937, La Follette Committee Hearings, 13937-41.

22. Sofchalk, 166-70; Mary Heaton Vorse, *Labor's New Millions* (New York: Modern Age Books, 1938), 118-27. For more details of the Little Steel strike and the Chicago incident, see Bernstein, 483-97; Brooks, *As Steel Goes . . .*, 137-45.

23. *Steel Labor*, 5 June 1937.

24. Tom M. Girdler to Edward J. Kelly, December 31, 1937 in Records of the Committee to Investigate Violations of Free Speech and Rights of Labor [La Follette Committee], United States Senate Records, Record Group 46, National Archives and Records Administration, Washington, D.C., 13944.

25. Edward Levinson, *Labor on the March* (New York: Harper & Brothers, 1938), 207.

26. Levinson, 206-09; Brooks, *As Steel Goes . . .*, 149.

27. *New York Times*, 1 August 1937.

28. T.M. Girdler, "What's Ahead in Industrial Relations?," Annual Banquet, Illinois Manufacturers Association, Chicago, IL, December 14, 1937, 11.

29. Vorse, *Labor's New Millions*, 131.

30. Walter Galenson, *The CIO Challenge to the AFL* (Cambridge: Harvard University Press, 1960), 108-09.

31. John David Lages, "The CIO-SWOC Attempt to Organize the Steel Industry: A Restatement and Economic Analysis," Ph.D. Diss., Iowa State University, 1967, 97.

32. *Steel Labor*, 5 June 1937.

33. Complete Presidential Press Conferences of Franklin D. Roosevelt, Vols. 9 and 10 (New York: Da Capo Press, 1972), 466-67.

34. Steel Workers Organizing Committee, "Proceedings of the First Wage and Policy Convention," December 14-16, 1937, 68.

35. *Proposed Amendments to the National Labor Relations Act*, 1923. For details on the companies and size of the units involved, see "Steel Workers' Organizing Committee elections under auspices of National Labor Relations Board," *Proposed Amendments to the National Labor Relations Act*, 1974-76.

36. Galenson, 109; *New York Times*, 11 April 1940; *New York Times*, 9 April 1940.

37. Elizabeth C. Sholes and Timothy E. Leary, "Eugene G. Grace," in *Iron and Steel in the Twentieth Century*, 172-81; Bethlehem Steel Corporation, [Executive Statements in Connection with Shareholder Suits Relating to Bonus Plan], January 28, 1935, 12, 10, Hagley Museum and Library [stacks], Wilmington, DE.

38. Munley, 67, 73; Galenson, 115-16.

39. Galenson, 116-18; Nelson Lichtenstein, *Labor's War at Home* (New York: Cambridge University Press, 1982), 71-72; Steel Workers Organizing Committee, In the Matter of Bethlehem Steel Company, Republic Steel Corporation, Youngstown Sheet & Tube Company, Inland Steel Company, [1942], 27. For more on the Little Steel Formula and its significance, see Joel Seidman, *American Labor From Defense to Reconversion* (Chicago: University of Chicago Press, 1953), 113-30.

40. Girdler, *Bootstraps*, 449.

41. Mark McCulloch, "Consolidating Industrial Citizenship: The USWA at War and Peace, 1939-46," in *Forging a Union of Steel*, Paul F. Clark, Peter Gottlieb and Donald Kennedy, eds. (Ithaca, NY: ILR Press, 1987), 52; Lichtenstein, 79-80.

42. Independent unions with close ties to management remained the collective bargaining agents for some smaller steel companies even after the Little Steel settlement. Two of the larger companies with independent unions were Wisconsin Steel and Weirton Steel.

Wisconsin Steel employees repeatedly chose an independent organization, the Progressive Steelworkers Union, over SWOC, as a reward for management's commitment to them as expressed through welfare capitalism. That union represented employees at Wisconsin Steel's Chicago plant until it shut down in 1980. See Lizabeth Cohen, *Making a New Deal* (New York: Cambridge University Press, 1990), 351-54; David Bensman and Roberta Lynch, *Rusted Dreams: Hard Times in a Steel Community* (Berkeley: University of California Press, 1987), 1.

The NLRB forced Weirton Steel to disband its company union in 1941, but an organization called the Weirton Independent Union continued to operate there until 1951 when a Federal Court ordered it to disband. This organization was replaced by the Independent Steel Workers Union, which continued to represent Weirton employees into the 1990s. Ironically, by that time Weirton had become an employee-owned company. See Teresa Lynn Ankney, "The Pendulum of Control: The Evolution of the Weirton Steel Company, 1909-1951," Ph.D. Diss., The Catholic University of America, 1993, Chapter IV.

43. John Hoerr, "Comments," in *Forging a Union of Steel*, 121; Steel Workers Organizing Committee, "Proceedings of the Second International Wage and Policy Convention," May 14-17, 1940, 26; Philip Murray, "Industry Council Program," 343-47; Morris Llewellyn Cooke and Philip Murray, *Organized Labor and Production* (New York: Arno & The New York Times, 1971/Revised edition published by Harper & Brothers, 1946), xi.

44. War Production Board representative quoted in John P. Hoerr, *And the Wolf Finally Came* (Pittsburgh: University of Pittsburgh Press, 1988), 277-78.

45. Hoerr, *And the Wolf Finally Came*, 277-78, 282.

46. Hoerr, *And the Wolf Finally Came*, 23, 161.

47. Paul Tiffany, *The Decline of American Steel* (New York: Oxford University Press, 1988), 186, 86, 85.

48. Mark Reutter, *Sparrows Point* (New York: Summit Books, 1988), 346, 390, 414.

49. Golden and Ruttenberg, 228.

50. Thomas Misa, *A Nation of Steel* (Baltimore: The Johns Hopkins University Press, 1995), 281.

Conclusion

During the 1870s and early 1880s, skilled iron workers exercised enormous influence over the manner in which they labored because their skills made them indispensable to the production process. As steel began to surpass iron, employers hired and trained large numbers of immigrants to operate new, nonunion production facilities. Easily replaceable, skilled workers could do little to prevent their obsolescence. The new workforce of the Nonunion Era, just as replaceable as the skilled workers who preceded them, had to work to survive. Therefore, they could not safely organize to make demands on their employers. They could only react to management labor policies rather than shape them through their own initiative. Although steel workers made isolated attempts to organize unions, the great majority of them remained nonunion for decades because management insisted on maintaining a direct relationship between the company and its employees, free from the constraints that organization would bring. Only in the 1930s, with the advent of new organizing strategies and new laws, especially the National Labor Relations Act, did steelworkers return to the union fold. By following this industry from highly-organized to nonunion and back again, this study has traced the decline and rise of an industrial relations system, the ever-changing relationship between American steel companies, their employees and, after the World War I era, the state.

In *Steelworkers in America*, David Brody cited the cost-cutting mentality of steel industry leaders and the divisions among steelworkers as the most important reasons for the long absence of organization from this industry. However, from management's perspective, other ideas were equally important. The ethos of individual achievement and the desire for the freedom of control were by no means the only ideals important to American steelmakers, but they come up again and again in the public and private statements of key management figures as explanations for all kinds of labor policy decisions. One might feel safe assuming that this kind of business thinking is just rhetoric: that whatever businessmen say about society is just self-justification for the relentless pursuit of profit (conservatives applaud that pursuit, of course, while liberals decry it). Hopefully, this study has demonstrated that this interpretation would be a mistake. Even if they did not actually determine anti-union labor policies, the ethos of individual achievement and the desire for the freedom to control certainly helped shape the form that such labor policies took. For this reason alone they are worthy of scholarly consideration.

In the case of the steel industry, the persistence and pervasiveness of management's ideas indicate their importance. Employers wanted to both make money and create policies that represented their beliefs, even though those policies were not necessarily profitable. This helps explain what might be deemed "irrational acts" on management's part, such as the dogged persistence of the ten and twelve-hour day at most firms in the industry long after other steelmakers had demonstrated that shorter hours paid for themselves by making workers more productive. The pursuit of the freedom to control also helps explain why steelmakers picked one seemingly profitable policy over another; for example, Little Steel's decision to fight organization in the late-1930s rather than recognize the union and prevent a costly strike as many other firms did.

The ideas that motivated employer anti-unionism are not specific to this industry. This study has focused on steelmakers, but all kinds of American employers fought unions for similar reasons. In late-nineteenth century America, businessmen venerated poverty as an obstacle to overcome in order to prove one's merit. That idea lives on today in the rhetoric of organized labor's enemies. Rather than argue against wage and benefit demands, they often attack the collective nature of organized labor in the hopes that this will deflect arguments about the ability of management to pay.[1] The roots of this defense, argues Sanford Jacoby, can be found in the early history of American economic development. Because the government's primary role in the nation's economic system until the 1930s was to serve the interests of capital, most businessmen of the United States became accustomed to a nonunion industrial relations system. "Late nineteenth- and early-twentieth century American employers did not have to make alliances with other social groups—such as landed gentry—to achieve their goals, and rarely had to share the levers of power with 'outsiders' like the government. Hence, they developed an especially strong belief in the virtues of free enterprise and apotheosized themselves as self-made men."[2] Andrew Carnegie's remarkable success and his deliberate policy of cultivating partners from the ranks of his mills strengthened this tendency among steelmakers. Industry leaders clung to their ethos of individual achievement long after technology and market conditions made rising through the ranks nearly impossible. The economic benefits of nonunion operation tended to reinforce management's attachment to these ideas; so much so that they poisoned the relationship between labor and management after government intervention helped trade unions return to the industry.

Culture, at its most basic level, is the framework through which individuals interact with their society. Labor historians writing since the 1960s have clearly demonstrated the way that working class culture has influenced American labor history. The "old" labor history, originally called the Wisconsin School because nearly all the practitioners of this scholarship studied at the University of Wisconsin, saw American labor history almost exclusively as a continual conflict between organized labor and management for higher wages and better working conditions. The practitioners of the "new" labor history were not interested in management. They believed that working people were subjects worthy of study in their own right—independent of their employers and their unions. Strongly influenced by British historian E.P. Thompson's analysis of English working-class culture,[3] these scholars who started writing in the 1960s analyzed the culture of workers in this country in order to show that class has been a fundamental element in the American experience. By doing this, they transcended the discipline's roots in economics to assume a role in the larger transformation of historical scholarship that also took place during this decade.

Only recently have scholars recognized the ways in which cultural traditions strengthened employers in the same way that they aided employees. This delay can be explained, in part, by the reluctance of businessmen to let their views be known on matters that did not seem to directly pertain to the enterprises they ran. As Thomas Cochran put it in 1947, they "have not left large collections of 'public papers' deposited in libraries for perusal by graduate students; their debates have not been preserved in congressional records or legislative journals; their policies and beliefs were not broadcast for the benefit of constituents. They went quietly, often secretly, about their tasks."[4] Nevertheless, a growing number of business historians have tried to show how cultural considerations affected the economic decisions of American corporations. One of them,

Kenneth Lipartito, defines culture as "a system of values, ideas and beliefs which constitute a mental apparatus for grasping reality." Lipartito defines business culture as the "set of limiting and organizing concepts that determine what is real or rational for management, principles that are often tacit or unconscious."[5] Those principles derived from a wide variety of sources: Republican ideology that originated during the American Revolution, religious beliefs, work habits unique to particular trades, etc. Delineating the exact influences acting upon a particular policymaking entity is an impossible task. However, understanding the collective influence of "producing-class culture" on the labor policies of the steel industry is not hard at all.

The ethos of individual achievement and the desire for the freedom of control formed an important part of the culture of American steelmakers. These ideas influenced these employers just as working-class culture influenced their employees. Therefore, in this study, I have tried to use the insights of scholars like E.P. Thompson and Herbert Gutman, and apply them to the other side of the industrial relations equation. Hopefully, this model can serve as a framework for other scholars of business history interested in the newly emerging subject of business culture. Even though management's ideas did not take hold among steel workers, the fact that so many important steelmakers believed in the same two cultural ideals tells you something about the intellectual underpinnings of our economic system. As John Kenneth Galbraith explained in his classic, *American Capitalism*, "Man cannot live without an economic theology—without some rationalization of the abstract and seemingly inchoate arrangements which provide him with his livelihood. For this purpose the competitive or classical model had many advantages. . . . By asserting it was a description of reality the conservative could use it as the justification for the existing order."[6] Since the classical economic model was and is still an important intellectual rationalization for the American capitalist system, historians should recognize that the economic justification of the past and those used in the present are linked.

At the turn of the century, the rationalization of the economic situation included the ideas described in the preceding chapters. Beginning in the 1930s, businessmen in and out of the steel industry began to use the same kinds of arguments designed to keep unions out of their shops to keep government from regulating many aspects of their operations. This included not only the regulation of industrial relations (such as the arguments against the National Labor Relations Act covered in Chapter Seven), but government restraints of all kinds. By the late-twentieth century free market principles were used to oppose environmental protection, tariffs, taxation and much more. In this manner, modern devotees of the free market have modified an old idea and projected it backward in order to affect our understanding of economic history. Modern anti-government sentiment among businessmen derives from more than just federal involvement in industrial relations, but since unions have been weak in recent decades one might forget how big a change government support for unions was in the 1930s and how far-reaching its effects proved to be. Anti-unionism, in effect, was an intellectual antecedent of modern conservatism.

Discerning the exact cause of a policy decision is a difficult task. People and institutions seldom offer explanations of how they made decisions; they may not even know themselves. For this reason, one should be suspicious of statements of certainty in these matters. To assume material considerations are the root cause of all economic behaviors not only assumes certainty, in the case of steelmakers during the Nonunion Era, it also contradicts a considerable amount of evidence that illustrates the industry's cultural aims with respect to its labor policy. Since these considerations cannot be quantified, the common response is simply to assume them away. By separating cultural from economic motives, culture becomes a subject worthy of consideration by itself, rather than simply because of its effect on material interests.

My intention in this work has been to present a broad, multivariate explanation for the labor policy choices of American steelmakers. I did not intend to single out the ethos of individual achievement and the freedom to control as the only forces behind anti-union labor policies—only as forces worthy of consideration by labor and business historians alike. Economic factors influenced the labor policy of steelmakers throughout the Nonunion Era, but to offer the minimization of costs and the maximization of profit as the sole variable for firm behavior does not credit steelmakers with the gift of complex thought. They cared about ideals, particularly when it came to labor policy, and any historian who ignores those concerns will get a distorted picture of labor's and management's history alike.

Notes

1. For example, driving across country during the 1997 Teamsters strike, I heard Rush Limbaugh repeatedly decline comment on the merits of the union's position. Instead, he just repeated the admonition that nobody needed a union to help them. He told his listeners that they could all succeed on their own.

2. Sanford Jacoby, "American Exceptionalism Revisited," in *Masters to Managers* Sanford Jacoby, ed. (New York: Columbia University Press, 1991), 176-77.

3. Thompson's most influential work is *The Making of the English Working Class* (New York: Vintage, 1966).

4. Thomas C. Cochran, "A Plan For the Study of Business Thinking," *Political Science Quarterly* 62 (March 1947): 82.

5. Kenneth Lipartito, "Culture and the Practice of Business History," *Business and Economic History* 24 (Winter 1995): 2. On the historiography of business culture, see William H. Becker, "Managerial Culture and the American Political Economy," *Business and Economic History* 25 (Fall 1996): 4-5.

6. John Kenneth Galbraith, *American Capitalism*, Revised edition (Boston: Houghton Mifflin, 1956), 17.

Index

About the Author

Jonathan Rees earned his M.A. and Ph.D. in history at the University of Wisconsin–Madison. He has taught at Whitman College, Southwest Missouri State University and is now an Associate Professor of History at Colorado State University–Pueblo.

His work has been published in the *Wisconsin Magazine of History*, *Pennsylvania History*, *Labor's Heritage* and *Business and Economic History*. He is also co-author of *The Voice of the People: Primary Sources on the History of American Labor, Working-Class Culture and Industrial Relations* (Harlan Davidson, 2004).